George Seward

America's First Great Runner

Edward S. Sears

THE SCARECROW PRESS, INC.
Lanham, Maryland • Toronto • Plymouth, UK
2008

SCARECROW PRESS, INC.

Published in the United States of America
by Scarecrow Press, Inc.
A wholly owned subsidary of
The Rowman & Littlefield Publishing Group, Inc.
4501 Forbes Boulevard, Suite 200, Lanham, Maryland 20706
www.scarecrowpress.com

Estover Road
Plymouth PL6 7PY
United Kingdom

British Library Cataloguing in Publication Information Available

Library of Congress Cataloging-in-Publication Data

Sears, Edward S. (Edward Seldon), 1943–
   George Seward : America's first great runner / Edward S. Sears.
      p. cm.
   Includes bibliographical references and index.
   ISBN-13: 978-0-8108-6133-6 (pbk. : alk. paper)
   ISBN-10: 0-8108-6133-X (pbk. : alk. paper)
   1. Seward, George, 1817–1883. 2. Runners (Sports)—United States—Biography. I.
Title.

GV1061.15.S38S43 2008
796.42092—dc22
[B]   2007051557

Contents

Foreword

Is it possible that George Seward ran so fast in 1844 that it took over a hundred years for any other human to match him? Common sense says no, there must have been something amiss with the timing, the reporting, the weather conditions or the level of the track. And yet, and yet . . .

Sprinting is the most basic of activities. A fast run over 100 meters by Jesse Owens in 1936 still looks fast when seen on film, even though modern sprinters go a few tenths better. Improvements measured in microseconds owe something to modern training and something to shoes and surfaces. Yet all the technology, the competition, the coaching, the incentives have resulted in what? A difference of less than a second in the 100-meter record since records began to be ratified in 1912.

A sprinter is a sprinter is a sprinter. George Seward was gifted with raw speed. Of that there is no doubt. He ran exceptional times on a number of occasions. He offered to give any man alive a 5-yard start for £100—a huge sum—and nobody would take him on. Contemporary reports called him "astonishing" and "wonderful." He *may* have done 9.25 on that September afternoon in 1844. You will read a full account in these pages, and you can judge how good he was. But I think when you have read all of the book, you will appreciate much more.

George Seward emerged as a talent at a critical time. Athletics was on the brink of huge changes. For centuries runners had met to decide wagers. They challenged each other for money prizes. Sometimes they had rich backers. The races took place on stretches of road, or horse-racing courses, or pieces of ground behind public houses. But while George Seward was still compet-ing, athletic arenas were being built with tracks we would recognize as such. More spectators were drawn to watch. With the development of railways, people were encouraged to travel some distance to be there. The sport of "pedestrianism" was joined by something not quite the same, but similar, called "athletic sports." Soon the first "gentlemen amateurs" would see the attraction of running. Histories of athletics used to be written as if the mod-ern era began in 1850. Any "professional" performances were viewed with suspicion. We now know that the professional timekeepers were exacting. They had to be. Serious money depended on it.

Ed Sears explained all this more thoroughly in his book *Running Through the Ages*. There, in a chapter headed "The Origin of Modern Running," he gave us the fullest account yet of Seward. It was fascinating stuff, rich in de-tail. Yet Ed believed there was more to tell about this phenomenal athlete, and he has spent the years since 2001 in extensive research. Somehow he re-cruited a team of unofficial research assistants in England who helped seek out the family history, the moves and the marriages and the children. I have followed the progress in an e-mail correspondence that itself must almost amount to a book, and I am amazed by the vivid material he has uncovered. We are given an unparalleled insight into the triumphs and tribulations of a runner in the early Victorian era.

George Seward is the first of a long line of world-beating American sprint-ers. His credentials are laid out in these pages, and I think you will agree that ultimately it doesn't matter if some people doubt that 1844 performance. Thanks to this book, his reputation is secure.

—Peter Lovesey, Chichester, England

Preface

A few years ago while doing research for a book on the history of running, I read everything I could find about outstanding runners of the past. Usually the best runners of each era ran similar times for a given race, but occasionally one runner stood out from the rest. For example, in 1886 British professional Walter George ran the mile in 4 min. 12¾ sec., a performance so outstanding for its time that it remained unsurpassed by either amateur or professional for twenty-nine years.

A tiny minority of performances stood out so much I began to wonder if they ever happened. They were "outliers" in a statistical sense—performances so much better than any others of their time that they seemed out of place. Outliers are often bad data, but it is a rule of statistics that they should be studied carefully. Many great discoveries in human history can be traced to researchers exploring some outlying or unusual event.

Examples of outlier running performances include those by Norwegian ultra runner Mensen Ernst. In 1831 several newspapers reported that he had run from Paris to Moscow, about 1,500 miles, in fewer than fourteen days. This feat would be difficult or impossible for the best modern ultra runners. Another example occurred in 1905 when R. P. Williams, an American professional sprinter, convinced some sportswriters he had run 100 yards in 9.0 seconds—a performance that neither the great Jesse Owens in the 1930s nor Bob Hayes in the 1960s could match.

On looking into these two performances I was surprised by how little first-hand reporting there was on them. The newspaper accounts consisted mostly of what the runners said they had done. This lack of supporting evidence led me to conclude that these two outliers could safely be dismissed as bad data.[1]

There was another runner whose performances were so far ahead of his time that I questioned them as well. On September 30, 1844, in Hammersmith, England, George Seward from New Haven, Connecticut, ran 100 yards in 9¼ seconds—an astonishing performance for that era. The time was accepted as a world record and remained in the record books for nearly fifty years until it was removed, mostly because no one could come close to matching it.

Unlike the previous two runners, Seward was not just a clever self-promoter who managed to fool the press. Seasoned reporters from the celebrated sporting journal *Bell's Life* in London as well as the *Era* and *Times of London* all witnessed his performance. After studying these and other contemporary documents, I was unable to find any evidence that he or anyone else faked his performances. Nor was there any indication that they were the result of unreliable timers, short or downhill courses, or tailwinds.

Sprinting was in its formative years in the 1840s and was popular mainly in England and to a lesser extent in America. Methods for starting races, running surfaces, training, and diet were all in primitive states of development. In one respect, however, Seward was like today's best sprinters—he was a professional. But professional running of that time was plagued with unruly crowds, fixed races, and double-crosses. It came to be looked down on and in the second half of the nineteenth century was almost replaced by the more socially acceptable amateur movement.

While today's professional sprinters have corporate sponsors and receive large appearance fees, sprinters of Seward's time earned most of their money from betting on themselves. Seward ran his first professional race in New Haven in 1840 and from the start won his races with almost laughable ease. After only three races he found he was so fast no sprinter in America would race him.

Unwilling to give up running, in 1843 he went to England, where running was more highly developed and racing opportunities more plentiful. He tried hard to keep his great speed a secret while running there, but when he raced William Robinson for the sprint championship of England in 1844, he went all out to win. The result was a 100-yard time that was nearly a second faster than most sprinters of that era could run. After that, he had a very difficult time finding opponents, even in England with its rich running tradition. To continue his career, he had to resort to such measures as offering long starts, starting on his knees, carrying weights, and racing against horses or several men in quick succession. He still had trouble finding opponents and worked hard to become competitive at longer distances such as the mile. Had he not made these extraordinary efforts, he would have been a champion with no challengers and no income.

Although Seward's major races were well reported in the newspapers of his time, many modern writers have neglected these documents and questioned or ignored his performances. Their doubts are based on his being a professional and so much faster than anyone else of his era. In addition, a dubious "eyewitness report" appeared in the *New York Clipper* forty-four years after he set his 100-yard record. The report claimed the course was downhill, Seward took a running start, and there was a strong tailwind.

This book examines this claim as well as other efforts to discredit Seward's performance. More importantly it presents, for the first time, a complete account of the life and running career of this legendary American sprinter. It is hoped it will set Seward's record straight or at least provide enough information to allow readers to make up their own minds about the validity of his records and his place in running history.

Note

1. For a discussion of Mensen Ernst's career, see Edward S. Sears, *Running Through the Ages* (Jefferson, N.C.: McFarland, 2001), 59–62. Information on R. P. Williams is on page 171 of the same book.

~

Acknowledgments

Researching this book was difficult. The events took place long ago on two continents and in an era when most newspapers gave minimal coverage to sports. It would not have been possible without several people who helped track down the details of Seward's life and running career.

I owe a special debt to British mystery writer and track and field historian Peter Lovesey. He convinced me there was enough material for a book on Seward, wrote the foreword, shared his research, and encouraged me at every step of the way.

John Goulstone, also of England and the author of two excellent articles on Seward, was very helpful with the manuscript as well as providing material on several other runners of Seward's era. I would especially like to thank Kev Seward (not related to George, it turned out) who was my "eyes on the ground" in Liverpool. He spent many hours seeking out George's residences there and tracking down his family members. I would also like to thank Maurice Rigby, who searched most of the cemeteries in Liverpool before finding the one where George is buried. The *Liverpool Daily Post and Echo* was helpful in publishing my "Lost Runner" letter asking for information. Tim Rainey of the Local Studies Library in Stalybridge, Paula Moorhouse of the Manchester Archives & Local Studies, and Doug Hindmarch of the Sheffield Local Studies Library all provided useful information. Carole Walsh and Susan Coull were helpful in tracking George's descendants.

In America, Carol Ganz of the Connecticut State Library helped uncover details on Seward's family in New Haven. Wendy Schnur of the Mystic Seaport provided valuable information on Azariah's ship, the *Greyhound*. Thanks also to Bill Mallon for reviewing the manuscript and lastly to my wife, Rebecca, for her help with the manuscript.

~

CHAPTER ONE

The American Wonder's
Last Race (1866)

You see the great ones, the legends, they serve a purpose. A challenge from out of the past that says "Match what I've done, boy, and make it better!"

—Fats Brown

It was a cold day in late February 1866 in Stalybridge, a small town about ten miles east of Manchester, England. Despite the weather and the poor economy, pedestrian fans had come from miles around to see the professional sprint race between Joe Horrocks of Halifax and the American George Seward from New Haven, Connecticut. Horrocks, about forty, was a veteran runner who had once been champion of England at 880 yards. There were few Horrocks fans in the crowd, however; almost everyone was there to see Seward, the famed "American Wonder."[1]

Seward had run but little in almost eight years. Several times he had tried to return to the sport he loved, but each time severe bouts of rheumatism forced him to abandon his comeback attempts. Much of the time he had been bedridden and so ill he had to be lifted in and out of bed. Recently the pain and stiffness had eased, if only temporarily, and he was eager to test himself one more time.

At forty-eight, he was far past the age where most men would be willing to subject their bodies to the rigors of a professional sprint race. Yet he still craved competition and still looked imposing—handsome and well muscled, if a little heavier than he had been in his youth. His neatly trimmed dark hair

1

with a few streaks of gray fell nearly to his shoulders. Long hair was not in fashion, but he had always worn it that way, sometimes wearing a hair net to keep it from flowing in the breeze as he ran.

The race was at 100 yards, Seward's favorite distance and one where he had once been unbeatable. After defeating all the best sprinters in America, he had arrived quietly in Liverpool in 1843 and flashed like a meteor across the British athletic firmament. In the next five years he ran sprint races in unheard-of times and for twelve years was champion of the world at short distance. During that period he effortlessly defeated all challengers until his rheumatism became so bad he could no longer defend his title. Others took his place as sprint champion, but none came close to matching his performances. Even though he was no longer able to beat the best sprinters, Seward did not retire, but continued to race when he was healthy enough to train for a few weeks.

The two men were competing in a "match" race. In these races the runners, or more often their backers, put up the stakes for which they ran. The stakes for this race were £25 a side, enough to support Seward and his family for months if he won. The fans also took part in the betting, and despite his age and illness, Seward's reputation was such that the odds were an overwhelming 5 to 1 in his favor.

They were running on the Stalybridge Recreation Grounds, a sports complex that Seward had once owned. In 1858 he had taken over the Hare and Hounds pub in Stalybridge and built a grand sports complex on a nearby seven-acre site that was surrounded by a high wall. It included a gymnasium, a dancing salon, a bowling green, fishponds, and two running tracks—a 440-yard oval and 250-yard straightaway. Although a foreigner, he had been the great star of his day, well liked and respected by sports fans. His continued popularity allowed him to earn enough to live comfortably and support his wife and three children by managing the complex.

His good fortune did not last. Hard times came to Stalybridge in the mid-1860s. The American Civil War led to a shortage of cotton in England, causing many mills in the Stalybridge area to close. The government set up soup lines to feed those out of work; now few of the citizens of Stalybridge could afford to drink beer in Seward's pub or watch the sports on his grounds. He was forced to close the Hare and Hounds pub and the sporting complex in 1864 and was then out of work himself. Soon he would have to leave to find employment at his old trade of silver plating in one of the larger cities.

Arriving at the familiar athletic grounds on foot, Seward walked slowly around, surveying the site one last time. He took long, wistful looks at the course and greeted old friends he recognized in the crowd. At last he removed his coat and began to take some easy warm-up strides on the straight-away. He moved stiffly at first, but after he loosened up, his running became more fluid and relaxed, and the crowd buzzed at once again seeing the "Won-der" in full stride. His warm-up complete, Seward paused to slip on a pair of light, flexible, spiked running shoes made of goatskin. He had pioneered the use of spikes for sprinting, and they were one of his most prized possessions.

Horrocks, whom Seward had known for many years, met him at the scratch—a line drawn in the dirt at one end of the straightaway. One hun-dred yards down the straightaway, two men held a long handkerchief to form a finish tape. The course had been carefully measured, roped, and staked. One rope went down the middle to separate the runners, and ropes on both sides kept the crowd from interfering.

The two men greeted each other and waited for the referee to toss a coin to decide the choice of sides. Horrocks won, and as the ground appeared a lit-tle firmer in the left lane, chose that side. They stood behind the starting line facing each other, and when the referee was satisfied all was ready, he de-clared the race ready to begin. Horrocks made the first attempt to start, step-ping over the line and sprinting a few yards before realizing Seward had not followed. He stopped, turned around, and walked slowly back for another try. They did this several times, each stepping over the scratch and sprinting away whenever he felt like it. Finally both went over the scratch at the same time, and the race was underway. The crowd cheered loudly as Seward got the best of the start by a small margin, and defeated Horrocks by a scant 12 inches.

Unlike most of his previous races, the narrow winning margin was not by design. He had exerted himself to his limit and still barely won. The thrill from winning was still there, although the narrow victory margin convinced him his twenty-six-year professional running career was finally over. Seward accepted congratulations from his friends and thanked the crowd for coming to see him run. Then he put on his coat and walked away with his head held high. He had gone out on his terms.

Note

1. *Bell's Life*, February 25, 1866.

CHAPTER TWO

~

The Emergence of America's First Great Runner (1817–1843)

New Haven, Connecticut, lies about eighty miles north of New York City. In 1779 British soldiers led by General William Tryon invaded the town and planned on burning it to the ground. They spared it, however, some say, because of the beauty of its elm trees. Today New Haven is best known as the home of Yale University, but it is also the birthplace of George Seward, one of the fastest runners the world has ever seen.

In 1815 New Haven was a picturesque, seafaring town of about 8,000. In April of that year on the faraway island of Sumbawa in Indonesia, a long-dormant volcano named Mount Tambora erupted. It was the most violent volcanic explosion in ten thousand years, and its effects were felt worldwide. Besides killing an estimated 100,000 people, the explosion sent thirty-six cubic miles of ash, dust, and grit high into the atmosphere, obscuring the sun and causing global temperatures to drop by three to six degrees. In 1816, spring and summer never came to New England. Frosts lingered until June and almost no seeds would grow. Newly shorn sheep froze to death, and other livestock died or had to be slaughtered because there was no hay or fodder to feed them. The inhabitants of New Haven called the year "eighteen hundred and froze to death." It was a time of hardship and hunger.[1]

On January 2, 1817, in the midst of the following winter, a dark, intense sailor named Azariah P. Seward married twenty-three-year-old Caroline Temple Bartholomew. Caroline was the daughter of Moses and Mary Bartholomew, a well-to-do New Haven couple. Thirty-year-old Azariah was from the small town of Durham about twenty miles northeast of New Haven.

He and Caroline did not migrate to a warmer climate as some New Englanders had after the long, harsh winter. Instead they bought a house near present-day Columbus Avenue and Spring Street in New Haven. Spring returned to New Haven in 1817, and the weather was almost normal. On October 16, 1817, the couple's first child, George, was born.

The following year Azariah was able to borrow enough money to become part owner and captain of the merchant ship *Greyhound*, a two-masted, eighty-five-ton schooner. We do not know if Azariah was a fast runner, but the greyhound on the masthead of his ship would prove prophetic for his son. Captain Seward plied the coastal trade, sailing the *Greyhound* from New Haven down the eastern seacoast to cities such as Charleston, South Carolina, and Savannah, Georgia, carrying oats, potatoes, hay, and passengers. By working as a coastal captain out of New Haven, he began to earn a comfortable income to support his young family.[2]

In 1819, with the help of a loan from his business partner Andrew Kidston, a New Haven shipping merchant, Azariah was able to become sole owner of the *Greyhound*. The Seward family grew to four that year when on Christmas Day a daughter, Mary, was born.

Just as Azariah was mastering being captain of a ship and had settled into raising his young family, tragedy struck. In March 1820 he put in at the port of New Orleans for extensive repairs to the *Greyhound*, and on October 1, as the work neared completion, he unexpectedly died. The cause of his death is unknown. It may have been from cholera, yellow fever, or perhaps an accident. Azariah's body was brought back to New Haven and buried in the Bartholomew family plot in the Grove Street Cemetery. Because he had no will, the New Orleans probate court seized the *Greyhound* and sold it at auction for $1,050, with $700 of the money going to pay for the repairs the ship had just undergone.[3]

To make matters worse, on October 28, 1820, there was a great fire on the Long Wharf in New Haven. Andrew Kidston, Azariah's business partner, suffered a severe financial loss when his storehouse of rum and other commodities burned. Although Kidston was a friend of the Seward family, he was in no position to forgive Azariah's estate the loan used to buy the *Greyhound*.

In 1822 the New Haven probate court seized the Seward home and sold it at auction to satisfy Azariah's creditors. Not completely heartless, the court allowed Caroline to keep a one-third "widow's share" of the house and garden, which made the property difficult to sell. It was valued at $530, but few people wanted to buy two-thirds of a house, especially if a family was living in the other third. Caroline's mother, Mary Bartholomew, herself a widow living at nearby 14 Fleet Street, bought the house for the bargain price of

$167. Her efforts gave Caroline, five-year-old George, and three-year-old Mary a home of their own where the children grew up.[4]

Caroline's feelings for Azariah were strong, and she remained unmarried for fifteen years after his death. It was a struggle to raise her two children on her own, but she did her best and taught both George and Mary to be honest and polite. We do not know where George went to school, but it is obvious from his later love of reading and thoughtful, well-crafted letters that he received a good education.

George grew up to be a handsome young man who wore his long dark hair in what would today be called "Prince Valiant" style. Had Azariah lived, George would probably have become the captain of a sailing ship, or being an intelligent young man, he might have attended nearby Yale College. Azariah's death closed these doors to George and made it necessary for him to learn a trade to support himself. He took up the trade of silver plating, but his destiny lay in a much different direction—that of a professional runner or "pedestrian."

The word *pedestrian* comes from the Latin *pedester*, meaning "going on foot." Today it is used to refer to someone walking or something dull or unexciting. In the nineteenth century it had a much different meaning. A pedestrian was an athlete who took part in walking, running, or jumping contests, usually for money. Pedestrianism was a working-class sport, and almost all pedestrians as well as their fans came from this group. Had Azariah lived and the family remained prosperous, it is unlikely that George would have taken up professional running as a career.

Although of average height and weight for his day (5 feet 8 inches, 160 pounds), George was an extraordinarily muscular and athletic young man who was also a fierce competitor. He could outrun his schoolmates at any distance they chose and excelled at both high and long jumping. Thaddeus Austin, one of his boyhood companions, said young George was always ready to make a small bet that he could take a short run and jump over a horse—a feat he performed many times. As an adult, he would refine the stunt and thrill his fans by jumping over three horses standing side by side. According to Austin, on another occasion, George took a run of about 15 feet and jumped across a stream. The feat so astonished his friends that they measured the stream where he jumped and found it to be 21 feet wide.[5]

In 1835 Caroline married Richard Trowbridge, a wealthy shipping merchant. The Trowbridge family of New Haven was the largest West Indies trading company in the United States at the time. George, now eighteen, was apprenticed to a silver plater named John Murphy to learn the trade, and he perfected his skills while working at a firm owned by Leverett Barnes of New Haven.

Today silver plating may seem like a quaint occupation, but in Seward's time, it was used to beautify and protect metal parts on carriages and harnesses. When Seward was an apprentice, silver plating could be applied only to copper objects. Plates of pure copper and silver were united by "sweating." The first step was to remove oxide from the surfaces of the plates. The plater then pressed the plates together and heated them until they fused. The two plates could then be rolled or worked without the two metals separating. For irregularly shaped objects, the procedure was different. The object to be plated was cleaned and then covered with sal ammoniac and tinned; then silver leaf was laid on and combined with the tin using the heat of a soldering iron.

About the time George was completing his apprenticeship, John Wright, a surgeon in Birmingham, England, discovered an electroplating process that proved to be a better way to apply silver to metal objects. He used a mixture of cyanide of silver dissolved in cyanide of potassium. A metal object could be plated by submersing it in the mixture and running an electric current through it. Despite the dangerous chemicals involved, Wright's method for silver plating spread rapidly throughout England and America, and George learned to use it as well as the older methods.

George was late in getting started as a runner. His first recorded race did not occur until 1838, when he was twenty-one years old and nearing the end of his apprenticeship as a silver plater. The distance was 330 yards, and the race was open to all comers with prizes for the first three runners. It took place in Wallingford, a small town about fifteen miles north of New Haven. There were eight other runners entered, including an outstanding runner of the time named Lee, who was undefeated in Connecticut. An inexperienced George finished second, a few feet behind Lee. Even though he lost, the thrill of competition and the cheering fans fascinated him. He was hooked on the sport and knew he had talent; all he needed was more experience.

In the next two years he grew stronger and faster, but opportunities for a New England sprinter in the early 1840s were limited. Horse racing, boxing, and running were the only sports with much following in the United States, and even they faced opposition. The influence of the Puritans was still strong, and many preachers considered sports evil as well as a waste of time and railed against them. Newspapers, with a few exceptions, either ignored sports or wrote editorials calling for their abolition. Horse racing was the most popular sport and thrived because it was considered a way to improve the breed. Gambling was the chief motivation for all three sports. There were no amateur sports in America and just a few professional footraces.

As bleak as this picture was, there were a few indicators that running might have a future in America. In 1835 John C. Stevens, a wealthy horse owner, brought national attention to foot racing when he offered a $1,000 purse for a 10-mile race on the Union Course in New York City. The race drew runners from all over the country and, surprisingly, 30,000 spectators.[6]

Unfortunately for Seward, no one in America had ever offered such prizes for sprint races.[7] Except for fairs and a few other special occasions, the only races available to him were match races. These races, originating in England in the seventeenth century, came about because of the British love of gambling. When British immigrants came to America, they brought match racing with them and American runners adopted it.

To take part in a match race, a runner, unless he could raise the money himself, had to find a "backer" who would put up his "stake" or money to bet on the race. With permission from his backer, one runner challenged another to a race. If the second runner accepted the challenge, the two met, usually at a pub, and drew up "articles of agreement," a written contract describing when, where, and how to conduct the race. After they signed the articles, both runners gave the money they had agreed to wager to a stakeholder, a trusted neutral individual. When the race was fairly decided, the stakeholder awarded the money to the winner, who divided it with his backer.

The split of the stakes between the winning runner and his backer depended on the generosity of the backer. Although the amount staked was usually listed in newspaper accounts of races, how the winning runner and his backer divided the money was not. The spectators of these races joined in by betting on their favorite runner at whatever odds they could agree on among themselves. It is easy to see why most professional runners did not prosper from match races. For every winner there had to be a loser—a zero-sum game. If a runner won half his matches, he and his backer would break even, but that would leave him with nothing to live on or to pay his training expenses. Few pedestrians could support themselves from these contests, especially if they were unwilling to be involved in fixed races. Most had to have at least a part-time occupation.

Despite the lack of significant monetary return for all but the best runners, the possibility of winning a stake that was more than a year's wages was attractive to many of the working class. Although the number of sprint races that took place were few, those that were held created much interest among the sporting public and often drew large, enthusiastic crowds.

Seward's first professional race was at 100 yards on October 18, 1840, against Henry Ainsworth, a local runner from New Haven. George put up his own stake of $50 and won by a small enough margin that Ainsworth agreed to another match. The second race was also at 100 yards and took place the following month near New York City. It was George's first race outside the New Haven area, and the stakes were $250 a side—more than George could make in a year as a silver plater. He was able to borrow his stake from friends who had seen him run and recognized his talent. In his second race with Ainsworth, he decided to go all out and impress his friends.

No time exists for the race. Watches that could time races to ¼ second had been in existence since the 1820s, but they were rare and expensive, so there were no official race timers. As a result, few newspapers or sporting journals published times for sprint races. In addition, the time for a match race, where the emphasis was on betting, did not have the importance we assign it today. In fact, pedestrians of Seward's era might well wonder at our modern custom of ranking sprinters solely by their times. Beating a highly regarded opponent and winning by a small enough margin to get a second race were what counted. In addition, many race fans, especially in America, did not have a well-developed sense of what was a good or bad time for a sprint race.

Although no time was recorded for his second race with Ainsworth, Seward surprised everyone with his great speed and easy victory. Those who saw the race agreed that a marvelous new American sprinter had emerged. With his speed now obvious, Seward had no trouble finding a backer, a wealthy jeweler from Newark, New Jersey, named Elias Van Arsdale. George also found another opponent in William Belden from New York. In August 1840 Belden had run 200 yards in 21 seconds in a race on Staten Island, defeating Peter Van Pelt by 20 feet before several thousand spectators. After this victory, the sporting press considered Belden the fastest sprinter in America.[8]

Seward and Belden signed articles in November 1841 to run 100 yards for $500 a side. The match took place at the old Centerville Course on Long Island on December 7. It attracted much attention, and many sports fans turned out to see Belden, the American champion, race the dashing young newcomer from New Haven. Champion or not, Belden proved no match for Seward, who won easily by 6 feet. There was much betting on the race, and one man who had seen Seward's previous races and bet heavily on him made $1,500.[9]

It had taken Seward only three races to rise from an unknown to the unofficial champion sprinter of America. Elated by his easy victories, he went on the road, traveling from town to town throughout New England for all of 1842 and the early months of 1843 searching for matches. To his surprise and great disappointment, he was not able to make a single match. He had earned the reputation of being a "flyer," and the few sprinters available had developed a wholesome dread of him. A few were willing to race him, but they could not find backers.

A drawback of match racing was that if a runner earned a reputation that put him above all the others, it became increasingly difficult to find opponents who could get anyone to back them. In addition, the number of outstanding runners in the United States was small. Frustrated, Seward realized that winning his races with so little effort and showing such blazing speed had scared away the few runners who might have gotten backing to race him.

The main exception to the poor coverage of sports in America in the mid-1800s was the *Spirit of the Times*. It was the country's leading sporting journal, published in New York City and edited by William T. Porter.[10] The weekly *Spirit* covered all the popular sports of the day, including the major footraces in the Northeast. The paper had reported on Seward's race with Belden but for some reason did not print his name. Instead it referred to him as a "Down-East Yankee."

Because there was not much foot racing in America, the *Spirit* often filled its pedestrianism section by reprinting descriptions of the major races from England. The newspaper copied these accounts without change from Britain's top sporting journal, *Bell's Life in London*, and reprinted them about a month after they occurred. It took that long for copies of *Bell's Life* to reach New York by steamer and for the *Spirit* to reprint the accounts.

Bell's Life sometimes reprinted reports of races from the *Spirit of the Times* although not nearly as often. Pedestrianism was much more developed and more popular in England. Since 1822 when Pierce Egan founded *Bell's Life*, it had teemed with glowing reports of footraces for large stakes and small in cities such as London, Manchester, and Sheffield as well as a multitude of smaller cities and towns.

By following these reprinted accounts in the *Spirit of the Times*, Seward realized that finding opponents would not be a problem there. Nearly every city and town in England had its own running heroes who competed with those from other cities and towns. The large number of races there impressed him, and he came to realize opportunities awaited him in the land of "John Bull."

Seward wondered if he could defeat the British sprinters as easily as he had the Americans. Sports fans had often debated the relative merits of the English and American runners. Some believed that times for footraces in Britain were faster than in America because of different atmospheric conditions. In truth, Britain had superior runners at both short and long distances, but the reasons had nothing to do with atmospheric conditions. Britain had the advantages of a large pool of runners, experienced trainers, frequent quality competition, and, most importantly, a running tradition dating back to the running footmen of the 1600s and 1700s.

Seward's desire to use his gift of great speed led him to decide to give up his trade of silver plating and leave his family and friends in New Haven. He would go to England. There was no other choice if he wanted to continue his calling as a professional sprinter. Although he was now the unofficial sprint champion of America, there was no money to be made because no one would race him. His quick rise to the top and sudden inability to find opponents had taught him a valuable lesson. He promised himself that when he arrived in England he would not repeat his mistake of making extravagant public displays of speed. He could make a fresh start there as his name had never appeared in the newspapers in England and no one there knew him.

His mother Caroline's remarriage into the wealthy Trowbridge family in 1835 and his sister Mary's marriage to William Ferree in 1842 made it easier for George to leave New Haven. He had no family obligations since he was unmarried and no longer had to worry about his mother's and sister's welfare. In late spring of 1843, at age twenty-five—middle-aged for a sprinter—he prepared to leave for England.

By the 1840s, many shipping companies catered to the massive number of migrants pouring into America, and the 3,000-mile journey across the Atlantic had become relatively inexpensive. A dozen steamships made the trip from New York to Liverpool charging $120 for a cabin, and passage on any of fifty sailing ships could be had for $20 less.[11] Even these amounts were too much for George, who had spent all his race winnings in his futile search for races in 1842.

Because he did not want *Bell's Life* to know the champion sprinter of America was coming to England, he did not tell anyone other than his family he was leaving. His mind made up to try his luck in England, he found a ship's captain willing to take him on as an unskilled sailor, and after telling Caroline and Mary good-bye, he quietly boarded and prepared to work his way to Liverpool.

Notes

1. Richard B. Stothers, "The Great Tambora Eruption in 1815 and Its Aftermath," *Science* 224, no. 4654 (1984): 1191–98.

2. Azariah was listed as a sea captain on George's marriage certificate.

3. Information on the sale of the *Greyhound* is contained in Azeriah (*sic*) P. Seward's inventory, October 26, 1820, City Archives, Louisiana Division, New Orleans Public Library. Voyages of the *Greyhound* are listed in the *Connecticut Journal* from

October 1818 to November 1819. According to the G. W. Blunt White Library, Mystic Seaport, The Museum of America and the Sea, Mystic, Connecticut, the schooner was registered at New Haven until March 27, 1820, when it was enrolled temporarily at New Orleans. Azariah Seward was listed as owner and master at the time. The *Greyhound* was registered again at New Orleans in January 1821, with New Orleans owners and a new master.

4. The distribution of Captain Seward's property is described in "Azariah P. Seward's New Haven probate" (LDS# 1024378).

5. "George Seward, The American Runner," *New York Clipper*, May 8, 1880.

6. Philip Hone and Allan Nevins, *The Diary of Philip Hone, 1828–1851* (New York: Dodd, Mead and Co., 1927), 156.

7. A "sprint race" or "short distance race" was considered to be any distance of 440 yards or less, although late in his career, Seward would argue that 440 yards was longer than a sprint.

8. *New York Herald*, August 7, 1840.

9. *Spirit of the Times*, December 11, 1841, 486.

10. Porter was a promoter of many sports. He gave wide coverage to horse racing and angling and opened his pages to cricket, foot racing, rowing, yachting, and baseball. He is credited with the first baseball box scores and "dope" stories and was the first to call it the "national game."

11. "Cheap and Quick Traveling," *New York Herald*, October 22, 1840.

CHAPTER THREE

~

Champion of England
and America (1844–1845)

Time is at the heart of all that is important to human beings.

—Bernard d'Espagnat

The sporting scene in England was much different from that in America. The Industrial Revolution there, coupled with improved railroads, led to the spread and increased popularity of sports in the years 1820–1870. Inexpensive rail travel made it possible for both athletes and their fans to cover long distances to attend athletic events. As in America, horse racing, boxing, and pedestrianism were the most popular sports. Boxing and pedestrianism were more developed in England, however, with many more participants and larger followings. These two sports provided excitement, heroes, and betting opportunities for the working masses.

Although the lives of many British factory workers were grim, even the most exploited had some free time to seek escape from the drudgery of their jobs. Many used this time to attend footraces or boxing matches, hoping for a betting coup or at least a diversion from the boring grind in the factories.

There was no season for pedestrianism in England. Runners could be seen racing bare-chested in the dead of winter or in the hottest days of summer. The sport was enjoying heady times in England in 1843. *Bell's Life* and a combination sporting journal–family newspaper, the *Era*, actively supported the sport. They reported on the major races throughout the country, listed future races, and acted as forums where runners could issue and accept challenges. It had long been the custom for *Bell's Life* to cover foot racing in its boxing section, but by 1838 pedestrianism had grown so much in popularity that the editor gave the sport its own section, and in the years 1840 to 1850 it was booming. A fan could take a quick look in *Bell's Life* or the *Era* and find thirty important footraces scheduled for the next two weeks, plus countless minor races for small stakes.[1]

The origin of many of today's track races, such as 100, 200, 400, and 800 meters as well as the mile and several longer races, can be traced to this period in England. There was no governing body to police the sport, so pedestrian matches reflected the character of the runners, their backers, and the fans attending a particular race. Many were contested fairly and the fans orderly, but unruly crowds, "fixed" races, and double-crosses were by no means unknown.

Since the eighteenth century, boxing and pedestrianism had been entwined in the sporting culture of England. Boxing of this era was not for the faint of heart. Until 1866 when the Marquis of Queensberry Rules made wearing gloves compulsory, boxers or "pugilists" fought bare-knuckled using gloves, or "mufflers," only for sparring.

With the popularity of sports and the rapid growth of towns and cities, sporting houses or pubs where runners met their fans, discussed their trade, and challenged other runners became popular. Trainers sometimes handled both runners and boxers, and followers of the two sports often attended the same sporting houses. If they were successful in their careers, both boxers and pedestrians occasionally earned enough in their competitive years to buy a sporting house and, after they retired, used their hard-earned fame to draw customers to their establishments.

On the long voyage across the Atlantic, Seward devised the strategy he would use for his first race in England. He had little money but came up with a plan to make the best use of what he had. At the time, the boxer Jem Ward kept the York Hotel, Liverpool's most popular sporting house, where most of the local boxers and pedestrians met and made their matches.

Seward arrived in Liverpool on June 26, 1843, and went straight to Ward's sporting house. Dressed in his rough sailor's outfit, he did not tell anyone he was the champion sprinter of America, not even Jem Ward or his brother Nick.[2] Instead, he pretended to be new to running, and using a put-on accent that almost made him a laughingstock, said he had just arrived in town and wanted to try his hand at sprinting.

He soon found he might be able to make a match with Jack Fowler, a native of Liverpool who was considered one of the fastest sprinters outside London. When Fowler's backers sized up the strange-talking young sailor, they jumped at the chance to take his money. With the help of Nick Ward, Seward made a 100-yard match with Fowler for £4 (about $20 in 1843) a side.[3] To complete the ruse, Seward insisted on a start, and Fowler agreed to give him 5 yards. Even with a 5-yard start, not a living soul was willing to risk a shilling against such a flyer as Fowler, so Seward had to back himself and put up his own stake. After giving £4 to the stakeholder Jem Ward, he left to find a place to spend the night.

The next day the runners, as well as many spectators, took the ferry across the river Mersey to the race grounds at Woodside, Cheshire, opposite Liverpool. These ferries were open wooden-paddle steamers that had to dodge the many sailing ships using the Mersey.

Seward still pretended to be a novice as he strolled around the ground in his plush cap, worsted shirt, and sailor's pants tucked into his cowhide boots. Many in the crowd wondered, "Who was this brash young man who had the nerve to challenge Jack Fowler, one of England's crack sprinters?" Fowler would surely put the young "Yankee" in his place, they believed, and some of them taunted Seward with "Do you think you can run?" and "Fowler will make you sweat before the race is over."[4]

Despite the American's 5-yard start, Fowler was a 10-to-1 favorite, and even at these odds not one person in the crowd was willing to bet on Seward. Having little more than £10 to his name, George bet £10 on himself, giving the money to the stakeholder Jem Ward, who held it and the £100 bet against him.

After he was told that Fowler was ready to start and did not like to be kept waiting, Seward made his way to the starting line. He sat down on his haunches, kicked off his boots, then pulled his worsted shirt over his head, revealing flesh-colored silk tights and a white cotton running shirt. As he slipped on a pair of spikeless running shoes, the crowd gasped as they got their first look at the American stripped and ready to run. With his muscular physique, the long-haired, handsome stranger looked the picture of a fast runner.

The "knowing ones" looked also, but said little, until Seward took a few warm-up strides to get ready for the start. Then even they stared in amazement. The crowd buzzed and thought aloud, "was this a 'flyer' from some far-away part of the British Isles that had been 'rung in' on them?"[5]

Despite the crowd's reaction, Fowler was still confident and wanted to get on with the race. At the start Seward took his position 5 yards in front of his opponent, and at the word "go" they were off. Midway through the race Fowler made up most of the 5 yards he had given Seward, and for a short time it looked as if he might win. Then Seward made his move, easily accelerating away from Fowler to win by a small margin. Although the outcome was close, Fowler realized he was no match for the Yankee sprinter.

The £100 Seward won was enough to pay for his food and lodging for several months.[6] He stayed in Liverpool for a few days trying to make another match. But by defeating a sprinter of Fowler's stature, he had closed the doors to racing there for the immediate future. He left Liverpool but decided to remain in the north of England far from London, the center of pedestrianism. *Bell's Life*'s and the *Era*'s coverage of racing in the North was not as extensive as in the London area, which meant he could keep out of the limelight, at least for a while.

Now that he had achieved his first goal of earning enough money to support himself for a while, he did not immediately try to make more matches with England's best sprinters. Finding a job and learning the geography and customs of England were his first priorities. He knew little of pedestrianism in England besides what he had read in the *Spirit of the Times*. Unable to find work as a silver plater, he took a job as a "putter" in the Durham coalfields. A putter was a laborer who pushed wheelbarrow loads of coal from the mines with the barrow's wheel running on a plank called the barrow-way. The work was dangerous and backbreaking, but Seward was strong and used to hard work, and it was the best he could do for the moment.

He settled in Cockfield, a village midway between Barnard Castle and Bishops Auckland, and worked at hauling coal from the mines. Although he was eager to continue his running career, he did not challenge any of England's fastest sprinters. Instead he started at the bottom, entering races open to all and running match races with second-rate opponents. During this time, he lived quietly in Cockfield and for nine months never ventured outside the North.

The first of Seward's races reported in the pedestrian section of *Bell's Life* was a "foot hurdle race" at Bellevue near Manchester on September 4, 1843, two months after he arrived in England. The thirty-five-acre enclosed ground at Bellevue was one of England's premier racecourses. Located two and a half miles from Manchester, it featured a running course with a splendid grandstand and rails along the track to keep the crowd from encroaching on the long straightaway. In addition, the grounds had a beautiful lake, a museum, a collection of animals, and a superb exhibit of rare birds.

A hurdle race in three starts or "heats," each twice around the 586-yard track, was the main sports event that day. The men were to leap sixteen irregularly spaced hurdles 3 feet 6 inches high. Hurdle racing had come into existence a few years earlier in England. Reports of "foot-hurdling" began to appear in British newspapers near the end of the 1830s. The event grew rapidly in popularity and would become a craze in 1844–1845.[7]

The winner of two of the three races was to receive £5, given by the landlord. Hurdles of this era were not like modern ones but evolved from sheep hurdles and were usually planks about 3 feet 6 inches high supported by poles in the ground. Because they were not designed to be knocked over, if a runner hit one he could suffer a serious injury. The athletes did not stride across them like modern hurdlers but leaped them with enough clearance to provide a safety margin. Seward had never seen a hurdle race as the sport was unknown in America. To add to his difficulty, 1,172 yards was well beyond the distance he normally ran.

It was the custom for British runners to have colorful nicknames. Among those present that day were Benjamin Badcock, "the Lurcher" of Birmingham; Richard Whitehead, "Barrel" of Crumpsall; and William Jackson, "the American Deer." Seward, who used the nickname "the American Youth," went off in the lead but found timing his jumps over the irregularly spaced hurdles more difficult than he had expected. When he neared the last hurdle, he began to tire. "The Lurcher," an experienced hurdler, passed him and won by 5 yards. After a 15-minute rest, they ran the second race, and Seward again finished out of the money.

Besides not being fit enough to race the full distance, he found hurdle racing required more than just superior speed and leaping ability. Later he would master the technique well enough to challenge anyone in the world to a match with him jumping the hurdles on ice while his opponent jumped them on land! Although he did not win anything that day, Seward learned a great deal about hurdling and met William Jackson, "the American Deer." The two men would later become close friends and their careers entwined.[8]

Seward's nickname "the American Youth" did not stick. Instead he soon became known as "the Cockfield Putter," from working in the mines there. He found a backer named Dan Dinsmore, a former boxer and noted walker, and began challenging runners in the North. His strategy was to make matches with second- and third-rate runners and try to win by as small a margin as possible to avoid drawing attention. By making the races close, he hoped the defeated runners would feel they might have a chance against him in a second match. Both Seward and Dinsmore believed this strategy would give them the most opportunities to make matches and earn money before all the local runners learned how fast he was and refused to race him.

His first match-race victory was at 500 yards against Samuel Wood of Levenshulme. The stakes were £10 a side, and the race took place at Bellevue, near Manchester, in early September. Later that month he raced John Jackson, "the Hewer Lad," 100 yards for £5 a side and won again, this time by a half yard. On October 21, 1843, at Cookton Hill, he raced John Chapman 120 yards for £3 a side. Chapman led until near the end, but Seward slipped by him and won in 13½ seconds.

Thinking ahead, Seward looked for a wealthier backer who could put up the stakes for the matches that he felt were in his future. He soon met George Colpitts, a tavern owner in nearby Bishop Aukland who was wealthy enough to put up the stakes for any races the American might run. Their association would last for many years and benefit both men. Not only did Colpitts have deep pockets, he was generous and treated Seward well and, like the runner he backed, was an honorable man who would have no part of fixed races. The two men would develop a deep and lasting friendship.

Seward next ran a disputed 100-yard race with Charles Metcalfe of Stockton at Darlington. The starter was alleged to be John Johnson, a farmer returning from market who had been pressed into starting the race. He sent the runners away by firing a pistol, but it was not a good start, and he ruled the race unfair and that the stakes should be withdrawn or the race rerun. Later Johnson could not be found, and some questioned whether he ever existed. The dispute raged on through the winter in the pages of Bell's Life, giving Seward some unwanted publicity.

Colpitts offered to give the £8 stakes to Metcalfe if he would agree to race Seward again for £50 a side, or offered to rerun the race for the original stake or with £10 to £20 added. Metcalfe, realizing he was up against a superior runner, refused, and reporting on the dispute finally petered out without revealing what happened to the stakes.

Seward's last race of 1843 was a 200-yard match against John Foster of Barnard Castle on December 21 near Cockfield. Foster's side of the road was slippery, and he fell at the start. Seward, trying to keep the race close, slowed when he saw Foster fall, allowing him to scramble to his feet and catch up. The "Putter" then burst ahead and won easily.

He opened 1844 with a 100-yard race against John Cooper, alias "Tearaway of Chester-le-Street," at Plawsworth Flats. After seven or eight false starts, Cooper went off with the lead and kept it until within 5 yards of the finish. Seward, as usual, tried to slip by him at the end but miscalculated, and the referee declared the race a dead heat. The two men agreed to rerun the race on January 15, but Seward had to forfeit his stake of £10 because of a sore ankle.

His first loss in a match race in England came on February 5 in a 130-yard race with Thomas Atkinson of Shincliffe. The race was for £25 a side, Seward's highest-stakes race since arriving in England. At 3 p.m. the men appeared at the scratch, the odds being 6 and 7 to 4 on Seward. To everyone's surprise, Atkinson won by 1½ yards. Much money changed hands, and many that had bet on Seward were angry with him, thinking he had sold the race.

The two men had started by "mutual consent," where they stood behind a line or "scratch" and either could start whenever he felt like it. If both did not cross the scratch, however, they had to return for another try. Seward was inexperienced at using this start, which required much practice to perfect. C. A. Wheeler, in *Sportascrapiana* (1867), described the prevailing method of starting and timing a mutual-consent race.

> Your man should stand on the mark, with his face to his opponent, perfectly upright. Here you will see at once the difference between a professional and a novice. The eye of the former tells him whether his opponent means going or not, and if he can start before his opponent's muscles become stiffened, generally gets the lead of half a yard. . . . Place a practical man with one of M'Cabe's stopwatches at the finishing point, with his eye on the feet of his man, and from the first motion of the 'spirter' set the watch off, still keeping his eye immovably on his man's feet, with his thumb-nail on the stop-watch, and directly he steps on the scratch of finish, either one or the other side, stop the watch, and you can tell to a beat what your man has done. If the timer should have his eye on the man, instead of his feet, he is very likely to lose time, as the foot starts before the arms or body, and finishes the same.[9]

Seward later recalled how he went over the line, but thinking Atkinson had not started, stopped and turned around to go back. Atkinson, taking advantage of Seward's inexperience, bolted past him and was several yards in the lead before the "Putter" realized what had happened. Seward turned and desperately tore after Atkinson and was able to cut his huge lead to 1½ yards at the finish. He never made this mistake again and eventually became so expert at the mutual-consent start that he preferred to have his races started that way.

Four days later, Seward ran Joseph Nixon of Gateshead 120 yards for £15 a side. He defeated Nixon with ease and a day later ran a 150-yard match for £25 a side with Gowens of Felton. This race took place near Morpeth in the presence of about a thousand spectators. After twenty false starts, they got off together, and continued that way until near the finish when Seward made his move and won in 16½ seconds. The time, one of the few reported for his races, suggests he was running just fast enough to win. Upward of £400 changed hands among those attending the race, and a "sporting female," who had bet every shilling she had on the handsome American, gave him a sovereign to express her gratitude. Seward, although he won, appeared exhausted after the race and complained that 150 yards was too far for him. It is likely he did this to encourage someone to challenge him at longer distances, as he would later show that he could also run the longer sprints faster than anyone else of his time.

Despite his efforts to keep a low profile, there was so much interest in pedestrianism in England that it was only a matter of time before a runner of Seward's caliber became known nationally. On February 25, the editor of Bell's Life received a letter from a reporter explaining why he had not reported on Seward's race with Nixon. "Steward, commonly called the Cockfield Putter, is a very superior runner and does not wish his victories to be published, that he may have greater opportunities of making matches with second and third-rate men. Our correspondent adds that it would be more manly for Steward's friends to throw down the gauntlet to Willox or Robinson."[10]

John Willox ("the Scotchman") was the fastest sprinter in Scotland, and William Robinson ("the Newton Moor Ranger") was considered the fastest short-distance runner in England. Since Seward's arrival in England, both Bell's Life and the Era had misspelled his name as "Steward." He did not correct the error because he was in no hurry to have it known that he was the champion sprinter of America.

Although he was doing well running in the North, Seward knew it would not last and that London, with its population of about two million, was where the big-money races came off. Now that he was beginning to make a reputation as a superior sprinter, fewer and fewer runners in the North would be willing to race him. If he wanted to advance his career, he would have to get some experience running in London.

After quitting his job at the Durham coal mines, he quietly traveled to London and soon found part-time employment as a waiter at Johnny Broome's "Rising Sun," a popular sporting tavern on Air Street, Piccadilly. Johnny Broome (figure 3.1), who kept the tavern, had won the boxing title of England in 1841 and retired as champion.[11]

Seward knew that in London he would be under the watchful eyes of Bell's Life and Era reporters who would do their best to discover how fast he was. To keep them in the dark, he decided to train at secret locations and use aliases when he raced. The names he chose included Sherrin, William Sherryn, Sherryn the Unknown, "Johnny Broome's Waiter," and possibly others.

It was acceptable in mid-nineteenth-century England for runners to use nicknames as well as their real names, but the editor of Bell's Life frowned on the "questionable practice" of using a fictitious name solely to hide a runner's identity. In time, Bell's Life reporters would discover Sherryn's identity, but before that happened, Seward hoped to become familiar with London and improve his hurdling skills.

JOHNNY BROOME'S SPARRING ARENA.

Figure 3.1. Seward was employed as a waiter at Johnny Broome's about the time this illustration was made. From *The New Tom Spring's Life in London and Sporting Times,* February 24, 1844.

His first race in the London area was a March 12, 1844, hurdle race of slightly more than 400 yards at the Crown Inn in Harlesden. Running as "Sherryn the Unknown," he found he had not yet mastered the finer points of hurdling when he fell going over a hurdle midway through the race and injured his ankle. Jumping up, he tried to continue, but the encroaching crowd prevented him from getting back in the race.

Two weeks later he raced Frederick Scott of Hammersmith at London's Hyde Park. The stakes were £10 a side, and several hundred people came to watch the race. Scott had created a stir four months earlier when he was arrested while running a trial near the Hammersmith Bridge. The police charged him with "unlawfully, wickedly and scandalously exposing to the view of persons present his body naked and uncovered, for the space of one hour." Scott had not run completely naked but wore shoes, a handkerchief around his head, and knee-length shorts. The only objectionable body part he exposed was his navel. Although running shirtless was commonplace, the judge and jury decided his outfit was too revealing for their tastes and found him guilty. They recommended mercy, and believing he was ignorant of the law, fined him forty shillings.[12]

Scott was more decently dressed for his race with "Sherryn" and won by better than a yard. Seward, who had been hobbled by his injured ankle, told *Bell's Life* after the race he was not satisfied with his defeat. He challenged Scott to run the same distance again for £5, but Scott refused.

Seward's next opponent was Benjamin Badcock, "the Lurcher" of Birmingham, at 100 yards for £10 a side. The race took place on April 1 at Hampton, and "Sherryn" won by three yards. Badcock must have recognized Seward because they had faced each other in a hurdle race at Bellevue a year earlier. The two men agreed to run a 250-yard hurdle race for £10 a side on April 9 at the Beehive Cricket Ground, Walworth.

On the day of the race there was a large crowd present, and Badcock was the favorite at 6 to 4. Seward had not yet mastered hurdling and, having given up the hard physical labor in the mines, was several pounds overweight. After a good start the two men were even for the first four of the fifteen hurdles, but by 100 yards Badcock was 3 yards in the lead and went on to win by 5 yards. *Bell's Life* wrote, "Badcock looked in admirable condition, but his opponent, a fine made young fellow, appeared a great deal too fat. If Sherryn can only make up his mind to go through a regular course of training, he would cut out the work for some of the best men of the day."[13]

In April 1844, Seward decided he had gained enough experience running in London and had improved his hurdling skills to where he was competitive with the best hurdlers in England. He was now ready to make his run at becoming the champion sprinter of England. Returning to Durham, he resumed running as "the Cockfield Putter." It is unclear whether he went back to work in the mines or was able to support himself solely from his running.

His first race after returning was at 440 yards over six hurdles on the Craven Course in Durham on April 18. The prize was a silver cup valued at 20 guineas. By now Seward was becoming well known in the North. His popularity, the celebrity of the other runners, and "the beautiful and romantic piece of ground selected for the run-in," led to an overflow crowd of 20,000 filling the ground and the banks of the river and adjoining woods. Seward's opponents were Booth, "the Yorkshireman"; Badcock, "the Lurcher"; Scarlett, "the Doctor" of Newcastle; Thomas Atkinson of Shincliffe, and John Atkinson, "the Teetotaler," of Durham.

There was a delay in starting caused by a misunderstanding with the clerk of the course about digging holes in the turf to put up the hurdles. Clearing the huge crowd from the course took even more time, and it was 7 p.m. before workers could string ropes along the sides of the course to hold back the huge crowd and get ready for starting. When the men came to the scratch, all of them appeared in top condition. Seward had shed most of the extra weight he had put on in London. The men wore tights and silk jackets and caps to keep from offending the delicate Victorian sensibilities of the women present.

When the starter fired his pistol, "the Teetotaler" took the lead followed by "the Lurcher," with Seward about 5 yards behind.[14] Everyone cleared the first hurdle except Thomas Atkinson, who misjudged it and had to back up a few yards and try again, causing him to lose 10 to 15 yards. By the fourth hurdle he had regained his lost ground. "The Teetotaler," who had run himself out in the early going, staggered across "the Lurcher's" path and collided with him, causing both men to fall. They got up quickly, but Seward was several yards ahead before "the Lurcher" could get back up to speed. Despite "the Lurcher's" desperate effort, Seward won his first major hurdle race by 10 yards to the deafening cheers of the crowd. Later in the evening, the runners and their followers met at the Puncheon Inn owned by John Colpitts, where Seward was presented with the silver cup and the crowd celebrated his victory.[15]

The following week F. Featherston of Durham wrote to *Bell's Life* demanding the race be rerun because "the Lurcher" had interfered with "the Teetotaler." Seward's bold reply left little doubt that he had made great strides in mastering the hurdles and was now supremely confident of both his sprinting and hurdling abilities.

In reply to Mr. Featherston, I have only to state that I received the cup by the decision of the judge, the rest of the runners being in the room at the time and no one made the least objection, however if the Teetotaler wishes for another chance I will stake the cup to his £5 and race him in the same race as before— the winner to receive both or I will run him the same distance 440 yards with or without hurdles for £20 a side. And to convince the cold water drinker and his friends that he is not a runner, I will give him 20 yards start and will be prepared at the Puncheon Inn, Durham tomorrow night to make the match.

Yours &c George Steward,
Cockfield May 8[16]

The last sentence of Seward's letter made it clear he was no longer pretending to be a novice or second-rate runner. Twenty yards is a huge handicap to offer in a 440-yard race. Still, he was unable to entice "the Teetotaler" into another match and a week later challenged both Atkinson, who had defeated him, and Metcalfe, with whom he had run the disputed race. Neither was willing to race him again, but on July 7 *Bell's Life* announced a much more important race, a match between "Steward from the North," and John Smith, "the Regent-street Pet," at 100 yards for £50 a side.

This race marked a turning point in Seward's career in England. Previously, his races had been for small stakes against second- and third-rate runners. Now he had made a match for a large stake against one of the fastest sprinters in England. At the time the average wage of a laborer in England was less than £100 a year. The willingness of George Colpitts (Seward's backer) to stake more than half a year's wages on the race meant he had developed enough confidence in Seward to back him for high stakes against one of England's best sprinters.

The *Era* described the public's anticipation of Seward's first major match race in England. "The match had created a lively interest among the lovers of pedestrian sports, and the result was looked forward to with feverish anxiety, as this race would test the genuine qualities of the American runner, about whom so long a veil of mystery has hung."[17]

John Smith, "the Regent-street Pet," was born in Leicester on March 2, 1819. He started his athletic career as a boxer but in his second match broke his hand and turned to sprinting and hurdling. Arriving in London in 1841, he defeated Charles Jenkinson, "the London Stag," in his first race there. In 1842, after beating his brother Edward in a 120-yard race across Waterloo Bridge, he announced he could be backed against anyone in the world at either 100 or 440 yards for £50 a side. Smith, who was also an outstanding hurdler, had one annoying tendency. He liked to keep everyone waiting at the start and in one match made 147 false starts taking more than two hours.[18]

According to the articles, Seward's race with the "Pet" on August 19 was to be on a macadamized section of the road leading to the Thatched House Inn in Hammersmith.[19] This was a scenic, level course that would become one of Seward's favorites. Large sums of money were riding on the race, as were the reputations of both runners. After signing the articles, Smith left town for intensive training at the Angel Inn at Sutton, Surrey. Seward trained himself and kept the location under wraps.

Tom Oliver, a popular retired boxer, roped and staked the 100-yard section of road to prevent the crowd from pressing in on the runners. He also placed a rope supported by stakes down the middle to keep the runners from interfering with each other. The time stated in the articles for the starting was 4 p.m., but the two men did not come to the scratch until nearly half past five, irritating many of the spectators. Early on, the betting had been even, but by race time the odds had changed to 5 to 4 in favor of Seward.

After making twenty false starts, Smith went over the line with a slight advantage. Seward, considering the "Pet" a first-class runner, took no chances. He made his move early and by 50 yards had passed Smith and was more than 3 yards in the lead. Realizing he had his man beaten and not wanting to show too much speed, he eased up and ran the rest of the way with his head turned to one side, keeping his "sinister ogle on the Pet of Regent-street." The result stunned the crowd, and *Bell's Life* wrote: "The time was said to be 10½ seconds but we thought it was not quite so much."[20]

As in America, there were no official timers at races, and *Bell's Life* correspondents did not normally time them either. The reporter wrote that the time was less than 10½ seconds but did not say by how much. In the instances when *Bell's Life* reported times, they were conservative. Unlike many other newspapers and sporting journals, *Bell's Life's* reporters were knowledgeable of the sport they were covering. They knew roughly what most runners were capable of running and reported few dubious or "too-good-to-be-true" times. Three days later at Broome's tavern, the stakeholder handed over the £100 to Seward and started a collection for Smith. Seward headed it with a sovereign.

Encouraged by his first victory in a high-stakes match in England, Seward challenged two more top sprinters. He challenged Charles Jenkinson, "the London Stag," to race at 160 to 200 yards and Jemmy Kitchener, "the Hampstead Stag," to run 100 or 120 yards, for £25 or £50 a side. There was no response, but on the same day the public received news of a far more exciting match—Seward and Robinson of Newton Moor.

In the summer of 1844 William Robinson, known as "the Newton Moor Ranger" and "the Wonder of the World," was clearly the fastest of the English sprinters. In addition, he was an outstanding middle-distance runner. In January 1844 he had given Charles Jenkinson, "the London Stag," who had previously run 440 yards in just less than 51 seconds, a 10-yard start in a ¼-mile race and defeated him by 6 yards. Afterward, Robinson offered to run any man in the world 440 yards for £100 and give a 10-yard start. He had also recently recorded a time of 3 min. 22 sec. in defeating William Jackson, "the American Deer," in a ¾-mile race. After that race, Robinson offered to run anyone in the world from 100 to 1,000 yards for £100 a side.

George Colpitts allowed Seward to accept Robinson's challenge but had so much respect for "the Newton Moor Ranger" that he would not stake more than £50 a side against him. On August 25, 1844, the *Era* published the articles for what would be the greatest 100-yard race of the nineteenth century.

George Steward agrees to run William Robinson, 100 yards, for £50 side on a fair, level, turnpike road, within 10 miles of London, on Monday, September 30th. In pursuance of this agreement £5 a-side are now deposited in the hands of Jem Burn who is appointed final stakeholder. The second deposit of £5 a-side at Johnny Broome's, tomorrow Monday evening, the 26th instant, and the third deposit of £5 a-side, at Mr. Halifax's, the Horse and Dolphin, St. Martin-street, Leicester square, on Monday, September 2nd; the fourth deposit of £10 a-side at Mr. Parr's, the Green Mary, Green-street, Grosvenor-square, on Monday, September 9th (when the place of running is to be named) the fifth deposit, of £10, at Mr. Halifax's, aforesaid, on Monday, September 16th and the final deposit of £15 a-side at Jem Burn's on Saturday, September 28th. Each and every deposit is to be made good between the hours of 8 and 10 o'clock or the party failing to forfeit the whole of the money down. The ground is to be roped and staked from end to end and each party is to pay an equal share of the expenses. The men are to meet at 12 o'clock and be prepared to start precisely at 2 o'clock.[21]

The articles clearly stated the race was to take place on a level course, although many years later, in an effort to discredit Seward, a supposed eyewitness would claim the course was downhill. Breaking up the stakes into several deposits increased public interest and drew customers to the various pubs. The meeting places were all popular sporting taverns in the London area, and each of them expected large crowds when the two famous runners met to make their deposits.

Bell's Life broke the news that the mysterious "Steward" was in reality an American from New Haven, Connecticut, and there were rumors he had already beaten Robinson in a private 100-yard trial. But after his loss to Atkinson, his friends at West Auckland had, for a while, refused to back him again. The article ended by saying Seward was "a very steady young man and as fast a runner as any of the most celebrated men."[22]

In their description of Seward's race with "the Regent-street Pet," the *Era* reported that Seward's old employer, boxer Johnny Broome, had been his trainer. Seward immediately wrote to the *Era*, correcting the error and challenging any runner in the world to run for the championship of England—an offer he would repeat countless times during his career.

CHALLENGE TO ALL THE WORLD.—Mr. Editor, -You would oblige me by correcting a small paragraph in your last stating that I was under the care of Mr. Broome; I wish you to state that I was not under his care, neither did he know where I was training. I trained myself, as I always shall do. You would oblige me also by inserting, that, although I am matched with Robinson for £50, I am still open to run any man in the world for the Championship of England, 100 yards, for £50.

Yours, respectfully, George Steward.[23]

Seward did not trust the prevailing training methods for sprinters and preferred to train himself. Perhaps he was wise in doing so. The book *Sportascrapiana* (1867) described how a British sprinter of Seward's time trained:

Training. -The first two days your man should be in what is called 'strong physic.' He should keep good hours; in bed by eight or half past; not lay too warm; rise at seven o'clock. He should be provided with plenty of clean Guernseys and drawers. Dress, and walk one mile out, and home; strip and take a good shower bath; he should be briskly rubbed for at least twenty minutes. Rubbing is particularly essential, as it extends the muscles. Dress well in flannel, keeping the wrists covered with flannel all day.

Wear heavy shoes for exercise. Breakfast at half-past eight, taking mutton chops, tea, and dry toast; not any slops, and not too much tea. Sit half an hour or so after each meal, read or write, so as to keep the mind occupied, not thinking too much of the coming match, as it is apt to make a man slower, or, in slang terms, 'fink.' After this he should take a steady five-mile walk out, and five back; on reaching home, take a tumbler of calf's-foot jelly and a dry biscuit.

Then take your man to the scratch, stripped, all but short drawers and slippers, the latter made as light and strong as possible. Select a piece of level turnpike-road or towing-path, rather loose, so that the spikes should not hurt his feet; put your man on the scratch for one hour, practicing starting, which is most essential, either starting himself or 'by pistol,' as per articles of match. If 'by mutual consent,' your man should have someone to keep starting with him; if 'by pistol,' to start and run about twelve yards out by report. After this, dinner; rump steak, or mutton (no vegetables), bread, and sherry (no smoking).

In the afternoon take a straggling walk of two or three miles across the fields, throwing stones, or shooting (skittles if you like), or other amusement or occupation, to keep the muscles in action; not too severe exertion of any kind, for fear of stiffness. Run the distance for which the match is made, about every third day at top speed. Take dry toast and tea about six o'clock. This repeated every day.[24]

It was unusual for professional runners of this era to train themselves. Most had trainers and followed their instructions without question. By this time, Seward had been racing professionally for four years and felt comfortable training himself. Dispensing with a trainer would prove a great advantage in the years to come, as he was free to develop the training methods that best suited him. Since he needed no trainer, he was also able to move around the country in a way most pedestrians could not. He usually kept his training locations secret and during this phase of his career did not like for his opponents or the public to witness his training.

Seward did not want to remain idle for a whole month waiting to race Robinson. In late August, he signed articles to race John Rush of Bradford 120 yards on September 16, two weeks before his match with Robinson. The site for the race with Rush was on the Market Harborough road near Leicester. Former boxing champion Peter Crawley agreed to hold the £50-a-side stakes, and according to the articles Seward was to give Rush a 2-yard start.

In a letter to the *Era*, Seward offered to run Robinson a second race of 120 yards for £50 a side on the same day as their 100-yard race. Usually runners took several days of rest between major races. Either Seward did not expect to have to give his best effort to beat Robinson or he had extraordinary recuperative powers. Robinson, who considered himself better at the longer sprints, declined the second race but offered Seward £5 to change their 100-yard match to 120 yards and run for £100 a side. Seward declined Robinson's counteroffer.

When Robinson and Seward met at Mr. Parr's Green Mary on September 9, Seward won the toss for choice of ground and chose to race on a section of the Hammersmith New-road near the Seven Stars Inn. The site was where he had previously defeated "the Regent-street Pet."

Seward now had all the racing he could handle and had achieved his goal of running high-stakes matches against the best sprinters in England. His preparation for the race with Rush did not go as expected, however. Five days before the race, while running a trial, he strained the sartorius muscle in his right leg. The sartorius is the long, narrow muscle running across the thigh from the hipbone to the inside of the leg below the knee.

In a match race, once a runner signed articles, he had to go through with the race. If he did not, his opponent could claim the stakes and often did. Seward's unexpected injury left him with a major problem. Not only did he have to race Rush in five days, but he also had a race with an even more dangerous opponent, William Robinson, looming two weeks after that. George Colpitts tried to delay the race with Rush for a week to allow the injury to heal, but Rush's backers insisted the match go on, as the articles required.

Both Seward and Rush arrived at Dick Cain's Castle Tavern in Leicester near the end of the week and stayed there until the race on the following Monday. Seward's recent defeat of "the Regent-street Pet" and his pending match with Robinson created much interest, and running fans came from all over the country. On the day of the race the crowd was so large it tied up traffic. The police soon arrived and told the men they could not race there and insisted they "move on." The runners, their backers, and the spectators all walked to a new location with less traffic, and the police allowed the race to take place. The police in London took special delight in harassing pedestrians and their fans. Not only were the races a hindrance to traffic but also most of the runners and their followers were of the working class. Dick Cain, owner of the Castle Tavern, later wrote indignant letters to both *Bell's Life* and the *Era*, complaining that the police had arrested and fined him £2 for merely trying to watch the race!

There was little wagering on the race because word had gotten out that Seward was injured and few would bet on him. Several men had come from London to back him, but Colpitts, unsure that Seward's leg would hold up, advised them not to, and 2-to-1 odds on Rush went begging. Seward remained silent, realizing that, injury or not, he must not only go through with the race but also make up 2 yards on a dangerous opponent.

Bell's Life described the match as "one of the best contests ever witnessed." The start was not by mutual consent, the normal method of starting match races. Instead, the men started at the drop of a hat. By 75 yards Seward had made up Rush's 2-yard start and then made a rush of his own to win by 2½ yards. Even with Rush's 2-yard start, Seward did not have to go all out, and his bad leg did not fail him. His friends celebrated his victory with great delight although there had been little money riding on the outcome.[25]

After he defeated Rush, Seward immediately resumed preparations for his race with Robinson. Not wanting anyone to know the extent of his injury or witness his trials, he trained at a secret location at Deal in Kent about ninety miles southeast of London. He was afraid to do any fast running. Instead he took easy runs and rested, hoping his injured leg would be sound for the most important race of his life.

There was much excitement in the weeks leading up to his race with Robinson. The public was split on who it thought would win. Most favored Robinson, "the Newton Moor Ranger," who had defeated all the top English runners at distances from 100 yards to ¾ mile. After his triumphs over John Smith, "the Regent-street Pet," and Charles Jenkinson, "the London Stag," knowledgeable fans believed Robinson had no equal in the world from 100 to 440 yards. Indeed, until Seward accepted his challenge, Robinson had been so feared that no one had been willing to race him.

Robinson, born on January 31, 1823, was from Cheshire. With a long stride, muscular thighs and legs, and a full chest, he was well made for running. His best running weight was about 150 pounds, and he stood 5 feet 9½ inches. He had run 440 yards in 51 seconds in a previous race, and there were rumors he had covered the distance inside 50 seconds in a trial. In addition, the *Era* reported that he had equaled the fastest time on record for 120 yards.[26] When he and Seward met at Jem Burn's tavern two days before the race to make their final deposits on the stakes, Robinson was so confident he bet £20 of his own money on himself.

At Newcastle the race was a hot topic of conversation, and the odds were 6 to 4 and 2 to 1 on Robinson, with few takers. Most sporting men from the North backed Robinson, but at Durham, Seward's adopted hometown, he was the favorite and several betting men planned to back him. The sporting enthusiasts at Blackheath, where Robinson had gone into training a month earlier, backed him to win. However, some thought he had trained too hard, because his weight had dropped from 168 to 145 pounds, 5 pounds below his normal running weight.

On the day of the race, a crowd of about 2,000 gathered just before noon at the straight stretch of the Hammersmith New-road where the race was to take place. They had come from all over the country. There were Seward's supporters from Durham and a great number of Robinson backers from Newcastle and the surrounding villages of Winlaston, Swalwell, and Blaydon. Many of Robinson's supporters had left the North by steamboat six days earlier.

Robinson, not known for his modesty, arrived in a "carriage and four" from his headquarters at the Seven Stars Inn a third of a mile away. When he reached the Thatched House Inn where the runners had agreed to meet, a band struck up "See the Conquering Hero Comes." Seward and George Colpitts, more modestly, walked from Mr. Parr's on Green-street, where he had spent the night.

Bell's Life described Seward as

> a particularly muscular and fine made young man, with a good-looking frontispiece. It is said that he never trained previously to his two or three last matches, but on this occasion he got himself in pretty good order at Deal. He had not, however, given a trial since he ran with Rush, it being feared that his right leg that had been strained in a spin previous to that race, would again receive some injury. It was well known that his time for 100 yards was most extraordinary, and although backed against such a first-rate man as Robinson, his friends appeared confident of the result, and they backed him freely.[27]

The police did not show up to harass the runners, and Tom Oliver had the course neatly roped and staked by half past two when the men came to the scratch. Seward wore white silk shorts and a white cotton shirt with blue trim. Robinson wore a similar outfit with a pattern of small diamonds, each having a dot in the center.

A spontaneous burst of applause broke out from the spectators when the two scantily dressed rivals appeared. The American looked so impressive and confident the odds changed from being in favor of Robinson to 6 and 7 to 4 in Seward's favor. George Colpitts had become so sure his runner would win that he offered odds of 2 to 1 on him. Robinson also looked to be in fine condition and appeared sure of himself and ready to run.

The tension was almost unbearable as the two men stepped to the scratch. The excited fans lining the sides of the course from end to end fell silent and strained their eyes to follow every move the two men made. After nine false starts, Robinson stepped over the line, Seward followed, and the race was underway.

Robinson's supporters shouted with joy as he held a slight lead for about 60 yards. Then Seward, ducking his head slightly, shot past him and in a few strides had a 2-yard lead. A look of amazed disbelief appeared on Robinson's face as he strained to regain the lost ground. He could not make up an inch, and the American finished an easy winner. Jem Burn, the referee, gave the victory margin as 1½ yards, but other observers thought it was a full 3 yards. Seward would later say his victory margin was 2 yards. *Bell's Life* reported: "The distance was run in *less than ten seconds*, but the American Deer said that by his first-rate watch, the time was *nine and a quarter seconds*."[28]

Seward's performance was one for the ages—far surpassing any other 100-yard race of the nineteenth century. C. A. Wheeler, in *Sportascrapiana* (1867), described the times sprinters were running in the mid-nineteenth century. "A good 'spirt' runner should be able to do one hundred yards in ten and a-half seconds; a 'clinker' can do it in ten, but there are not two men known that can do it in less. If you had a man that could do it in ten, you could win £10,000 at Sheffield with him."[29]

Seward had not only broken 10 seconds, he had done it by a huge margin. The *Times of London* wrote: "Sherrin, by this victory, has placed himself in the first rank of runners for a short distance, and it would be very difficult to find a competitor who would have any chance with him. It was generally remarked that more money was laid out upon this race than upon any similar event for a long time past."[30]

Many who watched the race might not have grasped the significance of running 100 yards in 9¼ seconds. But if they did not fully understand what had happened, they at least went home knowing they had witnessed something wonderful, something they could tell their children and grandchildren about.

After the race Seward challenged Robinson to a rematch and offered to race anyone in the world and give them a 1-yard start for 100 yards or a 2-yard start for 120. There was no answer to his challenges. In a little more than a year he had defeated a long list of increasingly formidable British runners and was now the sprint champion of England. Because he had already defeated all the best American sprinters, he could claim to be the undisputed sprint champion of the world. More significantly, he had run 100 yards in a time that no other runner would approach until well into the twentieth century.

In 1877 *Bell's Life* was still fielding questions from readers asking who had run the fastest 100 yards on record. The editor stood behind Seward's 1844 time, writing, "George Seward was, when in his prime, an extraordinarily muscular man, standing about 5 feet 8 inches. He could, after partaking of his breakfast, one and one half-pints of milk and four pancakes, run easily 100 yards in 9½ seconds, and we have timed him so to do frequently."[31]

His victory over Robinson in an unprecedentedly fast time made him famous throughout England. During the week following the race he "sat" for a young artist named John Mott, who painted his portrait. Moor's Picture Gallery at St. Martins Lane, London, published lithographic copies in early 1845.[32] After having his portrait made, Seward left London for a triumphant return to the Puncheon Inn in Durham, where his friends greeted him as a hero and the undisputed champion of sprinting.

Seward challenged Atkinson of Shincliffe and John Willox ("the Scotchman"), the two outstanding British sprinters left that he had not defeated, and agreed to give them both starts but was unable to make a match with either.

Now that he had achieved his goal of becoming champion of England, he was eager for friends back home to know of his success. While resting his injured leg and trying to make another match, he wrote to the *Spirit of the Times* in New York to tell of his success in England.

Letter of a Yankee Pedestrian,
The present champion of England.

Durham, England, Nov 1, 1844
Sir: You will oblige me by inserting a few lines in your paper which I think will be relayed to the American Sporting World, as coming from a countryman in a foreign land. There are comparatively few who are fond of Pedestrianism in the U.S. but knows or has heard of me. My name is Seward; I am from New Haven, Conn.

After I defeated William Belden of NY, and Ainsworth, I thought I would try my luck among the English pedestrians. I landed in Liverpool on the 26th of June 1843 and got a match on at that place the second day after I landed, which I won. I should have given an account of my races before, for I presume there are very few of my sporting friends in NY who knew where I am; they may have seen some of my races in "*Bell's Life in London*," I went by the name of *Steward*—a mistake on the editor's part, however in spelling it. I allowed it subsequently to be printed so, but I had made up my mind, if I arrived at the top class, to have my name spelled properly. I have won some *sixteen of seventeen races* since I have been in this country, and now have the honor to stand *Champion of England*.

You will see an account of my last race in "*Bell's Life*" of Oct 6th or "*The Era.*" It was with a man of the name of Robinson, considered by his countrymen to be the best man in the world; he went by the name of "the Wonder of the World." I ran him for £50; there were thousands to see the race from all parts of the country, and a good deal of money changed hands; I won it by two yards. I likewise challenged, in the same paper, to give any man one yard start in 100 yards, or two yards start in 120 yards, for £50 or £100; as yet no one has accepted.

I have had fair play in every respect, in every race I have run, and have done very well since I have been here. I likewise won a beautiful silver cup, open to all England, to run 410 yards and leap 6 hurdles.

By inserting these few lines in your paper, you will very much oblige.

Your obedient servant, George Seward

PS—I intend to be in New York in April or May next. My three last races I won in 6 weeks—each a match for £50 a side.[33]

Seward was proud of his success in England and wanted his friends to know about it, but he was careful not to mention running 100 yards in 9¼ seconds. He planned to return to America later that spring and knew that reporting such a fast time would make it almost impossible for him to find anyone willing to race him. American sprinters could tell by running time trials that they had no chance to beat him. The *Spirit of the Times* could not let such a great feat go unreported and reprinted the full *Bell's Life* account of the race in the same issue as his letter. His effort to keep his 100-yard time from being known in America was in vain.

The *Bell's Life* editor, after reading Seward's letter printed in the *Spirit*, wrote that he objected to one paragraph. "He says he went by the name of Steward, the mistake originated with us. Now such is not the fact, for in all the communications which reached us, either written by himself or friends, the name was so spelt and if he did not intend that it should be so he ought to have written to us to that effect." The *Bell's Life* editor went on to note that Seward also neglected to mention the races he ran using the alias Sherryn and added, "We always repudiate men running in fictitious names and ever endeavor to ascertain who they really are."[34]

William Robinson was a proud man and, despite his loss to Seward at 100 yards, believed that if the distance were longer, he could defeat the American. On October 16 he wrote to the *Era*, "I will run any man in the world from 200 yards to a mile; Seward the Cockfield Putter would be preferred at 200 yards for £50 a-side."

Seward was eager for a rematch but wanted it to be at 100 yards, which he felt was his best distance. When Robinson refused to run again at that distance, Seward proposed they split the difference and run 150 yards, but Robinson still held out for 200 yards. They settled on 160 yards and signed articles for the rematch to take place on December 23, 1844. Seward was still not able to do any rigorous training, fearing he might do more harm to his right leg. It had never fully healed since the injury he suffered while training to race Rush two months earlier.

He tested his sore leg by competing in a hurdle race of four 410-yard heats at the Northumberland Cricket Ground on November 11 for a silver cup valued at 20 guineas. There were nearly 2,000 people present. Many had come expressly to see the all-conquering American who had run such a wonderful time for 100 yards. His opponents were John Smith ("the Regent-street Pet"), his brother Edward Smith, and a runner called "the Flying Mouse" of Durham. The "Pet" won the first race and Edward Smith the third, but Seward took home the cup by winning the second and fourth races. Before the crowd left, American showman P. T. Barnum, who was touring England, had 2-foot-3-inch Charles Sherwood Stratton, better known as "the celebrated General Tom Thumb," ride through the ground in his miniature carriage, "exciting much admiration."[35]

Interest in the rematch of the fastest two men in the world was even greater than for their first race, but Seward's nagging injury caused him to worry. Two weeks before the race *Bell's Life* reported, "A correspondent states that Seward in his training is not enabled to do the work he could wish for fear of his leg which has never been quite the thing since he strained the tendon Sartorius when giving a trial previous to his race with Rush of Bradford."[36]

On December 23, there was a huge crowd at the race site in Blackheath when both men, dressed in their running outfits, arrived in carriages. To everyone's surprise, the police were waiting and insisted that if either runner got down from his carriage, he would be taken into custody. The officer in charge said the crowd was so large it was interfering with traffic and that he had received orders from the commissioners of Scotland Yard to put a stop to the race. Seward, Robinson, and their backers all argued that they had chosen a spot with little traffic and that no long delays would result from running so short a distance. The officer stood firm, and the disappointed crowd dispersed as the runners and their friends adjourned to the nearby Hare and Billet public house to decide what to do.

After some discussion, they agreed to run the race at the Tiger's Head, Lee, Kent, one and a half miles away. The runners rode to the new location in their carriages followed by the police on horseback and a long procession of race fans on foot. When they arrived at the Tiger's Head, the police superintendent of the R. division rode up and told them they could not run there either, or anywhere else within seven miles of the place. By this time it was getting dark, so the race party retreated to Robinson's headquarters, the Green Man, at Blackheath. They sat down to discuss what to do, and tentatively decided to run the race at the enclosed grounds at Bellevue the following week.

Most of the crowd left after hearing the new place and date for the race. Then Robinson, who had the choice of ground, made a startling proposal. Seemingly not realizing Seward was a heavy favorite, he offered to double the stakes and run the race the next day, Christmas Eve, at Wimbledon Common. Seward's backers smiled at one another when they heard Robinson's offer. They had been placing bets at odds of 6 and 7 to 4 on Seward. Doubling the stakes allowed them to bet another £50 at evens. To avoid further interference from the police, the men agreed to keep the new race site and time secret.

The next day when the runners arrived at Wimbledon Park, fewer than 100 people were there to watch them run. Robinson had trained at Blackheath while Seward had stayed at his old quarters at Deal in Kent but was unable to do much training because of the nagging injury to his right leg. When they came to the starting line at 2:30 p.m., both men looked in admirable condition although *Bell's Life* reported Seward was at least seven pounds over his normal running weight because of his forced inactivity. He sported "American colors" while Robinson wore blue bird's-eye.

Robinson had been surprised and disappointed by his loss to Seward in their previous match and felt he had taken the American too lightly. This time he had trained harder than ever and was in top form. In addition, they were racing at the longer distance of 160 yards, which he considered to be to his advantage. He had prepared well and was determined to regain his lost fame.

After six false starts, they bounded away, each man exerting himself to the maximum. Seward gained a slight lead at the start but did not increase it until they passed 100 yards. Then, as he had done in their previous race, he changed speeds and was soon 3 full yards ahead. Despite Robinson's best efforts, Seward kept the lead and won with ease by 2½ yards. Because the race had taken place in near secrecy, no time was reported. Since Seward won by at least as much as he did in their 100-yard race, his 160-yard performance that day would surely have been a record had it been timed.

Bell's Life described the race in glowing terms and coined a new alias for Seward:

> It was a highly exciting race, and the American, it is imagined, may defy any man in existence in sprint races. The stakes were handed over to Seward that same night at Jem Burn's, and the winner started a subscription for Robinson with £2, which was increased to £4 by others present. Robinson acknowledged that he had been fairly beaten by Seward, who was certainly a "wonder." [37]

The name was appropriate and stuck. Seward became "the American Wonder," although he was too modest to refer to himself by it. Years later when his great speed had all but left him, the press would shorten the nickname to just "the American."

The race cemented Seward's claim to being the champion short-distance runner of England and America. Afterward, he offered to run "any man on earth" 100 yards and increased the start he would give to 2 yards, or he would run anyone 200 yards level for from £100 to £1,000. No challengers came forward.

The *Era* described another painting of Seward. "An admirable likeness of this champion, at a short distance, of Yankee-land, in the act of his starting the 160 yards' race, in which he vanquished with ease, on the 24th of Dec. last the renowned Robinson, of Newton Moor, has been painted by Swandale, for Moore, of West-street, St. Martin's-lane, who has put it in the hands of an engraver of eminence for publication."[38]

William Robinson was never the same after his two losses to Seward. Although accepting the total domination the American displayed in their two races was difficult, he could have dealt with it. What he couldn't overcome was the "consumption," now known as tuberculosis, he had contracted. In 1845 he turned to longer races, including a mile handicap at Walworth's Beehive Cricket Ground and a 4-mile race against John Barlow, but without much success. His career plummeted further in 1847 when he had a disagreement with his backers and quit running for a while. He died of his illness in July 1853 in his thirty-first year, perhaps without ever reaching his full potential.

In early 1845 Seward rested and thought about his future. He had done well since arriving in England a year and a half earlier and had amassed about £300 from the races he had won. Although he was not rich, this was a tidy sum that would allow him to live well for some time. The problem was there were no runners left to challenge him. Even in England, with its great running tradition and large pool of talented runners, no one answered his frequent challenges. He was again a champion with no one to compete with in match races.

On March 21 he entered a 440-yard hurdle race over fifteen hurdles at Middle Deal, Kent, for a silver cup. Seward was the favorite in the betting as well as among the many ladies present who seemed delighted at watching him run. He won easily, defeating John Smith ("the Regent-street Pet"), John's brother Edward Smith, and William Jackson ("the American Deer").

With no humans willing to face him in a match race, Seward tried a four-legged opponent, running a 400-yard hurdle race against a horse named the Fox on March 31. He would race horses many times during his long career. Although he did not relish competing with them, it was better than not racing at all. Racing horses could be dangerous, especially going over hurdles, and the outcome was usually uncertain. A trained horse has much greater speed and leaping ability than a human and should win any race that does not take days to complete. Yet they were unpredictable, sometimes refusing to start, and because of crowd noise or a mistake by their rider, they might spook or even veer into the crowd or their opponent. They also might refuse to jump a hurdle, giving a human a chance. To make these races more interesting, promoters sometimes had the horse run a longer distance or handicapped it in some other way.

In this contest Seward had no advantage. They raced 400 yards over eight hurdles, best two out of three heats. The horse ran according to form, and although Seward was much admired for his hurdling skills, the horse won the first two heats easily.

While Seward was wondering how he could coax any of the British sprinters into racing him, other events were taking place that would have a major influence on his career. William Jackson, "the American Deer," was rising to the top at longer distances. Jackson, whose real name was William Howitt, was born in Norwich on February 14, 1821. He had taken the alias Jackson "for family reasons" and used it only in pedestrian circles. In 1841, while visiting his brother, who had left England to take a job as a typesetter in the United States, he picked up his other alias, "the American Deer." Jackson's brother later returned to London and worked for *Bell's Life* until he died of consumption.

Jackson (figure 3.2) was tiny—5 feet 3 inches tall—and weighed only 105 pounds, but he was all bone and muscle. He had large lungs, a full chest, muscular neck and arms, and thin legs. His best distances were from 2 to 20 miles, and he would become one of the greatest distance runners of the nineteenth century. Although he was intelligent, resourceful, and well mannered, Jackson had a dark side that would lead to his involvement in several double-crosses and "fixed" races.

On January 6, 1845, Jackson ran a race that would make him as well known at long distances as Seward was at sprinting. His opponent was William Sheppard of Birmingham, and the match was to see who could cover the greatest distance in 1 hour. It was for £100 a side on the Hatfield turnpike-road, about two miles from Barnet.

Jackson had started his career running sprint races but found he did not possess much speed and had only moderate success at short distances. On

Figure 3.2. Mezzotint of William Jackson, "the American Deer," in his prime (about 1850). From the Yale Center of British Art, Paul Mellon collection.

November 7, 1843, he defeated James Byrom of Birkenhead, in a mile race at Walworth Cricket Ground in 4 min. 40 sec. over heavy turf. Later he ran 3 miles in a respectable 15 min. 54 sec. and in one of his trials covered the distance in a sizzling 14 min. 45 sec.

William Sheppard, "the Birmingham Pet," was admired for the graceful way he ran. He had been running for about four years with only two or three defeats. A carpenter's toolmaker by trade, he was twenty-seven years old, 5 feet 6½ inches tall, and weighed 113 pounds. On July 31, 1843, Sheppard had run 1,000 yards in 2 min. 27 sec. A year later he defeated Thomas Birkhead of Sheffield at 10 miles in 56 min. 30 sec.

Although Sheppard had tried to keep his true ability secret, the *Bell's Life* editor believed he was at least 2½ minutes better than his best reported time for 10 miles. The editor pointed out that with more and more people timing runners, it was becoming difficult to keep a runner's abilities secret. This trend was aided by the availability of inexpensive watches for timing middle-distance and longer footraces. Watches for timing sprint races needed to be accurate to ¼ second and to have some method for quickly starting and stopping them. They were still expensive and rare, which hindered the timing of sprint races. *Bell's Life* wrote:

> It has been the object of men to keep their time as "dark" as possible, for they observe, and with truth, that if their races are run in less than what might be fairly expected at their hands (or legs), considerable difficulty is experienced in "getting on" other matches. But pedestrianism has of late become a sport of so much importance to a great many persons in various parts of the kingdom and of so much interest and amusement to others, that a *stopper* has in a material degree been put on the intentions of those who desire to keep the public in ignorance of their 'fleet-footed' doings, and innumerable *tickers* [watches] are now to be seen sported at races.[39]

The road selected for the race was a carefully measured mile with a moderate hill near one end. It stretched from the thirteenth milestone to the twelfth on the Hatfield turnpike-road toward Ganwick Corner. A machine scraped the course before the race, but it was still wet, and heavy in some parts. Jackson appeared in fine condition, naked to the waist, and wearing only cotton shorts and laced-up spiked shoes without heels. Around his head was a fancy plaid handkerchief.

Sheppard also looked well, but his face betrayed uneasiness and a less-than-confident appearance. His running outfit was similar to Jackson's except for a blue and white handkerchief around his head. At 1:30 p.m. they started with Sheppard sprinting into the lead (figure 3.3). Jackson passed him and led for about ¼ mile, when he allowed Sheppard to take the lead. They soon discovered they had started too fast and slowed a bit. Sheppard covered the first 2 miles in 10 min. 15 sec. with Jackson sticking to him like his shadow.

In the ninth mile Sheppard was still in the lead, but the "Deer" did not allow him to get far ahead. The crowd gathered at the 10-mile stone eager to see the runners go by. They were orderly and kept a path clear for the runners. After the turn at the ninth mile, Jackson slowed, then ran up to Sheppard and looked him in the face to judge how much he had left. Sheppard looked flushed and ran with his mouth open, but he otherwise did not seem distressed.

When he was within about 400 yards of the milestone marking the tenth mile, Sheppard gathered himself for a sprint and came down the hill at top speed. On nearing the handkerchiefs used to mark the turning point, Sheppard stuck out his hand, grabbed one of them, and fell on his hands and knees exhausted. His time for 10 miles was 53 min. 35 sec., the fastest 10-mile time yet recorded, beating John Barlow's record of 54 min. 21 sec. set on the Beacon Course in New Jersey in 1844. Why he stopped before the race was over is unclear—some reporters thought he collapsed from exhaustion while others insisted he had forgotten the race was for an hour rather than 10 miles.

Jackson was close behind when Sheppard fell, and after touching the other handkerchief, ran on up the hill to finish the race. Convinced Sheppard would not get up, he eased up, then began to walk. The fans, some of whom had bet Jackson would surpass 11 miles, encouraged him to resume running, and he complied. When the hour ended, he was within 100 yards of the 11-mile mark. Everyone wanted to know exactly how far he had gone, so the referee had the distance between the milestones accurately remeasured. When it was found to exceed a mile by 12 yards, the referee calculated Jackson's total distance as 11 miles 40 yards 2 feet 4 inches—the first time anyone had run more than 11 miles in an hour. Jackson had made himself world famous and risen to the first ranks of British distance runners.

A month later the *Spirit of the Times* in New York reprinted the *Bell's Life* account of Jackson and Sheppard's race, as it had done earlier for Seward's major races. C. S. Browning, owner of the Beacon Course in Hoboken, New Jersey, sent both Jackson and Seward special invitations to take part in the races he had scheduled for later that summer. In his invitations, Browning said he would be giving $4,000 to $5,000 in prize money for footraces that year. The Beacon Course was one mile west of New York City, and the races, ranging from 200 yards to 15 miles, would take place between May 20 and June 10, 1845.[40]

Figure 3.3. Sheppard leads Jackson, who became the first runner to cover more than 11 miles in an hour. From the *Illustrated London News*, January 11, 1845.

The prize money was enormous, enough to persuade both Seward and Jackson to start making plans to sail for America. On April 6, with no more worlds to conquer in England, Seward announced his decision to leave on April 18 to return to America. Expecting it to be a permanent move, he expressed his sincere thanks for the kindness shown to him in England. He added that he would run his last race on April 14 at Walworth Cricket Ground, and if anyone wanted to regain their lost laurels, he would give them a 3-yard start in 100 for £10 a side.

More than 4,000 spectators crowded the Beehive Cricket Ground, eager to see the American race for the last time. To their disappointment, no sprinter in England was willing to risk £10 running against him, even with a 3-yard start. Not wanting to disappoint the crowd, Seward agreed to run 440 yards over twelve hurdles against a pony. He started well and by halfway led by 6 yards. The rider, trying to catch up, spurred the pony too sharply, and it bolted off the course. It got back on again, but it was too late as Seward had gained a big lead and ran in a winner by several yards.[41]

On April 18, 1845, Seward and Jackson arrived in Liverpool and boarded the 624-ton sailing ship *Champlain* bound for Philadelphia. If Seward had not become wealthy in his rise to becoming champion of England, at least his financial status had improved to the point where he did not have to work his way back across the Atlantic. He carried only a small trunk filled with personal belongings including his clothes, running outfit, and spiked running shoes. Jackson, making his second trip to America, brought a bag of clothes and a small trunk. On the ship's manifest, Seward listed his occupation as silver plater while Jackson claimed to be a typesetter.[42]

In reality, they were an almost invincible, self-contained, two-man track team. Seward was unbeatable at short distances and, with enough training, could run excellent times up to a mile. Jackson's talents complemented Seward's. He was an exceptional runner at 2 miles and got better as the distance increased. The Seward-Jackson team had all the running distances covered from 50 yards to 20 miles. In addition, Seward was an expert hurdler and jumper, should anyone want to challenge them in those events. Both men were resourceful, independent, and self-coached. These traits would serve them well as they tried their luck in the great footraces on the Beacon Course beginning in June 1845 and afterward ran anyone, anywhere they could find competition in the "land of stars and stripes."

Notes

1. Montague Shearman, *Athletics and Football*, 3rd ed. (London: Longmans, Green, 1889), 39.

2. Known as "The Black Diamond," Jem Ward had been the English boxing champion for most of the years from 1825 until 1831, when he retired from the ring. He then had some success as an artist, and his paintings were displayed in London and Liverpool. Ward also sang in concerts and kept the York Hotel.

3. £4 was equal to $19.44 in 1844. The 2006 purchasing power of Seward's bet of £4 is £308 or $547 (www.measuringworth.com, accessed October 30, 2007).

4. "George Seward, The American Runner," *New York Clipper*, May 8, 1880.

5. "Ringing in" referred to a race promoter conspiring to fix the betting odds unfairly. "Roping" meant holding back in order to lose a race. "Running to the Book" was to disguise one's form to obtain a generous handicap. Peter Lovesey, *The Official Centenary History of the Amateur Athletic Association* (Enfield, England: Guinness Superlatives, 1979), 15.

6. The £100 Seward won would be worth about £6,350 or $11,690 in today's (2006) money.

7. In *Athletics and Football* (1889), Montague Shearman stated that the annual hurdles race at Eton could be traced back to 1845, but the Earl of Beaufort, in a foot-

note to his foreword, stated that he had a recollection of hurdling in sports organized by his Dame's House (the "house" social system) as early as 1837.

8. "Foot Hurdle Racing at Bellevue," *Bell's Life*, September 10, 1843.

9. C. A. Wheeler, *Sportascrapiana by Celebrated Sportsmen* (London: Simpkin, Marshall & Co., 1867), 215.

10. *Bell's Life*, February 25, 1844.

11. The illustration of Johnny Broome's is from *The New Tom Spring's Life in London and Sporting Times*, February 24, 1844, which described the tavern as follows: "For sporting information, a glass of good grog, a bottle of wine, and general civility, the Rising Sun stands high on the list of sporting cribs."

12. "Caution to Pedestrians," *Bell's Life*, October 22, 1843.

13. "Badcock and Sherryn's Hurdle Race," *Bell's Life*, April 14, 1844.

14. Using a pistol to start a race would become the preferred method of starting by about 1860.

15. "Durham Foot Hurdle Race," *Bell's Life*, April 28, 1844.

16. "The Durham Foot Hurdle Race," *Bell's Life*, May 12, 1844.

17. "Steward and Robinson," *Era*, August 25, 1844.

18. John Goulstone, *Turf, Turnpike and Track* (London: Author, 2003).

19. The macadamized road was invented by Scottish engineer John Macadam (1756–1836). It had a smooth, hard surface that consisted of an angular aggregate over a well-compacted subgrade. No tar was used, but the broken stone was bound together by fines generated by traffic. Sections of these roads were well packed and smooth, providing hard, fast running surfaces.

20. "Steward and Smith's race for fifty pounds a side," *Bell's Life*, August 25, 1844.

21. *Era*, August 25, 1844.

22. *Bell's Life*, August 25, 1844.

23. *Era*, September 1, 1844.

24. Wheeler, *Sportascrapiana*, 214–15.

25. "Steward and Rush's Race," *Bell's Life*, September 22, 1844.

26. *Era*, December 29, 1844.

27. *Bell's Life*, October 6, 1844.

28. *Bell's Life*, October 6, 1844. Unfortunately the only things we know about Jackson's "first-rate" watch are that it could be read to the nearest ¼ second and that it was one of the best watches in existence at the time. The pocket chronometer was invented in the 1780s, but these timing devices could not return the stop-seconds hand to zero, so the user had to note the hand's starting position when he timed an event. In 1844 Adolphe Nicole, a Swiss watchmaker who had emigrated to London, created the first return-to-zero mechanism and took out patent No. 10,348 on the invention. It allowed the watch's second hand to be quickly returned to zero by use of a heart-shaped cam. This so-called flyback mechanism is still used in mechanical stopwatches. Since it is doubtful Jackson's watch had a flyback mechanism, he would probably have had to stop his watch, note the time, then start it again when he detected the first movement of Seward's feet. He then stopped the watch again at the

end of the race and subtracted the starting time from the finishing time. It required a lot of effort to time a sprint race with a watch of this type but was probably not that difficult for a practiced timer.

29. Wheeler, *Sportascrapiana*, 217.

30. "Great Pedestrian Match," *Times of London*, October 10, 1844.

31. "To Correspondents," *Bell's Life*, June 23, 1877.

32. *Era*, January 19, 1845.

33. *Spirit of the Times*, vol. 14, November 2, 1844, 428.

34. *Bell's Life*, January 19, 1845.

35. In 1844, Barnum took young Stratton on a tour of Europe, making him an international celebrity. Stratton appeared twice before Queen Victoria while he was in England. He was born in 1838 in Bridgeport, Connecticut, making him only six years old when he toured Europe. He had grown to 3 feet 4 inches tall and weighed 70 pounds when he died of a stroke in 1883 at the age of forty-five.

36. "Robinson and Seward," *Bell's Life*, December 8, 1844.

37. "Seward and Robinson's Race for 100 Pounds a Side," *Bell's Life*, December 29, 1844 (reprinted in *Spirit of the Times*, vol. 14, February 1, 1845, 538).

38. *Era*, January 19, 1845. An extensive search has failed to turn up this painting. A lithographic copy of Swandale's painting of Seward owned by the Yale Art Gallery was displayed for many years in the Payne Whitney Gymnasium at Yale. It disappeared and its location is unknown. Source: e-mail correspondence from Yale University Art Gallery, May 12, 2004.

39. "Jackson and Sheppard's Race—£100 a Side. Unprecedented Performance—Upwards of Eleven Miles in the Hour," *Bell's Life*, January 12, 1845.

40. *Bell's Life*, March 23, 1845.

41. *Bell's Life*, April 6, 1845.

42. *Manchester Guardian*, April 19, 1845. The *Champlain* was provided with "a plentiful supply of good bread daily and an abundance of pure water which is included in the passage-money." Presumably Seward and Jackson had enough money to supplement this diet on their long voyage.

CHAPTER FOUR

~

The Seward-Jackson American Tour (1845–1846)

In the mid-1800s, America had no tracks built solely for running. Short races from 100 to 440 yards were run on city streets or any convenient straight and level spot. Longer races were usually run on horse tracks.

The Beacon Course in Hoboken, New Jersey, was the most splendid horse track in mid-nineteenth-century America. It was a mile in circumference with a 300-foot-long, three-story grandstand that was the largest and handsomest in the country. The stand, which doubled as a hotel, had three sections. The first was for ladies and their escorts. The second, called the "club" stand, contained a plush dining room. The third, a "citizens" stand, was for the general public. In addition, there was a separate "cheap stand" opposite the 2-mile post. In all, the course could accommodate 15,000 people. Costing more than $60,000 to build and intended for thoroughbred racing, it opened in November 1837 amid a recession. Because of the poor economy, the track did not draw the expected large crowds.

In 1838 the owner, C. S. Browning, looking for ways to make the track profitable, began hosting trotting races. In addition, he came up with the idea of holding a once-a-year series of athletic sports on the course. These sports included walking, running, wrestling, and leaping contests with purses totaling about $1,500.[1] At first, Browning's "athletic sports" drew only moderate crowds.

In 1844, the enterprising Browning added steeplechase races for horses—becoming the first racetrack owner in America to do so. In addition, he hosted three major footraces on the track that would make running history.

He billed them as being between England and America, and they drew large crowds and created much excitement in both countries.[2]

The first, held on October 16, 1844, was a 1-hour race for $1,000 in prizes. Among the seventeen runners entered was the first American to run more than 10 miles in an hour, thirty-three-year-old Major Henry Stannard, a farmer from Killingsworth, Connecticut. He had covered 10 miles in 59 min. 48 sec. in 1835, setting the first American running record and becoming a national hero. Although he was still a crowd favorite, at thirty-three Stannard would not be a factor in any of the races. Other Americans entered were New Yorkers, John Gildersleeve and John Steeprock. A fireman by trade, Gildersleeve was the son of a New York farmer. He was a handsome thirty-two-year-old, 5 feet 5 inches tall, weighing 130 pounds. John Steeprock, a Seneca Indian chief from Buffalo, was a talented runner hampered by being undisciplined and undertrained. He was known for a wild, bounding gait.

Two crack English runners, John Barlow and Tom Greenhalgh, plus a third Englishman named Ambrose Jackson opposed the Americans. Barlow and Greenhalgh had made the long trip to America solely to run for the prizes. John Barlow, or "Tallick," from Bolton, England, was twenty-four years old, 5 feet 7 inches, and weighed 140 pounds. He had earned a reputation at distances from 1 to 4 miles. Thomas Greenhalgh, also born near Bolton, was twenty-four years old, 5 feet 6 inches tall, and weighed 128 pounds. Greenhalgh had been successful in races from ¼ mile to 4 miles. Ambrose Jackson, from just north of Manchester, had been racing in America with varied success since 1842. His best performance during that time was 4 miles in 22 min. 10 sec.

On the day of the race, the stands at the Beacon Course soon filled. Then a dense multitude of 20,000 "tag-rag and bob-tail denizens of New York"[3] broke through the fences and poured onto the track. Men on horseback tried to clear the course by galloping through the crowd at full speed, knocking people in all directions as if they were bowling pins. The crowd, aware of the British reputation for distance running, bet heavily on Barlow and Greenhalgh, but surprisingly, American John Gildersleeve came from 200 yards behind to win the race, running 10 miles 955 yards in the hour (figure 4.1). The first five runners all covered more than 10 miles in the best distance race that had taken place in America. Still, some observers believed the English runners had not done their best, hoping to improve the betting odds in the races to follow.

The second race in the series took place on November 19, 1844, and produced the first "world's best" running performance on American soil. Browning strengthened the fences, making it more difficult to break in, and at least

Figure 4.1. John Gildersleeve covered 10 miles 955 yards in an hour to win the first America vs. England race in 1844. From the _Weekly Herald,_ New York, October 19, 1844.

30,000 paid their way to see the competition on the muddy racecourse. The entries were nearly the same as for the previous race. Gildersleeve was in even better condition but was suffering from a cold, and the crowd was expecting Steeprock, the Indian, to perform well.

Betting was almost even on Gildersleeve and Barlow against the field. Before the race, the two Englishmen devised a strategy where Barlow would set a blistering pace to draw out and exhaust Steeprock while Greenhalgh dueled with Gildersleeve. After a false start, Barlow jumped into the lead and covered the first mile in 5 min. 10 sec. It was impossible to control the huge crowd, and spectators and men on horses crossed the railings on both sides of the track and interfered with the runners. One reporter wrote: "Nearly every one of the pedestrians was more than once thrown off his stride by the obstructions of the horses, or the crowding upon them of the spectators."[4]

Despite the crowded track, Barlow covered the second mile in 5 min. 15 sec., built a sizable lead, and went on to win by 250 yards in a record-breaking 54 min. 21 sec. (figure 4.2). Steeprock followed in 54 min. 53 sec., Greenhalgh in 55 min. 10 sec., and Gildersleeve in 55 min. 51 sec. Barlow took the $700 first-prize money and sailed for Liverpool, but Browning persuaded Greenhalgh to remain and run another race against Gildersleeve.

50 ～ Chapter Four

GREAT FOOT RACE, AT HOBOKEN, NEW YORK.

Figure 4.2.   John Barlow fought his way through the crowd to win the second race in the America vs. England series in 1844. From the *Illustrated London News*, January 11, 1845.

This 12-mile race took place on December 15, 1844, and turned out to be the best of the whole series. The weather was bitter cold with a piercing wind and falling snow. Greenhalgh ran "nearly nude," with just a yellow cap and shorts. It was "cold enough to have frozen any other man as stiff as Lot's wife in five minutes,"[5] wrote one reporter. A small crowd of about 2,000 stamped their feet and danced to try to stay warm.

It soon became a tactical race between two evenly matched runners, both fit and mentally tough. Gildersleeve took the lead from the start, running slightly faster than a 6-minutes-per-mile pace for the first 5 miles, with the shirtless Greenhalgh a stride behind. Then Gildersleeve surged and covered the sixth mile in 5 min. 33 sec. but could not shake his rival. As they passed 10 miles in 57 min. 52 sec., sweat was pouring from both men despite the near-blizzard conditions. Greenhalgh ran the last mile in 5 min. 18 sec. and the 12 miles in 68 min. 48 sec. to defeat Gildersleeve and make it two out of three for the British runners.

Greenhalgh's victory ended the running season for 1844. It had been the greatest in the history of the sport. In England, Seward had brought sprinting to unprecedented heights in his rise to becoming champion, and Jackson had created similar interest in distance running with his 11-miles-in-the-hour performance. The American pedestrian fans had been able to read of these achievements in the *Spirit of the Times*, but they had witnessed the international races on the Beacon Course and would talk about them for years. Browning's success led to running contests on horse tracks spreading to the Cambridge Trotting Course in Boston, the Canton Course in Baltimore, the Hunting Park Trotting Course in Philadelphia, and the Metairie Course in New Orleans.

The coming foot-racing season looked even more promising. To build on his previous year's success, Browning offered even more prize money and improved his search for competitors to include advertising in the major newspapers in both America and England. In addition, he sent special invitations to the biggest two pedestrian stars of the day—Seward and Jackson. In advertising for the coming races, Browning noted that Jackson, who had agreed to come to America, was superior to either Greenhalgh or Barlow and that Seward, the sprint champion of the world, would be with him.

Seward and Jackson were late in arriving. Unfavorable winds and stormy seas led to a rough forty-two-day crossing on the *Champlain*. When the ship finally reached Philadelphia on June 3, 1845, both the 247 passengers and the crew were overjoyed to see dry land again. The trip had left the two runners wobbly, seasick, and out of condition.

One positive outcome of the long voyage was that the forced inactivity allowed the nagging injury to Seward's right leg to heal. Arriving in Philadelphia two weeks later than expected, the pair left immediately for Bergen, New Jersey. They checked into the New Hotel on June 4 and that same day began training on the nearby Beacon Course.

Three major footraces were on the program for the summer of 1845. Browning delayed them by two weeks because Seward and Jackson were late in arriving. He used the time to strengthen the fences and improve the seating for the large crowds he expected. To keep the unruly spectators from entering without paying, he built a fourteen-foot-high fence around the ground using two-inch-thick boards. Workers buried the boards about two feet deep and fastened them together at the top with cleats on both sides. They stayed and braced the whole fence on the inside and dug a deep ditch around the outside.

To further discourage fans from breaking through the fences, Browning built a new stand and charged a reduced admission to sit there. He improved the track by having it covered with ten inches of sandy soil and then grading it with a machine. With these improvements, the grounds were in first-rate condition and could hold nearly 50,000 spectators. Despite all these efforts, Browning would still be unable to prevent many of the fans from entering without paying.

The first race, now set for June 30, was at 1 mile. Strangely, this distance was the only one Browning could have chosen where neither Seward nor Jackson excelled. In addition, the long voyage had left them both out of condition. Although they were the headliners, both declined to run the race. Of the eleven entries, only six came to the post. The most distinguished were Billy Barlow, Henry Stannard, Ambrose Jackson, and an Iroquois Indian from Canada with a nearly unpronounceable name—Ignace Katanachiate.

The favorite, Billy Barlow, whose real name was William Freestone, came from nearby Williamsburg, Long Island. He was no relation to the English runner John Barlow who had set the 10-mile record on the Beacon Course in 1844. Nineteen-year-old Billy had come to America from London when he was nine, and by this time, the fans considered him an American.

The race was delayed until July 1 by heavy rainstorms that left it damp in some spots and in only fair condition. At the word "go," the Canadian, Ignace, shot into the lead and covered the first ½ mile in 2 min. 11 sec. At the three-quarter mark, Barlow caught up and tried to pass on the inside. He brushed Ignace as he went by, and the Canadian retaliated by shoving him into the railing. Barlow recovered and pulled ahead to win in 4 min. 36 sec., an excellent time on the slow course. The best time on record for the mile was 4 min. 30 sec. by Englishman James Metcalf in 1825. Ignace finished in 4 min. 42 sec., trailed by Ambrose Jackson in 5 min. 6 sec. and Henry Stannard in 5 min. 9 sec. Several fights that broke out among the unruly spectators marred the event. In addition, some men hired by Browning to prevent fans from entering without paying severely beat a young man who tried to climb over the high fence.

Rainy weather delayed the next race in the series until July 7. Although the day of the race was hot, thousands crossed the Hudson River on the Hoboken and Jersey City ferries to crowd the race ground. Many wanted to see Jackson, whose 11-miles-within-the-hour feat they had read about in the *Spirit of the Times*. Shortly after 4 p.m., seven men came to the start of the 5-mile race to try for the $400 purse. The runners were Jackson, Billy Barlow, Edward Kennedy, William Fowle, P. Hutchinson, Ignace Katanachiate, and C. Desmond. Jackson, with a month's training since arriving in America, was now fit and ran the first mile in 4 min. 53 sec., exhausting the runners who tried to stay with him. By the fifth mile he had built a huge lead. He stopped and walked, then trotted again, stopped and walked again, then sprinted to the finish in 27 min. 39 sec.

The *New York Morning News* wrote: "Jackson is a queer built man about 25 and not far from 5 feet tall—legs rather long in proportion to his body and shoulders drooped forward. His gait is easy and rapid of course and he appears to take the best care of himself."[6]

On July 9, Seward and Jackson made their first joint appearance since arriving in America. The first race featured Jackson against Gildersleeve at 10 miles. It was a fine, clear day, but the temperature was an unbearable ninety-two degrees in the shade. Despite the heat there was a large, enthusiastic crowd to watch the races.

Pedestrian fans in America were as rowdy or perhaps more so than those in England, and race promoters and law enforcement officials had not yet figured out how to control them. The state of New Jersey had recently passed a law making it a felony to break through the fences, and Browning hired extra workers to keep the fans from breaking in. He even patrolled the fences himself, but large numbers were still able to enter without paying. Frustrated, he realized that no matter how many fans he drew to his racecourse, he was not going to make money if they did not pay for their admission.

Before the first race, Browning spotted a large, black-whiskered man climbing over the fence. He rode up and ordered him to leave, but the intruder grabbed a strip of plank he had pried from the fence and struck Browning on the left jaw, cutting a deep gash. Stunned, Browning lashed back with his loaded whip, but the burly intruder grabbed the end of it, tore it from his hands, and struck him on the head with it. Browning drew his "pepperbox" revolving pistol loaded with bird shot and fired at the trespasser's legs.[7] The blast had no obvious effect, and as the enraged man aimed another blow, Browning fired again. The shot from the second barrel still did not faze the gate-crasher.

Finally, the county sheriff came to Browning's rescue. He subdued the angry gate-crasher, named David Ward, and carted him off to the Hackensack Prison. It was not Browning's day, as a few minutes later when he rushed in to break up a fight, someone accidentally poked him in the left eye with a lit cigar, blinding him temporarily.

Both those who had paid and those who had climbed or broken through the fences tried to stay cool in the brutal heat by drinking large quantities of ginger beer, lemonade, and "pop" as well as beer, ale, and whisky.

When the time came to start the "Great Ten Mile Race," Jackson refused to run, saying he had never before competed in such hot weather. He insisted that Browning delay the race until it cooled, arguing that to race 10 miles under such conditions was foolhardy. Because he was the runner everyone wanted to see, he got his way. After a long wait, it cooled enough for Jackson to agree to strip down to his running outfit, and five minutes before 5 p.m., the race got under way. Only Jackson, Gildersleeve, and Robert Williams, "the Welsh Bantam," started; the other entrants had been scared away by either Jackson's reputation or the heat.

The "Bantam" took the lead and covered the first ½ mile in 2 min. 32 sec. Jackson and Gildersleeve began to gain on him, but as the timer called out 5 min. 23 sec. at the mile, the "Bantam" was still leading. In the first quarter of the second mile, Jackson and Gildersleeve, still almost side by side, caught the "Bantam" and left him behind. At the end of the second mile Jackson was about a yard ahead of Gildersleeve, and by the fifth mile, he had gained 8 or 9 yards and was increasing his lead. By the end of the sixth mile, the "Deer" had broken contact with Gildersleeve and was a full ⅛ mile ahead. Gildersleeve quit, saying later he had gotten a stitch during the third mile. Jackson, knowing there were bets on time, did not slow down, but increased his pace to finish the 10 miles in 56 min. 29 sec. and claim the $600 prize.

Seward's reputation had preceded him, and there were no challengers willing to race him in a sprint race despite both his and Browning's searching in earnest for opponents. In order not to waste Seward's crowd-drawing appeal, Browning had scheduled him to introduce the new British sport of "foot-hurdle racing" to the American fans.

Before the race, the New York Herald wrote, "The hurdle race will be very interesting, but it is not sufficiently understood in the sporting circles of this latitude, to create much excitement; but must become in time very common on our courses."[8] Although hurdle races had taken place in England and Canada, most of the fans and even some of the contestants had never seen one.

Shortly after Jackson finished running, Seward made his way to the track. His opponents were Hiram Horton, described as a young man of "fine symmetrical proportion"; "the Welsh Bantam"; and four others. Seward, by this time a first-rate hurdler, cleared the fifteen 3-foot-3-inch hurdles in a "clean, beautiful style" and easily won both 440-yard races by 10 yards. His time for the first was 1 min. 11 sec. and the second 1 min. 9 sec.[9]

He was pleased to win these races but disappointed at the prize money. The $50 first-place prize was less than a tenth of the amount Jackson had received for winning the 10-mile race. Seward now had no source of income other than his running and needed higher-stakes races. After the race, he and Jackson stayed in a hotel in nearby Jersey City and resumed training on the Beacon Course while Browning continued to search for a sprinter willing to challenge "the American Wonder."

In 1845, New York City, about a mile east of where Seward and Jackson were staying, had a population of about 400,000 and was becoming the cultural and sporting center of the United States. Earlier that year, on January 29, the New York Evening Mirror had published for the first time Edgar Allan Poe's poem "The Raven." Later that year, on September 23, the New York

Knickerbockers would become the first organized baseball club in the United States.

About 3:30 in the morning on July 14, 1845, both Seward and Jackson were thrown from their beds by an enormous explosion. On going to a third-story window, they looked out to the east and saw New York City burning. The flames lit up the entire city, outlining dense clouds of smoke rising to meet the clouds. The fire had started in a whale-oil store near the corner of Broadway and Wall streets in the heart of the city. It soon spread to a warehouse containing a large store of gunpowder. Ten minutes later, the warehouse exploded, destroying seven buildings. The explosion was so powerful it shook the city like an earthquake, and the *New York Herald* reported that it broke a million windowpanes. Besides killing thirty-five people, the explosion and resulting fire destroyed more than three hundred buildings and caused an estimated $10,000,000 in damage.[10]

Seward and Jackson were shaken by the disaster, but both men had been asleep in their beds rather than out sampling New York City's nightlife and had avoided injury. The fire, although a major catastrophe, had little effect on the races taking place on the Beacon Course.

The following week, Billy Barlow challenged Seward to race a mile on the Beacon Course for $300 a side. Seward had mixed feelings about accepting the challenge. The money was to his liking, but a mile was far longer than his best distance. Because it looked as if he might never get any of the American sprinters to race him, he accepted the challenge and started training for the race.

On July 28 he interrupted his training to run another 440-yard "foot-hurdle race" on the Beacon Course. His opponents were again "the Welsh Bantam" and Hiram Horton. In the first race Seward struck the third hurdle and fell but jumped up and soon caught the other runners. He went on to win in 1 min. 8 sec. A few minutes later he won the second race in 1 min. 13 sec. and collected another $50 first prize.

Not everyone embraced this new sport of "foot-hurdling." After the race, the *New York Daily Tribune* wrote: "Then a couple of fools on foot just missed breaking their necks 'in gallant style' over the hurdles."[11] The *New York Herald*'s report was more favorable and finished with "George Seward is a fine made young man, a most beautiful and swift runner, and doubtless will astonish those present in his match with Barlow on Thursday. A mile is certainly more than he has ever been in the habit of performing, but those who know him well say that he is quite able for it."[12]

Billy Barlow had run the mile in 4 min. 36 sec. a month earlier, and Seward expected him to be at least as fast when they met. He knew his great sprinting ability would give him little advantage and that to defeat Barlow, he would have to do some serious training to improve his endurance.

The training methods he had learned in England were credited to Captain Barclay Allardice, a wealthy Scottish landowner. In 1804 he had run a match race of a mile in 4 min. 50 sec. and won 1,000 guineas. Five years later he became a British legend by walking 1,000 miles in 1,000 hours to win an even larger stake.[13] He described his training methods in the book *Pedestrianism* written by Walter Thom in 1813. British athletes and sports fans revered Barclay and used his training methods until late in the nineteenth century. The training was harsh. Besides running and walking it called for purgatives, artificial sweating, and severe dietary restrictions.

To prepare himself for his match with Barlow, Seward put himself through Barclay's rigorous training program. Instead of getting him into top condition as he expected, the training left him feeling sick and too weak to compete. A few days before the race he ran a mile trial and found he was not able to perform at anything like what he had expected. Not wanting to disappoint his friends who would bet on him, he consulted his backers and with their approval decided to forfeit the match, paying Barlow $100—all the winnings he had earned since returning to America.

Race fans were disappointed, but no one condemned Seward for backing out. The *New York Herald* wrote, "It must be borne in mind that a mile is a much greater distance than Seward has been in the habit of performing. In his other matches, his distance has seldom or never exceeded half a mile, and for which he seldom or never trains."[14] Seward's first effort at running the mile had been a failure, but he would have success as a miler later in his career using his own training methods.

Unable to find a sprinter willing to challenge him, he agreed to race a famous Canadian hurdle-racing horse named Hops, as soon as he recovered from his ill-fated mile training. The race was at ¼ mile over twelve hurdles, each 3 feet 6 inches high. Seward asked for a 25-yard start, but the horse's backer refused, and Seward, having no other choice if he wanted a race, agreed to run on even terms. At the word "go" he took off like an antelope and cleared the first hurdle before Hops's rider, Mr. Browning, could get the horse started. Hops reared and plunged, but when he got going, took the hurdles in stride, clearing some and knocking the upper planks off others. Browning used a long-lashed whip that cracked loudly as he urged the horse on. Seward's only chance was in the horse refusing to take the hurdles, but Hops either cleared or broke all of them and crossed the finish line while Seward still had two hurdles to go.

Despite the appearances of Seward and Jackson, the two best-known runners of the time, the foot-racing program on the Beacon Course in the summer of 1845 failed to produce as much excitement as the America vs. England races in 1844. Seward was unable to find any sprinters who would race him, and Jackson was so superior to Gildersleeve and the other American distance runners that his races failed to create much betting interest. In addition, the weather was so hot that many city residents left for the countryside in case the cholera epidemics that had plagued the city in the summer months of the 1830s returned.

At last a human challenger appeared who was willing to race Seward in a sprint race. George W. Morgan, who had just won a 75-yard race for $600 on the Canton Course in Baltimore, challenged Seward in the *Spirit of the Times*. "Mr. George W. Morgan will run Mr. Geo Seward or any other pedestrian in New York 75 to 100 yards for $500 or $1,000, to run over the Canton Course in the month of September. This offer is open until the 10th of September."[15] Unfortunately for Seward, he had become discouraged in finding a challenger and left New York to visit his mother and sister in New Haven and was unable to respond to the challenge in the short time Morgan allowed.

Jackson had also become discouraged at the lack of opposition and considered returning to England. Before leaving, he gave a challenge in the *Spirit of the Times*:

> I, W. Jackson, will run any man that can be produced in America, any distance, from two miles to fifteen. I will also stake $1,200 to any other man's $1,000, or $600 to their 500, provided they give me the privilege of naming the Union, Central, or Beacon Course, to run over. If anyone should think the above sum is not sufficient to run for, I will stake, in proportion, the above odds to any amount they think proper to name. This challenge will remain open until 25 September, at the expiration of which date I set sail for England.
>
> W. Jackson, at Mr. Jones's, Park Row, NY Sept 4th 1845

Billy Barlow answered Jackson's challenge and agreed to stake $500 to Jackson's $600 and race him at 2 miles. Jackson chose to run on the Beacon Course, and the race was set for September 30. In addition, Steeprock, who had rounded into shape and run some impressive trials, challenged Jackson to run two high-stakes matches on the Beacon Course—a 10-mile race on Monday, October 20, and a 20-mile race on the following Saturday. Each runner was to put up $500 a race and Mr. Browning agreed to sweeten the pot with $500, making the total purse $1,500 for each race. An elated Jackson canceled his plans to leave for England and stepped up his training to get ready for the three races.

Seward's fortunes improved as well. On September 25 the *New York Herald* published a notice from C. S. Browning, owner of the Beacon Course. "George Seward is requested to call immediately on the proprietor of this course as a match has been made on him to run 100 yards within two weeks." The match Browning made for Seward turned out to be with Hiram Horton for $500. After some negotiation, Seward agreed to increase the distance to 200 yards and give Horton a 2-yard start.

The Jackson-Barlow race created intense interest. The two men seemed evenly matched and observers expected a close race. Pedestrian fans were asking: "Did Jackson have the foot speed to keep up with Barlow? Did Barlow have enough "bottom" to last two miles?" The youthful runner was an unknown quantity at the distance. He had run a fast mile, but performed poorly at 5 miles.

On race day, September 30, both Jackson and Barlow walked over the Beacon Course. To cover 2 miles, the men had to run two laps. As they inspected the course, Jackson was reserved and quiet, Barlow confident and joking. A few minutes before 4 p.m. they appeared in front of the stands. Barlow wore light flannel shorts and a blue bird's-eye handkerchief around his head. Jackson wore pink silk shorts and sported a blue handkerchief. The press described Jackson as a "small man of spare habit, with a bilious complexion and dark skin," and Barlow as having a "ruddy face, clear cuticle and a much more compact and robust frame."[16]

Barlow won the coin toss and lined up on Jackson's inside. At the word "go," both sprinted away, Barlow taking a yard lead and the "Deer" following on his outside shoulder. Their running styles were similar: both kept their elbows well in to their sides and ran slightly stooped. Jackson tried to draw even, but Barlow sprinted ahead, widening the gap to 6 or 7 yards. The "Deer" did not respond to Barlow's surge but ran easily a few steps behind.

They passed the ½-mile pole, and on the turn Jackson began to close again. From ¾ mile on, the men were almost side by side. At the end of the first lap, their trainers handed both men sponges to moisten their lips and chest. They went by the mile in 4 min. 50 sec., Jackson having opened a small gap. Both men appeared more strained as they started the second mile, and there was a painful expression on Jackson's face. At 1¼ miles he was in the lead by a few yards, but at 1½ miles, Barlow was again in front with the "Deer" crowding him.

As they entered the last ¼ mile, the crowd noise became deafening. They were both going as fast as they could, each straining every muscle. Barlow's white skin showed out at last in the lead as they came to the finish. Suddenly Jackson slowed to a jog, conceding the race, and Barlow won by 10 to 15 yards in 9 min. 44½ sec. Barlow's winning time was only 3½ seconds off the best time on record of 9 min. 41 sec., which had been set in 1836 by the Englishman Metcalf, who also held the mile record.

Many in the crowd were pleased with the race, but Jackson's supporters were highly disappointed. He had been a solid favorite, and those who thought he would win had bet large sums at odds of 100 to 60 on him. His supporters were even more disappointed when three days later, the *New York Herald* reported: "We have heard some ugly rumors relative to the late affair between Jackson and Barlow as to the impress abroad, but we bide our time. We have a few facts that will tell on the subject."[17]

On October 4, the *Herald* broke the news that Jackson had "sold" the race. Who provided them with the details of Jackson's scheme is unknown. The news shook the fledgling sport of pedestrianism to the core. In the week leading up to the race, some men had approached Jackson and asked if he would allow himself to be beaten by Barlow if the money were right. After some thought, Jackson agreed to lose the race for $900 plus the $600 he had invested in the stakes. The $1,500 was to be held for him until after the race.

To make even more money, Jackson went to his backer, a man from New Jersey, and asked for a $750 loan, saying it was to bet with. His backer gave him the money, assuming he would bet it on himself, and said that whatever Jackson won with the money they would divide evenly. He generously added that in the unlikely event Jackson lost, he did not have to pay the money back.

A short time later, Jackson gave the $750 plus $1,250 of his own money to two men he thought were his friends and told them to bet it all on Barlow, no matter what the odds. The odds from this time up to the race's coming off ranged from 100 to 60 to 105 to 75 on Jackson. By losing the race, Jackson stood to win $2,800 to $3,300 from betting on Barlow plus the $900 he had already received for throwing the race.

When Barlow won the race, Jackson's backers, supporters, and friends lost about $10,000. The scheme did not work out as Jackson had planned. Not only was it found out, but Jackson was also double-crossed. The two men he had entrusted with his $2,000 to bet on Barlow denied ever receiving the money and kept it for themselves as well as the money they won betting with it.[18]

Jackson's backer, who had lent him the $750, was incensed when he found he had been double-crossed. He got a warrant for the "Deer's" arrest and, with the Jersey City sheriff and several angry men who had lost money on the match, went to Jackson's hotel to arrest him. Jackson spotted the party approaching and escaped by leaping out of a third-story window. He managed to elude the sheriff and his men and set off for Canada.[19] From this time on, he often complained of a problem with his ankle. It is possible his injury was a result of his escape.

The scandal enraged both the press and pedestrian fans. One New York City newspaper, the *Subterranean*, believed those who lost money on Jackson should have taken matters into their own hands.

> The throwing off of this race was so disgracefully palpable, that a schoolboy could not have avoided seeing it. A more shameless swindle was never before played off even in Jersey, and the thieving little scamp who cheated his friends and filled his own coffers on that occasion ought to have been so maimed on the spot, by those he victimized, as to have effectually prevented him from ever committing a similar crime, during his future career. An example or two of this description would have a very salutary effect in preventing the recurrence of these disgraceful frauds.[20]

New York City and the surrounding area was the center of sports and entertainment in the United States and Jackson's best hope of running for large purses in America. After the incident, his high-stakes races with Steeprock on the Beacon Course were canceled, as were all other races he might hope to run near New York City.

Seward was not involved in the scandal; nevertheless, he decided to follow Jackson to Canada. In doing so, he had to abandon his race with Hiram Horton, his first opportunity to earn a significant amount of money since returning to America. The reason for his loyalty to Jackson is uncertain. They may have had an agreement to stick together, and as Seward was having difficulty finding opponents, he may have felt his best hope for making matches was traveling with Jackson, as they had planned all along.

While the two men were on their way to Canada, William T. Porter, editor of the *Spirit of the Times*, in his "answers to correspondents" column, expressed surprise at their sudden departure. "The conduct of Jackson, the American Deer and Seward is inexplicable indeed. Both are o-p-h! Done gone, the Lord knows where. We do not imagine that Barlow had any idea Jackson was making game of him. There are two sides to a story and until we hear the explanations of Jackson and Seward we must decline expressing an opinion about Barlow and Jackson's race."[21] Both the *Spirit* and *Bell's Life* refused to condemn Jackson, even though there was little doubt of his guilt.

With the New York City area closed to them, their only choices were to return to England or go on a countrywide tour offering to race anyone anywhere they could find challengers. The two men had an exceptional product to sell. Not only were they superior runners, but both knew how to please crowds and had unique talents to display. They were also willing to travel widely to see if they could earn some money from their sport.

Travel was their biggest problem. In the Northeast, trains, coaches, and steamers were readily available. A couple of months earlier, writer Henry David Thoreau had begun his twenty-six-month experiment in simple living at Walden Pond, near Concord, Massachusetts. He wrote that he doubted there was a spot in Massachusetts where one could not hear a train whistle. His suspicions were confirmed when he found that the Fitchburg trains passed Walden Pond about five hundred yards south of his cabin. Seward and Jackson would find that travel in many other parts of the sprawling, undeveloped country would prove much more difficult.

Their first order of business was for Jackson to avoid going to jail, so they headed for Canada, where he would be beyond the reach of New Jersey law enforcement. By October 22, 1845, the two men had managed to persuade a Canadian racetrack owner to stage three races on the St. Pierre Course near Montreal. The prizes were £50 for a 3-mile race, £30 for a 250-yard hurdle race over five 4-foot hurdles, and £100 for a 10-mile race. Jackson easily won the 3-mile race in 16 min. 15 sec., then defeated Gildersleeve, his sole opponent in the 10-mile race, running 59 min. 56 sec. It is unknown whether Gildersleeve and Jackson had a formal agreement, but Gildersleeve would follow Jackson throughout most of the tour. Although he was not as talented as Jackson, he, like Jackson, was a crowd favorite, and could be counted on to give an acceptable performance and provide at least some opposition for the "Deer."

In the hurdle race, Seward's bad luck continued when he fell at the third hurdle. He jumped up and continued but was unable to catch Edward Lamontagne, who won the race. One positive outcome of the match was that Lamontagne agreed to run Seward a 100-yard match race for $500 a side three days later, on the same course. Lamontagne's backers paid Seward an undisclosed amount of forfeit when their runner hurt himself fighting a fire and was unable to run. Seward then won a 250-yard race over five 4-foot hurdles against Augustus Lamontagne, a member of the Montreal Olympic Club.

After leaving Montreal, Seward and Jackson traveled to Toronto and on November 2, 1845, Jackson ran 10 miles against Gildersleeve, who fell far behind and quit after 6 miles, allowing the "Deer" to win in 56 min. 52 sec. Seward ran a solo exhibition hurdle race, as no one would come forward to race him. Hurdle-race competitors were proving almost as hard for Seward to find as sprinters. The event was new in America and required much practice to master.

Seward's exhibition hurdle race led to a match race on College Avenue in Toronto the following day. He offered a "stranger from Down East" named Leakdigger a 5-yard start in a 150-yard race for $50 a side. Strangely, Seward lost the race. Near the middle he all but closed with Leakdigger, who then shook him off and won by 2 yards. Seward tried to schedule a new match on even terms, but Leakdigger refused.[22]

On November 5, while Seward and Jackson were in Canada, a tragic event took place on the Beacon Course that, coupled with the Jackson-Barlow scandal, would set back running in America for years. The main event that day was a much-publicized hurdle race between the horse Hops, who had defeated Seward, and another outstanding hurdle-racing horse, Black Douglas. The jockey who was to ride Hops was ill, and Mr. Browning, the owner of both Hops and the Beacon course, decided to take his place.

Hops started well by clearing the first hurdle and taking the lead. At the second hurdle he hit the top plank with such force that Browning was thrown 20 feet over the horse's head and landed on his own head and back. Hops turned a somersault and came to rest on top of him. The horse was not seriously injured, but Browning suffered massive head injuries and, despite bloodletting and a trephining[23] operation, died the next day. Running in America had lost its greatest supporter, and the accident proved to be the death knell for the Beacon Course. It closed in early 1846, never to reopen.

By November 12, 1845, the Jackson-Barlow 2-mile scandal had cooled enough for Seward and Jackson to return to the States, although they avoided the New York City area. Jackson ran a mile race at the Bull's Head Course in Albany before a large crowd. His lone competitor was Gildersleeve, who gave him a tougher race than expected. During the first six miles Jackson kept well ahead, but on the seventh, Gildersleeve began to catch up, and on the ninth, they passed the post neck and neck. The "Deer" gradually pulled ahead during the tenth mile and finished in 55 min. 30 sec. with Gildersleeve just 19 seconds behind.

From Albany, they traveled to Philadelphia, and on November 17, Jackson wrote to the *Spirit of the Times*, giving another challenge before he left for England:

> I do hereby challenge Barlow of Williamsburg and Steeprock, the Indian, and all America or any man that can be produced from any country. I will give three hundred yards start in twenty miles or two hundred in ten miles, one hundred in eight miles, fifty in five miles, twenty in four miles, ten in three miles, or run anyone that can be produced two miles level. As I do not feel satisfied with my defeat by W. Barlow, I will run him two miles again, or any of

the above distances that he may choose, to satisfy the public and myself which is the better man of the two.

With no immediate answer to his challenge, Jackson went to Baltimore to prepare for a race against time on the Canton Course. He had bet he could cover 10½ miles within an hour, and on November 24 a large crowd came out to witness the effort. The "Deer" covered the distance with 2½ minutes to spare, finishing fresh and confident of his ability to cover 11 miles in the hour when the betting called for it. If Seward accompanied him to Baltimore, he did not find anyone to race there.

By mid-December there was still no answer to Jackson's challenge, but he and Seward had received an invitation from Col. Y. N. Oliver, owner of the Metairie Course in New Orleans, to spend January and February there.[24] Col. Oliver offered generous prize money, and the climate in Louisiana was much more suited to foot racing in the winter. The offer was too good to refuse, and despite the cold weather and long journey, the two men set off for New Orleans.

The easiest route was to take a riverboat from Pittsburgh down the Ohio River to Cincinnati and then to Louisville. The Louisville & Portland Canal had been finished in 1830, allowing steamboats to bypass the Ohio River rapids at Louisville. This made it possible to travel all the way from Pittsburgh to New Orleans without changing boats or waiting for high water. Winter had already set in over much of the Northeast, however. Three-foot snows were on the ground in Michigan and Indiana, and a foot in many places south of Kentucky. When they tried to book passage, they found the Ohio River already blocked by ice, all the way from Pittsburgh to Cincinnati, forcing them to take a six-day coach trip to Louisville.

Soon after they left, another challenge from George Morgan appeared in the *Spirit of the Times*. Morgan challenged Seward to run 100 yards for $1,000 on the National Course in Washington, D.C., and requested a response within a week. Seward answered the challenge from Louisville, where he and Jackson were waiting to board a steamboat to New Orleans.

Challenge by Seward the Pedestrian Louisville, Ky. Dec 30, 1845
Dear Sirs:—I have seen a challenge in your paper of the 20th from Mr. Morgan to run me 100 yds for $1000. Now, this is the second challenge from him, and both came when I was away from New York. In the last he states he wishes me to accept or decline the challenge in your next paper. Now he must know that it would not be possible to do it from Louisville, when it takes five or six days to come. Now, I wish to ask him why he did not make the match when

he was in New York. He well knows he could have had the match for from $500 to $5,000 if he had wanted it very much.

Now, Mr. Editor, I wish to state that I will run Mr. Morgan or any man that can be produced from 100 to 500 yds for from $100 to $1,000 or I will give any man in the U.S.10 yards start in 500 yards, over 15 hurdles, 3 feet 6 in high, or 5 yards start in 200 yds level running. I will also give 3 yards in 150 to Mr. Morgan or anyone that can be produced. I don't intend to return before April or May, this challenge, therefore, is open until then. I give more than one week's notice. Anyone wishing to make the matches can deposit a forfeit of $250 in the hands of the Editor of "Spirit" with the conditions of the match, and I will forward the same to the Editor—the race to be run in May. I should like to accommodate them sooner, but it is impossible for I am going south.

Now, if Mr. Morgan can't make it convenient to run in May, he can be accommodated. If he will run me at New Orleans I will be happy to have a gallop with him on the Metairie course in Jan or Feb for $1,000. There will be no back out, I assure you.

Yours, respectfully Geo. Seward

On their tour, Seward and Jackson searched for anyone willing to race them. During their stay in Louisville, it is likely they visited the nearby Big Gun Tavern at Shippingport. It was similar to the sporting taverns in England and was kept by Jim Porter, "the Kentucky Giant," who was believed to be the tallest man in the world. Charles Dickens, on his way to St. Louis in 1842, had stopped at Shippingport and, after meeting Porter, reported that he was "21 inches more than 6 feet tall." Dickens called the gentle giant "a lighthouse among streetlights." Porter's tavern featured a display of his custom-made eight-foot-long rifle and a sword so long only he could draw it from its scabbard with one hand. Porter towered over the 5-foot-3-inch Jackson by 30 inches.

Finding no competition in Louisville, the two men boarded a steamboat to take them down the Ohio and Mississippi rivers to New Orleans. This five-day journey was not without risks. Earlier that year in New York a paddle-wheel steamer's boiler had exploded with devastating results. In addition, the Ohio and Mississippi rivers contained sandbars and submerged logs that could sink a steamer. In winter, ice in the river was also a problem.

On the trip down the Mississippi, Seward reflected on his return to America. So far he had little to show for it as he had yet to run in a single race for high stakes. His thoughts also turned to the stories his mother had told him years earlier about his father, Azariah. He had died in this strange city of New Orleans, and his ship, the *Greyhound*, had been seized and sold by the New

Orleans probate court. George wondered if his father would have approved of his career as a professional runner.

They arrived in New Orleans in the first week of January 1846. With its quaint streets and strange-talking people, the city fascinated them. It had a population of about 110,000 and was divided into three districts: Creole, American, and French. Although Col. Oliver had promised them races on the Metairie Course, the enterprising Jackson had written to the owner of the rival Eclipse Course in Carrollton, just outside the city, and scheduled an attempt to run 11 miles in an hour. This race against time was set to take place before he and Seward were to run on the Metairie Course. The New Orleans *Daily Delta*, January 1, 1846, advertised the race even before the two men arrived.

Eclipse Course—Carrollton
FOOT RACE AGAINST TIME.

William Jackson, The American Deer is backed to Run on Foot ELEVEN MILES IN ONE HOUR on the above race course on SUNDAY at TWO o'-clock P.M. Umpire and Referees to be chosen on the ground prior to starting.

The attempt, which was delayed by rainy weather until January 25, 1846, was a failure. Although Jackson gave his best effort, he missed covering 11 miles by just 10 seconds, and he and his backers lost $1,000 on the match. Although he was disappointed, it was by far the best long-distance running performance anyone had made in America up to that time. Jackson had already proved he could run 11 miles in an hour, but this time fate was against him. His training had been hampered by a severe cold that allowed him to run only 2 miles in the ten days before the match. In the end, he lost because of his shoes. Near the finish, a spike penetrated the leather sole of one of his flimsy running shoes, causing him so much pain he had to slow to a 6-min.-40-sec. last mile. His abrupt slowdown can be seen from his mile times (table 4.1).

Jackson's 4-min.-49-sec. first mile may also have been too fast for him to have his best performance, but runners of this era understood little of the advantages of even pacing. A fast first mile and a sprint at the finish were the traditional British strategies for running a distance race.

On the following day, the *Daily Delta* published a notice for Jackson and Seward's first appearances on the famous Metairie Course. The Metairie Course opened in 1838, and as New Orleans became a commercial and shipping center and a focal point for sports and entertainment, the course

Table 4.1.   Jackson's January 25, 1846, Attempt to Run 11 Miles in an Hour

Split times		Cumulative times	
Mile 1	4:49	1 mile	4:49
Mile 2	5:10	2 miles	9:59
Mile 3	5:13	3 miles	15:12
Mile 4	5:25	4 miles	20:37
Mile 5	5:22	5 miles	25:59
Mile 6	5:12	6 miles	31:11
Mile 7	5:30	7 miles	38:41
Mile 8	5:29	8 miles	42:10
Mile 9	5:37	9 miles	47:47
Mile 10	5:43	10 miles	53:30
Mile 11	6:40	11 miles	60:10

became the South's leading racecourse. On January 31 Jackson would run an hour-and-a-half race and Seward would again demonstrate his prowess over the hurdles.

Col. Oliver had agreed to give the winner of the longer race $750 if his total distance exceeded 15 miles. Seward again found no one willing to race him in a sprint race and agreed to run a 300-yard hurdle race. Col. Oliver had invited some other well-known runners to New Orleans to provide competition for Jackson. John Gildersleeve, Cornealius Desman of Boston, and John Nevils of Plattsburg were all in town and eager to test their running skills against the Deer.

After sizing up his competition, Jackson decided to make the 15-mile race more interesting by offering starts to all the other runners and on January 28 published a "card" in the *Daily Picayune*.

Having heard that if I entered in the Fifteen Mile Footrace for the purse of $1,000, to be run for over the Metairie Course, on the 8th of February, I might prevent others from starting, and having already given various challenges to any one in America, to give them half a mile in a race of twenty, I now propose—if the proprietor of the course (Col. Oliver) will consent—that I will give every other competitor 600 yards at the start. If the proprietor will signify his acceptance of this proposition in tomorrow morning's paper, I will remain and run the race, which will be the last I shall run in America before leaving for England.

WM. JACKSON "The American Deer."

Jackson had a motive other than generosity for making this offer. For the second time since coming to America, he had secretly agreed to "sell" a race. He was well known and a heavy favorite. By offering the other runners 600-yard starts, it would be less obvious he was intentionally losing the race.

An unsuspecting Col. Oliver agreed to Jackson's proposal and invited the press to visit the course to witness the pedestrians in training. The *Daily Delta*, one of the invited newspapers, believed Jackson had no chance to make up 600 yards on Gildersleeve.

> It really seems to us impossible that a man of Gildersleeve's power and compactness of form, added to his peculiar facility of "go along" can be beaten 600 yards in the given distance of 15 miles. Of Seward we can truly say that his performance in jumping hurdles surpasses belief and, we may say, the imagination of any one who has not witnessed it. The parties are daily at work in their preparations for this gigantic performance, and it really is worthy of the attention of the curious. The race comes off on Sunday next, and we expect a greater crowd than has ever been seen upon any occasion of the kind in this country.[25]

Although the crowd of five to six thousand was huge by New Orleans standards, had the races taken place in the New York City area, they would have drawn five or six times as many fans. The program opened with the 300-yard hurdle race over twelve 3½-foot hurdles between Seward and Irishman Cornelius Fitzgerald. Seward won without difficulty, giving a dazzling display of swift running and graceful jumping.

Although Jackson allowed all the other runners 600-yard starts, he was such a heavy favorite the timers paid no attention to them and kept all their watches on the "Deer." Overtaking his opponents proved easier than Jackson expected. He sped by them one by one until he caught the leader, Gildersleeve, after they had gone only six of the fifteen miles. From then on Jackson could have taken the lead whenever he chose, but did not. Instead, he ran on Gildersleeve's shoulder, never once making an effort to pass. As the race continued, it became painfully obvious to those watching that Jackson was not trying to win. He seemed unsure of himself, and the crowd stared in bewilderment when several times he veered away from Gildersleeve and ran over to one side of the track to consult with his backers.

When the two leaders had gone seven and a half miles, it began to rain. At first it was a sprinkle, but it soon grew harder, and the course became muddy and slow for the last three miles. Had it not rained, both Jackson and Gildersleeve would have finished within the allotted 90 minutes. But Jackson refused to take the lead no matter how much the pace slowed, even when it became obvious they were not going to meet the required time. He finished less than a yard behind Gildersleeve in 92 min. 30 sec.

Jackson's throwing of the race was even more obvious than his race with Barlow, and the New Orleans newspapers wrote stinging condemnations of his "outrageous" behavior. A gracious Col. Oliver gave the purse, pro rata, to Gildersleeve and Jackson although neither had covered the distance in 90 minutes. Oliver said that it was his opinion both men would have made the required time had it not rained. Jackson collected his money and quickly left town, leaving behind many angry fans who had lost money betting on him.

This time Seward did not go with Jackson. He may have become fed up with Jackson's behavior, but he also had another reason for staying—a high-stakes race of his own. The *Daily Picayune* published a notice of the race (figure 4.3).

The ad's claim that both men were undefeated and had run 100 yards in 9 seconds flat was obviously not true. Little is known of Collins, not even his first name. He is never mentioned again in the *Spirit of the Times* or any other major newspaper in America. This makes it unlikely that he ever ran 9 seconds flat for 100 yards. Seward, on the other hand, had been defeated in previous races, but there were reports he had run 9 seconds for 100 yards in practice.[26]

Their race took place on the day advertised, but Seward's association with Jackson led to the major New Orleans newspapers boycotting it. The *Jeffersonian* was the sole newspaper to print anything about the race, and it gave

Races!---Metairie Course.

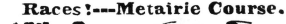

SUNDAY, 15th February, 1846.
THREE RACES!!!
☞ RACE TO COME OFF AT 2 P. M. ☜
*First Race...*GREAT FOOT RACE—100 YARDS.
A MATCH FOR **$1000** BETWEEN
MR. GEORGE SEWARD, of Connecticut,
....AND....
MR COLLINS, of Alabama.
☞ The two engaged in this Match are the fastest runners in the world, neither having ever met with a defeat, and both claiming to have run the distance in 9 seconds!

Figure 4.3. Advertisement for Seward's race with Collins, published in the New Orleans *Daily Picayune*, February 13, 1846. From the *Daily Picayune*, February 13, 1846.

only a short report saying Seward won. Nothing about the victory margin, time, or other details was ever reported. Nevertheless, Seward was happy to have won a major race for a good stake. Since returning to America, he had traveled from Canada to New Orleans, and the $500 was the first large sum he had been able to earn.

There is no information on how long Seward remained in New Orleans after the race. Jackson traveled to Savannah, Georgia, taking the sea route around the southern tip of Florida and up the East Coast. On March 11, 1846, he raced Gildersleeve at 10 miles on the Oglethorpe Course near Savannah and won in 58 min. 10 sec. He and Gildersleeve traveled on to Charleston, South Carolina, where they raced again on the Washington Course on March 20. This time Jackson covered 10½ miles in 59 min. 35 sec. in another easy victory. Large, enthusiastic crowds that appreciated seeing quality distance racing for the first time attended both races.

The race in Charleston was the last time Jackson faced Gildersleeve, the best American distance runner of the time. Gildersleeve continued to travel the country for several years looking for races. In October 1851 the *Spirit of the Times* reported he was in San Francisco and had made an effort to run 10 miles in less than an hour for $500 a side. On the day of the race, a "perfect gale" was blowing, and he could only manage 63 min. 37 sec.

In late February 1846, Billy Barlow challenged Jackson to a rematch at 2 miles for $200. By this time Jackson had lost his enthusiasm for another race with Barlow and wrote to the *Spirit of the Times* refusing the challenge. The $200 stake was "too trifling a sum and he had better fish to fry in England," he wrote. He countered with an offer to race Barlow for $400 a side in Baltimore or Philadelphia and ended his letter with "If any man in America thinks that he can beat me at any distance from two to 20 miles, for $1,000 or $2,000 a side, now is his time, as I leave shortly for England. I will give any man that can be produced in this country a half mile in 12, or three quarters in 20, for either of the above sums."[27]

Barlow was unable to raise the additional $200, and there were no other responses to Jackson's challenge. On April 6 he wrote again to the *Spirit* saying he was leaving for England from Boston by steamship on May 1 because he could find no more competition in America.

His letter was gracious and diplomatic. Jackson most likely hoped to soothe the hard feelings caused by his intentionally losing two races and may have had future trips to America in mind. The *Spirit* wrote:

He states that wherever he has traveled he has found innumerable friends, both North and South, alike ready to give him a friendly hand, and in returning his thanks he trusts that our countrymen in England will be received with the same cordiality which has ever been shown to him here. Jackson deprecates any interruption of the good feeling which should exist between the two countries—is decidedly opposed to a war for Oregon or any thing else, but hopes that this country will "increase in wealth and remain in peace under the flag of Liberty forever!" ["Hurrah for Jackson!"][28]

On April 25, just before he was to leave, his challenge to run 11 miles within an hour was accepted by a man from Philadelphia who bet $1,000 to Jackson's $700 that the "Deer" could not perform the feat. The match was set for June 15 on the Hunting Park Trotting Course near Philadelphia.

Seward also found another opponent for a high-stakes match. The *Spirit of the Times* on May 2 contained an acceptance of the challenge he had made to George Morgan back in December 1845 while he and Jackson were on the way to New Orleans. Morgan agreed to take Seward's offers of a 3-yard start in 150 and 5 yards in 200 and run two races in Washington City (now Washington, D.C.) in the summer.

By June Seward was in Washington City preparing for his race with Morgan. At the time, Washington City had a population of about 30,000. Morgan warmed up for the race on June 5 by easily defeating an English runner named Bannister, a relative of Richard Pakenham, the British Minister to the United States. His victory at 100 yards for $500 a side on the National Course made him the consensus fastest American sprinter besides Seward.

After his failure in New Orleans, Jackson was more eager than ever to complete the 11-miles-in-an-hour feat. Acting as his own trainer, he put himself through a rigorous conditioning program and got himself superbly fit, bringing his weight down to an ideal 105 pounds. Before making the attempt, he inspected the Hunting Park course looking for soft areas to avoid.

Confident of setting a new 1-hour record, Jackson left nothing to chance. To make sure there would be no dispute over the distance, he supervised a team of surveyors who accurately measured the course. They found one lap of the track to be 5 feet 3¾ inches longer than a mile. This extra distance was multiplied by eleven and subtracted from the eleven laps. The surveyors moved the starting line 58 feet 5¼ inches forward to make eleven laps the exact distance Jackson needed to run to win the bet.

Jackson started the race alone at a few minutes past 5 p.m. and ran the first mile fast as usual. For the first four miles he was ahead of the required pace, but after the fifth mile he began to lose ground. He made a supreme effort to get back on pace and was so exhausted after the race he was seized with convulsions. Still, he failed to complete the 11 miles in an hour by 28 seconds (table 4.2). His friends carried him to his lodging and he soon recovered.

Table 4.2. Jackson's June 15, 1846, Attempt to
Run 11 Miles in an Hour

| | His splits were: | | |
Mile	Time	Loss	Gain
1	4:55		0:37
2	5:13		0:14
3	5:16		0:11
4	5:25		0:02
5	5:27½		
6	5:34	0:07	
7	5:42	0:15	
8	5:44	0:17	
9	5:51	0:24	
10	5:43	0:16	
11	5:42½	0:15½	
	60:28		

There were conflicting reports why Jackson failed to cover 11 miles in an hour. Some claimed he had started too fast, but the real reason had nothing to do with pacing. In a letter to the *Spirit of the Times*, Jackson explained why he lost and complained bitterly of "the scandalous treatment he received while running." In the seventh mile, several men ran onto the track and stood in front of him, two of whom he had to knock down to get past.[29] The *Spirit* sympathized with Jackson, writing: "It is the general opinion of everyone that witnessed the Jackson race on Monday that he would have won it with ease had he but had fair play and a clear course."[30]

For the second time Jackson had failed to perform in America the feat that had made him famous in England. The first time had been because of bad luck, the second because the race was rigged against him.

Although Samuel Morse had demonstrated the telegraph in 1838, it was just coming into widespread use in America in 1846. One result was that the market for carrier pigeons quickly dried up. More importantly, the invention revolutionized news and sports reporting in the major cities in the Northeast. The editors of the *Spirit of the Times* in New York marveled at how they had received the outcome of Jackson's match by "Magnetic Telegraph," as soon as their Philadelphia contemporaries.

A disappointed Jackson traveled from Philadelphia to Washington City where he rejoined Seward, who was training for his race with Morgan on the National Course. Not wanting to waste the hard training he had done, Jackson arranged another attempt to run 11 miles within the hour on the Canton Course in Baltimore. The racetrack owner assured him he would receive fair treatment and a clear course. On July 6, a large crowd came to watch him make his third try at running 11 miles in an hour in America. Seward opened the program by running a ¼-mile hurdle exhibition. It had been advertised as a race, but no opponents came forward. Seward started alone and bounded over the twelve hurdles "with the agility of a deer"[31] and pocketed the $50 first prize.

A short time later Jackson appeared and started alone, but he soon realized the weather was much too hot to perform the feat. After going 3 miles he tripped and fell heavily. He got up and limped from the course, giving up the effort. Whether the fall was intentional is unknown. Jackson may have felt it was a more face-saving way to end the attempt than just quitting. The next day the *New York Herald* wrote: "Jackson is certainly either very unfortunate in his matches against time or he is playing a game that is not generally understood by his admirers."[32]

While Seward continued training for his race with Morgan, he and Jackson took part in a 1-mile hurdle race on the National Course near Washington City. The course had been built in 1802 to satisfy Congress's obsession for horse racing and was located about a half-mile east of what is now Bolling Air Force Base. The purse was $200 and the race was over fifty hurdles 3 feet 3 inches high, best two of three starts. Besides Seward and Jackson, there were two Indians and what the *Spirit* called "other things that talk" entered. Seward won the first race in 5 min. 48 sec. and the second in 5 min. 58 sec., so there was no need for a third. Jackson finished second in both races.[33]

On August 1, the *Spirit of the Times* announced that the much-awaited match between Seward and Morgan for $500 a side and the sprint championship of America would come off at the National Course on August 8. Morgan, who was part Cherokee Indian, came from the West and had made quite an impression in the Northeast. Instead of taking the starts of 3 yards in 150 or 5 yards in 200 that Seward had offered, he decided to start even in a 100-yard race. He coveted the unofficial title of champion sprinter of America and knew he would have to run Seward on even terms to get it.

Morgan was about thirty-two years old and 6 feet 2 inches tall with long, thin legs that bowed out at the knees. He had broad shoulders and walked with a spring in his step but ran with an awkward style, twisting his body from right to left with each stride. His backers felt his prodigious strength and speed more than made up for his less-than-perfect form.

On August 8, despite the severe heat, a large crowd arrived at the National Racecourse. Many came in carriages and willingly paid 25 cents each to watch the race between the fastest two sprinters in America. Seward had prepared well, spending six weeks in Washington City getting into top shape.

A group from Philadelphia came to town for the race and gobbled up every bet they could, placing their money on Seward. The odds for the previous week had been 2 to 1 on Morgan, but the last-minute betting on Seward caused them to swing around to his favor. At the starting line, Seward showed his confidence by betting Morgan $10 to $50 he would beat him by at least 6 feet, but Morgan declined the bet.

They both had a good start, with Morgan getting the best of it. He was leading by 2 to 3 feet at 75 yards when Seward shot by him and took a 2-yard lead. At 90 yards, Seward looked back, then slowed, allowing Morgan to cut the gap to about a yard at the finish. An observer, believing Seward was not going all out, wrote: "His [Seward's] way of getting along is so graceful and easy that many suppose him to be doing only a part of what he is able to do."[34]

After the race, Seward tried to promote a rematch, saying he was "astonished at the way Morgan dug out the last ten yards."[35] He offered to repeat the race allowing Morgan a 2-yard start, but Morgan declined. The race was the last Seward ever ran in America although he and Jackson made one last challenge in the *Spirit of the Times*.

Challenge by Seward and Jackson

To the editor: Seward and myself are about to visit Canada, but before going so far North we put forth the following challenge to America and the World, neither country nor color excepted. We hereby publicly declare that we will run any man that can be produced, from 100 yd to 20 miles for from $300 to $5,000 a side—Seward to give any man 5 feet in 100 yards, 8 feet in 150 yards, and 10 feet in 200 yards. And I will give to any man a half mile in 20 or a quarter in 10, 200 yards in six miles or 100 yards in four miles, or any man can be accommodated by me with a race of one, two or three miles level, for any amount they wish to name. And to show the public that I can run 11 miles within the hour, I will bet any gentleman $1200 to $1000, or $600 to $500 and run the match anywhere 200 miles from NY to Philadelphia.

Yours resp'y W. Jackson   U.S. Hotel NY, Aug 12, 1846
Geo. Seward[36]

Since the letter was mailed from New York City, the warrant for Jackson's arrest must have no longer been in effect there. He had won and lost large sums of money since fleeing New York City and may have been able to reach an agreement with the backer he had double-crossed the previous summer. Jackson was eager for another shot at running 11 miles in an hour, but there were no answers to his or Seward's challenges. With no immediate prospects for a race, they decided to forgo the trip to Canada and left Boston in early September to return to England. Not wanting to endure the ordeal they had experienced on the voyage over, they traveled by steamer.

During their fifteen-month stay in America, they had searched the entire country looking for races, visiting twenty-three of the twenty-eight states as well as the major cities in Canada. Their tour marked a change in American sports. It showed that travel had improved enough, even in the sparsely populated parts of the country, for an athlete to compete on a national scale. With Gildersleeve, they were the first athletes to tour the entire country.

Seward behaved honorably, and the crowds and race promoters treated him with admiration and respect wherever he went. His victories over Collins and Morgan, the fastest two sprinters he could find in America or Canada, added to his fame and reinforced his status as the fastest sprinter in the world. But the tour had earned him little money. He had endured the hardships and expense of mid-nineteenth-century travel without finding a single runner who could come close to matching his speed. Little had changed since he had toured New England from end to end looking for races in 1842. Given his enormous talent, it is unlikely he would have found any real challengers no matter where he went. Without quality opposition and with the public not having a well-developed sense of what made up an outstanding sprint race, he was underappreciated by many of the Americans who saw him run. His decision to return to England where racing opportunities were more plentiful was a good one.

Jackson, like Seward, was intelligent, resourceful, and a superior runner but did not have Seward's sense of fair play. This trait made him more representative of professional runners of his time than Seward was. Jackson had no qualms about "selling" a race if the money was right. His races were more financially rewarding than Seward's as he ran for larger purses and had more challengers. Promoters discovered that an hour that could be filled with a 10-mile race or an attempt to run 11 miles was a better drawing card than a sprint race lasting only a few seconds.

Except for Barlow at 2 miles, Jackson had proven far superior to the American distance runners of the time. Although he said he refused Barlow's challenge for a rematch because the stakes were not high enough, he must have doubted that he could beat Barlow at 2 miles. On this tour and on another he would make in 1849–1851, Jackson helped popularize distance running in America with several quality races that were exciting and fairly contested. On the other hand, he also showed the ugly side of professional running of the time by "selling" races and falling victim to double-crosses and foul play himself.

Notes

1. *Spirit of the Times*, May 19, 1838.

2. J. A. Cuddon, *The Macmillan Dictionary of Sports and Games* (London: Macmillan, 1980), 767.

3. *Spirit of the Times*, October 19, 1844.

4. *Spirit of the Times*, November 23, 1844.

5. "The Best Foot Race of the Season," *American Turf Register*, December 1844, 738.

6. *New York Morning News*, July 8, 1845.

7. The pepperbox was an Allen Thurber six-shot .31-caliber pistol with six rotating barrels. The pepperbox system offered serious competition to Col. Colt's revolving-cylinder revolvers in the mid-1800s. It was self-cocking and could fire all six barrels in three seconds. A serious design flaw was that it sometimes fired all six barrels at once when the trigger was pulled.

8. "Sporting Intelligence," *New York Herald*, June 29, 1845.

9. "Clean, beautiful style" (*New York Morning News*, July 10, 1845). We do not know how Seward actually went over the hurdles. Mid-nineteenth-century illustrations show hurdlers clearing the hurdles in an ungainly fashion with both legs bent. The first amateur to lead over the hurdles with a straight leg was Oxford student Arthur Croome in 1886 (*C. B. Fry's Magazine*, March 1909, 495–500). Seward probably used the bent-leg style but with skill and speed.

10. *New York Herald*, July 20, 1845.

11. "Beacon Courses Races," *New York Daily Tribune*, July 30, 1845.

12. *New York Herald*, July 29, 1845.

13. Peter Radford, *The Celebrated Captain Barclay: Sport, Money and Fame in Regency Britain* (London, Headline, 2001).

14. "The Foot Race Between Barlow and Seward—No Go," *New York Herald*, July 31, 1845.

15. "Foot Race at Baltimore," *Spirit of the Times*, August 23, 1845.

16. *New York Morning News*, September 30, 1845.

17. "The Late Pedestrian Match," *New York Herald*, October 2, 1845.

18. "The Recent Pedestrian Match a Sell.—The Biter Bitten," *New York Herald*, October 4, 1845.

19. *New York Herald*, October 4, 1845.

20. *Subterranean*, October 11, 1845, 2.

21. "To Correspondents," *Spirit of the Times*, October 11, 1845.

22. *Spirit of the Times*, November 15, 1845, gave the runner's name as Leakdigger; however, the *Toronto Herald*, November 6, 1845, gave his name as Hastings.

23. A trephining operation consisted of cutting a circular hole in the patient's skull. In this case it was apparently done to relieve pressure on Browning's brain.

24. *Métairie* means "farm" in French. The Metairie Course in New Orleans was located at what is now Metairie Road and Pontchartrain Blvd. There is a story that in

the 1860s, Charles T. Howard, who was refused membership in the Louisiana Jockey Club, vowed to turn the track into a cemetery and, sure enough, the Metairie Cemetery now located on the site of the course was chartered in 1872.

25. *Daily Delta*, February 3, 1846.

26. *Bell's Life*, November 24, 1850, stated that Seward could run 100 yards in 9 seconds.

27. "Pedestrian Challenge: Charleston S.C.," *Spirit of the Times*, March 21, 1846.

28. *Spirit of the Times*, vol. 16, March 21, 1846, 42.

29. "Jackson 'the American Deer,'" *Spirit of the Times*, vol. 16, April 11, 1846, 78.

30. *Bell's Life*, July 19, 1846.

31. "Foot and Hurdle Race," *New York Herald*, July 8, 1846.

32. "The Jackson Race," *Spirit of the Times*, vol. 16, June 27, 1846, 210.

33. "Foot and Hurdle Race," *New York Herald*, July 8, 1846.

34. "Match Between Seward and Morgan," *Spirit of the Times*, August 15, 1846, 294.

35. "A Foot Hurdle Race," *Spirit of the Times*, vol. 16, July 25, 1846, 253.

36. *Spirit of the Times*, vol. 16, August 15, 1846, 294.

CHAPTER FIVE

∿

George Seward in His Prime (1847–1848)

Seward's style of running surprised every person and his legs went like lightning.

—*Bell's Life*, May 9, 1847

Seward and Jackson arrived back in England in early October 1846. Jackson returned to Birmingham, where he had been staying before leaving for America. Seward did not go back to Durham or Cockfield; instead, he settled in Sheffield, the northern center of professional sprinting. By 1857 the Sheffield Handicaps, held seven to nine times a year, would become the premier sprint races in England, attracting runners from all over the country and later the world. Seward had another reason for going to Sheffield. It was also the center of the metal trade, and steel from that city is still famous today. He knew he might have trouble finding opponents and reasoned, if worst came to worst, he could find work in Sheffield as a silver plater.

His second trip to England was much different from the first. Everyone in England who followed pedestrianism had heard of him now, and there would be no running under assumed names or competing with second-rate runners. On the plus side, he had a good understanding of British pedestrianism and knew his way around. He also had made many friends and, as he approached thirty years old, had fully mastered his sport of professional sprinting. Sheffield would be his home for the next two years—the most productive time of his career.

Just after he had left for England, the *Spirit of the Times* in New York received a letter from George Morgan asking for a rematch. It appears that Morgan always waited until Seward was out of town to challenge him. One of Seward's first tasks after arriving back in England was to write to the *Spirit* accepting Morgan's challenge. He proposed they run for $1,000 a side and offered Morgan £50 for travel expenses if he would run in England. If that were not acceptable, he agreed to take the same amount and return to America for the race. As an added incentive, he offered Morgan a 3-yard start in 100 or 4 yards in 150. Morgan never responded and faded into obscurity.[1]

On October 26, 1846, both Seward and Jackson traveled to Sheffield's Hyde Park for their first running appearances since returning to England. Hyde Park was located on scenic Park Hill, three-quarters of a mile east of Sheffield Market and about a mile from the railway station. It featured a 508-yard circular track built from a pony course in about 1836. The track was 9 yards wide and surrounded by a wall that allowed the owner to charge for admission. The popular multipurpose ground, which was also used for cricket and pigeon shooting, would become Seward's favorite running course during his stay in Sheffield.[2]

Jackson entered an 8-mile handicap and started from scratch alongside his old rival William Sheppard. Neither he nor Sheppard was in top condition. Jackson was suffering from an illness that *Bell's Life* attributed to his travels. William Williams of Gorton, who had a 150-yard start, won the race. Seward, who suffered no ill effects from their travels, was more successful. He ran a 508-yard handicap in three starts and needed only two to take home the £10 prize. Starting from scratch, he took the lead in both races at 200 yards and won them easily, beating Henry Molyneux of Halifax and William Matthews of Birmingham, both of whom had 10-yard starts.

While Seward and Jackson had been away touring America, a young former medical student named Charles Westhall had developed into England's finest sprinter and boldly claimed to be champion of England at sprinting. Westhall, whose real name was Charles Hall, was born in London on March 6, 1823. At 138 pounds and 5 feet 10 inches tall, he was a thoughtful, literate man who would later write four books on training for pedestrians. His contemporaries described him as "a civil, well-behaved, unostentatious man, highly respected by all."[3]

Not only was Westhall an outstanding sprinter, but also he may have been the most versatile pedestrian of the nineteenth century. During his career, he ran 150 yards in 15 sec., 200 yards in 20 sec., a mile in 4 min. 28 sec., and 2 miles in 9 min. 55 sec. He was even more adept at walking, covering a mile in 6 min. 54 sec., 7¾ miles in an hour, 14½ miles in 2 hours, and 21 miles in

3 hours. Walking 21 miles in 3 hours became known as the "Westhall feat" because he was the first to do it. He was a fast walker and was also praised for his walking technique. No one questioned the fairness of his walking. John Levett in *How to Train* (1862) rated him the best pedestrian England ever had.[4]

Westhall and Seward were similar in many ways. Besides being the fastest two sprinters in England, both were well-educated, honest men trying to earn a living in a sport where most of the athletes were barely literate and many dishonest. The two men would later become close friends, but initially Seward pretended to be miffed at the young Englishman for claiming his sprint title. In reality, he relished the chance for some high-stakes races and wrote to *Bell's Life* to promote the rivalry. Seward opened his letter with an Old Danish proverb, a playful put-down of Westhall's bragging.

Mr. Editor:

Deep rivers flow with silent majesty;
Shallow brooks are noisy.
I was greatly surprised at Westhall challenging me to run a quarter of a mile, when he and his backers well know that a hundred yards is my distance. The desire to see his name figure in your widely circulated journal is, however, very excusable. His boastful statements all over the country, in my absence in America, that if ever I came back, he would lick me five yards in a hundred, now remains to be proved, and I now offer him the opportunity of 'licking' me at one hundred yards, for £50 and as much more as he can raise. If he does not make a match, I trust he will be more moderate in his assertions of what he can do for the future. At any rate he need not specify the number of yards he can give one whose performances have given satisfaction to the public, unless prepared to prove his words. I will send a £10 note to Temperance to make the match or any letters addressed to me there will receive immediate attention; and as I have always had good treatment in London, I am willing to run there.

Yours, &c George Seward.
Sheffield, Nov 4[5]

Seward was proud that he had "always given satisfaction to the public," that he had performed honestly and put on good shows at his races. Westhall answered the challenge in early December, and the two men signed articles to run 120 yards for £50 a side. Although Westhall had claimed to be the sprint champion in Seward's absence, he was not too proud to accept the 2-yard start the American offered. The race was to come off on December 14 within fifteen miles of London.

On the day of the race a large crowd came to Ganwick Corner to see the two popular pedestrians race. They began to express their disappointment, however, when at 12 p.m., the time the men were to meet, Westhall had not shown up. He had still not arrived at 2 p.m., the time set in the articles for both men to be at the scratch. Seward arrived at the appointed time, ran over the course, and claimed the stakes.

At a quarter to three Westhall and Harry Broome drove up in a horse-drawn cab and explained that the slippery roads had delayed them, as they had neglected to roughen their horse's shoes. Westhall was eager to race, but Seward's backer, George Colpitts, refused, saying that after running over the ground, Seward had eaten. "Temperance" (Edward John Drinkwater), the stakeholder, after much negotiating, got the two runners to agree to reschedule the race for the following Tuesday. By this time, Colpitts had already left, leaving instructions to claim forfeit, and Seward had no choice but to comply.

An irate Westhall wrote to *Bell's Life* claiming Seward had taken unfair advantage of him. *Bell's Life* sided with Seward, saying: "Westhall's excuse for not being present is at the best a very lame one as the frost was just as intense in town as it was in the country and he ought to have taken the very ordinary precaution of having the horse's shoes roughed before starting from town."[6]

Westhall still wanted to race Seward and proposed they run four races each for £50 a side. He had to withdraw the challenge, however, when his backers refused to risk so much money against the consensus champion of sprinting. Seward responded with a polite letter to *Bell's Life*.

Mr. Editor I wish in a friendly manner to bring myself to Mr. Westhall's notice. Westhall, a short time since, challenged me in *Bell's Life* to run four races— 100, 120, 150 and 200 yards and though the three last mentioned races would have been far over my distance I could have found friends in this good town to have backed me. The following week however Westhall withdrew, in polite terms, his challenge, on the ground that his friends who had promised to stand with him had declined doing so. I was disappointed but there was no help for it.

Westhall has this week come out in *Bell's Life* with a number of challenges to first-rate men at various distances offering them all good starts and I am therefore in hopes that he is now in a position to run me according to his challenge. I propose the four races shall be for £25 or £50 a side and that you Mr. Editor be stakeholder and should name the referees and place of running but as I claim to be the champion runner at one hundred yards, I would rather stake £50 to £40 or £100 to his £90 and run Westhall one hundred yards the four races above mentioned.

Now is the time or never for the public to judge our respective merits. Westhall is in his prime and I am getting old and stiff and if Westhall declines I must retire and trust he will not hereafter challenge me when I am quite done as a runner.

In conclusion, I beg for the last time to throw down the gauntlet to any man in the world at 100 yards for from £50 a side or as much more as may be desired and any person disposed to make a match will find my money ready at Mr. George Naylor's Matilda Tavern, Matilda-street Sheffield[7] or they can remit a deposit to you and I will do the same.

Begging the favor of your inserting this that I may have the pleasure when I get back to America of being able to point to it as a proof of your courtesy to a stranger, I am, Mr. Editor, with many thanks for your frequent kindnesses, your humble servant,

G. Seward—Sheffield, Feb 4

Seward planned to return to America, but first he wanted to exhaust his racing possibilities in England. His statement that he was getting old and stiff may have been a hint that he was feeling the early effects of "rheumatism," which would plague him in his later years. But he was far from finished. On the contrary, he would soon show that he was at his peak. He and Westhall signed articles for a match at 200 yards for £50 a side to take place at Frank Key's, Duke of York, Ganwick Corner, on Monday, March 22.[8] They agreed to start by a 3-yard scratch and have the course roped and staked the whole distance.

On March 9, Seward ran a 508-yard hurdle race (3 starts) for £10 at Hyde Park, Sheffield. By this time his fame had grown so much that all his opponents were given long starts. J. Searles had 15 yards, Benjamin Badcock 15, Rhodes 20, Willus 20, and Stainsby 20, while Seward started from scratch. In the first race Seward came in first with Badcock second. Badcock won the second race, but Seward came home first in the third to take the prize money.

His long-awaited 200-yard match with Westhall took place on March 22, at the enclosed grounds near Frank Key's, the Duke of York, at Ganwick Corner. Enclosed (fenced) grounds were just coming into use in England. Previously, most races were run on turnpike roads, but because of the popularity of pedestrian matches and their accompanying large crowds, they became a hindrance to traffic. In 1850, the police would stop all pedestrian matches on the turnpike roads around London, and tavern owners would scramble to build fenced-in tracks near their pubs. They promoted races on these tracks and charged admissions to watch. Fans patronized the pubs, which often did a booming business on race day. Sometimes the pub owners invented delays in starting the races to sell more drinks to the waiting fans. The tracks were made to fit the available space and their sizes and shapes varied: some were straight, some circular, others were rectangular with rounded corners. Their circumferences ranged from 200 yards to a third of a mile, and they were not always level.

Westhall had gotten himself in top form for the race. The *Era* reported that both he and Seward were "sticking to the stringent rules of training with the constancy of Anchorites."[9] The paper also reported that in his trials Westhall had repeatedly run 200 yards in "level time" (20 seconds) and felt confident he could defeat Seward. Interest in the race was high, and spectators came from Birmingham, Sheffield, Nottingham, and other distant parts of the country. Frank Keys had spared no expense to make his ground first-rate for this race billed as "England versus America." He prepared a level sprint course of about 230 yards, with ropes and stakes down the middle. A hedge on one side and posts and rails on the other kept the spectators from crowding the runners. Seward had always insisted that 100 yards was his best distance, and the betting men in London, considering 200 yards beyond his range, made Westhall a slight favorite, but on the ground the odds were even.

Bell's Life, however, believed that despite the increased distance, Seward was in a class by himself. "Both in America and England for some years past, Seward has shown speed rarely equaled, and when he defeated the celebrated William Robinson, certainly never surpassed. He is a most unassuming and well-conducted man and fully entitled himself to the confidence placed in him by his backer."[10]

At 4 p.m. the men appeared at the start dressed in their running outfits and wearing spiked shoes. *Bell's Life* wrote that Seward's spikes were the best in existence. George Colpitts had made them from goatskin, and they were very light and admired for their "neatness and pliability."[11]

As a warm-up, each runner took some strides over a portion of the course, causing their admirers to break out in loud cheers. The race was to start by a "three-yards scratch," meaning the runners could stand up to 3 yards behind the starting line and start whenever they felt like it. It was some time before they got away, and when the cry "they're off" was heard, Westhall took a yard lead and held it until they had gone about 90 yards. His supporters cheered loudly, thinking he would win. Then Seward, who had been running well within himself, ducked his head slightly, and with his long black hair flying, sped by Westhall with such speed the spectators gasped.

When Seward went by him, Westhall was as surprised as the fans and began to lose his usual form. Seward soon had a yard lead and increased it to three when they passed 180 yards. Having the race well under control, he turned his head and with his left hand playfully signaled for Westhall to come on. Westhall was unable to respond, and Seward coasted to the finish to win by 2½ yards in 19½ seconds. Although the time was a record that would stand for nearly fifty years, *Bell's Life* wrote that "it was evident that Seward could have done it in less time had the occasion required."[12]

Westhall appeared groggy at the finish and wept bitterly over his defeat. *Bell's Life*, however, was ecstatic, writing:

> We have no hesitation in declaring that neither Westhall nor any other man that we know of at the present time has a chance with such a really wonderful runner as Seward, who in his last six flat races has proved victorious beating Badcock, Rush, John Smith, Robinson (two races) and Westhall. He can be backed to jump with skates on ice against anyone jumping on land, and to throw a quoit with anyone in the world. As a fast skater, he is said to be un-equaled, and during the past winter he astonished many by his feats on the ice especially in clearing hurdles with skates on.[13]

Despite his defeat, Westhall was not willing to concede that Seward was the superior runner at distances shorter than 200 yards. After the race he challenged the American to run a 100-yard race for £50 a side. He later con-sulted his backers and they were unwilling to risk so much money against Sew-ard. The two men then agreed to change the distance to 120 yards and re-duce the stakes to £25 a side.

On April 6 Seward ran in a 120-yard handicap race at Birchfield, located two miles from Birmingham, for £10. He was now at the height of his popu-larity, and more than 8,000 fans came to see him run. Most of the other run-ners withdrew from the race when they heard Seward would compete. Those that remained were Edward Gregg (2-yard start), Benjamin Badcock (3 yards), and Henry Davis (3 yards). Seward looked to be at the top of his form and was backed against the field at 2 to 1. Badcock went away with the lead and kept it for about 90 yards, where Seward caught him and won by a cou-ple of yards. Although Seward won the race handily, the grass running sur-face hampered his usually fluid running style. The following Sunday's *Bell's Life* contained a challenge from Seward offering to give any man in the world a 3-yard start in 200.

A week later Seward appeared unannounced at Bellevue, Manchester. He had come as a spectator to watch the races and was not wearing his running outfit. *Bell's Life* noted the great change that had taken place in the Ameri-can's appearance since he first made a name for himself four years earlier while working as a coal miner.

Considerable curiosity was excited by the unexpected appearance of the great star of the day, Seward (the American Wonder) who, although no stranger in Manchester, at first sight was only recognized by a few familiars, his appearance being more aristocratic than when he resided in the northern metropolis; and such was the sensation produced by the challenge of the luminary in *Bell's Life* of Sunday last, that the speculators, from the juvenile in their teens to the senile octogenarian, viewed him as he perambulated the grounds, with as much interest as if he had been the hero of a hundred battles.[14]

On April 18 Seward wrote again to *Bell's Life* challenging anyone in the world and offering to increase the start he would give in a 200-yard race from 3 to 5 yards for £50 or £100. He still did not receive a response.

The 120-yard race with Westhall took place on May 3, 1847, at Mrs. Emmerson's Sprint Ground, Old Hat, Ealing.[15] Although the weather was bad, many spectators still came to watch. Westhall's defeat at 200 yards at Ganwick Corner combined with Seward's dazzling display of speed in winning the race caused "the American Wonder" to be the favorite at 2 to 1. Both men appeared looking fit and confident. Seward had easily defeated him at 200 yards, but Westhall believed he could win as he had never lost at a distance shorter than 200 yards.

On the second attempt to start Seward slipped and fell, cutting his leg. He was still eager to race, however, and as soon as he got the bleeding stopped was back at the scratch and ready to go. On the fourteenth try they bounded away and ran abreast for the first 40 yards. Then Seward shot into the lead and at 80 yards was 2 yards ahead. As in their previous race, he turned to Westhall and urged him to speed up. Despite his great effort, Westhall could not gain an inch, and Seward finished an easy winner by 3 to 4 yards, covering the 120 yards in 11½ seconds.

Without exerting himself, he had set another record that would not be beaten for half a century. *Bell's Life* wrote, "Seward's style of running surprised every person and his legs went like lightning. Westhall also ran well, at least four yards better than he had ever done at the distance, which makes the easy victory of the American Wonder much more astounding."[16]

Westhall was not as surprised at the outcome of the race as he had been in their earlier match and was now in awe at his rival. He told the press that Seward's accelerating away from him was like the firing of an arrow from a bow. "Seward seemed to bend his body in a sort of 'doubling' all the muscular powers into his legs and 'bow' away at a speed never before witnessed in any other in the world."[17]

A few days later Seward wrote to *Bell's Life* hinting of retirement and offering even longer starts.

Many of the first-rate runners are fond of talking of match making. Now in order that the public may judge of their capabilities, I hereby, before retiring from pedestrianism, offer to give any man in the world white, black, or of no color, five yards start in 120, or 10 yards start in 360 for £100 or £1,000 a side. Anyone can be accommodated at Temperance's on Monday next; the first deposit for £100 a side not to be less than £10 and for £1,000 not less than £50. If neither of these challenges be accepted, I trust I may not be deemed presumptuous in claiming to be the champion of sprint running and I accordingly avail myself of the opportunity of thanking you for your frequent kind attentions. I remain, Mr. Editor, your very humble servant.

George Seward:—May 5, 1847[18]

There was no answer to this offer or to any of Seward's frequent challenges. He was at the height of his popularity, much admired by running fans, and had soundly defeated Westhall, his only real challenger in England. Their second race proved to be the last epic match race at 200 yards or less that Seward ever ran. There were simply no runners left willing to race him on even terms in a sprint race. His career was not over, however. He could try to make matches by offering long starts or run in handicap races open to all. The prize money for handicaps was not large, and he knew he would be severely handicapped because of his reputation. His only other choices were to race against horses and run longer distances where he was not invincible.

On May 27, he wrote to *Bell's Life* from the Hope Tavern, St. Pierre, Calais, offering almost unbelievable starts at short distances and to run matches at longer distances. "I will, to show the public that I am not particular to a yard or so, now shorten the distance and give any man in the world 5-yards start in 100, or 10 yards in 250; or run anyone any distance up to 1,000 yards, for £50 or £100 a side."

A 5-yard start in 100 is roughly half a second. Professional sprinters sometimes offered handicaps this large to novices, but to offer 5 yards in 100 to anyone in the world was unprecedented. The lack of responses meant the other top sprinters wanted no part of racing with Seward no matter how long the starts he offered. Only Westhall was willing to race under these terms, but his backer did not share his optimism and refused to put up the stakes. Westhall decided to bet his own money and take the 5-yard start, but later thought better of it and declined to go through with the match.

Longing for a race, Seward wrote again to *Bell's Life*.

I have so repeatedly, by your kind favor, challenged without being able to get on a match, offering starts that never were offered before that I am at a loss to think what has become of the pluck of the runners of old England, what start do they want? Let some of them say in your next. I have some American friends over here who are eager to see me run, and I shall be glad to have an opportunity for a large or small sum. I have never tried it, but will carry a 10-lb weight and run any man in England 100 yards. The match can be made at Temperance's any time.

Your humble servant, George Seward.[19]

There were still no takers, and there is no record that Seward ever ran a race carrying weights to handicap himself. With no prospects for a match race in sight, he ran in a 440-yard handicap hurdle race (three starts) open to all on July 5 at the Sunderland Cricket Ground for a purse of £10. His opponents were Atkinson, "the Teetotaler of Durham," 10-yard start; Jackson (not "the American Deer") and Thwaites of Durham, 15-yard start each; Place of Sunderland, 12 yards; and Anderson of Tudhoe, 12 yards. In the first race Jackson slipped and broke the third hurdle. Seward, running close behind, cleared the top of Jackson's head by an inch and took the lead and kept it, finishing an easy winner. He also won the second race easily.

After offering Thomas Atkinson a 10-yard start in 130 and receiving no response, Seward did what he had always done before when he could find no human opponents: he turned to racing horses. On the Bishopwearmouth Cricket Ground on July 26 in the presence of about 4,000 spectators, he ran 200 yards in three starts over eight hurdles against a steeplechase horse named the "Sailor." They got off well, with Seward getting a slight lead. Both took the hurdles in excellent style, but Seward kept his advantage and won by a few yards. On the signal for the second start, Seward bounded off with the lead, followed by the horse. At the sixth hurdle they were even, but some rain had fallen between races and the horse slipped on the circular course. The jockey had to pull in a little, allowing Seward to win by 6 yards.

On August 5, Seward wrote to *Bell's Life* from Newcastle offering even longer starts. "Mr. Editor, you will be much obliged by stating in your next that I will give any man in England ten yards start in 160 if they will stake £200 to £100 and start by mutual consent; to run in six weeks from first deposit." Despite this handicap, which amounted to a full second, no one answered the challenge.

Seward was unwilling to give up his running career and, after much thought, devised a plan that would not only allow him to race regularly but would also showcase his running talents to the maximum. He explained his idea in a letter to *Bell's Life*.

Mr. Editor: I wish to give one more challenge although I believe it is useless. I will now run any four men in England in one hour, each one in succession, 120 yards and give them five yards start for £50 to their £50 between them, and if I lose one race out of the four to forfeit the £50 which can be divided among the four if they can make it agreeable; each man to start either at or before the expiration of 15 minutes. I will also give £5 for choice of ground. Any letter addressed to me at the Red House, Meadow-lane, Leeds will be immediately attended to.

Yours &c George Seward Sept 23, 1847.[20]

Seward's stunning challenge is unique in the annals of sprinting. No other sprinter is known to have raced four first-class sprinters separately in an hour and defeated them all. During the next year he would run many of these matches. He did not stop with four, but increased the number of races to as many as ten within the hour. These multiple races within the hour satisfied his appetite for racing and added to his fame, but did not make him wealthy.

On September 30, 1847, at the Victoria Cricket Ground, Leeds, Seward defeated Westhall and six others in a 500-yard handicap hurdle race. He then agreed to give Westhall a 5-yard start in a 120-yard race at Hyde Park, Sheffield, for a £10 purse. He also offered to run anyone in the world for £25 or £50 a side 30 minutes after he finished with Westhall but got no takers. The race with Westhall took place on October 11 on a flat area near the top of the hill. More than 2,000 spectators watched the two men make seven or eight false starts before they got away. Seward was equal to the task, overcoming Westhall's 5-yard start and winning by a yard to the shouts and applause from the crowd.

The victory had come with a cost. In making up the 5 yards he had given Westhall, he had gone all out and irritated the old injury he had received while training to run John Rush three years earlier. The injury did not reveal itself right away, and Seward ran the next race of the day, a 160-yard hurdle handicap in three starts. He and Luke Furness started from scratch, giving Westhall 5 yards, Henry Walsall 15 yards, and Joseph Redfern 25 yards. Seward won the first race easily with Westhall finishing second and Furness third. Only Seward, Furness, and Redfern started the second race, which Seward won also to claim the £10 prize money.

Three weeks later he entered a 500-yard hurdle race at the Talbot, Bowling Green, Stafford, but soon after starting found his right leg so painful he had to withdraw. Despite the injury he was still eager to try running several opponents in quick succession. In less than two weeks he appeared at the

Leicester Cricket Ground to run his first match of this type. Because of his bad leg, he shortened his opponents' starts from 5 to 3 yards. The first competitor to come to the scratch was Nutty Bodycoat, of Leicester, whom Seward beat with ease. John Handley of Nottingham was next and had no better luck. Joseph Robinson then tried his speed, and although he ran a game race, he had no chance with Seward, who took only enough time between races to return from the finish to the starting line.

After defeating Robinson, Seward felt fatigued and took a 30-minute break. The crowd waited eagerly for him to return and race Westhall, by far his most dangerous opponent. His race with Westhall turned out to be closer than expected. Although Westhall had the same 3-yard advantage as the others, Seward soon caught and passed him, and it appeared he had the race won. But nearing the finish, he felt a sharp pain in his right leg and slowed almost to a walk. Both men breasted the handkerchief together and many thought it was a dead heat, but the referee declared Seward the winner by 3 or 4 inches. Some medical men who had attended the race examined Seward's leg, and their prognosis was that he would not be able to run again for a long time.

They were wrong. Two weeks later he was back running and made his most startling challenge ever. Since his races with Ainsworth and Belden in 1840 and 1841 Seward had done his best to keep the winning margins in his races to a minimum. Even against such first-rate sprinters as Morgan and Westhall, he had eased up at the end trying not to show too much speed. His injury convinced him that his running career might be nearing its end. In addition, he had given up hope of finding any more challengers for short-distance match races. Now there was no longer any reason to hide his talent. He reasoned he might as well let the public see him at his best and earn some money doing it. His records at 100, 120, and 200 yards were so outstanding that no one would come close to them for fifty years, yet he knew from his trials that if he went all out, he could run faster. *Bell's Life* for November 21, 1847, printed his challenge to run three races in record times.

> Mr. Editor: As I have challenged so frequently without success, I will now try against Old Time. If anyone will stake £100 to £50 against my running 200 yards inside 19½ seconds; or 120 yards in 11 seconds or 100 yards inside 9¼ seconds, or if they will stake £50 to £25.
>
> George Seward, Nottingham, November 18.

Because watches of this era read to the nearest ¼ second, he would have to run 200 yards in 19¼ seconds or faster to win the first challenge. He should have been able to run this time because his 19½-second record for the distance was set in a race where he turned and motioned to his opponent, Westhall, to speed up. Running 120 yards in 11 seconds would be much harder. His best public performance at the distance had been 11½ seconds in another easy victory over Westhall. To beat that time by ½ second he needed to run an unprecedented 10 yards "inside even time." It is puzzling that he bet he could run the distance in 11 seconds because that was ¼ second faster than necessary to beat his existing record.

His most remarkable challenge was to run 100 yards inside 9¼ seconds, the time he was already world famous for running. To win that bet he would need to run the distance in 9.0 seconds, an incredibly fast time for an era when training methods were primitive and sprinters started upright on turnpike roads or sand-covered tracks.

Had he run any of these times in public, he would have solidified his place in sports history as one of the greatest sprinters that ever lived. No one was willing to bet against him, however, and he saw no reason to run the races just to break his own records. It is likely he had already run the times in trials, however, as he was not a man to make bets he had no chance to win. In 1850, Bell's Life gave their assessment of Seward's sprinting ability, which suggested that he would have won his challenges. "Three years ago Seward was the fastest runner in the world. He could run 100 yards in 9 seconds, 200 yards in 19 seconds, and 300 yards in 29 seconds."[21]

Unfortunately, the Bell's Life reporters did not say how they knew Seward could run these times. The first two times agree closely with his challenges, and it is possible the reporter had timed him running them. The 29-second 300 yards is a revelation because Seward was never timed for that distance in public. Nearly forty years later, Harry Hutchens would become world famous for running the distance in 30 seconds. No sprinter would officially beat 30 seconds for 300 yards in the nineteenth century, and even today the feat is no easy task.[22]

On November 22 at Trent Bridge Ground, Nottingham, a large crowd gathered to see Seward give Westhall and three other noted runners 3-yard starts in 100 and run them all separately in half an hour for £15 a side. The "Wonder" complained of being lame, however, and to test whether his leg would hold up, he selected William Birks of Tyson Green, the slowest of his opponents, to run first.[23] After a little dodging they got away, but before Seward could get up to speed, the large tendon in his left thigh gave way and to the great astonishment of the crowd Birks won by a yard. Seward collapsed at the end of the race and had to be carried from the course. Westhall agreed to help his injured friend by running the rest of the men. Giving each a start of 2 yards, he rose to the occasion by defeating them all. On Thursday, three days later, Seward was still lame, and it appeared he might be unable to run for months.

This time there was no quick recovery. The injury took three months to heal. While he recovered, Seward tried to make matches at longer distances where there would be less strain on his injured leg. He made a 1,000-yard match with John Leyland (alias Chip of Bury) for £100 a side, but after a deposit of £1, Leyland refused to go on with the match. Although 1,000 yards was well beyond his best distance, Seward wanted the match badly because it was for high stakes. He offered to give Leyland a 10-yard start in the 1,000-yard race or the same start in a 150-yard race, but Leyland still refused to run.

By early February 1848, Seward's injury was better, and he was again offering long starts in sprint races. He stated in Bell's Life he would run any man in England 140 yards and give them 7 yards' start for £50 to £100 a side.

His first race after his injury was at Hyde Park, Sheffield, on March 20, 1848. Despite the freezing weather and heavy snowfall, several hundred hardy fans paid their threepence to see the sports. The main attraction was a handicap hurdle race in three starts, once around the ground (508 yards) over eight hurdles. About 4 p.m., Seward, Luke Furness, Isaac Howard, and William Parrott came to the scratch, but after taking a good look at the icy ground, the men decided it was not safe to jump the hurdles. Instead they ran a flat race of once round the ground, with Seward giving all his opponents starts and winning easily.

Some of the fans were not satisfied, saying the men could not jump the hurdles because they were a full 4 feet high. Seward, not wanting the crowd to go away disappointed, ran a 100-yard race against William Parrott. Bell's Life reported that he "astonished all present by winning by at least a score yards."[24] Then, to silence those who had doubted his hurdling ability, he ran the ice-covered 508-yard course alone, clearing all the hurdles in "admirable style."

On April 17, Seward tried to run six men 100 yards each, one every 10 minutes, for a purse of £10. He agreed to give the purse to any of them that beat him. Soon after 4 p.m., he stood at the mark with his first opponent, John Mappin, who had a 5-yard start. He disposed of Mappin without much trouble, winning by 2 yards. Next was Hopewell, who had 4 yards and gained 2 more at the start, but it was not enough, and Seward defeated him by a yard. The next runner, Westhall, was by far the most dangerous of the lot and, with his 2-yard start, was favored by many of the crowd. After several tries, they got off to an even start. At 50 yards, Seward caught Westhall and the struggle began in earnest. They ran side by side until near the finish where Seward made an extraordinary effort to win by a foot, amid the wild cheers of the crowd.

Exhausted from his struggle with Westhall, he left the track to rest but in fifteen minutes was back at the mark. His opponent this time was Samuel Brammar, who had a 5-yard start. Both men got off well, and Seward won a good race by a foot and a half. Next came the celebrated John Shaw of Doncaster, to whom Seward had also given 5 yards. After several tries they started, but Seward got off badly and found himself another 2 yards behind. He tried desperately to catch up, but could not make up the 7 yards, and Shaw won by a couple of feet. Despite his prodigious effort, Seward got nothing for his efforts. The *Era* credited the defeat to his not taking more time for the first three races.[25]

At Bellevue, Manchester, on May 1848, upward of 4,000 came to watch Seward race six well-known runners 100 yards separately in 60 minutes for a purse of £20. Seward was not well, and the *Era* wrote:

> The spectators were on the tiptoe of expectation to witness the extraordinary powers of the Connecticut pedestrian, G. Seward, whose fame is not confined to Old England, but extends far west across the Atlantic. On stripping, Seward became the observed of all observers, his muscular development exciting universal admiration, but as he paced the ground it was evident he was amiss and not likely to accomplish the extraordinary task.[26]

His opponents included the best sprinters in England—Thomas Hopwell of Nottingham, Charles Westhall of London, H. A. Reed of London, George Martin of London, J. Flockton of Leeds, and Samuel Wood of Levenshulme. At a little after 3 p.m. Hopwell came to the scratch to face Seward. The betting was 4 to 1 on the "Wonder" versus each of the runners, and the odds were even he would win all six races. At the fifth try, Hopwell got away with the lead. Seward caught him and won the first race by a yard, hopping in on his left leg. Many thought he was just showing off, but he had reinjured his bad leg and had to withdraw.

Westhall again substituted for him and defeated the next two runners but declined running the last two because he had to save himself for a 14-mile walking match later that day. Undaunted, Seward vowed that "when himself again, and on the same ground he would run any six men on the same terms to show the good folks of Lancashire he was of superior metal."[27]

He was true to his word and in less than two weeks was back racing. For the next several months he was injury free and embarked on a historic tour of England performing the feat that had become his trademark. On May 22, at the Huddersfield Cricket Ground he defeated six men, running each 100 yards separately, for a purse of £10. Running with little rest between races so his bad leg would not become stiff, he defeated them all easily in 21 minutes.

A month later, at Wolverhampton in the Albion Tavern Enclosure, he astonished the fans by defeating eight men in separate races for a purse of £10. They were Benjamin Badcock, "the Birmingham Lurcher," William Taylor, "the Temple Street Pet," and six other lesser-known runners. He ran each 80 yards and defeated them all in 16½ minutes! It took him less than 2 minutes to run each race then return to the start and begin again.

On July 10 at the Albion Tavern Enclosure he raced separately "Young Badger," William Taylor, George Yeyrick, "Ruffler," and six others at 80 yards. He defeated them all in 29 minutes for a purse of £10. Two days later, on the same grounds he ran four men 100 yards each for £5. His opponents were Benjamin Badger, Greatbach (suspected to be Ralph Penk) of the Tetteries, William Taylor, and Henry Ruggler. Seward took only 5 minutes to defeat all four opponents.

Seward loved running these matches. They drew large crowds and allowed him to at last showcase his extraordinary sprinting ability to the fullest. At Vauxhall Gardens, Manchester, on July 31 upward of 5,000 came to watch him race six of the most celebrated men in Yorkshire, Cheshire, and Lancashire separately at 100 yards. Wearing netting around his head to keep his long black hair from flowing in the breeze, he defeated them all in 25 minutes "to reap a bountiful harvest in threepenny gate money."[28]

Unfortunately, these races were beginning to take a toll on him. The *Era* reported he did not seem well. "To our eye he appeared much more worn than we should have imagined from his temperate mode of life and though he fleeted gracefully along, we thought he had not quite that surpassing speed he was wont to have. He is somewhat reserved, rather haughty, with unmistakable signs about him that he thought no small-beer of himself."[29]

In August, William Jackson, "the American Deer," answered Seward's long-standing challenge to race a mile. Since his return to England Jackson had been out of action because of illness for most of 1847. His one significant race that year was on October 13, when he beat Richard Manks for the 10-mile championship running 53 min. 10 sec. and lopping 25 seconds off Sheppard's record.[30] The following April he clocked 54 min. 20 sec. for the distance on a partly uphill course at the Bury St. Edmunds Cricket Ground.

Seward and Jackson met at Tom Spring's Tavern in early September 1848 to sign articles to run 1 mile on November 6 for £200 a side. Although the stakes were twice the amount Seward had ever competed for, he was not worried. He was at his peak as a runner and though a mile was far beyond his best distance, he was so confident and eager to test himself at that distance he agreed to give Jackson a 15-yard start. Having the choice of ground, Seward selected the enclosed grounds at Hyde Park in Sheffield where he and Jackson could share in the gate money.

Seward also had other plans. For some time he had been seeing a young woman named Mary Mascall, the twenty-two-year-old daughter of Thomas Mascall, a Sheffield stonecutter. After his high-stakes race with Jackson, which he was confident he would win, Seward and Mary planned to marry and use the money from the race, plus what he had been able to save, to return to America.

On September 11, he traveled to London to run six 100-yard races in half an hour at Mrs. Emmerson's, Old Hat, Ealing. He was at his best that day, and his performance on the familiar course was the stuff that legends are made of, as an awed *Era* reporter described:

At five p.m. Seward came on the course and was soon afterwards followed by H. A. Reed, a man that can run a bit when he likes. The start was performed without any ceremony and away they dashed for the goal. Of the race nothing remains to be told for Seward won with ease.

The second "ped" that took his station to contend with the all-conquering Seward was that rising star Newman, who in turn was defeated with all imaginable ease.

The third competitor was Morris, who ran bravely and gallantly and proved himself to be a lad possessing much speed and though he did not come in successfully in this event, we feel confident he will on some future day run with better success.

The fourth competitor that stood forth to "run a course" with the champion was Thompson, a lad who has frequently figured before the sporting critics of this metropolis, and is considered to be a swift and plucky runner. They got off well together and for a few yards were abreast, but as they approached the goal Seward once more displayed his abilities as a runner and won with all the ease possible.

Then came Cook, but his opposition was quite useless and ended in his goose being most effectually cooked.

Thompson, who was ambitious to have another struggle for supremacy, again betook himself to the scratch to contend for the second time with the great American runner. Fate doomed this last pedestrian once more to defeat and thus he stood a foe over which a double triumph had been achieved. This last spin made up the proposed number of men Seward was to run all of whom he beat into utter insignificance, much to the surprise of many present.[31]

On October 2, at Mr. Cheese's new race ground, Flora Grounds, Bayswater, Seward tried his most ambitious feat ever—defeating ten men separately in 100-yard races, all within an hour.[32] The Flora Grounds had two race-courses, an oval for longer races and a straight course for sprints of up to 120 yards. Seward, running on the straight course, easily defeated his first five opponents in only 10 minutes, but by the sixth race, the excited spectators had crowded onto the course, leaving the men little room to run. Seward ran into one of them and the collision knocked the wind out of him, causing him to lose the race and the match.[33]

Bell's Life called these races "monster matches." In less than a year, starting in late 1847, Seward ran at least eighteen of them. Each required him to race several opponents separately with little recovery between races. At first he was hampered by injuries, but when he became healthy and gained experience in judging how much rest he needed, he was nearly unbeatable. In many of the matches the time between races was as little as a minute or two, and sometimes the matches themselves were only a day or two apart. He did not choose inferior opponents but competed against the best sprinters he could find, including Westhall and Reed, and often made his task more difficult by giving starts. There is no evidence any of the matches were faked. He needed little rest between races because he was so much faster than his opponents that he did not have to exert himself greatly to win.

Seward traveled all over England, running these matches anywhere he could find an audience and a suitable number of opponents. He was treated as a celebrity and was often the guest of well-known sporting figures. The feats attracted large crowds, and most were held in enclosed grounds where he could share in the admission money. Because he ran so many of these races, not all of them were reported in *Bell's Life* or the *Era*, but of those reported he won seventy-four individual races, lost three, and withdrew from one match because of an injury. The losses are most telling. The loss to Birks came when Seward came up lame. The loss to Shaw, who had a 5-yard start, came when Seward got off to a bad start. The loss in his effort to run ten men 100 yards in an hour came when he ran into a spectator.

He was at last getting his fill of running, performing to large crowds, and making a comfortable income. If he was pushing the limits of what his thirty-one-year-old body could withstand, it was better than not racing at all. This frequent, strenuous racing eventually led to a major breakdown, and his running came to an abrupt end in mid-October 1848.

On October 22, *Bell's Life* wrote that Seward was ill, and later that week George Colpitts sent one of his employees to Sheffield to check on him. On arriving, he was shocked to find Seward so ill with rheumatics that he had to be lifted in and out of bed. The attack of rheumatism was the first of many Seward suffered as he grew older.[34] He blamed this bout on his match to run six men in an hour at Bellevue, Manchester, on May 8, 1848, when he injured his leg, but his many other "monster matches" probably contributed as well.

There was no way he could run his high-stakes mile match with Jackson on November 6. Colpitts offered to give Jackson £10 and pay his training expenses if he would postpone the match for three weeks. The "Deer" said he had no objection, but he needed to get his backer's approval. After talking to his backer, Jackson reversed himself and refused to postpone the race, saying that under similar circumstances in one of his races, he had been forced to run on the day named or forfeit. He added that had their positions been reversed, he did not think Seward would have granted his request for a postponement.

The stakeholder, boxing legend Tom Spring, having no other choice, handed over the £265 stakes to Jackson at Spring's Castle Tavern on October 30.[35] Jackson was saddened that his old friend was so ill. He made a short speech saying he would be happy to make a new match when Seward recovered and left a generous £10 of the stakes for him. After calling for some champagne, Jackson left with the rest of the money.

For some time, Jackson had wanted to return to America and resume racing there. After dividing the stakes with his backer, he would not have had enough money to finance the trip. The entire stakes were more than enough, however.

After waiting a few days, Jackson's backer discovered that the "Deer" had "bolted" with all the money. The outraged editor of *Bell's Life* wrote:

> It is one of the most cruel cases that ever occurred, for the gentleman in question has been to him the best and most liberal patron he ever had during his long career as a pedestrian. It would appear that the ingrate had packed up his portmanteau at his mother's on the previous day and took it to some place ready to carry off on the following night. Every means will be adopted to find out his whereabouts, and it is to be hoped they will prove successful.[36]

In early December, Jackson was sighted traveling by rail from Lewes to Brighton and sometime in early 1849 discreetly boarded a ship bound for America. He planned to use the stakes to finance a three-year running tour of America similar to the one he and Seward had undertaken in 1845–1846.[37]

Since Seward's return from America in late 1846, he had decisively defeated Westhall, his only real challenger at sprinting, as well as everyone else who had been willing to race him. In addition, he had added best-on-record

times at 120 and 200 yards to his 100-yard record. None of these performances would be beaten in his lifetime, and his feat of defeating up to ten top
sprinters separately in an hour has never been repeated. These events had
made him a legend, but now he was a cripple who would spent the rest of
1848 and the spring of 1849 unable to get out of bed without help.

Notes

1. *Spirit of the Times*, vol. 16, November 14, 1846, 450.
2. Sheffield Handicaps were held in Hyde Park from March 31, 1857, until 1884.
3. *Illustrated Sporting News*, March 22, 1862.
4. John Levett, *How to Train* (London: Newbold, 1862).
5. "Seward and Westhall," *Bell's Life*, November 8, 1846. "Temperance" was Edward John Drinkwater, a noted walker. He bought the Blue Boar's Head in Long
Acre, near Trafalgar Square, in 1842. His establishment sold engravings of pedestrians and dealt in sporting art in addition to the usual pub fare. He was a noted judge
and timekeeper for pedestrian matches. He also kept his own records of pedestrian
performances and, like the editor of *Bell's Life*, was a popular stakeholder for pedestrian matches.
6. "Seward and Westhall's Match.— No Race," *Bell's Life*, January 3, 1846.
7. The Matilda Tavern at 100 Matilda Street dates from 1825, becoming a
coaching inn around 1840. The archway provided access to the stables, which still
exist, to the rear. Until the demise of the brewery a good pint of Wards was always
available. Seward's letter appeared in *Bell's Life* on February 7, 1847.
8. The Duke of York still exists as the Beefeater Restaurant & Pub.
9. *Era*, March 14, 1847.
10. "Seward and Westhall's Race," *Bell's Life*, March 28, 1847.
11. "Seward and Westhall's Race," *Bell's Life*, March 28, 1847.
12. According to *Modern Athletics*, 2nd ed. (London: "The Field" Office, 1875), by
H. F. Wilkinson, the *Bell's Life* reporter who timed this race as well as the one when
Seward ran 120 yards in 11¼ sec. was E. Smith. The 19½-second time was reported in
the May 28, 1847, *Bell's Life* and listed in the record books. The *Era* of the same date
apparently had no timer present and seemed unsure of the time, writing, "The time
that the distance was done in is stated to be as good as any on record, the 200 yards
being run in nineteen seconds; but whether the time was correctly taken we cannot
say."
13. *Bell's Life*, March 28, 1847.
14. "Doings at Bellevue, Manchester," *Bell's Life*, April 18, 1847.
15. Old Hat was a sprint ground attached to the Old Hat public house. It opened
in April 1844 and was originally referred to as Emerson's Ground but was later just
the Old Hat, Ealing. It was reported to be "a very excellent enclosed ground," 160
yards long and 17 feet wide, which is just over four lanes wide by today's measure-

ments. The ground was advertised for sale in April 1849. Source: UK Running Track Directory, at www.runtrackdir.com/details.asp?track=london-eal-oh (accessed September 22, 2007).

16. "Seward and Westhall," *Bell's Life*, May 9, 1847.

17. *Bell's Life*, May 9, 1847.

18. *Bell's Life*, May 9, 1847.

19. *Bell's Life*, June 22, 1847.

20. *Bell's Life*, September 26, 1847.

21. "Seward and Reed Race," *Bell's Life*, November 24, 1850.

22. Although no time for 300 yards has ever been ratified by the IAAF, Peter Radford of Great Britain ran the distance in 29.9 sec. on August 1, 1960, at Hornchurch Stadium, London, and the performance was widely recognized as legitimate. In 1999 Doug Walker, the European 200-meter champion, made an unsuccessful attempt to beat Hutchens's 30-second time for 300 yards. Walker's time was 30.05 seconds. "Time runs out as Walker wins but misses an age-old target," *Herald* (Glasgow), January 1, 1999.

23. *Illustrated Sporting News*, August 8, 1863, published a portrait of William Birks, calling him "Champion Pedestrian of France." The article listed as one of his greatest achievements his victory over Seward at Trent Bridge in 1847. It did not mention that Seward broke down during the race.

24. "Matches at Hyde Park, Sheffield," *Bell's Life*, March 26, 1848.

25. "Pedestrianism at Hyde Park, Sheffield," *Era*, April 23, 1848.

26. "Bellevue, Manchester," *Era*, May 14, 1848.

27. "Doings at Bellevue, Manchester," *Bell's Life*, May 14, 1848.

28. "George Seward and His Six Competitors," *Era*, August 6, 1848.

29. "George Seward and His Six Competitors," *Era*, August 6, 1848.

30. Richard Manks, "the Warwickshire Antelope," was born in Solihull on May 3, 1818. Manks was a versatile pedestrian who raced all distances up to 50 miles. He was best at longer distances and his performances included 11 miles in an hour on December 3, 1855; 20 miles in 1 hr. 52 min. 51 sec. on December 16, 1851; and 50 miles in 6 hr. 47 min. on February 7, 1853. John Goulstone, *Turf, Turnpike and Track* (London: Author, 2003).

31. "Racing at Ealing," *Era*, September 17, 1848.

32. The Flora Grounds opened in March 1849. It was also referred to as the Flora Race Ground or Flora Gardens and was an extension of some horticultural grounds. The ground was enlarged and reopened on February 26, 1850, although it was still very small and there were no stands. It was a 240-yard "broad and hard gravel walk" (circuit) and a 130-yard sprint straight in the center of the ground. It was also described as being 73 times round for 10 miles, which is fractionally over 241 yards. Source: UK Running Track Directory, at www.runtrackdir.com/details.asp?track=london-bay-f (accessed September 22, 2007).

33. "Seward and Jackson's Race Off," *Bell's Life*, October 29, 1848.

34. Rheumatism is a diagnosis no longer used and in Seward's day was a catchall phrase to describe almost any inflammation and pain in the joints, muscles, or fibrous tissue, especially rheumatoid arthritis. It is impossible to say precisely what brings on the disease. It was fairly common among runners of the nineteenth century, and the great British sprinter Harry Hutchens, who ran in the 1880s, was also dogged by the ailment.

35. The Castle Tavern opened as a Sporting House in 1810 and was the haunt of boxers, pedestrians, and their admirers. A previous host, Bob Gregson, ended up in a debtors' prison, but Lord Byron stepped in and bailed him out. Under Spring's orders, all actual fighting was prohibited though one of the main reasons for people's frequenting the establishment was to talk about or listen to stories of boxing matches and foot races. Some came to see Spring, whom they had read or heard so much about. Regulars included Pierce Egan and Vincent Dowling, the editor of Bell's Life from 1822 until his death in 1852.

36. "Jackson and Seward," Bell's Life, November 5, 1848.

37. The New York Herald, June 9, 1849, had an ad for an hour run on the Union Course scheduled for June 29, 1849. The prize for breaking 11 miles was $500, and Jackson was listed as an entrant.

CHAPTER SIX

~

Merely the Shadow of
His Former Self (1849–1852)

For three long months Seward languished in bed in Sheffield. In addition to the match with Jackson, he had to forfeit matches at 200 and 440 yards to Henry Allen Reed. Preparations for the races with Reed were in the early stages, so forfeiting them was not as financially devastating as the match with Jackson had been. Through the early months of 1849, Reed repeatedly challenged the ailing American, and by March Seward felt well enough to respond in *Bell's Life*:

> Mr. Editor: Mr. Reed asks me if I mean running him. My answer is yes. The following proposition I will make to him, which I think is no more than fair, namely to run 200 yards and 440, the same distance he received forfeit for through my illness; the two matches for £50 each match. The 200 yards I will run in London, not exacting anything for my expenses; but for the 440 yards race, I will give him £10 for choice of ground or take £10 to run on a turnpike road within 20 miles of London. This, Mr. Editor, I think is a fair offer. The first race to come off in six or eight weeks from the first deposit. If this suits Mr. Reed he can leave £10 or £20 with you, Mr. Editor, and articles and I will sign them. If he means running, he cannot object to £10 or £20 for the first deposit.
>
> —Your obedient servant, G. Seward, Sheffield, Mar 1[1]

Reed, although confident in his ability at 440 yards, had lost decisively to Seward in all their races at shorter distances and wanted no part of a match with him for high stakes at 200 yards or less. He refused to run the 200-yard match, pointing out that Seward had often challenged to run anyone in the world at any distance from 100 yards to a mile without any conditions attached. Seward let his pride get the best of him and agreed to skip the 200-yard race, which he was almost sure to win, and race Reed only in the quarter mile.

By mid-March he was feeling well enough to resume training. He had seldom done much training for sprint races; instead he would run a trial at the distance he was going to race. If the trial were in a time he felt his opponent could not beat, he did little further training. That strategy would not work this time because the quarter mile was beyond his best distance and required endurance as well as speed. He was also uncertain how fast either he or Reed could run 440 yards. George Colpitts encouraged him to start a rigorous training program to prepare for the match, and Seward agreed to do so.

The race was scheduled for May 28, but Reed developed a boil on his right shin, which had to be lanced. He asked for a month's delay, and instead of insisting on his "rights" and claiming forfeit, Seward readily agreed and used the extra time to prepare for the race. He had become more compassionate since he had claimed forfeit from Westhall two years earlier. In addition, he wanted badly to defeat Reed at 440 yards and was willing to accept almost any terms to get the opportunity to race him at that distance. On April 9, Seward tested his fitness in a minor handicap race of once around the ground at Hyde Park, Sheffield. The result was encouraging; he ran from scratch and won easily by 10 yards.

Being ill for so long and having to forfeit such a large sum to Jackson had forced Seward to delay his return to America. He could not put off his marriage, however, as he and Mary were expecting a child. They were married on Saturday, April 14, 1849, in the Parish Church in Sheffield. Seward hoped to recoup the money he had lost because of his illness and take Mary back to America with him.

His epic 440-yard race with Reed created more interest than any pedestrian match in years. An excited public was eager to see if the talented Reed could dethrone the American legend. Neither Seward nor Reed had ever been associated with fixed races, and the *Era* expected a fair and exciting race.

The distance to be run, it will be borne in mind, is a quarter of a mile, while the stakes invested on the result by the backers of the men amount in the aggregate to £200. This magnificent sum is now in the possession of the final stakeholder, who will hold the same until the time arrives for the lucky winner to receive the reward of what is hoped may be a fair and honorable victory.

That this will be the result of their meeting we are confident, for the position of the men and also the position held by their backers, at once convinces us that the competition is one in which both will honestly and manfully struggle for supremacy in speed.[2]

Destined to become the greatest quarter-miler of the Victorian era, Henry Allen Reed was built for running. He had a "broad chest, slender waist, and thin limbs, with remarkably muscular thighs, very long from the hip to the knee and walked as if his legs were hanging on wires."[3] Although of average height (5 feet 7 inches), he was famous for his long stride. After a 120-yard race in September 1847, officials measured the distance between his footprints and found his stride to be a remarkable 9 feet 4 inches.

Reed had started his racing career in 1846 while working as a linen-draper's assistant in Lamb's Conduit Street, London. After losing his first match to Londoner Edward Smith, he returned to his job. In September 1847, using the alias "William Allen of Holborn," he beat George Martin by 5 yards in a 120-yard race at the Old Hat, Ealing. The following year, in a race against Robert Inwood on a rising course at Wandsworth Common, he ran 440 yards in 53½ seconds without being pressed. Later that year, before 5,000 spectators packed into Hyde Park Ground, Sheffield, he beat James Sherdon at 1,100 yards.

Reed did not like to train and often depended on his unquestioned natural ability to win races. Instead of training, he preferred spending time with his friends in London's Newgate Market, which was lined with pubs that served juicy steaks.[4] As a result, he sometimes showed up at races 25 pounds over his best running weight of about 126 pounds. His tendency to gain weight and his lax training caused him to lose several races to men who had nowhere near his ability. Still, before his career was over, he would run two races that would give him a solid place in running history—the first sub-50-second quarter mile and the first sub-2-minutes half mile.

The long-awaited 440-yard race took place on Monday, June 28, 1849, on the turnpike road near the Magpies Inn at Harlington Corner. Seward wanted badly to defeat Reed. Not only were the men rivals but also Seward desperately needed the money from winning. As was his custom, he trained at a secret location, and *Bell's Life* wrote that he had worked harder and paid more attention to his diet than he had ever done before.

Great care had, however been taken of him [Seward] by his liberal backer and that gentleman's brother in training him for this important event, and if Seward was not quite so strict in his diet or work as could be desired, it must be remembered that in no former race can it be said that he trained at all, for drinking bowls of milk and eating cabbage, and having but little exercise, as was the case in his other matches is a system certainly not by any means general among those who are preparing for feats of this description.[5]

The reporter went on to tell of the great physical change that had taken place in the American's once remarkable physique.

He is 5' 7", wt. 11 stones [158 lb], with a display of muscle that excited the attention and admiration of all beholders. But alas! What a falling off in this respect was witnessed on Monday; he appeared merely the shadow of his former self, his severe illness at Sheffield during the past winter having given him a terrible shaking. Indeed, as he observed, it was the hardest match he ever had to overcome, and therefore, taking all the circumstances into consideration, it was a matter of surprise he even looked so well as he did, and so full of confidence as to the result.

The *Era* also noticed the devastating effects of his illness, writing: "Seward, with his fine commanding figure, looked well, but still his muscular proportions did not appear to be so fully developed as in times of yore, when, as the 'American Wonder,' he first astonished us with a display of his fleetness as a runner."[6]

Reed had trained near the Magpies Inn under the care of William Sheppard and had gotten himself in the best possible condition. His training was so rigorous that he had reduced his weight from 154 to an ideal 126 pounds. On the day of the race he appeared alert and dashing with rapid eye movements that signaled a "boldness of his daring spirit."[7] Reed and Seward were both confident of victory because in their trials leading up to the race, each had easily beaten William Robinson's best-on-record time of 51 seconds for 440 yards.

It was one of the hottest days of summer. Despite the heat and clouds of dust kicked up by carriages, 6,000 excited fans gathered early in the afternoon on the road leading from the Coach and Horses to the Magpies Inn. All were eager to see the race between two men whose trials at 440 yards *Bell's Life* had reported as "most wonderful."[8]

The articles required the runners to be at the scratch ready to start by 3 p.m., but when they met at the Magpies Inn, they agreed to postpone the race until 5 p.m. to avoid the intense heat. It was past 7 p.m. when they came to the start, much to the chagrin of the many spectators who had waited over four hours in the sweltering heat to see the race. Early on, Reed had been the favorite, with the odds at 5 and 6 to 4 on him. By race day, however, the betting was even, and when Seward appeared confident and seemingly recovered from his illness, odds of 6 and 7 to 4 went almost begging on him. George Colpitts had been so impressed by Seward's recovery and training that he brought £1,000 to speculate but had trouble finding takers. Reed showed his own confidence by betting his last £20 on himself.

Tom Oliver had carefully measured the straight 440-yard course and roped the last 200 yards. As the men got ready to the start, the referee took his position in a carriage halfway between start and finish. A fast race was expected, and many were curious to know the winning time. Timing a 440-yard race on a straight course was no easy task. The timer stationed himself on the roof of the Magpies Inn, about midway along the course, where he had a good view of both start and finish.

A dense crowd pressed in on the ropes on both sides of the course, trying to get a better look at the runners. Many of them wore handkerchiefs displaying the "colors" of their favorite runner. Despite Seward's popularity and all he had accomplished in his four years running in England, he was still a foreigner, and spectators wearing Reed's colors outnumbered his by almost two to one. *Bell's Life* reported that every spectator imaginable was there. "The rough, the smooth, pickpockets, laborers with rough hands, well-dressed idlers who lived by their own means, and even better dressed idlers who lived off others—all came to watch and among them were those who love sport and manly exercises for their own sake."[9]

Although confident he would win, Seward tried to gain an edge at the start by doing his best to rattle his less-experienced opponent. After twenty-five false starts, however, Reed assured him it would not work. He said he "did not mind waiting as long as he pleased, for he was sure to prove victorious when they did run."

Seward responded with a smile and when Reed asked, "Do you mean to go now, George?" replied "Yes," and away they went.[10]

Reed surprised everyone by sprinting away so quickly it looked as if he would not be able to hold the pace for half the distance. Seward, who had won the toss for choice of sides, stuck with him on his left for the first 100 yards, then began to fall back. At 150 yards Reed, still going all out, increased his lead to 2 yards. On approaching the Magpies Inn, Seward fell even farther behind. Reed turned his head slightly to see where his opponent was, then went on to win by 14 or 15 yards.

Loud cheers greeted "the Great H. A." as he crossed the finish line so "done up" he could hardly walk. His time was announced as a new record, a staggering 48½ seconds. He had taken remarkably long strides and run with a beautiful bounding style throughout. Seward had exhausted himself by 300 yards but gamely pushed on to the end, exerting himself so much his face was nearly black when he crossed the finish.

It was a crushing defeat. Although Seward was a foreigner, he had become an institution in England. After the race, the *Era* wrote: "The defeat of the renowned and supposed to be unconquerable George Seward created quite a panic in the city of Manchester where Seward was a great favorite. In its way, a Bank of England had failed and the distance of the defeat made people vow they could not read it."[11]

Seward's illness had weakened him, but Reed must be given credit for a great race. His performance was the first 440-yard race run under 50 seconds. The time would go unbeaten until October 4, 1873, when another professional, Dick Buttery, "the Sheffield Blade," ran the distance in 48¼ seconds on a track at Newcastle. Reed had good reason for being confident. His backer, Mr. Parker, said that before the race he had twice timed Reed inside 47 seconds for the distance in trials on the turnpike road.[12]

On July 5, the stakeholder from *Bell's Life* gave the £200 to Reed at the Red Cross Tavern, Barbican, where Reed was the proprietor. The large, joyful crowd drank to the health of the new 440-yard champion and celebrated his great victory. Seward was too despondent to attend, but Reed agreed to give him £5 of his winnings and collect what money he could "to comfort the American and his 'better half' on their way back to the United States." Reed's backer generously presented him with the entire £200 stakes and in addition paid for a lavish dinner for the new champion and his friends.[13]

Seward's backer, George Colpitts, although disappointed in losing so much money, wanted to help his defeated runner any way he could. Satisfied Seward had done everything possible to win, he scheduled a benefit for him at the Flora Grounds, Bayswater, for July 9.

Even the best professional runners of this era were often only one race away from poverty. When they were ill, injured, or unable to win races, their friends and fellow pedestrians sometimes held benefits for them. An owner of a running ground where the pedestrian had been a favorite would grant the use of his grounds, and pedestrians who wanted to help would perform with the gate receipts going to the stricken runner.

Seward was a proud man, yet he accepted this arrangement and received many benefits after his career began to falter because of illness and advancing age. Most of his benefits were poorly attended and failed to raise much money. Some were hindered by bad weather, and despite all of Seward's accomplishments, he was still a foreigner. In addition, pedestrian fans were almost all from the working classes and few had much money to spare, even for their running heroes.

Reed promised to appear at the benefit as did Westhall and several other pedestrians who admired and respected the American. Afterward, Seward still intended to leave with his new wife for America but decided he would also take leave of his Sheffield friends at his favorite course at the Hyde Park Cricket Ground.

The attendance at the Flora Grounds was disappointing; only six or seven hundred came. Seward was still thankful and said the reception was "friendly, fair, and honorable,"[14] and all agreed the races were first-rate. The highlights were Seward and Reed racing 120 yards. Reed won by a foot—the only time he ever defeated the American at a distance shorter than 440 yards. Seward then raced William Jones 120 yards and won easily, and Reed defeated Westhall by half a yard in a 140-yard race. Afterward, Seward announced he would expand his farewell tour to include many of the towns where he had been a crowd favorite. Reed graciously agreed to go with him on the tour.

On July 17 Seward received another benefit, this time at his favorite running ground, Hyde Park in Sheffield. The attendance was again small, only about 500. He and Reed ran once round the ground (508 yards) for a small purse, with Seward winning by a yard.

Seward never returned to America as he had planned. Publicly he gave no reason for changing his mind about returning, but his long illness had drained him physically, and his forfeit to Jackson and loss to Reed had left him nearly penniless. In addition, it is likely that he did not want to risk taking his pregnant wife Mary on the long voyage across the Atlantic. Their child, a girl named Clara, was born on November 1, 1849, at 26 Burgess Street in Sheffield.[15] Instead of going home to America, he did what he had always done when unsure of what to do next—he went back to racing against horses.

On August 6 he ran Mr. J. Harwood's mare Black Bess a 400-yard hurdle race in three starts over twenty 3-foot-6-inch hurdles for £25 a side at the Barrack Tavern Cricket Ground, Sheffield. The turnout of 5,000 spectators proved that even if he had declined as a runner, he could still draw a crowd. In the first race Seward led, closely followed by Black Bess, for 200 yards, where the mare caught up. Seward, however, kept at it and won by a yard. After a short rest they ran the second race and Seward won again, this time by a foot.

In Manchester on September 3, there were two novel events competing for the attention of entertainment seekers. Lieutenant George Burcher Gale was making an ascent from the Pomona Gardens in the "Prince of Wales," a balloon designed to make aerial fireworks displays safer. It had two baskets, one inside the other. The outer basket could be lowered by ropes and pulleys and the fireworks set off from a safe distance below—if setting off fireworks from a hydrogen-filled balloon could ever be considered safe. The audience got another thrill when Gale climbed from the top basket into the lower one.[16]

Despite the competing balloon display, an overflow crowd of 5,000 came to Bellevue to watch Seward race Mr. Harwood's mare, Black Bess, 200 yards over ten hurdles for £25 a side. At the signal to start, Seward sprinted away with the lead and cleared the hurdles in excellent style up to the seventh, where he caught the hurdle with his left foot and fell heavily, enabling the mare to pass him. He jumped up and finished the race but could not recover his lost ground. Game to the end, Seward insisted on starting the next heat as soon as possible before his injured hip and bruised hand could get stiff, but the black mare won the second race anyway.

He raced the same horse for a third time in early September in Liverpool, running 120 yards for £20 over eight hurdles. The novelty of the match drew a huge crowd. Seward displayed his talent for showmanship by appearing in an all-white running outfit, providing a stark contrast to the jet-black mare. Unfortunately for Seward, the course was not level, with the last hurdle being at the top of a small hill. In both races he ran even with Black Bess until the last hurdle, but each time he had difficulty clearing it, causing him to lose both races.

On September 17 at Broadholm, near Belper, upward of a thousand people assembled to see a match between Seward and Mr. Nix's chestnut pony, Maid-of-all-work. The conditions were to run 200 yards and jump ten hurdles. About 4 p.m. both man and horse came to the post and at the word "go" went off at full speed and cleared the first hurdle together. The spectators cheered loudly, causing the "Maid" to veer across the course straight into the crowd. In doing so, her hooves passed within inches of Seward's shoulder and a spectator's head. The rider gained control of the pony and got it back on course, but the "Wonder" was so shaken by his hairbreadth escape that he gave up the contest.

John Moor then came to the scratch to run Seward once over the hurdles. Both got off at the first try, but by the second hurdle Moor was so far behind he gave up hurdling and tore after Seward on the flat but was unable to catch him. The owner of Maid-of-all-work challenged to run 200 yards and jump ten hurdles in 18 seconds or give any pedestrian in the world 2 seconds for £10 a side.

Tired of racing horses, Seward decided to try a running-related business venture. He wanted to do something to keep himself in the pedestrian circles he had grown to love, and like many famous athletes, he hoped to capitalize on the fame he had achieved. Because the number of spectators attending pedestrian matches dropped off in winter when the weather was bad, he hit on the idea of holding athletic events in a traveling covered racecourse. He found two men, Mr. Harwood, the owner of Black Bess, and a man named Heath, who put up most of the money for the venture, which he called "The Great American Arena."

Seward was perhaps too extravagant in his venture, having a huge, portable, circus-like tent built that contained 20,000 square feet of canvas and could hold 10,000 people. He planned on traveling from town to town in northwest England starring in his own circus that featured various old English sports and footraces. The highlight was a race between Seward and a horse over hurdles. The tent protected the fans from the weather and allowed him to charge a small admission.

The popularity of circuses in England had started with Philip Astley, who held his first circus in 1768. Astley's early circus featured trick horses riding in a ring. He later added musicians, clowns, jugglers, tumblers, tightrope walkers, and dancing dogs. This laid the foundations for the modern circus.

Improvements in the railroads and improved tent technology in the 1820s led to the circus becoming mobile. In 1825, American Joshuah Purdy Brown was the first circus owner to use a large canvas tent for circus performances. Circuses in canvas tents soon became common both in America and England. Seward's was different only in that it featured sports rather than trick horses, trained animals, and other entertainment acts.

He opened his "monster pavilion" on Monday, October 1, 1849, at Walness, Pendleton, near Manchester. The weather was bad; about 2,000 people came, including a good number of women. Few women attended pedestrian events, but Seward's circus was novel, and many women wanted to see the handsome American perform. Seward managed to get some first-rate pedestrians to take part in his venture. The preliminary event was a wheelbarrow race by men blindfolded. Then George Martin, Edward Roberts ("the Ruthven Stag"), J. Smith (alias Major), T. Flockton ("the Yorkshire Plant"), T. Kearney, B. Maguire, and J. Portlock ran a 300-yard hurdle race for a silver snuffbox, which was won by Martin.

The finale was "the American Wonder" himself running a 100-yard hurdle race in three starts against Mr. Harwood's mare Black Bess. Seward won the first two races in fine style, and the crowd went home happy with the afternoon's entertainment. On Tuesday the weather was better and the attendance not as large. The program included most of the same pedestrians, and the sports were the same as before except for slight variations including bell and sack races. Seward then packed up his arena and moved it to Rochdale to repeat the performances.

The venture did not prove successful. Attendance was not as large as he and his backers had hoped. In addition, moving and erecting the huge tent was difficult and expensive. Seward's traveling arena was a little premature. It might have been more successful a year later when races on turnpike roads were banned in and around London. Runners had to turn instead to private grounds and several, such as Flora Grounds, Bayswater, cashed in on the need.

George Martin, who had won the hurdle race on opening day, put Seward's innovative idea to good use twelve years later when he managed the great American distance runner Deerfoot's tour of England. Martin used a portable enclosed racecourse for his "traveling Deerfoot circus" and charged admission to see the Indian run in towns without enclosed tracks. His "traveling circus" enclosure was more easily transported than Seward's was because it had no cover but was merely a portable canvas fence, 12 feet high and a quarter of a mile in circumference. Inside he would set up a makeshift 200-yard track and provide room for spectators to stand and watch the races.

Giving up on the traveling arena, Seward went back to match racing, running his next major race on November 12, 1849, at the Norfolk Cricket Ground, Sheffield. This unusual race was both a 200-yard and a 500-yard race at one start. There were two finish lines, and the runner who was ahead at 200 yards would be declared the winner of the first race. The runners then continued running to 500 yards to decide the winner at that distance. His opponent was Edward Roberts, "the Ruthven Stag" of Manchester, and the stakes were £25 a side for each distance. The match created much interest both in Manchester and Sheffield, and a large crowd came to watch. Roberts was a twenty-two-year-old Welshman, born at Ruthven, Denbighshire. He had made his debut in 1846 and had run many races with varied success.

Shortly after 4 p.m., both men appeared on the ground, and Seward, having won the choice of sides, put Roberts on his right. They dodged at the start for about ten minutes before Seward got away with a 3-yard lead, increasing it to 8 at 100 yards. He eased his pace, and Roberts decreased the distance to 2 yards at 180. A struggle then followed, and Seward won the 200-yard race by half a yard. They continued to the 500-yard mark, and despite the best efforts of the Welshman, Seward won by 5 yards.

By late 1849 Seward had recovered more fully from his illness and wanted another crack at Reed in a 440-yard race. He wrote to *Bell's Life* on December 9 challenging Reed to another match.

Mr. Editor: Not being satisfied with my defeat by Reed of London, I will now run him or any man in England 440 yards for £50 a side and give £10 for choice of ground if they will run me at Sheffield. As I came to all of Reed's terms in my last match, I hope he will accommodate me this time to run in four or six weeks from the first deposit. Your humble servant, G. Seward.

Reed, realizing Seward was eager for a rematch, was in no hurry to race him again unless it was on his own terms. He refused to run in Sheffield, insisting the race take place in London and for £100 to £500 a side. Seward wrote that his backer would not allow him to run in London, adding:

> As £50 is but a trifle for him [Reed] to train and run for, in four or five weeks, he can surely make it convenient to train one week for £50. If he consents to that I will run him any distance he pleases, from 50 yards to 500, and give him £10 to run at Sheffield. I never defeated a man yet but I would give him another chance if I went to the furthest part of England and hope Reed will give me the same chance if he is not afraid of Yours &c. Geo. Seward Sheffield, Dec 13.[17]

Reed continued to stall, and Seward finished out 1849 by winning a 500-yard handicap race for a patent lever watch at the Barrack Tavern Cricket Ground, Sheffield, on Christmas Eve. He beat Thomas Birkenhead, who had a 25-yard start, and two others.

Although Reed put off the 440-yard rematch with Seward, he continued to race at that distance. In late March 1850 at Harlington Corner near the Magpies Inn, he gave Edward Roberts a 5-yard start in 440 for £100 a side and defeated him easily, running 49½ seconds. After the race Reed said he was ready to race Seward. He added that "it was not, as Seward claimed, from fear of defeat that he had not accepted the American's challenge, but from the fact that he (Reed) does not like two matches on at once."[18] A confident Reed offered to give Seward a 5-yard start and run him for any amount more than £10 a side.

On March 4, Seward won a 440-yard hurdle race at the Huddersfield Cricket Ground for a watch valued at £5, and shortly afterward *Bell's Life* sent Seward's articles to Reed, who refused to sign them. Reed said his backer would not allow him to run at Sheffield, or in any enclosed ground. He claimed his long bounding stride and "slovenly" style of getting around corners put him at a disadvantage on anything but a straight course. Reed proposed either running on a turnpike road at Rugby, halfway between London and Sheffield, or offered the "Wonder" £10 and a 5-yard start to run near London.

Seward, disappointed in Reed's continued stalling, proposed running once around Hyde Park, 508 yards, for £25 a side and then racing wherever Reed pleased. He added if Reed did not accept this proposal he would dispute his claim to being the quarter-mile champion. He also declined the 5-yard start Reed offered.

Reed refused the offer to run at either Sheffield or London, repeating his proposal that they run halfway between the two cities. He also insisted on giving Seward a 5-yard start, which was unacceptable to Seward because it was not the custom to offer or accept starts in championship races. If Seward did not agree to this proposal, "he had better worry someone else," Reed added.[19]

While the negotiations with Reed dragged on, Seward won a 440-yard hurdle race on Trent Bridge Cricket Ground on May 6 for a £10 prize. He was still popular enough that about 1,000 fans wanting to see him run stormed the gate and entered without paying. Pleased with his improved fitness, after the race he challenged any man in England to run 100 yards for £50 a side and the championship of sprint running. After his defeat of Seward at 440 yards, Reed had claimed to be the champion at "short distance," yet he refused Seward's repeated 100-yard challenges. John Howard of Bradford, however, accepted, and the two men agreed to a match for June 10.

On June 3 Seward ran a ¾-mile race with Richard Conway of Preston at Hyde Park, Sheffield, for £25 a side. Seward looked well, yet because of the distance, Conway, who was in first-rate condition, was the favorite at 3 to 2. He took an early lead, but Seward did not let him get far ahead. At the end of the first lap (508 yards), Conway was 7 yards in the lead and increased the gap to 12 yards as they went up the backstretch onto the flat. Seward gradually gained on him, and on coming to another rise in the course, the American shot past into the lead. Conway was not through and caught Seward at the top of the hill, 100 yards from the finish. The two men became locked in a desperate struggle as the cheers of the 4,000 spectators became almost deafening. They were even with 30 yards to go, but Seward's superior speed gave him the victory by half a yard in 3 min. 22 sec.

Seward's next opponent was John Howard (figure 6.1). According to the *Illustrated Sporting News*, Howard, born in 1824, ran 100 yards in 9¾ seconds in a race with Robert Low in February 1850. For some reason the time was not widely accepted. Howard was better known as a long jumper and for ten years was the champion of England, having once jumped the astonishing distance of 29 feet 7 inches. He took off from a wedge-shaped board raised 7 inches from the ground at the end and threw two 4-pound dumbbells backward as he sprang from the board. These aids make his jump difficult to compare with present-day long jump marks although he was obviously well ahead of his time. He also cleared 27 feet across a stream in Denmark and could

Figure 6.1. John Howard, one of Seward's friends, was noted for his jumping. From the *Illustrated Sporting and Dramatic News*, May 10, 1862.

leap lengthwise over a billiard table. He once tried jumping in theaters, but his performances did not prove popular as the spectators could see nothing but a man flying across the stage and thought there must be some trick to it.

When they raced on June 10 at the Flora Grounds in Bayswater, Seward had regained much of his old form. The 100-yard course was roped and staked down the middle, and the sides were well barricaded to keep spectators from interfering with the runners. Seward was a heavy favorite with the odds being 2 to 1 in his favor, with few takers. Among the spectators were two famous boxers, Tom Paddock and William Perry, "the Tipton Slasher."

After nearly a dozen false starts, Howard got away with a lead of about 1½ yards, and kept it for more than half the distance. Seward drew even and at 80 yards sped by Howard in his "usual astounding manner." *Bell's Life* reported Seward's winning time as 10 seconds. *The Illustrated Sporting News* later reported it as 9½ seconds.[20]

Bell's Life, October 13, 1850, contained the exciting news that Reed had left articles for Seward to sign for their long-awaited rematch at 440 yards. Reed, knowing that Seward was eager to avenge his defeat, had stalled for nearly a year to get exactly the terms he wanted. Seward agreed to run on a turnpike road within 20 miles of London for £50 a side and did not insist that Reed also run him an additional shorter race. He was so annoyed at Reed's foot-dragging that he insisted on only one condition—that they start even so the winner could claim to be champion at 440 yards. After winning the toss for choice of ground, Seward chose to run at Boxmoor, about 24 miles from London down the Birmingham Railway. Boxmoor was 4 miles farther from London than the distance named in the articles, but Reed agreed to run there.

Heavy rains fell on the day of the race and never let up. Although the contest would normally have drawn a huge crowd, few people were willing to brave such bad weather. Both men appeared in good health, but it was obvious to keen observers that Reed was heavier than he had been when he defeated Seward in their previous 440-yard match. Still, the odds were 3 to 2 in his favor. His illness now one and a half years in the past, confidence shone on Seward's face and he looked to be in great condition although he had never regained his old physique. The *Era* wrote that before his illness Seward

> was, without all question, the fleetest man that had ever stood forth in a public match, to contend for pedestrian honors. But a protracted and severe illness caused this "clipper" to remain for a long period in a state of inactivity, and many of his friends, at the time, were extremely doubtful as to whether he

would ever be able to run again with anything like his former extraordinary speed. Time, however, works wonders, and certainly, in this instance it had the effect of putting Seward once more upon his pins, although leaving him anything but like his former self. Since then he has been taking all-possible care of himself, and was at last deemed by his backers sufficiently well up to the "mark" to struggle once more for superiority with his dashing competitor.[21]

At a quarter past 4 p.m. they came to the scratch. Seward made no effort to rile Reed as he had in their previous race, and after one or two false starts they sprinted away. Neither gained any important advantage at the start, and after 100 yards they were even. When they had gone 200 yards, the "Wonder" was leading by 4 yards, still keeping up his speed. Reed was beginning to struggle, and at 350 yards it was obvious he was beaten. Seward looked around and, seeing that his opponent could not keep up, slowed, allowing Reed to regain some of his lost ground. Seward won by 6 yards, and because it was getting dark, timing the race proved difficult, but *Bell's Life* gave him 51 seconds on a muddy, slow course.

The result shocked the crowd. Reed's backer, Mr. Parker, accused him of being unfit and overweight. He had him weighed soon after the race and found he was 10 pounds over his normal running weight. Reed, who had been overconfident and had not trained as hard as he should have for such a demanding race, not only lost the race but also his backer.

Seward had taken the race seriously indeed and afterward told *Bell's Life* he was in the best condition of his life. He said that in a trial before the race he had run 30 yards better than when he lost to Reed in their previous 440-yard race.[22] Since Reed had run 48½ seconds and won by 15 yards in that race, Seward had prepared himself to run 15 yards faster than 48½ seconds or just under 47 seconds for their rematch. It is unfortunate that the muddy course and out-of-shape Reed kept him from displaying this potential. Nevertheless, it was a most satisfying victory. He had come back from an almost career-ending illness and atoned for a crushing defeat at the hands of his greatest rival.

Seward made his familiar challenge that he was ready to run Reed, or any other man in the world, from 100 yards to a quarter mile for £100 a side. When no one answered, he rested for a few days, then left London for a week's visit with his old friend Mr. Briggs at Calais.

Exhausted by his intensive training, Seward ran only once more in 1850, a 120-yard handicap for £10 on November 25. The race was in two sections. In the first Seward was at scratch, George Cook had a 5-yard start, and Smith and Thompson 8 yards. Seward won easily by 3 yards. The second section had Westhall at scratch, Thomas Reed of Bedlington with a 2-yard start, J. Smith and Dehany at 5 yards. Westhall "cut down" all his opponents and won by 5 yards. Instead of having a third race to decide the overall winner, Seward and his friend Westhall agreed to divide the prize money.

Uncharacteristically, Seward started 1851 with two straight losses. On January 20, during a rainy afternoon at the Barrack Tavern Cricket Ground, Sheffield, he ran in an 880-yard handicap for a gold watch. Seward's handicap proved to be more than he could make up. Running from scratch, he finished second in his heat to Alfred Simpson of Sheffield, who had a 40-yard start. Two days later, Seward suffered a rare defeat in a sprint race. He raced Mark Parramore at Hyde Park for £5 a side. The race was only 50 yards, and Seward gave his opponent a 4½-yard start. They got off well, but Seward did not gain any in the first 20 yards. By 30 yards he had narrowed the gap to 3 yards. He then made a bound and got within a yard of Parramore, but could get no closer.

On January 27, he raced Joseph Pinder once around Hyde Park, Sheffield, for £10 in the presence of several hundred spectators. Seward gave Pinder 10 yards and the betting was in his favor at 5 and 6 to 4. Neither of the men had been in training, and Seward appeared too heavy for a fast race. Pinder got a good start and Seward barely gained on him in the first 300 yards, but the "Wonder" eventually caught up and won by 6 yards.

Seward then ran a series of races with horses that highlighted the dangers and uncertain nature of these races. At the Barrack Tavern Cricket Ground, Sheffield, on March 3, he ran a hurdle race against Mr. Williamson's black horse for £40, the best of three heats, to leap sixteen hurdles. About halfway through the first race, Seward stopped from fear of being trampled by the horse, giving the animal an easy victory. In the second heat, Seward led until he came to the last hurdle but caught the top of it with his foot and fell, leaving the horse to finish the race without him.

Three weeks later at the same location, Seward ran Mr. Broadbent's steeplechase horse, Jack. At the fourth hurdle the horse fell, injuring the rider. Mr. Broadbent found a fresh jockey for the next heat, which the horse won. During this heat Seward ran a spike into his foot going over a hurdle and declined running any more.

On March 10 Seward ran 350 yards for a purse given by Mr. Broadbent of the Barrack Tavern Cricket Ground, Sheffield. He beat John Howard, who also started from scratch, and four others. Seward and John Howard appeared at the Vauxhall Grounds, Boston, on March 31, where a man backed Seward to run a quarter mile and jump four hurdles in a minute. He performed the feat with 3 seconds to spare. Howard long jumped 24 feet on the second try without any takeoff aids or dumbbells. A day later at the Redford Cricket Ground Seward beat Howard in a 200-yard race over eight hurdles.

Seward, now thirty-three years old, ran what turned out to be his last major match race on June 25, 1851. Nearly 5,000 came to Hyde Park in Sheffield to watch him race William Matthews of Birmingham over a hilly course for £50 a side and the championship of England at 1,100 yards. Much betting had taken place at all the sporting houses in Sheffield, at 12 to 10 on Seward, and a special seventeen-car train brought spectators from Birmingham, arriving in Sheffield at 9:30 in the morning.

Seward had trained at Barnet near London and was in first-rate condition. Matthews, who was 5 feet 7½ inches tall and weighed 122 pounds, was famous for a mile he ran in 1849 against Charles Westhall on the turnpike road at Lansdown, Bath. He defeated Westhall by 30 yards, running 4 min. 28 sec., the fastest mile ever run up to that time.

Matthews won the toss and placed Seward on the left. They got away on the first try with Matthews leading by a yard, which he increased to 3 going down the first hill. On reaching the bottom, he sped up and was at least 6 yards ahead starting up the next hill. Seward stayed behind until they neared the last hill, where he sprinted by Matthews and in a few strides was a dozen yards ahead. He turned his head once to find Matthews before going on to win in 2 min. 45 sec. After the race Seward said that he would accept H. A. Reed's challenge to run another 440-yard match for £100 a side within 20 miles of London.

On July 29, Seward and George Grantham, "the Eton Pet," ran a mile race near Slough for £25 a side with Grantham receiving a 30-yard start. The race took place on the road known as "Maxfield's Mile" where in 1845 Thomas Maxfield, "the North Star," had become the first man to run 20 miles in less than 2 hours.

At a quarter past five the men appeared at the start, and both looked well. On the given signal they bounded off, and by the quarter mile Seward had made up about 10 yards of the 30-yard start. By the half mile he reduced it to 8 yards but had overextended himself in making up the handicap. He slowed and Grantham finished the race about 40 yards ahead. Because of the unruly crowd, the race could not be timed, but the first half mile was very fast.

The spectators had been even more rowdy than usual, and Seward was lucky not to have been trampled. *Bell's Life* wrote: "We regret to add that the conduct of most of the parties (not all) riding and driving was most censurable; it certainly was a wonder that both men were not knocked down by the wheels of the carts or by the horses, Seward in particular."[23]

On September 7, 1851, Seward offered to try high jumping off a board against any man in England. Frank Theobald, who could high jump 6 feet, answered his challenge. The match took place two weeks later at the Flora Grounds for £5 a side. The heights achieved by high jumpers in Seward's day were quite modest by today's standards. This was at least partly because the jumping style differed from the modern flop. The rules also varied from match to match. For this one, the athletes took a short run and jumped from a 1-foot-wide "dead" board, 6 inches from the ground. Seward and Theobald started jumping at 5 feet 4 inches and after two hours had reached only 5 feet 8 inches. It was a hot day and both were baked by the sun. They agreed to double the stakes and jump it off the next week. There was no reporting of the outcome.

One of the defining moments of the nineteenth century was the Great Exhibition held in London's Hyde Park in 1851. Prince Albert came up with the idea for this exhibition, which was designed to symbolize the industrial, military, and economic prowess of Great Britain. The organizers decided to make the exhibit international and sent invitations to most of the industrialized countries. It took place in the magnificent Crystal Palace, which covered 700,000 square feet (19 acres), not including the 217,100 square feet of galleries. The exhibit opened on May 1, 1851, with more than 13,000 displays and was attended by more than six million visitors. On display were the technological wonders of the time, including the Jacquard loom, an envelope machine, tools, kitchen appliances, steel-making displays, and a reaping machine from the United States.

Although Seward was past his prime, almost anyone in the world who followed running had heard of "the American Wonder." A group of Americans visiting the Great Exhibition decided that, despite the technological wonders they had just witnessed, their trip to England would not be complete without seeing their fellow American "Wonder" perform. They collected £10 for Mr. Cheese, owner of the Flora Grounds, Bayswater, who offered it to Seward if he could perform his "world famous" feat of beating six men separately at 100 yards in 30 minutes. For Seward's opponents, Mr. Cheese selected James Mayne, William Jones, Thomas Perch, George Langsdale, John Delaney, and William Richards. Seward easily defeated them all in 24 minutes.

Two weeks later Seward and H. A. Reed happened to meet at the Flora Grounds. The two men were friends, and Reed had gone out of his way to help Seward when he had been ill. They were also fierce rivals, and for years Reed had longed to dethrone Seward and become the new champion at short distance. Neither was scheduled to race that day, but after some discussion the two men decided they could not go home without a race. They agreed to run 120 yards for £5 a side, and Seward allowed Reed a 2-yard start. An *Era* reporter wrote that "both Reed and the mighty George Seward looked well, although the once Herculean American Wonder is now but a shadow of his former self, as regards muscular development."[24]

As they stood on the line, Seward smiled at his opponent, and at the word "off" Reed led the way for 70 yards, where Seward flew by him to win the race. *Bell's Life* reported no time for the race but described it as "one of the finest and quickest races ever witnessed. Reed had booked winning a certainty and after his defeat was so chagrined he shed tears of vexation."[25]

On October 8, Seward ran at the Copenhagen Grounds for the first time. This venue had opened as a cricket ground in 1835, but to take advantage of the 1850 ban on racing on the turnpike roads near London, Mr. Garratt, the owner, had a fine, level gravel track built around the grounds. The track was completed in early March 1851 and was originally a third of a mile around and almost square. Later, he improved the course by rounding off the sharp corners. It included a 200-yard straight section that was ideal for sprint races.

Seward's opponent was his old rival H. A. Reed in a 150-yard race for £25 a side. He gave Reed a 2-yard start and before they had gone 10 yards had made it up. They ran side by side for 120 yards when the American took a slight lead and turned and playfully smiled at Reed. They raced on to the finish, where the referee called the race a dead heat although many of the spectators thought Seward had won by half a yard.

The following week in *Bell's Life*, Reed challenged Seward to another 440-yard match for £25 a side. Again Reed insisted on running on a level turnpike road within 25 miles of London. This time Seward was in no hurry to comply with Reed's terms. Two weeks later he replied: "I beg leave to say that I will run him for £50 a side and give him his expenses if he will run in the north of England as I consider £25 not enough to train six weeks for."[26]

Further down in the same paper Seward and John Howard announced a novel challenge of their own. They would run any eight men in England 100 yards, each separately in 2 hours, and stake £50 between them against their opponents' £25 apiece. If any of the eight defeated either Seward or Howard, they would receive the £50. The eight men were to draw lots for their places, and each man had to start within 5 minutes after appearing at the scratch. There was no answer to this challenge, but on December 15 at the Sunderland Cricket Ground, Seward ran four men 100 yards separately, over four hurdles, for £10. He lost the match when he hit one of the hurdles, fell, and had to withdraw.

In April 1852 Reed agreed to run Seward 440 yards in the North but for only £25 a side. Seward answered saying he would not run a quarter of a mile for less than £50 a side, but he would run Reed 100 or 200 yards for £25. Seward was reluctant to run Reed 440 yards on a turnpike road because he knew the race would draw a huge crowd and wanted to run in an enclosed ground where they could share the gate receipts. In addition, 440 yards was beyond the distance he could run well without intensive preparation. He knew that to beat Reed in the quarter mile he needed to be at his best at that distance, which he believed would take six weeks of hard training. Reed wrote back that he was surprised Seward would not run him a quarter mile for £25 a side when he had run 1,100 yards and a mile for the same amount. He added that to run at Sheffield, he would have to travel 250 miles and raise his own stake because he no longer had a backer.

Although Seward had too much pride to take a start from Reed at any distance, one of his backers did not. In May there was a letter to *Bell's Life* from "J. E." saying Seward would take an 8-yard start from Reed and run him 440 yards for £25 a side on a turnpike road within 20 miles of London. J. E. believed that with an 8-yard start, Seward could defeat Reed even without extensive training. He added: "Giving Reed the merit of being of the first-class, Seward is content to hold that of second until better entitled to a more forward position; but he shall run any man in the world for from 50 to 300 yards for £100 a side."[27]

Reed replied that he thought Seward ought not, "for shame sake," ask for an 8-yard start because they had split their two previous races at 440 yards. He offered to give Seward 5 yards for £25 a side if Seward would give him choice of ground. Seward countered saying he would give "the great H. A." a 6-yard start in exchange for the choice of ground.

In the fall of 1851, while Seward and Reed were trying to agree on terms for their third 440-yard race, William Jackson, "the American Deer," returned from his second tour of America. After he fled with the forfeited stakes he received from his and Seward's November 1848 mile race, Jackson sailed for America. He turned up at the Union Course, Long Island, on June 29, 1849, where he failed in a bid to run 11 miles in an hour. After races at Saratoga and Buffalo, he settled in Brooklyn. In early 1850 he went south, racing in New Orleans and Mobile, Alabama, and returning via the Mississippi and Ohio rivers to Cincinnati, Ohio, where he ran a 5-mile race with Coffee, an Indian. It was another "fixed" race, and the "Deer" narrowly escaped a lynch mob when he lost after building a commanding lead.

He returned to New York and in June 1850 challenged "any man, white, red or black, from one mile to ten"[28] and offered to run against horses. Another long trip took him to Nashville and as far west as St. Louis, where he stayed six months. On this tour Jackson raced many Indians, offering starts of as much as a mile in twenty. The native Americans came to regard him with awe for his great distance-running ability. Although he tried several times, he was still unable to run 11 miles in an hour in America.

By October 1851, he was back in England, where he found that after his three-year absence, professional runners had largely switched from running on roads and horse-race tracks to fenced-in tracks. He had done well financially on this tour and arrived home in good health with much luggage and dressed in expensive clothes. How he avoided being arrested for fleeing with the stakes from his 1848 mile race with Seward is unknown.

On March 29, 1852, in a memorable 20-mile race at the Copenhagen grounds, Jackson set several records before having to stop at the end of the sixteenth mile because of the pain from his bad ankle. He covered 11 miles in less than an hour (59 min. 20 sec.) and 15 miles in 1 hour 22 min. His 13-, 14-, 15-, and 16-mile times were all records; the 15-mile time would not be beaten until 1892.

On May 31 at the "Cope," Jackson ran the race of his life to win the 10-mile championship belt. He defeated John Levett by more than 500 yards in a time of 51 min. 34 sec.—a new record. Jackson was on pace to run even faster. Levett, on being lapped, stepped off the track. When Jackson saw his opponent had quit, he also stopped running and walked the last 200 yards.

Seward wrote to *Bell's Life* challenging the British milers. He offered 10-yard starts to Grantham, Levett, Chadwick, Tetlow, Jesse Smith, and Jackson, and 20 yards to Richard Manks. In addition, he challenged the elite milers Sherdon, Siddall, and Pudney or any man in the world to run even for £25 to £50. He received no answers and two weeks later wrote again praising Jackson's success at 10 miles and chiding the English milers.

America v England.—Mr. Editor: The "little adopted Deer" having gained the proud title, and now holding the post of the 10 miles champion, I ask the peds of England of what metal they are made? Is there no mile runner left? Am I to claim the empty honors and hold them without dispute? Where are the Mathewses, Sherdons, Conways, Tetlows, Siddles, Pudneys, Byroms, Mankses, Granthams, Levetts, and Jacksons?—*Cum multis aliis* [with many others]—all of whom at the Cope and elsewhere treat distance as naught.

Well may an "Old Pedestrian" wish to back time. Mile runners there can be none, when I, old George Seward, one of the oldest school, offer a start a *small start*, at a distance far from my fork, and, to suit all, for a small sum. Small indeed must be the hearts of mile men, for I get no response. Am I the Mile Champion of the World? Has Yankee Land been cute enough to adopt the 10-mile champion, and to furnish the mile ditto?

For some seven long years have I been champion of sprint distances; who dare *even now* to dispute it? And it would seem that by a little "large talk" (for doing has been out of the question), I hold the glove for a mile. My next stride must certainly be 10 miles! Seward and 10 miles is rather rich.

Once more; I will run one mile against any man or against any number of men for £25 a side each race; the first to take place in four weeks from the first deposit and run a fresh man every fortnight, the more the merrier; and to suit all I am willing to give or take a reasonable sum to run *anywhere*, all being on the square.

I think your last week's correspondent "An Old Pedestrian" must be satirical. 30 under indeed! I should satisfy my backers to beat five by 20; who is there that can? Certainly not.—Yours George Seward.[29]

The "Old Pedestrian" Seward referred to had written to *Bell's Life* the previous week saying he had seen William Matthews set the record of 4 min. 28 sec. for the mile. However, he claimed the course was mostly down a steep hill. The writer offered to bet £50 that no one could be found who could run the distance in 4 min. 30 sec. on level ground.[30] Seward's remark that his backer would be satisfied if he could "beat five by 20" referred to running the mile in 4 min. 40 sec. He was being conservative, as he would later run the distance in slightly less than 4 min. 30 sec. on a muddy track.

On June 7, Seward ran James Patterson a hurdle race of 200 yards over ten hurdles for £25 a side at the "Cope." Patterson surprised Seward by giving him all he could handle. He took the lead at the sixth hurdle and by the seventh was a full yard in front. He tired, however, and Seward caught him in the last 50 yards. As Seward was leaping the ninth hurdle, he turned his head to one side to see where his opponent was. He had done this many times before and with the same result. He caught his spike on the top of the hurdle and knocked the plank partly off. Mr. Garratt, the referee, decided Seward won by a yard, but a dispute arose over whether it was necessary to clear all the hurdles to win. A meeting was held later that week at *Bell's Life*, and after much discussion, the stakeholder awarded the £50 to Seward. In addition, Seward finally got his wish to try himself in a mile race as both Westhall and Jackson accepted his 1-mile challenge. A three-man sweepstakes was set for July 26 at the "Cope."

On June 14, at the "Cope," Seward raced E. Barnsley, an amateur who had a 4-yard start in 100, for £4 a side. After they had gone 40 yards Seward slipped and despite his famous "rush" could not make up the lost ground, and Barnsley won by half a yard.

A month later at the "Cope," the main event was a race of once around the ground (a third of a mile) for £20. Seward, Reed, and Westhall entered, scaring away all the other runners except James Mayne and John Lovell. Seward was in top shape, and H. A. Reed, although a little overweight, was also confident of success. Westhall was ill. Finally the five men started, with Mayne leading for the first 150 yards. Westhall then took the lead but with 80 yards to go became exhausted and dropped out. Seward ran in an easy winner with Reed finishing second.

On July 26, 1852, the Copenhagen House ground was a scene of great bustle and excitement. Seward, Jackson and Westhall were there to run a mile for £75. Only H. A. Reed, who did not enter because the mile was beyond his distance, rivaled the fame of these men, and the crowd sensed it was in for a rare treat. But the weather did not cooperate. A thunderstorm had passed over London and its suburbs on the preceding day and turned the normally firm, well-maintained track into a sea of mud that was in some places ankle deep. Although there was a good crowd, it would have been huge if not for the weather. At 5 p.m., the time announced for the race, the rains came again in torrents and delayed the start for an hour.

All three runners were in fine condition. Westhall had trained at Harebore's, the Hare and Hounds, at Northolt, under the care of James Newman. Seward had trained himself at Barnet with his headquarters at the Albion, Union Street. The "Deer" had stayed at his old quarters at Sutton and had gotten himself in top condition. Before the race a reporter heard him remark quietly, almost to himself, "They would have to run and run fast to beat me."[31]

The trio appeared at the scratch on the muddy track amid the loud cheering of the crowd. Seward was the favorite as Westhall had been ill and the distance was thought too short for Jackson despite his 10-yard start. As they warmed up, Seward offered to bet £10 on himself, but neither of his opponents accepted.

They started by pistol, with the "Deer" getting away slowly and losing two yards. Jackson then sped up and Seward went after him while Westhall tried to stay in contact. On turning the first corner Seward caught Jackson, but the "Deer" fought him off. At the end of the first ⅓-mile lap Jackson still led with Seward on his shoulder. Westhall had fallen back and appeared not to have a chance. On the second lap Jackson extended his lead to a full 10 yards, but Seward soon caught up and the two men ran even faster.

By the end of the second ⅓-mile lap Jackson had taken a small lead, but on the last lap Seward passed him. Westhall lagged at least 30 yards behind, seemingly out of the race. Just before the final turn Seward made his move and sprinted by Jackson. Most of those present thought Seward had the race won. Westhall, who had been conserving his energy, had other ideas. He first shot by Jackson and then drew even with Seward, who strained every muscle to fight him off. About 100 yards from the finish Westhall made another surge and Seward, who had exhausted himself dueling with Jackson, could not respond, and Westhall won by 10 yards.

After the race Westhall was exhausted, as was Seward, but Jackson was still fresh and said he "only wished the race had been a little longer." *Bell's Life* in its odd way of reporting times gave Westhall *"four minutes and a half* and *something under,* over heavy ground."[32] Other timers gave him 4 min. 28 sec., the first time anyone had run a sub-4:30 mile on a track. Seward, realizing that if he had not been so absorbed with beating Jackson he would have won, challenged his two opponents to another race. Westhall declined but Jackson accepted, and the race was set for September 20 with Jackson to again have a 10-yard start.

On the day of the race, rainy weather again kept the attendance down at the "Cope." In their previous race both Seward and Jackson had tried to "cut each other down" and were defeated by Westhall running a more even pace. The pouring rain delayed the race for some time, but when it became obvious it was not going to let up, the two men agreed to go ahead and run. Both were fit although Seward looked a little heavy and the "Deer" looked thin owing to his hard training for his match with Levett for the 10-mile Champion's Belt. Jackson was also suffering from "shin-ache" (shin splints). With the mud ankle deep and amid a "perfect hurricane," they started at the first try. Jackson again got a bad start, losing 3 yards of his 10-yard start. The "Deer" tried to push the pace and draw Seward out as he had done before, but Seward would have none of it and waited 10 yards back.

On starting the second lap Jackson made a spurt, but Seward kept him within reach and going past the post the second time was only 2 yards in the rear. The "Deer" again tried hard to pull away, but on the backstretch of the last lap they were shoulder to shoulder. With 200 yards to go, Seward left Jackson and won by 5 yards. His time in the pelting rain and deep mud was 4 min. 53 sec.

The two men had signed articles to run a third race at 2 miles with Jackson agreeing to give Seward a 10-yard start. It would have been the longest public race of Seward's career, but again the weather refused to cooperate. On race day it rained for fourteen straight hours. Jackson, scheduled to race Levett for the 10-mile championship, did not want to chance catching cold and paid Seward £5 to postpone the race for two weeks. Before the race could take place, Seward was seized with another severe attack of rheumatism and had to forfeit to Jackson. This bout with the crippling disease would mark the end of his career as a champion runner.

Notes

1. "Reed and Seward," *Bell's Life*, March 4, 1849.
2. "Reed and Seward," *Era*, June 24, 1849.
3. *Era*, June 24, 1849.
4. Lee Jackson, *Victorian Dictionary*, at www.victorianlondon.org (accessed September 22, 2007). The Newgate Market, located between Newgate Street and Paternoster Row, was a popular meat market in the Victorian era.
5. "Reed and Seward Race for 200 Pounds," *Bell's Life*, July 1, 1849 (reprinted in *Spirit of the Times*, vol. 19, July 28, 1849, 269).
6. "Important Match between G. Seward and H. Reed, for 200 Sovs," *Era*, July 1, 1849.
7. "Important Match between G. Seward and H. Reed, for 200 Sovs," *Era*, July 1, 1849.
8. *Bell's Life*, July 1, 1849.
9. *Bell's Life*, July 1, 1849.
10. *Bell's Life*, July 1, 1849.
11. *Era*, July 1, 1849.
12. *Bell's Life*, January 2, 1875, stated that Reed had twice been timed inside 47 seconds for 440-yard trials, and in *Bell's Life*, October 28, 1849, William Matthews, one of Reed's opponents, said Reed was capable of running ½ mile in 8 seconds less than 2 minutes.
13. "Reed and Seward," *Bell's Life*, July 8, 1849.
14. "Seward's Benefit," *Bell's Life*, July 15, 1849.
15. Seward listed his occupation on the birth certificate as silver plater rather than pedestrian. One wonders how much time he devoted to silver plating instead of running.
16. "Doings at Bellevue, Manchester, Monday, Sept 3, Man v Horse," *Bell's Life*, September 9, 1849.
17. *Bell's Life*, December 16, 1849.
18. *Bell's Life*, March 3, 1850.
19. "Seward and Reed," *Bell's Life*, March 17, 1850.
20. *Illustrated Sporting News*, May 17, 1862, 76.
21. "Seward and Reed," *Era*, November 24, 1850.
22. "Seward and Reed's Race," *Bell's Life*, November 24, 1850 (reprinted in *Spirit of the Times*, vol. 20, December 21, 1850, 524).
23. *Bell's Life*, August 3, 1851.
24. "Seward and Reed," *Era*, October 12, 1851.
25. "Doings at the Flora Grounds, Bayswater," *Bell's Life*, October 5, 1851.
26. "Reed and Seward," *Bell's Life*, November 30, 1851.
27. *Bell's Life*, May 23, 1852.
28. "Pedestrian Challenge," *Spirit of the Times*, June 15, 1850.
29. "America v England," *Bell's Life*, June 13, 1852.

30. *Bell's Life*, June 6, 1852.

31. "Great Match Between Westhall, Seward, and Jackson, for the Championship," *Bell's Life*, August 1, 1852.

32. "The Mile Sweepstakes Race Between Westhall, Seward and Jackson," *Bell's Life*, August 1, 1852.

CHAPTER SEVEN

~

Sinking into Oblivion (1852–1883)

The supremacy of a sprinter is sometimes short-lived, as a man's best pace often leaves him when he is still young and perhaps only a year or two over his majority.

—Montague Shearman, 1888

In November 1852 William Beswick, owner of the Royal Oak Gardens near London, announced a benefit for Seward, who was confined to bed by his second major attack of rheumatism. The sporting newspapers did their best to promote the event. The *Era* wrote: "Seward, as a fine, honest, manly pedestrian, has always stood high among the patrons of pedestrianism, therefore it is hoped that he may be well supported."[1]

The benefit took place on November 22 and was supervised by Seward's old friend William Jackson, who managed to get all the best-known pedestrians including Charles Westhall, Jem Pudney, H. A. Reed, George Frost, and many others to perform. It was not a success because the handbills advertising the event omitted the date and few spectators showed up. Jackson, Westhall, Reed, Lovell, and Pudney went ahead and ran a mile handicap race that Jackson won. Seward, although too ill to attend, wrote to *Bell's Life* thanking all those who had given a helping hand.

Beswick, disappointed at the turnout, agreed to allow Seward the use of his grounds again on December 6 and donated two watches and a silver snuff-box for prizes. Most of the pedestrians from the previous benefit promised to return. Both *Bell's Life* and the *Era* again promoted the event, with the latter writing: "It is hoped that on this occasion the ground may be well attended for the purpose of rendering poor George that assistance he stands at present so much in need of."[2]

The promoters had no better luck the second time. The weather was so bad no races could be run. In an unprecedented effort to help the ailing American, Mr. Wilson, John Garratt, John Thomas ("the Salopian"), and William Sheppard each contributed £5 to Seward, and the former 10-mile champion George Frost added £2.

From 1844 when he defeated William Robinson at 100 yards until his defeat by Reed in their 440-yard race in 1849, Seward had been the consensus champion of short-distance running in England. After Reed's victory at 440 yards, the picture was not as clear. Reed had taken the championship at that distance, but 440 yards is a bit longer than a sprint. In addition, Seward had evened the score in their second 440-yard match in 1850. During the twelve years from 1840 until his second illness in 1852, Seward had not been seriously challenged by anyone in the world at distances shorter than 440 yards. Now he was so crippled by rheumatism that he was unable to run even his favorite distance of 100 yards. His reign as champion was over, and other, younger men were ready to take his place. One of them, H. A. Reed, wrote to *Bell's Life*:

> There having been within the last two or three years several candidates for the title of Champion of Sprint Running, and as there seems to be some doubt on the mind of the public (*though not on mine*) as to who is fairly entitled to that distinction. I beg to state, in order to set the matter at rest, and prove who it belongs to, that I will run any man breathing from 120 yards to a quarter mile, for from £25 to £100 a side.
>
> H. A. Reed, Champion of England[3]

Reed was still unwilling to offer a direct challenge to Seward at 100 yards and did not say at what distance he claimed to be champion. Seward was too ill to respond, but John Howard answered Reed's challenge. Howard agreed to race Reed for the sprint championship of England but said he could not make the match until the leg he had broken leaping over horses healed.

Although Seward had been able to regain most of his old form after his first bout with rheumatism, this time there would be no such recovery. He began to feel better in March 1853 and all the rest of the year struggled to regain his fitness. In his heart, he must have known his days as champion of sprinting were over, but he was unable to give up the sport that had been such a big part of his life. Seward believed that when healthy he was still the fastest sprinter in England. He wrote a long letter to *Bell's Life* saying he considered himself the champion of sprint running until Reed or someone else beat him. Hoping that he would soon recover, he challenged Reed or John Lovell to a match at 100 yards for the sprint championship and £25 or £50 a side. Thinking Seward might be recovering, neither responded.

Unable to get up a race through the sporting journals, on May 16 Seward went to the Flora Grounds, Bayswater, to seek out Reed and try to make a match to run 100 yards for the championship. He was unable to get Reed to agree to a race, but the crowd of 3,000 wanted to see the "Wonder" perform. In his first race since his illness, the fans applauded his style of taking the hurdles as he won a minor hurdle race of once round the ground for £5.

A week later he returned to the Flora Grounds to again try to make a match with Reed. The main attraction that day was a 2-mile race for a £5 prize. Two miles was longer than Seward had ever run in public, and on this occasion he used the race as a training session. His opponents were John Howard, who was also subpar as he was recovering from a broken leg, Edward Pocock, and William Newman. After the start, Seward and Howard ran at the rear taking it easy, now and then putting on some surges. When Pocock dropped out at the mile and Howard at 1½ miles, Seward realized he might have a chance to win and felt his old competitive fires stir. He did his best to overtake the remaining runner, Newman, but could not, and Newman won by 100 yards.

H. A. Reed was there, and after the race Seward approached him about making a 100-yard match for the sprint championship. Reed refused. He wanted no part in a race with even an ailing Seward at 100 yards but instead challenged him to run for the 440-yard championship for £50 a side. Seward was far from being recovered from his illness but again let his pride get the best of him and agreed to run a third 440-yard race with Reed. The match was set for August 8, 1853, at the New Surrey Pedestrian Ground, Wandsworth.

Although he had not been able to schedule the 100-yard race he wanted, Seward was happy to be back in his familiar routine of preparing for races. He went into training and, as a tuneup, ran John Howard a quarter mile for £15 on June 6, at Hove near Brighton. The results were not encouraging. After giving Howard a 10-yard start, Seward lost the race when he slipped about 7 yards from the start and was unable to make up the lost ground.

As his running fortunes continued to decline in the summer of 1853, he was saddened to read in *Bell's Life* of the death of his old foe William Robinson. Victories over him in 1844 had catapulted Seward to worldwide fame and started Robinson on a downward spiral from which he never recovered. He had died of consumption in early July at Newcastle.

The third Seward-Reed 440-yard race paled in comparison with the previous two. Seward had been unable to regain even a semblance of his old form and must have known he had no chance against Reed. On August 8, 1853, a large crowd came to the New Surrey Ground to watch the two famous runners race to break the tie in their 440-yard series. The odds were in favor of the confident and buoyant Reed, who admitted to not being in top form but was well aware of how devastating Seward's illness had been. Seward had tried hard to get in shape, but his second bout of rheumatism had left him with a handicap he could not overcome. To make matters worse, he injured his leg training for the match and had been unable to run for several days.

After two false starts they got away and Reed took a slight lead. At 300 yards the pace began to tell on Seward. He fell back, and it was soon obvious to all he would lose. Reed won by 5 yards in a mediocre 54 seconds.

Still unwilling to hang up his spikes, Seward tried to get up another mile sweepstakes with Westhall and Jackson, but nothing came of his challenges. Although he did his best to regain even part of his old fitness, it was not to be, and it was becoming increasingly obvious that his reign as champion, even at 100 yards, was over. On August 21, 1853, he made what proved to be his last challenge to the world, writing in *Bell's Life*: "G. Seward will run any man in the world 100 yards for £25 a side in four weeks, Articles and a deposit sent to *Bell's Life* will be attended to. As Howard has challenged so often Seward will run him any distance from 100 yards to 10 miles."

As it turned out, he was unable to respond to his own challenge. Reed agreed to race him and proposed they run the match in two weeks. Before the race could take place, Seward had a relapse of rheumatics and was again confined to bed. He wrote to *Bell's Life* saying he would give Reed a chance when he recovered and continued to insist that if anyone wanted to claim his championship of sprint running, they must beat him at 100 yards. He added that just because Reed had defeated him at 440 yards he could not claim to be the champion of sprinting.[4]

Seward never recovered enough to defend his sprint title. His only other race in 1853 was at the Flora Grounds on September 5, when he took part in a benefit for George Frost ("the Suffolk Stag"), who had himself been laid up for several months with rheumatism. Seward won a 500-yard race beating George Martin, William Newman, and Benjamin Badger.

Unable to regain his fitness, Seward knew he must look for other means to earn a living. In December 1853 he decided to try his hand at training other runners. He helped Lieutenant Fred Sayers of the 23 Royal Welsh Fusiliers prepare for his two races with Captain John Astley of the Scots Fusilier Guards. Even though £50 a side was riding on each race, the men were considered amateurs because of their high social standings. Astley later became a Member of Parliament and was one of the few men of the British upper classes who publicly supported professional running. Sayers won the 150-yard flat race, but in the second race, which was the same distance but over seven hurdles, he slipped at the fourth hurdle and Astley won easily. Seward decided not to make a career of training other runners, and there is no record of him training anyone else.

In January 1854 Seward was staying in Birmingham and appearing at the Aston Cross Grounds. Even if he could not compete with the best runners, he was, after all, a legend and could still draw fans. On January 23, he performed his old feat of racing several men 100 yards in quick succession. This time the men were the best runners in Birmingham, not in England. Seward beat four in 20 minutes and on February 6 at the same grounds defeated a horse at 160 yards over eight hurdles. The crowd for the latter race numbered about 1,000 and Tom Barry, a well-known clown, rode the horse.

Although he was no longer at the top of his profession, when his rheumatism allowed, Seward still showed flashes of his old brilliance. On February 27 at Pitt's Ground, Lee Brook, Wednesbury, he ran from scratch in a 200-yard handicap race over four hurdles and won easily. He then performed some jumping feats, including jumping 6 feet high from a 4-inch block of wood. Next he long jumped over two 4-foot hurdles, 6 feet apart, then repeated the feat for two 3-foot hurdles 12 feet apart and 21 feet from the take-off. He finished with a standing long jump of 12 feet over a 2-foot hurdle.[5]

At Acton Cross on April 1, Seward and his old friend John Howard teamed up and ran eight Lancashire men 100 yards in an hour. They each ran four men separately. Howard had never fully recovered from breaking his leg jumping over horses and like Seward was on the decline as a pedestrian. The two veteran runners were still able to muster enough speed and endurance to defeat all eight men. A *Bell's Life* reporter doubted some of their opponents were giving their best efforts as they were being paid to take part rather than competing for a stake. After this match Seward had another bout with rheumatism, and there is no mention of him in the sporting journals for more than a year.

Several of Seward's rivals were also approaching the ends of their careers. After his running and jumping days, John Howard lived near Bradford, managed the High Sheriff Inn in Rochdale, and later became a billiard marker. He died on October 14, 1875, at age fifty-one.

H. A. Reed, who was a few years younger than Seward, continued to race and was most successful running middle-distance races. On February 28, 1854, he won the 880-yard championship belt from Joseph Horrocks, then successfully defended it against Thomas Horspool on April 11, running a record 1 min. 58 sec. on the track at Westhill Park, Halifax.

With Seward no longer able to challenge him at short distances, Reed raced James Hancock of Salford for the sprint championship of England. The 130-yard race for £50 a side took place on November 26, 1854, on the turnpike road near the Ship Inn, at Rempstone in Nottinghamshire. Hancock, born near Manchester, was twenty-one years old, 5 feet 7 inches tall, and weighed 132 pounds. He had been running for about two years and had been impressive from 100 to 200 yards. *Bell's Life* wrote: "With regard to Reed and Hancock, as pedestrians, it is the general opinion with the public that they are the two fastest runners upon record, and in this we agree, always excepting George Seward (the American) who, we regret to say, is now used up."[6] Hancock ran an excellent race and won by 3 to 4 yards in 13 seconds flat.

Reed defeated Hancock on February 13, 1855, in a 300-yard race at Bellevue, winning by 25 yards in 32 seconds, the fastest 300-yard time recorded for eight years. Thirteen days later he gained permanent possession of the half-mile belt with a victory over Joe Horrocks. In 1858, however, Reed told *Bell's Life* he had broken down during an 880-yard race against Horspool and had decided to retire from running. After a few handicaps and minor matches, he ended his career with a veteran's race at Hackney Wick in London in 1863. He then managed the Red Cross Tavern in London's Barbican and later became well known as a reporter for *Bell's Life* and the *Sporting Life*, attending shooting grounds and sports arenas across England. He died at age forty-nine on December 6, 1874, in Hanwell Asylum.

Seward's old friend William Jackson was at the top of his form in 1853 when he won the "Champion of the World" silver cup given by William Beswick, owner of the Royal Oak Grounds. The cup went to the runner who won the most of three races at 1, 5, and 10 miles. James Pudney[7] won the mile race, but Jackson claimed the belt by winning at 5 and 10 miles. On July 4 he regained the 10-mile belt by beating Frost at the Royal Oak. On October 5 at the Portsmouth Cricket Ground, he tried the 11-miles-within-the-hour feat that had given him so much difficulty in America. This time he covered the distance with ease in 58 min. 40 sec. despite having to run on heavy, damp grass.

The following year he retired from running and invested all his winnings in building cucumber houses and nursery grounds at Norbiton Common in Surrey. He neglected to insure his business, and on the morning of December 7, 1854, a fire destroyed it, causing him to lose everything. His friends and fellow pedestrians raised a subscription for him, but it was not enough to ease his poverty, and he had no choice but to return to running. By now he was, like Seward, "used up" and unable to regain the form necessary to contend with England's top young distance runners. Despite being too old to beat the best runners and having a history of fixed races, he was still a fan favorite. Wherever he went, the name "American Deer" on the race program was always enough to draw a good crowd.

In 1861, he raced Deerfoot, the American Indian, who was making a successful tour of England. Deerfoot soundly defeated him in a 4-mile race at Brompton, but Jackson was still so popular that in 1862 George Martin hired him to take part in his "Deerfoot Traveling Circus." Although Jackson usually finished dead last in the daily exhibition races, Martin still considered him a valuable addition to the tour. His association with Martin ended badly when Jackson took Martin to court for nonpayment of his £4-a-week wages. The trial created a sensation when one of Martin's other runners, John Brighton, revealed that the traveling circus races were rigged for Deerfoot to win. With his running days finally over, Jackson (figure 7.1) returned to his old calling of raising vegetables and flowers commercially.

Thirty years later, in 1892, he was so "short of coin" that John Astley, sporting baron and patron of pedestrians, held a benefit for him at Stamford Bridge. Astley put on a 10-mile veteran's handicap race for men more than fifty years old. The most famous of the thirty-three starters were Jackson and Bill Lang, the famed "Crowcatcher," the 2-mile record holder. In Astley's handicap race each runner received a 50-yard start for every year he was more than fifty years old. At age seventy-one Jackson had a start of 1,050 yards, but it was not enough; he had to drop out at 1½ miles because of his bad ankle. William Howitt, alias Jackson, "the American Deer," is believed to have lived into the twentieth century, dying in 1902 at age eighty.[8]

Charles Westhall's career was also winding down. After his mile victory over Seward and Jackson on July 26, 1852, he continued to specialize at that distance. On August 23 he won the 1-mile belt at Hyde Park in a leisurely 4 min. 53¾ sec., becoming the mile champion of England. In his first defense of the title on January 31, 1853, at the Hyde Park Cricket Ground, he lost by 35 yards to Robert Chadwick, whose time was 4 min. 38¼ sec. The loss so disappointed the betting public that after the race an angry mob went to Westhall's quarters and accused him of selling the race. He denied their accusations, and when they threatened to cripple him, he lashed out at the ringleaders. He was no match for the thirty roughs who beat him senseless.

Figure 7.1.   William Jackson was still racing in 1864 when he was forty-two years old. The artist has copied Jackson's body from the 1850s portrait (chapter 3). From the *Illustrated Sporting News*, July 2, 1864.

Although he recovered from the beating, the incident caused him to lose his zest for running, and at age thirty he was no longer a force as a runner although he still performed well at walking. He retired in 1859 and reported on pedestrianism and the ring for *Bell's Life* and wrote four books including *Hints Upon Training* (1860), *The Modern Method of Training for Running, Walking, Rowing & Boxing* (1863), and *Training for Pedestrianism, etc.* (1868). Like Reed and Howard, Westhall (figure 7.2) did not live into old age, dying on October 12, 1868, at age forty-five, leaving a widow and a large family.

Seward did not retire, but continued to race and perform jumping feats when his rheumatism allowed. Although illness and advancing age prevented him from challenging the fastest runners, when healthy he could still give a good account of himself. Occasionally he issued the same bold challenges as in his youth. In June 1855, while staying at Mr. Clark's Runmer Hotel in Cardiff, he wrote to *Bell's Life* saying he had "been on the shelf for some time but was anxious for another shy." He challenged the six best men in Wales to run 100 yards and to run each man separately every 10 minutes for £25, or he would run any man in Wales a mile for the same sum.[9]

Nothing came of these challenges, but on October 29, 1855, he ran the most bizarre race of his entire career. It was with William Thomas, a tailor from Newbridge, a small town in South Wales. The 200-yard race came off near the "Rock of the Common" in Newbridge for £10 a side. The weather was good although the ground was slippery from the heavy rains that had fallen earlier. Some of Seward's friends from Merthyr Tydfil, a hamlet about ten miles away, backed him, and the people of Newbridge supported Thomas, the local runner.[10]

The attendance was large, and the Newbridge gentry were confident Thomas would win. In fact, they were dead sure of it because of a little "business transaction" they had made earlier. Some of the residents of Newbridge had approached Seward and offered him £20 to lose the race. Seward, who had always disdained fixed races, thought their offer over and decided to teach them a lesson. The once-champion runner pretended to agree to their proposition. He took their money, refusing the notes they offered and insisting they pay him in gold—£10 before the start and the remaining £10 afterward.

At 4 p.m. the runners came to the scratch, and after a fair start, they went away at a good pace. Thomas's Newbridge backers smiled knowingly as he forged a 15-yard lead and seemed on his way to an easy victory. At 150 yards, to everyone's surprise, Seward ducked his head slightly and sped by Thomas like the "Wonder" of old. He crossed the finish line with such speed that the men holding the handkerchiefs were astounded. Not stopping to take the stakes or even to put on his coat, Seward kept right on running.

Figure 7.2. Charles Westhall was one of England's greatest pedestrians. From the *New York Clipper,* 1856.

As soon as the would-be bribers realized what was happening, they gave chase, trying to trip him or stop him any way they could. Their leader yelled at the top of his voice, "Stop, if you are a man!" Seward paid no attention and was soon out of town and on his way to Merthyr Tydfil. *Bell's Life* reported that he "reached High street, Merthyr in safety, where his friends congratulated him on his extraordinary adventure."[11]

In the winter of 1855 Seward suffered yet another severe attack of rheumatism, ending his running for many months. George Cook, the owner of the New Copenhagen Grounds at Shepherd's Bush who had once acted as Seward's attendant, agreed to give the ailing American a benefit on his racecourse. The event took place on June 3, 1856, with an attendance of 700 to 800. Unlike many of Seward's previous benefits, this one was a modest success. Champion walker William Spooner was backed to walk 7¼ miles in an hour, a feat he performed with 8 seconds to spare. D. Kennedy, the champion weight thrower of Scotland, threw the hammer against all comers.

During the latter part of 1856 Seward lived near Bellevue, Manchester. He ran no races but had recovered enough from his illness that *Bell's Life* printed a notice that he would, "on the first occasion of the ice being sufficient strength, go through his wonderful feats in skates on the large lake, including hurdle jumping, jumping for distance, backward jumping, etc."[12]

In the spring and summer months of 1857, Seward, now almost forty years old, occasionally ran in handicap races in Manchester. He seldom won anything but continued to race anyway, unable to give up the sport that meant so much to him.

On July 11, Thomas Hayes granted him the use of his grounds near Manchester for another benefit. The weather was good, but as was often the case for the many benefits held for the American, the attendance was sparse. The first event was a hop-skip-jump contest with the winner clearing 30 feet 9 inches and receiving as a prize a portrait of Seward in his earlier days. During the afternoon, Seward performed some of the jumping feats that a few years earlier had helped make him so famous. The spectators watched in amazement as he jumped over three horses standing side by side, sailing over them with the greatest ease. He went on to acquit himself well in his other efforts and proved that at age forty he could still lay claim to much of his previous fame as a jumper. The crowd went home pleased at having seen the great athlete perform his old feats.

Seward, although well past his prime, knew how to please crowds and was still a superior athlete when his illness did not confine him to bed. He tried another business venture, becoming partners with William Gale, a famous long-distance walker. Gale was adept at performing variations of the Captain

Barclay feat of walking 1,000 miles in 1,000 hours. In 1854 he duplicated Barclay's feat and surpassed it in 1856 by walking 1,500 miles in 1,000 hours. His crowning achievement came several years later in 1879 when he covered 2,500 miles in 1,000 hours. Gale had what it took to excel at these feats—an almost superhuman capacity to endure fatigue and go without sleep.

Seward and Gale bought a circus tent that was a scaled-down version of Seward's "Great American Arena" and traveled throughout Wales giving pedestrian exhibitions. The two men experienced mixed results with their venture. Seward performed jumping feats and raced horses while Gale displayed his ultra-distance skills. They did well in some locations and made a good amount of money. At other towns the public had little interest in pedestrian exhibitions, and the performances were poorly attended. Eventually, the two men disagreed over their business arrangements and had a falling-out. They abandoned the venture and separated with Gale going to Cardiff and Seward to Stalybridge.

Besides his many illnesses, Seward suffered misfortunes in his life off the track. His wife Mary died in December 1857 in Liverpool at age thirty from unknown causes. The couple's only child, Clara, had already died in childhood.

On July 6, 1859, Seward remarried, wedding twenty-four-year-old Jane Evans of Cheetham, the daughter of John Evans, a farmer. That same month he took over the Hare and Hounds pub at Ridge Hill on the highway to Hyde near Stalybridge and announced he "intended giving several money prizes to be contended for in old English sports." Seward's pub had a large building attached known as "Seward's Gym." He converted it for wrestling, ratting, and various other sports and games. The pub and gymnasium proved popular, and sports enthusiasts came from miles around to take part in or watch the sports.

George and Jane had their first child in 1859 and named her Caroline after his mother. On June 18, 1860, their first son, Edward, was born. A short time later Seward expanded his business by opening an amphitheater near his Hare and Hounds pub on a seven-acre site surrounded by a high wall. His sports complex now boasted a dancing salon, a bowling green, a fishpond, a gymnasium, a straight 250-yard course for sprinting, and a 440-yard track for longer races. The latter was one of the fewer than half a dozen quarter-mile tracks in England at the time. This distance set the standard for tracks now represented by the metric equivalent, 400 meters. The venture was initially successful as Seward was well known and respected by sports fans.

In June 1863 Seward, forty-five years old and unable to run for several years, wrote to *Bell's Life* saying he wanted to return to racing. He agreed to accept E. Lowe's challenge to run 100 yards for £25 a side in not less than eight weeks at the Copenhagen Grounds, Manchester. Seward became ill with rheumatics, however, and was unable to run the race.

Mr. Cheese, owner of the White Horse public house, heard of Seward's effort to return to running and his subsequent illness and scheduled a benefit for him at Hackney Wick for September 28. This pear-shaped, 260-yard track attached to the White Lion Inn had opened in late 1857 and, despite its sharp turns and one end being higher than the other, had become one of England's most popular running grounds.

The main attraction at Seward's benefit was a veteran's race featuring "the most renowned and fastest men ever known."[13] They included Seward, Charles Westhall, H. A. Reed, William Jackson, Jem Pudney, "the Epsom Stag," "the Regent-street Pet," and many others. In addition, there was to be a quarter-mile handicap race with a large field, and a canine match between Jemmy Shaw's dog Jacko and Seward's Venture, a renowned rat catcher. The big program also included sparring and other sports.

Seward had been so popular and well respected that almost every outstanding pedestrian of his time agreed to appear at his benefit. He stayed with his friend Jemmy Shaw while he was in London and visited with many of his old friends and former rivals. The benefit itself was not so successful as heavy rains caused the attendance to be sparse.

On October 12, Seward and his dog Venture appeared at Mr. Cheese's White Horse public house in Shepherd's Bush, where Venture displayed his skill by killing 100 rats in 7 minutes. William Lang, "the Crowcatcher," who had earlier that year created a sensation by running 2 miles in 9 min. 11½ sec., was also there and showed his trophies and championship belt. The Illustrated Sporting News for October 17 published a portrait of Seward and Venture on the front cover (figure 7.3).

Although he lived 3,000 miles from America, Seward could not escape the effects of the American Civil War. By 1862 the war had disrupted British imports of cotton from the United States. The cotton mills in the Stalybridge area were idled by a severe depression known as the Cotton Famine. Many of the mills closed, and the government set up soup kitchens to feed the large numbers who were out of work and faced with starvation. The few mills that were able to stay open paid their workers in scrip, which could not be used to buy beer at Seward's pub or pay admission to his sports complex.[14] In 1864, he reluctantly closed both the Hare and Hounds pub and the sports complex.

On February 24, 1866, Seward made his last public appearance as a runner. He had been unable to do much running since 1858 but was still eager to race his opponent, Joe Horrocks, the former half-mile champion. Their 100-yard race took place at the Stalybridge Recreation Grounds. Seward

SEWARD AND HIS FAMOUS DOG "VENTURE."—*(From a Photograph.)*

Figure 7.3. Seward, age forty-six. His dog Venture performed at his sports complex in Stalybridge. From the *Illustrated Sporting and Dramatic News*, October 17, 1863.

started well and after a fierce struggle managed to defeat Horrocks by 12 inches.

Having finally given up running and unable to find work in Stalybridge, Seward moved his family to the Liverpool area and took up his old trade of silver plating. The next ten years proved to be the lowest part of his life. His second wife, Jane, died on October 5, 1867, at Malo, about thirty miles from Liverpool, leaving him a widower with three small children—eight-year-old Caroline, seven-year-old Edward, and two-year-old Ann. Another child, Mary Elizabeth, born in 1863, had died in 1865.

Seward had written countless letters to *Bell's Life* and other sporting journals during his running career trying to get runners to race him. After he had to give up his running grounds in 1864, he tried to support himself and his family by working as a silver plater in Liverpool. He was unable to earn a respectable income at this trade. His frequent illnesses may have been the primary reason. Being a proud man, he went into a self-imposed seclusion and disappeared from public view for the next ten years.

During these years, he did not respond to letters from fans or the sporting press. He had too much pride to let them know that he and his family were living in a slum in Liverpool. There is no evidence that he asked for or received any financial support from his well-to-do relatives in America. Whether he was too proud to ask them for help is unknown. Few who met him knew that the polite but impoverished silver plater had once been the fastest sprinter the world had yet seen.

He lived on Torbock Street, a run-down section of Liverpool, where he struggled to raise his three children and earn a living from silver plating. On December 5, 1869, at age fifty-two, he married again. His third wife was Ann Stevens Duncan, a thirty-three-year-old widow and the daughter of John Stevens, a Liverpool builder. After their marriage, George, Ann, and the children lived in a "court" house on Torbock Street. The densely packed court buildings with their poor lighting and ventilation were rampant with diseases such as "fever" and tuberculosis. He and Ann had four children of their own, Eliza Jane, born in 1870, George Jr., born in 1874, Mary, born in 1876, and William, born in 1879. George taught both Ann and his older sons silver plating, and as adults the boys took up the trade.

By 1877 his fortunes had improved enough that he was able to move his family away from the depressing courts on Torbock Street to a more desirable location at 21 Langsdale Street in Liverpool. No longer embarrassed by his economic status, Seward emerged from his voluntary seclusion and answered a letter from Ed James, the sports editor of America's most prestigious sporting journal, the *New York Clipper*. James asked for details on Seward's running career, and in response, Seward sent a photograph of himself and a list of his major races. Later that year James published a book, *Practical Training for Running, Walking, Rowing, Wrestling, Boxing, Jumping and All Kinds of Athletic Feats*, which featured an illustration of Seward as the frontispiece (figure 7.4). Strangely, James did not use the photograph Seward had sent him but instead used a composite made up of Seward and another runner.[15]

In 1878 the Seward family moved again, this time to 45 Clare Street in Liverpool. The *Clipper* published a long tribute to him in the issue of May 8, 1880, with an engraving of Seward made from the photo he had sent to James (figure 7.5).

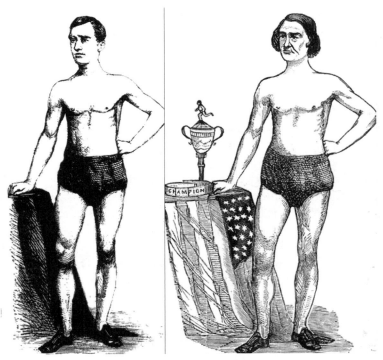

Figure 7.4.   The illustration of Seward on the right is from Ed James's 1877 book *Practical Training for Running, Walking, Rowing, Wrestling, Boxing, Jumping and All Kinds of Athletic Feats*. Seward looks to be in his fifties or sixties. Seward's body from the neck down was copied from the earlier illustration of William Jones on the left that appeared in *Illustrated Sporting News*, December 23, 1865. From frontispiece, Ed James, *Practical Training for Running, Walking, Rowing, Wrestling, Boxing, Jumping and All Kinds of Athletic Feats* (1877).

GEORGE SEWARD, the American Runner.

Figure 7.5. This illustration was made from a photo Seward sent to the *New York Clipper*. He said it was a good likeness. From the *New York Clipper*, May 8, 1880.

The portrait which we present above is that of a man who for nearly forty years has enjoyed worldwide fame as a runner—the result of the remarkable achievements credited to him when in the full vigor of youth and manhood, and which have through these years remained unequaled. Few persons who have within that period manifested any interest in pedestrianism, or athletic sports are unfamiliar with the principal performances of the celebrated American who still stands ahead of all others in his time records for 100, 120 and 200 yards, but they are unacquainted with the long list of other successes which go to make up the career of this fleet pedestrian, and will doubtless read with peculiar interest the sketch which we have prepared.

In early 1883 the Sewards moved across the river Mersey to a still better location at 48 Cleveland Street in nearby Birkenhead, but his stay there was short lived.

George Seward crossed his final finish line on April 10, 1883, when he died of a heart attack at his home at 48 Cleveland Street. Although invincible in his best years as a sprinter, he had been beaten by Death, who in the end claims victory over all. Seward's family could not afford a grave with a headstone. Instead, he was buried on April 14 in an unmarked common grave at the Walton Park Cemetery in Liverpool, only about five miles from where he ran his first race in England forty years earlier.[16] Since his grave has no marker, its exact location is unknown. It was a quiet, almost unnoticed exit, far from his native land. *Bell's Life* published a short obituary.

Death of George Seward, the American Wonder.— This celebrated pedestrian, who was born at Newhaven, Conn on Oct 16, 1817, and was, therefore, in the 66th year of his age, died at Birkenhead on April 10 last. He came to England in the year 1847, and resided at Green-street, Grosvenor-square, when he immediately displayed his skill as a sprint runner at 100 yards by polishing off all the best men in England at that distance. Seward was a thickset and very muscular man, stood 5' 8½" and weighed 159 pounds. He was peculiar in his habits, and trained but little for his undertakings; he lived widely different in those days to other pedestrians, and partook very sparingly of animal food. His *forte* evidently was 100 yards, which he once ran in 9¼ sec, though he accomplished 120 yards in 11½ sec, 200 yards in 19½ sec, and a quarter of a mile in 49 sec. He was particularly well behaved, very intellectual, and a great reader. He ran his first race in Hyde Park, and his second on Waterloo Bridge.[17]

The obituary was obviously not written by anyone who actually knew Seward as it contains several errors. By this time, the once-heralded *Bell's Life* had declined from being the best sporting newspaper in the world and would end publication in 1886.[18] In America, the *New York Clipper* for May 5, 1883, published a more substantial obituary, heaping praise on Seward and his running career.

Sixty-three years earlier George's father, Azariah, had died suddenly, far from home and leaving his family in need. Like the father he never knew, George too died far from his homeland and left his family in need. His running career had paradoxically provided him with little wealth, and the poor economic conditions in Stalybridge had led to the failure of his pub and sports complex. Frequent bouts with rheumatism also contributed to his inability to prosper after his running career was over.

A little more than a year after his death, the editor of *Bell's Life* published a plea for aid to his family.

> The Late George Seward.—We regret to hear that the widow of this celebrated pedestrian is in reduced circumstances and sadly in need of pecuniary assistance. It has been the fashion of late amongst the present class of writers on athletic subjects to sneer at the performances of the "giants of old." Probably they do not know that when Seward was the recognized sprint champion he not only offered long starts to all the best men of his day but would even allow some runners to start in the ordinary way, whilst he remained on the mark in a kneeling position. He also frequently undertook the task of beating several at intervals of a few minutes each with the provision that he was to receive nothing unless successful in every instance. Of all the champions we ever had he was perhaps the most unassuming, and anyone of the old school who desires to offer a graceful tribute to his memory cannot do better than send a trifle to those he held most dear, viz., his widow and four little children. Mrs. Seward's address is 48, Cleveland Street, Birkenhead, and any contributions will be gratefully acknowledged by her, or if preferred they can be sent to the care of the Editor of *Bell's Life*.[19]

There is no record of whether this plea raised any money to help Ann and the children. Ann was a remarkable woman who took over George's silver plating business and eked out a living for the family. She and the children lived at the Seward home in Birkenhead until 1886, when the city directory lists no occupants at 48 Cleveland Street. The 1891 census had her living at 1 Chapel Place, Liverpool, occupation silver plater. George Jr., now a silver plater's apprentice, and three of Edward's children were living with her. Edward had died earlier that year at age thirty. None of George's children took up running, or if they did, they were not successful enough to be mentioned in the sporting journals of the time. His daughter Eliza Jane, born in 1870, married a Swede named Carl Knudsen and in the early 1890s emigrated to America, settling in New Haven.

Ann remarried in 1895, at age sixty. She then took Edward's children and emigrated to the United States, settling in Rutland, Vermont. What happened to George and Ann's younger children, Mary and William, is not known, but they do not appear in the 1891 census and probably were no longer living.

George Jr., the only son to live into the twentieth century, also emigrated to America, arriving in 1902. He and his family had just $10 among them when they reached Newark, New Jersey, but in the following years he used his metal-plating skills to land a job in the fledgling aircraft industry and the family prospered.

Although George never made it back to America, a large part of his family returned to the place of his birth.

Notes

1. "Benefit of George Seward," *Era*, November 21, 1852.
2. "Seward's Benefit," *Era*, December 5, 1852.
3. *Bell's Life*, September 11, 1853.
4. *Sporting Times*, December 8, 1875, and *New York Clipper*, May 8, 1880, both listed these jumping feats in their compilations of Seward's performances. The last feat, a 12-foot standing long jump, would have been remarkable. Ray Ewry set the amateur record for this type of jump in 1904 when he cleared 3.47 meters (11 feet 4⅞ inches). Jumpers of Seward's era, such as John Howard, sometimes used weights that they threw behind them as they jumped. They also sometimes took off from a raised board. The reporting does not say Seward used weights or a board, but if he did, they would greatly reduce the significance of the feat.
5. *Bell's Life*, March 5, 1854.
6. *Bell's Life*, November 26, 1854.
7. James Pudney, born May 13, 1830, in Lambeth, was an outstanding distance runner who ran in the 1850s. His best performances included 2 miles in 9 min. 38 sec. in 1852 (*Bell's Life*, April 11, 1852) and 10 miles in 53 min. 18 sec. in 1857.
8. *Spirit of the Times*, May 31, 1851, reported that "he [Jackson] is a studious trainer, a careful man, the father of a small family in Brooklyn N.Y." Jackson never returned to America after this trip and what happened to his family in Brooklyn, if he had one, is unknown. According to the 1881 British census William Howitt was living in Barking, Essex, and working in a flower shop. His wife, Mariam, was born in 1824 in Nottingham, and he had a daughter, Ada Helen, born in 1858 at Battersea.
9. *Bell's Life*, June 3, 1855.
10. It was in Merthyr Tydfil in 1992 that the side effects of a new angina drug, Viagra, were discovered during safety trials. Previously, the blue-collar town was known for producing a different kind of iron.
11. Newbridge is about ten miles southeast of Merthyr Tydfil "as the crow flies," but the area is mountainous. Seward would probably have gone along one of the roads west from Newbridge, to link up with the road now called the A4049, and then north up the valley to Merthyr Tydfil. The trip would have been close to fifteen miles whichever route he took. This distance was probably beyond his range as a runner. Perhaps he had a horse or some other transportation waiting at a prearranged spot.

12. *Bell's Life*, December 14, 1856.

13. "Benefit for G. Seward at Hackney Wick, Monday Sept 28," *Bell's Life*, September 26, 1863.

14. "The Lancashire Cotton Famine," *Times of London*, June 4, 1868. In March 1863, a serious riot broke out in Stalybridge that was triggered by an attempt to reduce the scale of relief and impose harsher conditions on those receiving it.

15. The illustration of Seward in James's book is strange. It appears nowhere else and does not appear to be a true likeness of Seward. A previous illustration of William Jones that appeared in the *Illustrated Sporting News* on December 23, 1865, was apparently used as a basis for the Seward illustration. The illustration in James's book uses Jones's body but has Seward's head. If you look closely at the illustration, you can see that Seward is standing on the American flag. The significance of this is unknown. There is no evidence that he was unpatriotic or disliked America. Seward's face looks like he might be in his fifties or sixties although the body of Jones looks much younger. Apparently the illustration is a "cut-and-paste job" of an old Seward and the younger Jones.

16. George Seward was buried in a common grave at the Parochial Cemetery, Rice Lane, Walton, Liverpool, on April 14, 1883. His entry is in the "paid ground" book in section B grave 38, at a cost to his relatives of 15 shillings, and ministered by the Rev. R. Y. Leslie. The Liverpool Record Office reference for the above is 283 WAL (short for Walton) 4/2/7, entry number 2989, page 374. Nine other people ages two months to twenty-eight years are interred with him in the unmarked grave. The cemetery is now known as Walton Park Cemetery, and was considered to be the churchyard of the parish church of Liverpool. This site is also the resting place of Robert Tressel, author of *The Ragged Trousered Philanthropist*, Edgar Allan Poe's illustrator James Carling, and a number of pirates. In contrast, Seward's American family members, including his mother, father, sister, and one of his grandparents, are buried in the 15 Magnolia plot in the Grove Street Cemetery, Magnolia Avenue, New Haven. This elegant cemetery was the first in the United States to have family plots.

17. *Bell's Life*, April 21, 1883. Other obituaries were in the *Manitoba Daily Free Press*, May 10, 1883; *Liverpool Echo*, Monday, April 23, 1883; *New York Clipper*, May 5, 1883; *Wilkes' Spirit of the Times*, May 5, 1883; and *Boston Daily Globe*, May 3, 1883.

18. Seward first arrived in England in 1843 instead of 1847 and first lived in Cockfield rather than London. His first race was in Liverpool rather than Hyde Park.

19. "The Late George Seward," *Bell's Life*, August 2, 1884.

CHAPTER EIGHT

~

The Fastest Runner the World Has Ever Seen? (1884–1905)

When Seward died in 1883, his performances of 100 yards in 9¼ seconds, 120 yards in 11½ seconds, and 200 yards in 19½ seconds were all still listed as world records. He set the 100-yard record in his first race with William Robinson, a man Seward considered a dangerous opponent. In that race he made no effort to control the winning margin and ran as fast as he could although he was nursing a bad leg.

In setting his 120- and 200-yard records, he did not go all out. In these two races his opponent was Charles Westhall. Although Westhall was a fine sprinter who could run 150 yards in 15 seconds, Seward was at least 5 yards or ½ second faster than Westhall at 100 yards and did not have to run at his best to beat him. Because he did not want his best times known, he eased up in both races with Westhall, causing his records for these distances to be inferior to his 100-yard record.

Seward set all three of his sprint records using the mutual-consent start that was prevalent in the 1840s. About twenty years later, the starter's pistol became the preferred method of starting sprint races. The use of a starting pistol caused an additional delay that had to be added to a sprinter's time. Instead of starting his watch on the first movement of the runner's feet, a timer now had to see the flash or smoke of the pistol and react to it. Times for races started by a pistol were about ¼ second slower than those started with the mutual-consent start. Seward's records could perhaps have been retained and denoted by an asterisk to set them apart from the later records made with the pistol start, but this did not happen. Instead, more underhanded means were used to get his 100-yard record off the books.

There was no worldwide governing body that certified track and field records until 1912, when the International Amateur Athletic Federation (IAAF; now the International Association of Athletics Federations) began listing approved amateur records. Athletic records are much older, however. Compilations of professional "best on record" running performances had been kept since the early nineteenth century. Lists of amateur records started appearing in the 1860s and 1870s soon after the movement took hold. These early records were not "official" or certified, but efforts were made to weed out questionable performances. For a sprint record to be widely accepted, it could not be made using a running start, downhill, on a short course, or with a strong tailwind.

While Seward was in his prime, no one doubted his performances. In fact, he would have welcomed people questioning his records, especially if they had been willing to bet a sizable sum that he could not equal or exceed them. As the decades rolled by and no sprinter approached his performances, his 100-yard record came under intense scrutiny. Record keepers were content to let the records for the seldom-run 120- and 200-yard races stay on the books, but by the late 1800s, many wanted to find a way to get rid of his troublesome 100-yard record. In 1874, the first analysis of the record appeared in the London newspaper *Land and Water*. This analysis is significant because the writers were near contemporaries of Seward.

REMARKABLE PEDESTRIAN PERFORMANCES.
George Seward's historical 9¼ seconds.

For the last twenty years the time alleged to have been made by this celebrated pedestrian in a match with William Robinson of Newton Moor has remained unbeaten and it is therefore interesting to consider whether the same is really correct or merely one of the many worthless so-called fast times which have been foisted on the public through the stupidity or design of ignorant or unreliable officials.

In order to arrive at any definite conclusion as to this, it is evident that there are several things to be taken into consideration, namely, was the time taken by a reliable person? Was the distance accurately measured? Did the runner ever before or since show similar form? Were there any circumstances likely to qualify the performance?

For this purpose it is necessary to refer to the only full reports obtainable, viz, that contained in the columns of *Bell's Life* for Oct 6, 1844, from which we learn the race was for the championship, each of the competitors being considered by their respective partisans fully capable of holding the title; that Robinson was in his best form, having recently defeated such flyers as C. Jenkinson (the London Stag) and J. Smith (the Regent Street Pet), whilst Seward, for the first time in his life had undergone some slight preparation and the race was a clinker throughout. . . .

In a number of *Bell's Life* about that date, in answer to correspondents, we read that "Wantling has run 100 yards in 9 sec, and 100 yards has *never been run in 8 sec,*" which, to say the least of it, shows that pretty conflicting ideas then prevailed in *Bell's* mind as to what time a first-rate pedestrian would accomplish the distance in. The time, too, was then nearly every instance taken from the [knee] bend, and not the flash of the pistol—a difference of quite two and a half yards.

The account, also, does not state what we believe was the case—on no less authority than that of G. Cook, of Shepherd's Bush, Seward's trainer and attendant—that the wind, if not in favor of the runners, was at all events by no means against them, an item that should meet with its due consideration.

With reference to the American Deer's trustworthiness in watch-holding, it must be borne in mind that he—W. Howitt, of Norwich—was a runner himself who used to compete against the best men out with a more than usual amount of success and for large sums and therefore would be anxious to obtain the correct measure of the performers and if the watches were not then made on such scientific principals as now, at all events he would be in a position to obtain the best that was procurable and in order to make no mistake, would do so.

Next comes the distance. This it seems was trusted to T. Oliver, the commissary of the prize ring, and without offering an opinion either way, it is only necessary to call attention to the fact that in all matters connected with that now defunct institution, extreme accuracy was invariably insisted on, and therefore a person so used to measuring would not be likely to make any mistake; and had an intentional "error" been committed, surely, with so much at stake, some one would have detected it. Robinson's *forte*, also, was a longer distance, and therefore his party would take every precaution to see the full distance was run.

The point arrived at now is the "form" of the men. Firstly let us take their previous running which may be briefly summarized as follows:— Seward, who also used to run in the names of Steward and Sherrin, was an American by birth and prior to his race with Robinson had proved himself a first-class sprinter, having won all his races in America, and since his arrival here, defeating Fowler of Liverpool, Wood of Levenshulme, J. Jackson, J. Chapman, Routledge of Essington, Foster of Barnard's Castle, (doing in this race 200 yards in 23 sec), Badcock of Birmingham, and finally beating J. Smith, the Regent street Pet over 100 yds level, and successfully conceding John Rush 2 yds in 120.

Robinson's claim to supremacy in the pedestrian arena were also striking; he was at the time considered the champion, having beaten John Sale, of Denton, over 200 yds for £50; Coates of Sheffield, at the same distance for £100; Black Jack of Bellington over 300 yds for £40; J. Smith, the Regent Street Pet, at 440 yds and 100 yds, for £50 each; J. Duckworth of Droydson, over 100 yds for £50; and C. Jenkinson, giving him 10 yds in 440 and having won several other matches of slightly lesser note. So confident too, were his friends that he was brought down to the scene of action—the turnpike road near the Seven Stars, Hammersmith—in a four-in-hand and on his arrival a band struck up, "See the conquering hero comes."

Immediately after his match with Robinson, Seward offered a series of challenges, which, by being unaccepted prove that the runners of the time (many of whom were considered nearly, if not level time men) had a wholesome dread of the American's prowess, and if they did not believe the 9¼ seconds, at all events thought something wonderful had been done. For instance in a week later issue of *Bell*, Seward offered Atkinson of Shincliff, 2 yds in 100, and 1 yard in each 20 up to 200 for £25 or £50, or as he had heard Atkinson would run him for £5 sooner than not have a match, he would concede 3 yds in 100; the "Aspiring" Footman, 3 in 120. Willox in the same paper, offered to take 2 yds in 100 or 1 in the same distance of Robinson, and take £50 to £40 or to run Whyler of Manchester, Hopwell of Nottingham, or J. Smith 120 level for £50. Soon after Atkinson offered to take 3 yds in 100, if Seward would lay £20 to £10 and go by report of pistol, but it came to nothing, the stipulations being too binding for Seward; the latter, however, got on another match with Robinson and in December of the same year, defeated him 2 yds in 160.

In 1845 Seward beat J. Smith and E. Smith in a 440 yards hurdle race soon after which he went to America, but returning the following year, received forfeit from C. Westhall to whom he was to give 2 yds in 120, and in 1847 made two more still unbeaten fastest times, winning a 200 yds match in 19½ on March 22, and a 120 yard match in 11½ sec on March 3, overthrowing in each C. Westhall, after which he offered to give anyone, black, white or no color 5 yards in 120 or 10 in 300 for £100 or £1,000.

This sweeping challenge was unaccepted and on May 30, Seward offered 5 in 100 or 10 in 250, to run 1,000 yards level, or to give Westhall 10 yards in any distance he most fancied, from 200 to 1,000, and a month after, finding starts useless, Seward stated he would carry 10 lbs and run any man 100 yards level. Westhall at this time was in best form and before his 200 yards match with Seward, had repeatedly run the distance in level time according to J. Roberts, late of West London Grounds, who at the time was certainly capable of clocking a race.

All these matters tend to prove that Seward, without doubt was a long way ahead of anyone of his day, and, although it is almost too much to expect anyone to credit that a pedestrian could cover 100 yards in 9¼ sec, under any circumstances whatever, it certainly is within the range of probability that, on the occasion alluded to, it was closely approached. Running men, as a rule, do not make matches without a chance to win, and, to give a level time man 5 yards in 100, Seward must have been doing half a second better, which we are inclined to believe was about his form.[1]

Although neither of the authors, Thomas Griffith, pedestrian editor of *Bell's Life*, and J. Jenn, a running expert, witnessed the race, they did talk to some of the key people involved. This analysis by two of the top running experts of their day is the first time anyone tried to look into all the circumstances surrounding Seward's extraordinary performance. It is the best evidence we have that there were no obvious reasons to invalidate the record. Their conclusion that 2½ yards or ¼ second should be added to the time to account for the additional delay of starts made with a pistol is reasonable. This ¼-second difference between the two starting methods has been borne out by modern timing studies.[2]

The IAAF has set the lowest possible reaction time (from the flash of the gun to the time the sprinter exerts pressure on the starting block's pressure-sensitive pads) to be 0.100 seconds. Any sprinter who reacts faster than this is charged with a false start. These reaction times seldom drop below 0.130 sec, and average about 0.150 sec.[3] Allowing another 0.10 seconds for the timer of a mutual-consent race to detect the first movement of the runner's feet would give a difference of about ¼ second between a pistol start and a mutual-consent start. This difference agrees with Griffith and Jenn's estimate.[4]

If one accepts their analysis, then Seward's time would have been about 9½ seconds had he started by the flash of a pistol as modern sprinters do. This time is still faster than anyone else ran 100 yards in the nineteenth century. The first runner after Seward to officially beat 9½ seconds was Frank Wykoff, who ran 100 yards in 9.4 seconds in 1930, some eighty-six years after Seward's performance.

Here is a summary of questions that have been asked about Seward's 100-yard record and answers based on the best available information.

Q. Was the course accurately measured?

A. Yes, when so much money was at stake it had to be.

Q. Was it level?

A. Yes, they would never have chosen a stretch that was downhill. The object was not to produce a fast time, but to have a fair course for both men. In addition, the articles of agreement for the race required the course to be level.

Q. Was there a tailwind?

A. No. George Cook, Seward's attendant, stated after the race the wind was not in favor of the runners. Also, there was no mention of a tailwind by *Bell's Life*, the *Era*, or the *Times of London*.

Q. How many watches were used?

A. Only one, Jackson's, gave the official result, but others in the crowd would certainly have made their own clocking and would have disputed any discrepancy.

Q. Why was the odd timing of 9¼ seconds used?

A. Watches of this era were calibrated to the nearest quarter second.

Q. In that case, could the time have been closer to 9½ seconds?

A. It could. It may have been 9.375. Equally it may have been as fast as 9.125.

Q. How was the race started?

A. By mutual consent.

Q. Was the start a fair one?

A. Probably fairer than many "by word of mouth" or pistol starts.

Q. Did Seward take a running start?

A. No, the mutual-consent start required that the runners stand behind the scratch. The timer started his watch on the first movement of the runner's feet, which meant the runner had to be standing still at the start.

Q. Where would Jackson, the timekeeper, have been positioned?

A. At the finish, in the same place as modern timers.

Q. What was the running surface?

A. It was most likely a macadamized surface common in London at the time and made up of crushed stones without tar. When properly packed, this was a smooth, fast running surface.

Q. What was the finish line?

A. Not reported, but it would most likely have been a finish tape made up of one or more handkerchiefs knotted together and held by two men, one on each side of the course.

Q. How good was Seward's opponent?

A. Until the race, William Robinson was considered the fastest man in the world at distances up to 440 yards. He held the best time on record for 440 yards (51 seconds) and had equaled the record at 200 yards.

Q. What was Seward's winning margin?

A. It was reported as being from 1½ to 3 yards. Seward himself said it was 2 yards.

Q. Did he ever repeat the 9¼-second time?

A. None of Seward's other recorded sprint race times are this fast. Few of his times were recorded, so we have no way of knowing if he ran this fast or faster in other races. There is some evidence he could run faster. Bell's Life stated in 1850 that three years earlier he had run 100 yards in 9.0 seconds, presumably in a trial. Seward also made a bet in 1847 that he could beat his existing record or 9¼ seconds, which would have required him to run 9.0 seconds. In 1877 Bell's Life reported they had timed Seward many times during his career easily running 9½ seconds in practice, just after he had eaten breakfast.[5]

By the late 1880s few people were still around who had witnessed Seward's performances. No sprinter, amateur or professional, had come close to his 100-yard time, and many doubted that anyone ever would. Had 100 yards turned out to be a distance seldom run, it is unlikely anyone would have bothered to question Seward's record. In the second half of the nineteenth century, the "100-yard dash" became the premier sprint race in English-speaking countries. To beat "even time" (10 seconds) for 100 yards became the dream of every outstanding sprinter, amateur or professional.[6] The 100-yard sprint would reign supreme, especially in England and America, until replaced by the 100 meters in the 1970s when all track and field distances were changed to their metric equivalents. This change was made to conform to the metric units that had by then been adopted by almost every country in the world. Of the traditional English distances, only the mile is still occasionally run in modern track meets.

Amateurism began to dominate running in England and America in the 1870s and 1880s. As the movement gained momentum it almost replaced pedestrianism, which had fallen into disfavor because of widespread race fixing, unruly crowds, and double-crosses. Amateur sprinters found beating 10 seconds for 100 yards so difficult that they began to think there must be something wrong with Seward's record. By 1890, amateur sprinters had run 10 flat for 100 yards more than one hundred times in their race to "break evens." On October 11 of that year, American John Owen ran 9⅘ seconds at Analoston Island near Washington, D.C., to become the first amateur sprinter to officially "break evens" for 100 yards.[7]

The pros did not come much closer to Seward's time. Frank Hewitt was said to have run 9¾ seconds for 100 yards on March 7, 1870, in Melbourne although the time was not universally accepted. Timing standards in Australia were not rigorous at the time.

Harry Hutchens, probably the fastest nineteenth-century sprinter besides Seward, ran 131¼ yards in 12½ seconds in 1882 in a losing effort in a Sheffield Handicap. In May 1885, in an attempt to break Seward's 120-yard record, he ran the distance in 11¼ seconds. If we add ¼ second to Seward's 120-yard time to account for his mutual-consent start, then Hutchens equaled it. Like Seward, Hutchens cared little for setting records, and he never made a public attempt to beat Seward's 100-yard time.[8] American professionals H. M. Johnson and Harry Bethune were both credited with 9⅘ seconds for 100 yards in the 1880s, but no professional came closer to Seward's record than Hewitt's questionable 9¾ seconds.

Shortly after Seward's death in 1883, some British compilers of record lists began to drop his 100-yard mark although they kept his records for the less-popular 120- and 200-yard distances.[9] At the time, many British sports-writers thought that no amateur would ever break 10 seconds for 100 yards and therefore there must be something amiss with Seward's 100-yard record. These writers also thought the record was unfair to the current generation of the "morally superior" amateurs. To justify dropping the record, someone in England put out a story that it was made from a running start. This claim first appeared many years after the race and contradicted the original reporting in *Bell's Life*. The *Sporting Chronicle Annual* dated 1897 lists Seward's 100-yard record but states in brackets "from a flying start of 10 yards." This disclaimer appeared in every edition subsequently up to 1936.

The demise of the record in America can be traced with more precision. As in England, the decline of pedestrianism and the rise of amateur track and field played a key role. Many of the late-nineteenth-century American sportswriters worked to advance amateur athletics even to the point of suggesting that the old professionals were unreliable in every sense. The three major sporting newspapers in America in the last quarter of the nineteenth century were *Wilkes' Spirit of the Times*, the *National Police Gazette*, and the *New York Clipper*. All three sided with the amateur movement and came to discount Seward's 100-yard record.

In 1883, shortly before Seward died, William B. Curtis, sports editor of the *Wilkes' Spirit of the Times*, published a long article arguing that Seward's 100-yard record should be erased. Curtis, one of the founders of the Amateur Athletic Union in America, promoted amateurism any way he could, including discrediting the professionals. Although it had occurred almost forty years earlier and 3,000 miles away, "Father Bill" made his own analysis of Seward's record and argued that he never ran 100 yards in 9¼ seconds. Here are the reasons he gave for discounting the performance:

1. The measurement of the course was doubtful.
2. The men started not by pistol, but by mutual consent, with a 9-foot scratch start, so the exact distance was not run.
3. The timing could not have been correct, for no man can time a mutual-consent start with exactness.
4. As there were a dozen false starts, and the watches of those days did not have any flyback attachments, the announcement of the time for a watch that had been started and stopped a dozen times must have been a matter of guesswork or memory, as there could have been no way of knowing the exact position of the hands of the watch when the men finally started.

5. The official time was "less than 10 seconds."
6. The private time taken by "the American Deer" was ignored by the sporting publications of the time and remained unnoticed for seventeen years.
7. If Seward ran 9¼ seconds, Robinson must have beaten 9½ seconds, a manifest absurdity for a runner of his caliber.[10]

To his credit, Curtis did not claim that the course was downhill or that Seward had taken a running start or that there was a strong tailwind. Griffith and Jenn had already addressed most of his objections in their earlier analysis of the record. Although not considered a problem by Griffith and Jenn, objection number 7, that Robinson must have beaten 9½ seconds, may seem to have merit until one looks at the race more closely. Bell's Life's original reporting said that Seward beat Robinson by 1½ to 3 yards. At the speed they were running, that would have been by 0.15 to 0.3 second. Robinson would have run from 9.40 seconds to 9.55 seconds, but the ¼-second-reading watch used to time the race would have read from 9½ to 9¾ seconds. If we add ¼ second to account for the mutual-consent start, as Griffith and Jenn did for Seward, then Robinson's time would have been 9¾ to 10 seconds, fast for that era but probably within his ability.

Although Curtis's article caused some American sportswriters to doubt Seward's 100-yard record, most kept it on the books until the late 1880s. In 1887 the National Police Gazette published a list of "best on record" performances containing all three of Seward's records without any qualifications except that a professional had made them. A year later William Harding, sports editor of the National Police Gazette, began to express doubts about the record and wrote: "I never believed that George Seward did make this time [9¼ sec]. Not because of any prejudice, however, but simply from the fact that nearly 44 years have elapsed since the great runner was credited with the performance, and with all the new improvements in training, etc there has been no one to equal the performance."[11]

For many years the New York Clipper, America's most prestigious sporting journal of the late 1800s, published a yearly annual listing the fastest times on record for various sporting events. The Clipper Annual for 1889 contained the following listing of amateur and professional sprint records.

Amateur performances are designated by a *.
   100 yards - In England: 9¼ sec., George Seward (American) turnpike road, Hammersmith, Sept. 30, 1844; *10 sec., A. Wharton, July 3, 1886. In America

> 9⅘ sec, H. M. Johnson, Cleveland, Ohio, July 31, 1886, *10 sec, R. L. La Montagne, N. Y. City, June 29, 1878; W. C. Wilmer, Mott Haven N. Y. Oct. 12, 1878; L E. Myers, N. Y. City, Sept. 18, 1880; E .J. Wendell, Cambridge, Mass., May 24, 1881, R. S. Haley, Oakland California, Sept 23, 1882, and W. Baker, Boston, July 1, 1886.
>
> 120 yards - In England: 11½ sec, George Seward, London, May 3, 1847 *11⅘ W. P. Phillips, March 25, 1882. In America: *12 sec, L. E. Myers, NY City, May 30, 1882
>
> 200 yards - In England: 19½ sec., George Seward, London, March 22, 1847. *20 ⅕ sec, E. H. Pelling, London, August 8, 1887, In America: *20⅕ sec, L. E. Myers, NY City, Sept. 15, 1881

In the 1890 edition of the *New York Clipper Annual* the editors dropped Seward's forty-six-year-old 100-yard record and gave as an explanation:

> Note.—George Seward the American sprinter, was given a record of 9¼ sec, for a race run at Hammersmith, Eng., Sept, 30, 1844. Although the time was phenomenal, the runner was yards faster than any sprinter of his day, and the record remained virtually undisputed until after the lapse of many years, the few who at the time presumed to question it being silenced by a standing offer by Seward, through *Bell's Life*, to repeat the performance for a good sized stake.
>
> In those days, however, record making was not hedged about with the safeguards of later years, and the failure of the fleetest runners of modern times, with all the advantages of superior paths, equipment and training, to nearly equal Seward's figures strengthened the conviction of those who discredited the performance. Their arguments were directed mainly against the watch, with which the race was timed, which of course was hardly as worthy of dependence as the stopwatch of the present day. That fact alone, however, was not conclusive proof that the race was not run in the time stated, and we allowed the performance to remain among the records. Now, however, we are in possession of the evidence of an eye witness that not only was the race run from a flying start, but the piece of turnpike on which it took place was down hill—facts that warrant us in expunging it from the record.

The "eyewitness" account was described in a June 29, 1889, letter from M. J. Finn to the *New York Clipper*. Finn, a sportsman from Natick, Massachusetts, had just returned from England, where he had attended the famous Whitsuntide Handicaps in Sheffield. Besides his description of the races he wrote:

> I have actually been in conversation with a man who saw George Seward do his performance and he says it's true, but the conditions of the race are not generally understood. At the beginning and end of the hundred yards was a tape

and Seward standing ten yards away had a flying start through the first tape, when a pistol was fired, the time being taken from the crack of the pistol till the tape was broken at the post. The track was slightly downhill and a good wind was blowing from behind.

It is hard to believe that anyone knowledgeable of running in Seward's time took this account seriously. The "eyewitness" description is in total disagreement with the original *Bell's Life* and *Era* reporting of forty-five years earlier. It may have been an outright fabrication since it included every "sin" a sprinter could make in setting a record. According to the 1844 reporting in *Bell's Life*, the *Era*, and the *Times of London*, Seward did not take a running start nor was the race started with a pistol. The tape at the start is bizarre, as it has been impossible to find any newspaper accounts of tapes being used at the start of sprint races in Seward's era. There was also no noticeable wind, and the articles of agreement for the race stipulated that the course be level. *Bell's Life* would never have considered a race run under the conditions described in the "eyewitness" account to be a record. Because of the importance of the race, any of these problems would surely have been pointed out in the original reporting.

No one questioned the "eyewitness" account, however, or made any effort to check its validity. Those wanting to get rid of Seward's troublesome record now had all the ammunition they needed. In less than a year *Outing* magazine, citing the "eyewitness" report, also declared the record invalid:

> The record of 9¼ s for 100 yards which has been credited to George Seward since the date of the performance at Hammersmith, England, September 30, 1844, must be considered as incorrect. Considerable doubt has always attached to the genuineness of the record, since the means of obtaining accurate time in those days were somewhat limited. However, an eyewitness has been found who declares that Seward ran the race from a flying start and that the track was down hill, which of course invalidates the record. This leaves H. Johnson and H. Bethune in possession of the fastest professional time in the world for 100 yards—9⅗ sec. The former record was made at Cleveland, July 31, 1886, and the latter's at Oakland, Cal., February 22, 1888. Nevertheless, it is but just to Seward to give him credit for having probably been the fastest runner the world has ever seen. He was a wonder at distances under 200 yards, and for a long time had a standing challenge to give any man in the world 5 yards in 120, or 10 yards in 300 for any amount of money.[12]

Soon, almost every sports authority was using the "eyewitness" account to get rid of Seward's record. From this time on, the record books in America, if they mentioned Seward's 100-yard record at all, always qualified it with "set on a downhill course" or "with a flying start."

One late-nineteenth-century sports authority who still believed Seward had run 9¼ seconds for 100 yards was Sir Montague Shearman. He learned of Seward's extraordinary speed from walker William Gale, who had toured with the American in 1858. Although he believed Seward's records were genuine, Shearman failed to mention him in his groundbreaking history of nineteenth-century track and field, *Athletics and Football* (1887). This glaring omission may well have been because Shearman was a strong supporter of amateurism. In an 1884 article in the magazine *Ashore or Afloat*, Shearman heaped praise on Seward, calling him an even greater wonder than Harry Hutchens, the great professional sprinting star of the late 1800s.

It may not be generally known that some twenty-five years back Seward and Gale, the wonderful endurance pedestrian, bought a large canvas booth, which they turned into a hippodrome, and traveled the country in partnership as circus proprietors. Seward, being almost as good an equestrian as he was a pedestrian, undertook to do the horsemanship, while Gale used to amuse the company with some feats of walking.

During their travels the topic of conversation at the inn where they used to make headquarters frequently turned upon running, and Gale, who always had an eye to the main chance, often made a match for his partner to run the local champions. Seward, who was a man of very retiring disposition and spent nearly all his spare time in reading, would sometimes decline to run, and even when he did consent it was only by dint of a considerable amount of persuasion, although the business always proved more profitable than that of the circus. Of course, in these off hand matches Seward ran entirely untrained, and generally had to meet the fastest men in the district. In spite of this Gale has told me that he never lost, and frequently would let his opponent get several yards' start before he would leave his mark, but would be at his shoulder before running fifty yards, and win as he liked.

In one of these affairs Seward met an opponent who was said to be a sound half-second man.[13] The local champion was very unsteady in toeing the mark, and frequently got over before the pistol was fired. At length Seward, to the consternation of Gale, went down on his knees and told the starter to fire. Away went the local celebrity, but Seward was up like a cat, and ere sixty of the hundred yards they were running had been covered was on level terms, and shooting out like a flash of lightning in the last thirty, won by fully four yards.

The above are but a few of the many instances of Seward's remarkable speed that Gale related to me, and if space permitted I could enumerate many others equally astounding. Now, if Seward could (and I have not the slightest doubt he did) perform like this out of condition, there is some reason to believe that when fit he was capable of having run as fast as he was credited with on the records of *Bell's Life*.[14]

Few others objected to getting rid of the record, and by 1900 Seward and his 100-yard record were approaching the status of a myth. The 1905 book *Rowing and Track Athletics*, by Walter Camp, included a paragraph about Seward's performance. Although Camp discounted Seward's 100-yard time, he praised his other records, which were set under almost identical conditions. Known as the "father of American football," Camp was also a strong supporter of amateur athletics.

> Of the men who ran in this country in those days of quaint half-caste athletics, one stands out rather noticeably from the rest. This man was George Seward, who even in an age when training was only guesswork and established records unknown, so astonished his contemporaries here and abroad that his name has been handed down as that of a phenomenon. Seward was a professional, of course. He ran in this country and he ran in England—the same year that the Whigs were carrying log cabins in political parades "Tippecanoe and Tyler too"—and everywhere he met the best men and defeated them at every distance up to the quarter mile. Although his apocryphal 100-yard dash in 9¼ seconds is no longer accepted, his name stands on the record book beside a 120-yard dash of 11½ sec and 200-yard dash of 19½ sec done as far back as 1847.[15]

A more modern track and field historian, Roberto Quercetani, in *Athletics: A History of Modern Track and Field Athletics (1860–1990), Men and Women*, wrote:

> If one adds ignorance of the wind factor to the above considerations on starting and timing the least one can say about the times of early sprinters is that they must be taken with a sizeable grain of salt. The fastest times were usually registered in professional races where the financial terms made all tricks possible. Under these conditions, one can hardly express any judgement on such legendary exploits as those credited to George Seward of the United States.[16]

Although they had no wind gauges, timers of Seward's era were well aware of the effects of winds on sprint times, as Griffith and Jenn pointed out in their 1874 analysis. There is also no evidence Seward used trickery to set his records. Quercetani, like many of his predecessors, disregarded Seward's record not because he had evidence the record was incorrect, but because Seward was a professional.

With his greatest public achievement discounted by sportswriters of the late nineteenth century, Seward, whose fame on both sides of the Atlantic had been unrivaled during his running days, became a footnote in the history of sports.

To run 100 yards in 9¼ seconds requires enormous athletic talent. Could someone have run that fast so long ago? The answer is yes; modern sprinters, under more favorable conditions, have gone even faster and humans have not evolved in any way in the last 150 years that would have made Seward's feat physically impossible in 1844.

Based on his record against the best sprinters of his era, the starts he offered other runners, his many victories and other fast times, as well as the newspaper report of his having run 9.0 seconds for 100 yards in practice, it is quite likely Seward ran 9¼ seconds on that day. At least there were no doubters among his fellow runners or reporters who saw him run. Yet it is also possible that there was some error in timing or course measurement that we do not know about. Even today, with our sophisticated, fully automatic timing, errors still occur.[17] One thing is certain. The "eyewitness" account of a downhill course, running start, and tailwind could not have been accurate. Its purpose was to get rid of a record no other runner of the nineteenth century could approach.

Notes

1. *Land and Water*, October 17, 1874, 304.

2. To find their player's 40-yard speed, many modern college and professional football coaches still start their watches on their player's first movement rather than using a starting pistol.

3. J. R. Mureika, "A Simple Model for Predicting Sprint Race Times Accounting for Energy Loss on the Curve," Department of Computer Science, University of Southern California, Los Angeles, California, June 25, 2006.

4. Seward bet he could run 9.0 seconds for 100 yards in *Bell's Life*, November 21, 1847. "Three years ago he could run 9.0 for 100 yards," is from *Bell's Life*, November 24, 1850. "Could easily run 9½ after eating breakfast," *Bell's Life*, June 23, 1877.

5. R. L. Quercetani, *A History of Track & Field Athletics 1864–1964* (London: Oxford University Press, 1964), 2.

6. "World's Records Broken," *New York Times*, October 12, 1890.

7. *Bell's Life*, May 12, 1885.

8. Tom Malone tied Seward's 120-yard record on April 12, 1883, in Australia only two days after Seward's death. American Tom Keane ran 11⅔ at Ball Inn Grounds, Sheffield, September 5, 1898, to break the record. Seward's 200-yard record was still on the books in 1890.

9. Frank Zarnowski, *The Decathlon: A Colorful History of Track and Field's Most Challenging Event* (Champaign, Ill.: Leisure Press, 1989).

10. "The Seward Myth," *Wilkes' Spirit of the Times*, January 20, 1883.

11. *National Police Gazette*, March 31, 1888, 11.

12. *Outing*, February 1890, 43.

13. He is probably referring to someone capable or running 100 yards in 10½ seconds—a good, but not outstanding, time for that era.

14. Quoted in *Otago Witness* (New Zealand), January 26, 1884, 21. Seward would have been forty-one years old in 1858, far past his prime but still able to beat all but the very best sprinters.

15. Walter Camp, *Rowing and Track Athletics* (London: Macmillan & Co., 1905), 253.

16. Roberto L. Quercetani, *Athletics: A History of Modern Track and Field Athletics (1860–1990), Men and Women* (Milan: Vallardi, 1991), 1.

17. On May 15, 2006, ESPN reported that Olympic champion Justin Gatlin had broken the 100- meter world record with a time of 9.76 seconds at the Qatar Grand Prix. On May 18, 2006, ESPN reported that a timing error had been made and that Gatlin had actually run 9.77 and only tied the existing record. Gatlin was later found to have used steroids and was stripped of even a share of the record.

CHAPTER NINE

~

The Seward Legacy

Seward's speed put him head and shoulders above other sprinters of his time and would have set him apart in any era. He also had several other traits that made him stand out from other runners of his time and influenced those who followed.

He was an honest pedestrian, a trait sadly lacking in many professional sprinters. His sense of fair play probably came from his mother's influence when he was a child. If we discount the 200-yard race he ran in 1855 against William Thomas where he double-crossed the race fixers, there is not a hint of his "selling" a race or double-crossing anyone. Throughout his career, he showed that he cared about his friends and supporters and did his best not to let them down, even to the point of sometimes running injured or risking injury. Seward's backer, George Colpitts, must be given some of the credit for Seward's sterling reputation. There is no record that he ever encouraged his runner to perform other than honestly.

Seward's fondness for books, disregard for accepted training principles, and eccentric eating habits also set him apart from other runners of his time. Many pedestrians of Seward's era were illiterate or barely literate. Although his formal education ended at age eighteen when he started his apprenticeship as a silver plater, he was intelligent and well behaved. He loved to read and was literate enough to write thoughtful, polite letters to the press. Unfortunately, he never wrote anything describing his running experiences.

Barclay's training methods, consisting of long walks, a strict diet, purgatives, and artificial sweating, were used widely by both short- and long-distance runners of Seward's time. He did not follow these methods but instead took pride in training himself. In one respect his training philosophy foreshadowed that of the great distance runner Paavo Nurmi from Finland, who ran in the 1920s. Both were superior runners whose training included frequent timed trials. If a trial was in a time they felt no one else could match, they saw little reason for further training.

During the first part of his career Seward kept his practices closed to the public, but later he allowed some trusted reporters from *Bell's Life* to watch him train. One reporter said that in his trials Seward could "run easily 100 yards in 9½ seconds, and we have timed him so to do frequently."[1] Since few other men of Seward's day could beat 10 seconds for 100 yards, he knew he had a ½-second cushion to work with. Late in his career, while preparing for longer races, he trained much harder, sometimes for weeks or even months to get ready for an important race.

Seward had an uncommon ability to accelerate during a race. He loved to run behind his opponent for 70 percent or more of a race. When he decided it was time to make his move, he would duck his head slightly and, as Westhall put it, "'bow' away at a speed never before witnessed in any other in the world."[2] Once he changed speed, he would usually have the race won in just a few strides. This tactic allowed him to control races and keep his winning margins small to encourage future races. A more modern runner who used the ability to quickly change speeds to great advantage was Percy Williams from Canada, who won gold medals in both the 100 and 200 meters in the 1928 Olympics.

Seward's diet was also unusual for his time. While most pedestrians ate beef or mutton with stale bread and toast and drank old ale, he ate whatever he chose. Newspapers reported with near disbelief that he subsisted on bowls of milk, cabbage, pork, pancakes, and confectionery.

Despite his injuries and many bouts with rheumatism, his professional running career spanned twenty-six years, an unusually long time for any professional athlete, especially a sprinter. Beginning with his victories over Ainsworth in 1840 in New Haven and continuing until his devastating illness in the fall of 1848, he was the best runner the world had yet seen at short distances. Although he never fully regained his lost form after his bout with rheumatics, he was still fast enough to remain champion of sprinting in England until October 1852 when a second attack of the disease left him too crippled to defend his title. Even then, he did not abandon running but still ran whenever his illness would allow it. He continued racing until he was forty-eight years old.

We can only guess at how many races he ran in his long career. About 180 were recorded in the newspapers of his time, but he surely ran many other matches and races for small stakes that were never reported. It is likely the total number was in the thousands. Counting all of his races reported from 1838 to 1866, including those where he gave starts, came up lame, competed against horses, or ran after he was no longer a first-rate runner, he won 158 and lost 26.[3] Of the men who beat him, none was able to do so more than once in a sprint race. In their many races, H. A. Reed defeated him three times, once at 200 yards and twice at 440. All the losses to Reed came after November 1848 when Seward suffered his first severe bout of rheumatism.

Although Seward was a professional, he was not in the sport just for the money. During his career the largest stake he ran for was $500 a side in 1845.[4] For most of his races, the stakes were much smaller—in the £5 to £10 range. Seward, like many other runners, enjoyed winning and being the center of attention of race fans, but despite being the best sprinter of his era, he did not become wealthy from running. Why he continued to compete after his crippling bouts with rheumatics when he could no longer beat the best runners or earn a significant amount of money from running is not clear. Most likely it was his insatiable desire to compete and his love of the sport.

There is no question that Seward had great natural ability as a sprinter and could defeat most sprinters without doing much training or even putting forth much effort. He did not have this natural superiority at longer distances but still managed to compete successfully with the best middle-distance runners of his time. Competing at longer-than-sprint distances required much training and hard work. Few other great sprinters have been willing to put forth this effort. He was a first-rate miler, a distance he enjoyed running but admitted was "far beyond his fork." His best mile time of 4 min. 30 sec. on a muddy track in losing to Westhall in 1851 was the fastest mile by an American until May 31, 1880, when Lon Myers ran 4 min. 29½ sec.

In 1850, when increased traffic around London caused officials to ban footraces on streets and turnpike roads, pedestrians moved their races to enclosed grounds. Stadium owners charged admissions and often shared the gate receipts with their star performers. Seward took advantage of this change by pioneering the use of special feats and exhibitions to attract fans to his races. His hurdling, running against horses, and running against multiple opponents in quick succession drew large crowds. He sometimes made these races more interesting by giving other runners long starts, even starting on his knees.

Another way he entertained fans was by performing jumping feats such as leaping over hurdles or horses. Jumping contests were not as common as footraces in his era, and there are few reports of his taking part in them other than as exhibitions. Strangely, although he and John Howard were friends, there is no record of their competing with each other in a jumping match. Howard was for ten years the long jumping champion of England, and it should have been a natural rivalry. Seward was an outstanding jumper and was credited with a standing long jump of 12 feet over a 2-foot-high hurdle. This performance would have been a world's best, assuming he did it without weights and did not jump from a board or raised platform. Newspaper accounts sometimes neglected to mention the use of these aids.

He also excelled at hurdling and became so skilled at it that he had no qualms about jumping hurdles on ice. In his book *How to Train* (1862), John Levett, a champion distance runner of Seward's era, wrote: "Seward was a great hurdle jumper, and a splendid skater; and on the ice, in skates, could do some wonderful things, over hurdles. In fact he appeared to have been born with skates on, and his speed, for distance, long or short, on the ice was almost fabulous. On skates he was capable of 30 miles in an hour as well as jumping more than 23 ft."[5]

On December 20, 1846, shortly after he returned from America, Seward challenged any skater in England to a long-jumping match on skates and to race any distance from 440 yards to a mile on ice and jump five hurdles. Early in 1847 he received a challenge for a 3-mile match from the skater Joseph Clark of Yoxley, but it came to nothing. Seward described his exploits on ice in a letter to the *London Field*, January 3, 1880.

JUMPING IN SKATES—LIVERPOOL, Dec 23.—Sir: Will you kindly let me say a few words about skating, as I see my name mentioned in your valuable journal?

A good many years ago I was very fond of that exercise, and there has been so much said about skating, and the speed of skaters, that it revives old recollections. In looking through the papers I have often wondered that jumping on skates is so rarely mentioned. I suppose it looks too dangerous a feat to many. Let me tell them that jumping on skates at full speed is not nearly as dangerous as it looks and I think I have had some experience. It is when going slow and jumping where the danger lies. I have fallen hundreds of times at full speed and was never hurt, but often hurt when going slow. It is of no use anyone attempting to jump unless he can go a good speed, for it is the pace that throws you. Let a skater put on all the speed he is possessed of, and put his feet together the same as for a jump on land and he will soon make a jumper if he is not timid. In my younger days I practiced nothing but speed and jumping. That was in America, where there are more opportunities for this exercise. I have never had a match on in England, except a jumping match, where a gentleman laid me £20 to £10 that I did not jump 20 ft with skates on which I won.

I once advertised to jump over an open piece of water 16 ft wide, and through a fire balloon 3 ft high; but that did not come off, as the ice melted. I will give you another jump that came off in St. James Park. My late friend, Mr. Charles Westhall, was with me. It was one severe winter; there were some thousands of people and skaters on the little island opposite where the wild-fowl are. They had cut a piece of ice out and pushed it under so that the wild-fowl could get in the water. The width was about 16 ft, which I leaped, and was told by the Humane Society officers that if I attempted it again I should be put off the pond. I was giving them with their ladders too much trouble for thousands followed to see another jump. I should not have hesitated in my day a moment to have matched myself to skate a mile and jump four water jumps 12 ft wide in three minutes.

Geo. Seward

In this letter Seward understated his skating ability if Levett was correct. It is unfortunate that we have no such letter from him assessing his sprinting.

British pedestrians accepted Seward as one of their own, and his talent and showmanship made him a crowd favorite despite his being a foreigner. He drew large crowds to watch him run and perform his jumping feats. When he became ill with rheumatics, his friends held many benefits for him—more than for any other pedestrian of his era. These efforts show that he was well liked and appreciated by race fans, his fellow pedestrians, and the press.

His 1845–1846 American tour with William Jackson, "the American Deer," introduced world-class sprinting and hurdling to several American and Canadian cities. Jackson did the same for long-distance running. Their tour, covering most of the states of the union and the major cities in Canada, set a precedent for nationwide athletic tours.

Seward's major sprint races, especially those with William Robinson, Charles Westhall, and H. A. Reed in England and William Belden and George Morgan in America made him famous worldwide. His 100-yard performances helped establish the distance as one of the most glamorous in track and field. In contrast to his physical gifts, popularity, and success at running, Seward suffered misfortune and hardship in his personal life.

He never knew his father and spent most of his adult life far from New Haven and his family and boyhood friends. His bouts with rheumatism cut short his unmatched sprinting career and surely diminished his ability to earn a living after running. In 1849 his pioneering portable indoor arena, although not financially successful, was ahead of its time and was later used successfully by others. He tried a scaled-down version in 1857 that was more successful, touring most of Wales with walker William Gale.[6] Seward's indoor track and field efforts predate the official introduction of indoor track and field by ten years.[7]

Although the Hare and Hounds pub and his sports complex were initially successful, this venture also failed, not because of Seward's mismanagement but because of the poor economy. Seward suffered the loss of his first two wives, who both died in their early thirties, and several of his children did not live to be adults. After his running days, he could not earn enough at his trade of silver plating to keep his family out of poverty, which caused him to go into a self-imposed seclusion. Seward fathered nine children with his three wives. The last four were born when he was in his fifties and sixties, and he left them unprovided for when he died.

Setting records was not a priority for Seward. It was more important to keep the winning margins of his races small to promote future races. In addition, running records did not have the importance we give them today. He was talented enough to have set records at any distance up to 300 yards. When he challenged to break his own 100-, 120-, and 200-yard records and found no one willing to bet against him, he lost interest in setting records. This leaves us guessing about how fast he really was, and we will never know if he could run 100 yards in 9.0 seconds as *Bell's Life* claimed or, if he did, the conditions under which he was timed.

Seward wrote many letters to newspapers challenging other runners, and *Bell's Life* and the *Era* did a thorough job covering his races in England. The *Spirit of the Times* and other American newspapers covered most of his races in America. No diaries or personal correspondence have been found and there are no published interviews with him, leaving us with few details of his nonrunning activities.

After his death *Bell's Life* wrote, "Of all the champions we ever had he [Seward] was perhaps the most unassuming."[8] In contrast, when Seward was at the height of his career in 1847, the *Era*, far from portraying him as a modest man, wrote, "He is somewhat reserved, rather haughty, with unmistakable signs about him that he thought no small-beer of himself."[9] How do we reconcile these two assessments? It may be that both are correct. Most great sprinters have been supremely confident of their running abilities, and Seward was no different. He believed he could beat anyone on the planet in a sprint race, yet off the track, he was polite and humble.

When he was making a good income from running, he liked to live well. His business partner William Gale wrote in 1877 that "whenever money was to be had, [Seward] denied himself nothing that could be obtained that would add to his comfort."[10]

At sprinting he had no equal in his time. He was the first American athlete in any sport to be considered a world champion. In addition, he was the first American to set a world record in a running event. He went to England in 1843 because his sport of professional sprinting was not sufficiently developed in America for him to race regularly there. In England he was able to race more often, although not as often as he would have liked. Had he stayed in America it is unlikely he would have achieved as much as he did because he would have had little competition there. In addition, the timing of races in America was questionable until the 1880s. Had Seward set his 100-yard record in America, it is doubtful anyone would have believed it.

Comparing sprinters from different eras is difficult, but Seward was surely the fastest sprinter of his time. Considering that he usually ran just fast enough to win and on streets and primitive tracks, he might well have been the fastest American sprinter up to the time of Jesse Owens in the 1930s. All of which brings up the question of how he eluded the compilers of the *Dictionary of American Biography*, F. Boase's *Modern English Biography*, or any other listing of the greatest American athletes of the past.

One reason was that his sport of professional sprinting had such a reputation for dishonesty, a reputation that was partly justified and partly the result of the struggle between professionalism and amateurism to control track and field. His many years of running in England may also have played a part. Although he was respected and well treated there, British sports fans and sportswriters did not embrace him as they would have had he been born there. It is human nature to root for someone from your own country in a race with a foreigner, and many of Seward's races were billed as being England vs. America.

In a sense he was a man without a country. Because he did his best running in England, he was underappreciated in America. Although descriptions of many of his performances in England were reprinted in the *Spirit of the Times* in New York, it was difficult for Americans to follow his career from the month-old accounts they were receiving from 3,000 miles away. Other Americans who did their best running while living in England and whose fame suffered for it were Deerfoot in the 1860s and marathoner Buddy Edelen in the 1960s. These reasons help explain Seward's obscurity, but the removal of his 100-yard record from the books based on a bogus eyewitness report undoubtably played the greatest role.

Most of today's elite American sprinters are of West African descent. So far, it has been difficult to trace Seward's ancestors on his father's side. There is no record of his father Azariah's birth, so we do not know who George's grandparents on his father's side might have been. That makes it impossible to say whether he had ancestors from West Africa.

Seward set high standards indeed for all sprinters who followed. Paradoxically, his being so far ahead of his time may have contributed to his current obscurity. Perhaps if had not been so far ahead of the other sprinters, his 100-yard record would have remained on the books and he would be more appreciated today.

Besides being unequaled at sprinting, his greatest legacy was being an honorable man who performed with grace and style in a sport often deplored for fixed races and double-crosses. Since his time America has produced many great sprinters, but none stands out more than George Seward, "the American Wonder."

Notes

1. "Answers to Correspondents," *Bell's Life*, June 23, 1877.

2. "Seward and Westhall Race for £50," *Bell's Life*, May 9, 1847.

3. These figures were obtained from the list of Seward's races at the end of the book.

4. $500 in 1845 money would today be worth about $14,000 (www.measuringworth.com, accessed November 2007).

5. Quoted in "How to Train by John Levett Ex-Champion of England," *Illustrated Sporting News*, March 22, 1862, 15.

6. Autolycus, *Life and Performances of William Gale* (London: J. A. Brooks, 1877), 3.

7. The earliest account so far discovered of an indoor track meet is the "Grand Entertainment of Rustic Fetes" at Lambeth Baths, Westminster Road, London, on January 17, 1859. This was on the initiative of the well-known swimmer Frederick Edward Beckwith (1821–1898), who had taken over management of the baths. The building was too cold for swimming in the winter months, so other events were staged there by gaslight. The venue was also known as Beckwith's Gymnasium. *Bell's Life* reported that William Priestley was to jump 500 hurdles, 10 yards apart, in under 40 minutes, for a bet of £22, and also several prizes were to be given for running and jumping. From Peter Lovesey, "The Beginnings of Indoor Athletics," *Track Stats* 43, no. 3 (August 2005): 40–44. In the United States, an unofficial U.S. Championships was held at the Empire City Skating Rink in New York on November 11, 1868.

8. "The Late George Seward," *Bell's Life*, August 2, 1884.

9. The phrase "thought no small-beer of himself" is from *Era*, August 6, 1848.

10. Autolycus, *William Gale*, 3.

~

CHAPTER TEN

A Brief History
of Professional Sprinting

To put Seward's achievements in perspective, it is helpful to know something about the history of his profession and the men and women who took part in it. Although many professional sprinters were outstanding—a few even great—athletes, a history of professional sprinting has never been written. This chapter does not try to fill that void as the subject would easily fill a book. Instead, it covers the highlights of the sport and points out its greatest participants so the reader can more easily see how Seward compared with his fellow pros.

There are three reasons for the obscurity of professional sprinters. They had reputations for dishonesty that were often justified. The *Los Angeles Times* for December 1886 wrote: "It is a fact much to be regretted that professional sprinters, as a class, are by no means above reproach, for the annals of the cinder path teem with examples of their treachery, and to such an extent have races been thrown that at the present day no branch of sport is held in such low esteem by lovers of genuine sport as that of foot racing."

In the struggle between the amateur movement and pedestrianism, starting in the 1870s, most sportswriters took the side of the more socially acceptable amateurs. They either did not write about the professionals, or if they did, they stressed the seamier side of the sport. This slight of the pros is ironic because many of the top amateur sprinters of the nineteenth and twentieth centuries earned more than their professional counterparts. This corruption of amateurism was known as "shamateurism," which referred to the widespread practice of the best amateurs accepting under-the-table payments or excessive expense money.

Some have made light of the performances of both amateur and professional sprinters of old because their marks do not stand up to today's standards. One must remember however, that they did not have the advantages of weight training, drugs (legal and illegal), good coaching, starting blocks, composition tracks, and our knowledge of physiology and nutrition. In addition, the sprinters of the past had no incentive to run times that would compare well with those made by modern sprinters. They were just trying to beat the other runners of their time or the then-existing records.

Until accurate watches became available, it was difficult to say much about the outcome of any short-distance race other than who won and by what margin. Fortunately, time is an easy quantity to measure accurately, and it was possible to time races with reasonable accuracy early on. The pendulum spring that made accurate timing possible was invented in 1670, but these early timers were not portable enough to time races.[1]

By 1800 watches timing to ½ second were becoming widely available. In the 1820s, watches accurate to ¼ second were being made, and they were in widespread use by 1840. By the 1860s watches timing to ⅕ second with flyback mechanisms allowing them to be quickly reset were in general use in England and America. These ⅕-second watches became the standard for timing footraces for many years. It was not until the mid-1920s that they were replaced by models timing to 0.1 second. In the late 1800s and early 1900s, timers of professional sprint races also used watches accurate to ¹⁄₁₆ and ¹⁄₆₄ seconds as well as a curious watch called the "side-movement" watch. Using a side-movement watch, a timer could not tell the fractional part of a second but he "could tell at a glance if a runner was a foot worse than evens or a half yard better."[2]

Experiments with automatic timing began as early as 1874, but practical, fully automatic timers (FATs), accurate to 0.01 second, were not developed until 1932. FATs were initially bulky and expensive and were used only on special occasions like national championships and the Olympic Games. As their size and price dropped, their use gradually became more common, and by 1976 they were compulsory for setting sprint records.[3]

Even after reliable ¼-second timing became available, outstanding professional sprinters usually did not want their best performances known. If challengers learned of a pro's best times, it was easy for them to run time trials to decide whether it was wise to risk their money in a race. Professional sprinting was never about fast times and setting records. It was about athletes trying to earn money from the sport, and until the 1980s they did so by betting on themselves or running for prize money.

The old-time professional sprinters were professionals because they ran for money, but only a few (perhaps Seward, Frank Hewitt, Tom Malone, Harry Hutchens, and a few others at the peaks of their careers) were able to support themselves at it. Most followed a trade (such as shoemaking, mining, butchery, or farming) or kept a public house. Many took up the sport hoping for great wealth, but few ever found it.

One of the earliest sprint times we know of was 11½ seconds for 120 yards by a sprinter known as "the Lancashire Hero," who beat "the Italian Jew" for a stake of £1,050 in the reign of George II (1727–1760). The runners' real names were not revealed.[4]

Match racing, where two men ran for a stake, dates from the seventeenth century in England and was well developed by the early 1800s. A notable early time for 120 yards (which was often preferred to 100 yards) was 12½ seconds by Grinley (or Grindley), "the Boot Closer" (one who closed the uppers of boots), in beating Curley, "the Brighton Shepherd," by half a yard on the gravel path in Hyde Park, London, November 25, 1805. They met again on Hampton Court Green on August 25, 1806, when Grinley improved his time to 12 seconds and won by 2 yards.

The first dominant British sprinter was Harry Leach (1787–1849), who had fifty-six consecutive victories during 1813 to 1818, defeating all the picked men in England. He ran barefoot and bare-chested. Other fast sprinters of this era were Tom Wilson, who recorded 12 seconds for 125 yards on October 17, 1825; Sam Beddoe, 21 seconds for 210 yards on October 3, 1823; and William Jackson (no relation to Jackson "the American Deer"), who was credited with a hard-to-believe 19¾ seconds for 250 yards on June 6, 1826.[5]

James or "Jem" Wantling, the most famous sprinter of the early 1800s, was born about 1801 and was apprenticed to a potter in Derby. He was so muscular that he ran with his calves and thighs wrapped tightly with leather straps to prevent pulling a muscle. Despite this handicap, in 1824 he became the champion sprinter of England. Some of his times were recorded in newspaper reports, notably 200 yards in less than 21 seconds in a match with Sam Beddoe in 1823; 300 yards in 30½ seconds on April 12, 1824; and 400 yards in 47 seconds on August 28, 1823. Although not recorded in newspapers of the time, Wantling was also credited with 9 seconds for 100 yards and 19 seconds for 200 yards.

The latter two times as well as all others of this era have to be treated with much caution. The reporting is typically a sentence or two, which leaves us with no way of knowing if the timekeeping and course measurement were accurate. Nor do we know if the races were run on level ground without excessive tailwinds. The times were taken to the nearest half second or even the nearest second, so Wantling (and Leach) may have been doing around 9½ and 19½. If even some of these times are accurate, they argue for sprinting being of a high quality surprisingly early in the history of the sport. It is likely that many of these runners could do even time or better, as they did later in the century.

Wantling was a genuine national hero, and in 1822 two songs were composed in his honor. It is interesting that the songs praise Wantling for his honesty, a commodity sadly lacking among many professional sprinters even at this early date.

The Derby Hero.

Of all your modern Heroes
That rank so high in fame,
There's one that takes the lead of all,
Young Wantling is his name;
For when he takes the field
So nimbly he doth run,
His feet is at the destin'd mark
Ere the race is well begun!
Fol de rol, &c.
This youth's been lately tried
Against a man of great renown,
And to run the Stafford hero
He was back'd for fifty pounds;
O he is the bravest lad
That ever eyes did see,
For he won the race quite easy,
When the bets were five to three!
Fol de rol, &c.
Now ye men of sporting talent
I would have you all to know,
On the eighteenth day of March
You've a chance to see him go,
For this Hero he is match'd to run
Three hundred yards we're told,
Against the Stafford Bragger
For one hundred guineas in gold!
Fol de rol, &c.
Then keep your spirits up, my lads,
For he will show the way,

He is as swift as Mercury,
And is sure to win the day;
For Wantling's of such good mettle,
And his honour is as good,
He is sure not to deceive you,
As some other Runners would.
Fol de rol, &c.
Of all the Runners now in vogue
Young Wantling takes the lead;
You would think him jealous of the wind
When you view him in his speed:
He will make that Braggadocia
Afraid to show his face,
To be beat by an apprentice boy—
It will be such disgrace.
Fol de rol, &c.[6]

Before about 1850, sprinters usually ran on level stretches of turnpike roads. For important matches, courses were often roped and staked to prevent crowd encroachment and the runners' interfering with each other. The runners sometimes ran barefoot but more commonly ran in a pair of short pants and light "half-boots." The earliest references found to spiked running shoes were those worn by William Jackson and George Seward in 1845.[7]

The most common method of starting sprint races was by mutual consent, but by 1847 the *Era* was insisting a pistol be used.

Men in sprint races ought not to be allowed to start themselves, for the time spent in useless maneuvering is immense. Men will not go off until they fancy they have got the pull, and we could recite many instances wherein an hour or more has been spent in dodging for an advantageous start. . . . This tedious mode of getting away ought, in our opinion, to be abolished. It can easily be done, for men who wish to contend honorably for victory, will at once consent to go off by the report of a pistol, or the lowering of a flag.[8]

Many of the pros preferred the mutual-consent start because, if they were skilled at it, they could use it to their advantage against less-experienced runners. By 1860 it had, in most places, given way to the starter's pistol.

The next notable pro sprinter after Wantling was George Eastham, "the Flying Clogger of Preston," who had some fast times over 220 yards: 21½ seconds on the Blackburn Road on March 17, 1845; 22 seconds at Manchester in 1845; and 22½ seconds at Manchester on October 28, 1845. Although they were active at the same time, Eastham and Seward never faced each other. In November 1846 Seward challenged Eastham, offering a 3-yard start at any distance up to 300 yards, but Eastham declined the challenge. Other outstanding sprinters of the time were Charles Westhall, Henry Allen Reed, John Howard, and James Hancock, who were described earlier.

Sheffield, famous for its iron and steel production, became the center of professional sprinting in England in the late 1850s, and the first major handicap was run there in 1857. Queen's, Bell Inn, and Hyde Park grounds all hosted handicaps and offered large monetary prizes. Seven to nine Sheffield handicaps were held each year, and first-place prizes of £100 were offered. These events were well conducted, and the promoters managed to keep them free of fixed races for more than forty years.

Although later writers have questioned professional sprint records, at least at the major handicaps timing was accurate, as pointed out by David A. Jamieson, author of *Powderhall and Pedestrianism*.

> There may be some skeptics to whom all these records may appear of doubtful accuracy. But watch-holders in these times were scrupulously exact in their calculations—fortunes depended on their accuracy and in their estimate of their nominees at Sheffield, and they left nothing to chance or speculative advantage as far as the runner was concerned. These old-time 'gaffers' were hard holders and times had to be done to them under various circumstances before they were finally satisfied.[9]

At Sheffield, runners were given starts or handicaps. Handicaps enabled competitors of varying abilities to compete on an equal footing and provided closer races with more betting interest. Each runner's handicap was determined by the handicapper of the meeting, who based it on the runner's past performances and his assessment of each runner's ability.

Sometimes the fastest runner received no handicap and started off "scratch" and ran the full race distance. At Sheffield, however, the handicapper based his assessments on a fixed standard, not on the fastest runner entered. He gave each runner a start based on the number of yards he was estimated to be slower than this standard. This method resulted in the fastest runner, called the "backmarker," usually not starting from scratch but some yards ahead of it and running an odd distance.[10]

Basing handicaps on a fixed standard saved a handicapper time because he did not have to readjust the starts for each race according to the merit of the man at "scratch." The big disadvantage was that times were nearly irrelevant because sprinters almost never started from scratch or ran the full distance. Instead of times for a race, fans at Sheffield and Powderhall spoke of a runner's distance inside or outside even time.

The winner of the Queen's Ground Sheffield Handicap in 1865 was Frank "Scurry" Hewitt. Born in Limerick, Ireland, on May 8, 1845, Hewitt developed into a great all-around professional runner while running in Ireland and England. He moved to Australia in 1869 and a year later ran a 9¾-second 100-yard race at the Melbourne Cricket Ground. His other outstanding performances were 50 yards in 5¾ seconds (England), 300 yards in 30½ seconds at Melbourne, 440 yards in 49 seconds (England), 880 yards in 1 min. 53½ sec. (best time on record, New Zealand), and one mile in 4 min. 20 sec. (England). While racing in England he had the most opposition from George Mole, Johnny Clowry, and Dick Buttery (who ran 440 yards in 48¼ seconds).[11]

Powderhall Stadium in Edinburgh, Scotland, was named for the nearby gunpowder factory. Professional races were run there for more than 120 years, starting in 1870 and ending in the 1990s.[12] From the outset, the Powderhall organizers tried to keep their races scrupulously honest, even once having a man jailed for deception. One of the greatest stars in the early years at Powderhall was Dan Wight of Jedburgh. In 1877 he was the backmarker in the New Year's 150-yard handicap and tied for first place with F. Kilgour, who had a 13½-yard start. Wight's time was a remarkable 14¼ seconds or 7½ yards inside even time. In his career, Wight won more than one hundred races at distances from 100 to 880 yards.

In the late 1870s Harry Hutchens (figure 10.1), whose real name was Henry Hutchins, became professional sprinting's biggest star and was considered by many to be the greatest professional sprinter they ever saw run. On March 5, 1878, the twenty-year-old Hutchens entered his first Sheffield Handicap. Starting 5¼ yards ahead of the backmarker and champion, George Wallace, a 6-foot-2-inch coal miner. Hutchens won the 130-yard race by a foot. The following year when he returned to Sheffield the handicapper had reduced his start to 1 yard over Wallace. Before he had gone 70 yards Hutchens had passed all the runners, including Wallace, and won the race "in fine style" by 2 yards. He offered to run Wallace or any other man in the world for £500 but, like many great professional sprinters, found no takers.

In 1882, at the Hyde Park Sheffield handicap, Hutchens ran what he considered his greatest race. Running as the backmarker and covering 131½ yards, he showed the speed that would become his trademark. In a desperate finish, he lost by 6 inches to two runners who started 6¾ and 3½ yards ahead of him. Although he lost, Hutchens finished in 12 1/5 seconds, 7¼ yards inside even time.[13]

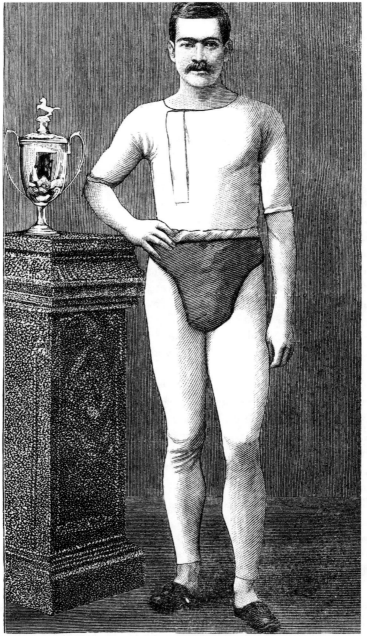

HARRY HUTCHENS, Champion Sprinter of the World.—Photo by Wood.

Figure 10.1. Harry Hutchens at age twenty-four. He was the greatest sprinter of the second half of the nineteenth century. From the *Illustrated Sporting and Dramatic Journal*, New York, November 22, 1884.

Hutchens's other legendary feat took place at the January 2, 1884, "New Year's Handicap" at Powderhall. Despite the cold weather and soft, sloppy track from a snowfall the previous night, Hutchens easily won his heat of the 300-yard race in a record 30 ⅔ seconds. Starting the final from scratch with his nearest opponent 18 yards ahead of him, he swept around the first curve well on the outside. With a "beautiful raking stride," he ran through the field "like a deer through a frightened flock of sheep."[14] He caught the last runner with 12 yards to go, dropped his arms, and smiled as he won the race in 30.0 seconds. This record lasted well into the twentieth century.

Like Seward before him, Hutchens suffered from bouts of rheumatism. In late 1886 he traveled to Australia, where he hoped a change in the climate would ease his aching joints. Since its settlement, Australia had enjoyed a rich tradition of professional running. Centered in Victoria, professional running was at its peak from 1870 to 1912. Many pros from all over the world made the long trip to Australia to try their hand in match races and the "Gifts." The "Gifts" were patterned after the Sheffield Handicaps and named for the tradition of wealthy gold-mine owners giving a gold nugget for the winner's prize. The famous Stawell Gift, first run in 1878, lives on as one of the two nineteenth-century professional sprint races still in existence. In 1887 all the world's top professional runners went to Australia to test themselves and try to earn some money. These included Hutchens and mile champion Walter George from England and half-mile champion Lon Myers from America.

In January 1887 Hutchens ran a series of races with Charlie Samuels, a Queensland Aborigine known as "the Prince of Black Pedestrians." Samuels had distinguished himself by winning a 136-yard Botany handicap in 13½ seconds. The first two races went to Samuels, but Hutchens later admitted that in these races, he was running "under orders" to lose to build interest for a betting "coup" in a later race. In the 150-yard last race of the series, with large sums of money riding on the outcome, Hutchens ran 14½ seconds and easily defeated Samuels.

Hutchens then ran a series of races with "Peerless" Tom Malone, an outstanding Irish runner. Thomas Michael Malone was a fine all-around athlete who competed as both an amateur and professional in Ireland and England. The allure of big prize money in Australia tempted him to emigrate, and he arrived there in November 1882. In 1884 Malone was at his peak, running 9⅘ for 100 yards, 21½ for 220 yards, 47⅗ for 440 yards, and 1:53½ for 880. In November 1886 he injured his hamstring in a race with William Clarke, and the injury had not healed when he raced Hutchens in January 1887. With Malone injured, Hutchens won the first two races easily and there was no need for a third. Before leaving for home Hutchens received a special award for running 50 yards with a running or "flying" start in 4½ seconds.

When Hutchens returned to England in the summer of 1887, he found a rival waiting to challenge him for the title of "Champion" sprinter of England. The new sprint sensation was twenty-six-year-old Harry Gent, a Darlington cabbie. On May 31, 1887, Gent had won the Sheffield Handicap by running 122 yards in 11⅗ seconds. Promoters for the two men arranged a 120-yard race at Lillie Bridge for the "Championship of the World" and £200. On September 19, 1887, 15,500 fans paid a shilling each to watch the two men race.

Race fans were never sure if Hutchens was going to give his best effort or was "running under orders" (ordered to lose by his backers). There are varying accounts of the events leading up to this infamous race. The most likely one is as follows: A rumor had been circulating that he was "hog fat" and not fit to run a good race. Hutchens did nothing to dispel the rumor, and his erratic training led many to believe he planned to lose.

Gent's backers bet heavily on their man, and Hutchens and his backers snapped up the bets. When Hutchens appeared, fit and ready to run the race of his life, Gent's backers panicked. To avoid losing their money, they hurriedly removed Gent from the ground by an underground passage. Hutchens's backers, sensing trouble, also removed him from the ground.

When the crowd discovered there would be no race, they demanded their admission money back, but the money taker had already left with the gate receipts. The enraged crowd decided to get their shilling's worth of entertainment by destroying the stadium. They demolished two grandstands and used the debris to make six bonfires. Then they set fire to the wooden railings along the railroad before looting nearby liquor stores. The mob pelted the firemen called to the scene with empty bottles, and to make matters worse, low water pressure made fighting the fire almost impossible. Next they destroyed most of the buildings on the grounds, and a stationmaster with a weak heart died of a heart attack from the excitement. The riot and burning of the stadium ended professional sprinting in London.

Hutchens, like most nineteenth-century professionals, used the upright start known as the "dab" or "Sheffield." To the end of his days he insisted it was faster than the crouch start that came into use near the end of his career in about 1890.[15]

The fastest runner at Sheffield was given the honor of being the backmarker (given the greatest handicap). Hutchens was the backmarker in Sheffield handicaps fifty-one times during 1879 to 1888. The next best, George Mole, "the Walsall Flyer," born June 6, 1842, was backmarker forty-four times during 1862 to 1869, and George Wallace was backmarker twenty-seven times during 1874 to 1879. Hutchens had three victories at Sheffield, winning from the back mark once. Mole won twice, Wallace never.

Like so many of the pros, after his running days Hutchens (figure 10.2) fell into poverty and obscurity. He died in 1939, fifty-five years to the day after he ran 300 yards in 30 seconds.

Alfred R. Downer, born in Jamaica in 1873, was the best of the nineteenth-century British sprinters after Hutchens. Downer moved to Edinburgh with his mother in 1880. As an amateur, he had many duels with Charlie Bradley, the champion amateur sprinter of England in the mid-1890s. In 1896 Britain's Amateur Athletic Association charged Downer with taking under-the-table payments from meet promoters and declared him a professional. Undaunted, he continued running as a professional and was at his peak in 1898. He later wrote *Running Recollections and How to Train*

Figure 10.2. As he grew older, Harry Hutchens struggled to make a living and ran wherever he could find a payday. From the author's collection, 1896.

(1902), a significant book that gives an insider account of professional sprinting of his time and describes his best performance, a 130-yard handicap he ran in 1898 at Powderhall. He conceded 8½ yards to George Duncan in a heat of the world-famous New Year's Handicap and lost by 1½ yards. In losing, he finished 4½ yards inside even time, a brilliant performance. Downer, who lived life to the fullest, died at age thirty-nine.

Efforts to trace sprinting in America before the late 1830s have proven unsuccessful. There were undoubtedly fast American sprinters in the early 1800s and perhaps earlier, but American newspaper coverage of sports was almost nonexistent in those days and accounts of footraces are fragmentary at best before about 1835. Up to that time there was no national-level sprinting in America.

The first world-class American sprinter after Seward was John Westley Cozad from Iowa. On November 23, 1868, at the Fashion Course on Long Island, Cozad, "the California Plowboy," ran a 125-yard race against Edward Depew Davis, "the Flying Boy of Kingston," from Kingston, New York. Cozad broke the handkerchief marking the finish 8 feet ahead in 12½ seconds. Two weeks later, on the same course, Cozad easily defeated "Poke" Perry from Trenton, New Jersey, at 70 yards in 7¼ seconds.

Now the champion sprinter of America, Cozad (figure 10.3) challenged all comers, but as Seward had found almost thirty years earlier, few sprinters were willing to take on the champion, and Cozad had to be content with exhibitions and offering starts to rivals. He raced for several years with many of his races "not on the square." In Salida, Colorado, on April 24, 1882, he was found in his room dying, robbed of his money and watch. Although poisoning was suspected, a coroner's jury found no satisfactory explanation for his death.[16]

In the 1880s American professional sprinting came to worldwide prominence. As in England, the sport had no governing body and crooked races were common. None of the American sprinters of this era raced Hutchens, the consensus world's fastest sprinter, so it is difficult to say how they compared with the best in the world.

George H. Smith of Pittsburgh was the first of a series of outstanding American professionals who ran in the 1880s. He was also one of the few American professionals of the time who would have nothing to do with crooked races. Smith traveled to England in 1881 and won the Sheffield Whitsuntide 208-yard handicap, beating sixty-two competitors. He was credited with running 125 yards in 12¼ seconds in December 1886 in Pittsburgh.

Harry M. Johnson was born in London on March 23, 1865, and came to New York as a child. At 6 feet ½ inch and weighing 186 pounds, he was big

THE FOOT-RACE ON "FASHION COURSE," LONG ISLAND, November 23, 1868.

Figure 10.3.   John Westley Cozad was the next superior American sprinter after Seward. From *Harper's Weekly*, December 12, 1868.

and strong, with a physique more akin to a modern-day sprinter than one from the nineteenth century. He ran in the American amateur 100-yard championship in 1881 and turned pro in 1882. After several races in Canada, he started training under George W. Gardner of Allentown, New York. In just six weeks of Gardner's coaching, Johnson improved his 100-yard time from 10¾ seconds to 9⅗ seconds, a time he considered himself consistently able to run when he was in top condition.[17]

Johnson entered the famous 120-yard Shrovetide Handicap in Sheffield, England, on March 8, 1886. The best sprinter in England, Harry Hutchens was the backmarker but was so severely handicapped he was beaten out in his heat. In the second round there were four starters separated by strings 2 feet high. Johnson was in lane one, Isaacs in two, W. Lockwood in three, and South in four. Johnson gave Isaacs 4½ yards, Lockwood 3¼, and South 1¼.

Isaacs and South were from the same "school" and teamed up to try to ensure that South would win. When Johnson caught Isaacs at 50 yards, Isaacs elbowed him, causing the American to lose 2 yards. Johnson got going again and just managed catch South in his last stride and win by inches. Isaacs's foul did not go unnoticed, and he was banned from all future handicaps at Sheffield.

In the final there were two runners starting ahead of Johnson, George Edge by 3½ yards and Walter Hudson by 3¼ yards. They all broke at the snap of the starter's pistol, but the pistol failed to fire. Although the starter shouted, "Come back," all three ran to the finish with Johnson winning by a yard. Officials declared the race invalid and ruled that it be rerun after a ten-minute rest. Johnson won the rerun, finishing a yard ahead of Edge.

In Cleveland, Ohio, on July 31, 1886, at the summer meeting of the Cleveland Athletic Club, Johnson ran down all his competitors and finished 6 yards ahead of the nearest in 9⅘ seconds. Five watches were held on him and the track, when remeasured, was found to be 2 inches more than 100 yards. Three of the watches caught him in 9⅗ seconds and two in 9⅘ seconds, which was the allowed time. The watches had been regulated and run together for three days before the race to ensure accuracy. When Seward's 100-yard time was removed from the record books in 1888, Johnson's performance made him the new professional 100-yard record holder.

Johnson (figure 10.4) was later credited with 50 yards in 5⅖ seconds and 130 yards in 12½ seconds. He also held several jumping records and was adept at putting the shot. In July 1890, he traveled to Grass Valley, California, to run a 100-yard race. There he came down with typhoid fever and died a few days later. He was only twenty-six years old and probably still had his best years ahead of him.

Mike K. Kittleman of Harper, Kansas, was another "fast man" of this era. On August 18, 1884, he defeated H. M. Johnson in a 125-yard open race in Pittsburgh, in 12¼ seconds for each of two heats. Kittleman won several races in England disguised as an amateur, a criminal offense that would have cost him six months of hard labor had he been caught.

Harry Bethune (figure 10.5) from Cornwall, Ontario, Canada, was a speedy but crooked runner. He began his professional career in 1886, plying his trade throughout the United States and Canada. Bethune probably made more money than any sprinter until modern times ($600,000, according to some accounts) but he was often on the run from the law and the people he swindled.[18] The *Ohio Democrat* for March 22, 1888, gives an account of one of his many misadventures.

HARRY M. JOHNSON, American Sprinter.—Photo by Wood.

Figure 10.4.   H. M. Johnson, who had a physique like many modern sprinters, died in his midtwenties. From the *Illustrated Sporting and Dramatic Journal*, New York, November 22, 1884.

Harry Bethune, who at one time posed in New Philadelphia as a sprinter and general masher, is in trouble again. A woman named Ida Baird has caused his arrest at San Francisco, California, on a charge of embezzlement. She claims Bethune embezzled $800 of her money. She tells a curious story of her relations with the sprinter which began in Montreal, where she alleges Bethune married her. He left her in Kansas City when he went on to the coast to arrange a big foot race. He took her baggage with him, and, hearing he was lavishing her goods on other women, she went west. She found another woman wearing her best bonnet, and her husband making violent love to another woman called the Idaho Cattle Queen. She [Baird] wanted money to return East, but Bethune refused, so she was determined to cause his arrest.

More important than her story are the letters from Bethune which she possesses and which clearly prove his swindles in Montreal and other places. They give the details of the throwing of the race in Montreal in which Bethune and his pals divided $15,000. Bethune was compelled to fly from Montreal to save his life. This exposure of his record will end his sporting career on the coast. He would probably have cleaned up many thousands on the race which was to come off next month.

There are many stories of professional sprinters of the late 1880s who traveled from town to town in the American West looking for prey. Using aliases, they challenged the best local runner to a race, and often gave starts of as much as 5 yards in a 100-yard race. The townspeople would usually back their local "fast man" and would almost always lose their money. British athletics historian Tom McNab vividly described these men in his novel *The Fast Men* (1986).

Although Bethune's conduct may have left something to be desired, he was one of the fastest sprinters of the nineteenth century. At Plattsburg, New York, on September 1, 1887, he tied George Seward's 200-yard record with 19½ seconds. He was also credited with running 100 yards in 9⅘ seconds at the "Olympic Games," of the Olympic Club of San Francisco on February 23, 1888. Bethune was so much faster than most runners of his day that he would often finish his races running backward, laughing at his opponents.

In 1890, he inherited a large sum of money from an uncle in Scotland and did little running after that. Although he made a fortune from running, he was a fast spender as well as a fast runner and wound up broke. He died of tuberculosis in 1909 in Cleveland, Ohio, and was buried in an unmarked pauper's grave in Potter's Field cemetery.

Seven Americans won Sheffield Handicaps. George Smith won the Whitsuntide in 1881. H. M. Johnson won the Shrovetide in 1886. Stephen J. Farrell won in July 1889 and again in 1894. Jim Collins won the Shrovetide in

Figure 10.5.   Harry Bethune, known for his outrageous behavior, was one of the fastest American pros of the late 1800s. From the *National Police Gazette*, January 29, 1887.

1890. Mike Donlan won the Bank Holiday in 1890. Edward S. "Piper" Donovan won the Shrovetide in 1893 running as "J. Early of Leeds." On February 18, 1899, Tom Keane won at Bill End Grounds—the last Sheffield Handicap ever held and his third Sheffield victory in a space of nine months.[19]

Professional sprint handicaps in the United States did not survive into the twentieth century, but there were some outstanding American pro sprinters near the turn of the century who raced in England, Australia, and South Africa. They included W. D. Walker, Charlie Holway, and Nate Cartmell. The best American pro of this era was most likely Tom Keane, known as "the Red Demon" for his shock of flaming red hair. Keane was born in Rochdale, England, in 1872 and emigrated to America as a child. He began sprinting in Boston in 1889 and five years later won the national Amateur Athletic Union (AAU) quarter-mile championship. Then he turned pro and competed in more than 3,000 races before retiring in 1906.

Keane went to Britain in 1895 and competed in twenty-six races in twenty-six days in a tour of the British Isles. He used the crouch start that had become popular in America but was new abroad. At one race, the Scottish starter, who used a double-barreled shotgun to start the race, glanced suspiciously at the crouching Keane, who stood out because all the other runners were starting upright. The starter walked over to Keane and tapped him on the shoulder and asked: "What are you doing, man?"

"Waiting for you to fire that cannon of yours," Keane answered.

"That's no way to run," remarked the starter. "Get up on your feet and run like a man."[20]

Besides his unprecedented three victories and two second-place finishes at Sheffield, Keane was a popular performer at Powderhall, and his appearances in the Scottish Highland Games provided the main attraction for several years. After his running days Keane (figure 10.6) coached the Syracuse University track team from 1906 to 1945 and served as an Olympic track coach for the United States from 1920 to 1936. His best sprint performances were 120 yards in 11⅖ seconds at Ball Inn Grounds, Sheffield, on September 5, 1898, and 220 yards in 21⅗ seconds in Scotland on February 4, 1905.

After their running careers, professional sprinters of this era were in big demand as coaches for major American universities and contributed to American dominance in track during the early 1900s. Besides Keane, other ex-pros who became coaches were Keene Fitzpatrick, who coached at Princeton, "Pooch" Donovan at Harvard, Johnny Mack at Yale, and Mike Murphy at Yale and Penn. In 1905 the University of Pennsylvania offered Murphy, considered the best American coach of any sport in that era, $5,000 a year

Figure 10.6. After his running days, Tom Keane had a long career as a college and Olympic team coach. From *Running Recollections and How to Train* by A. R. Downer (1902).

and free housing to lure him away from Yale. The amount was huge compensation for a coach at the time.[21]

Many professional sprinters did their best to fool handicappers and bookmakers. If a runner could get to the finals of a handicap without revealing his true form, he received a generous start. His backers could then place bets at high odds and possibly make a "killing." It was a battle of wits between the runners and the handicappers, who took pride in being able to spot runners trying to improve their handicaps by some devious means. To fatten their handicaps, some sprinters wore lead insoles in their shoes in the races used to decide their handicaps; others drank large quantities of beer or ran to exhaustion the day before.

Several amateur sprinters were forced into the professional ranks when they ran afoul of the amateur rules. Besides Downer in England, American Arthur Duffey, the first amateur to run 100 yards in 9⅗ seconds, had a brief pro career starting in 1905. Duffey became a pro after being too open about how amateur sprinting at the top levels worked. He wrote an article for Bernarr MacFadden's *Physical Culture Magazine* about the corrupt practice where star amateur athletes took excessive expense money. Instead of praising Duffey for uncovering this dark side of amateurism, an enraged James E. Sullivan, secretary of the AAU, tried to have Duffey arrested. He was unsuccessful, but did manage to have him banished from the amateur ranks and have all of his world records erased.[22]

In the fifteen years before World War I, professional sprinting was at its peak in Australia. Arthur Postle and Jack Donaldson were two sprinters from that country who were unsurpassed by either amateurs or professionals of their time. Postle, known as "the Crimson Flash" because of his red running singlet, turned pro in 1902 and was almost unbeatable up to 80 yards. In 1906, before a crowd of 20,000 at the Kalgoorlie gold fields in Australia, he beat Irishman Beauchamp Day at 75 yards in a record 7⅕ seconds. At Durban, on February 15, 1908, Postle set a professional record for 50 yards of 5⅕ seconds and in March of that year added another record by running 60 yards in 6¹⁄₁₀ seconds. Postle also ran 80 yards in 7⅘ seconds three times in his career. His biggest asset was a quick start (figure 10.7). In his heyday he claimed he never met a sprinter to whom he could not give 2 yards and beat in a 40-yard race.

Jack Donaldson, "the Blue Streak," raced in all blue and is still considered Australia's greatest sprinter. He was born in Raywood, Victoria, on March 16, 1886, and had a remarkable career racing in Australia, New Zealand, South Africa, England, and Scotland.

Figure 10.7. Arthur Postle was one of the early masters of the crouch start. From the author's collection.

Postle challenged Donaldson and American pro champion C. E. "Bullet" Holway to race for the 100-yard pro championship of the world at Johannesburg, South Africa, on February 12, 1910. Postle, as expected, was quickest away and was out in front at 20 yards. At 50 yards his lead had grown to 3 yards and at 80 he was still in front, but "the Blue Streak" was closing fast. With 15 yards to go, Donaldson caught and passed Postle and won by 2½ yards. Donaldson's astounding time of 9⅗ seconds broke the professional record of 9⅘ seconds held jointly by Johnson and Bethune.[23] Officials in the American AAU made light of it, claiming the course was downhill, although this claim was not borne out by the South African newspapers of the time.

Holway and Donaldson met again at the Sydney Sports Ground on September 23, 1911, for a 130-yard race. The match created much excitement, and an enormous crowd came to watch. Both men got off to perfect starts. At 80 yards Donaldson was 2 yards in front of the American, which he increased to 5 yards when he breasted the tape. The three timekeepers all caught Donaldson in 12 seconds flat—an astonishing 10 yards inside even time. Officials remeasured the track and found it to be long by 4 inches. Of course no wind measurements were taken in 1911 and it was admitted there was a breeze. How much it contributed to the time we will never know. Journalists in Britain and America refused to believe the fast time.

Donaldson went to Britain, where sports journalists were convinced he would never be able to match the "ludicrous" times he had run in Australia and South Africa. On October 10, 1912, at Taff Vale Park in Pontypridd, Wales, he raced South African Reggie Walker, the 1908 Olympic 100-meter champion, for the world professional 130-yard championship. Donaldson won by 5 yards in 12³⁄₁₆ seconds. With such a huge winning margin, he had time to turn and watch Walker finish. The time was 8 yards inside evens, and showed the fans sprinting of a quality not seen since the glory days of Harry Hutchens in the old Sheffield Handicaps.

The remarkable run convinced the British press that Donaldson was for real. His greatest critic, W. L. Sinclair of the *Sporting Chronicle*, wrote, "Donaldson in his earlier career had put up some records, which I would not accept. But after seeing the Australian defeat Walker on Saturday, I must admit today the greatest sprint runner in the world is with us. I refer to Jack Donaldson."[24]

As a further test, the *Chronicle* offered £100 to anyone who could break Harry Hutchens's hallowed record of 300 yards in 30 seconds. Donaldson made the attempt on August 4, 1913, at a Sports Carnival in Weaste, Manchester. "The Blue Streak" started from scratch, giving Tom Brandon of Edinburgh a 28-yard start and allowing two other runners starts of 23 and 19 yards. Brandon won, beating Donaldson by a distance officially reported as 2 yards, but some observers thought it was more like 3 to 5 yards.

Officials timed Donaldson with "Williams" dog-racing watches that recorded to ¹⁄₆₄ second. Two timers had him inside 30 seconds, but the third recorded 30³⁄₆₄. An average of the three times was calculated, and Donaldson was credited with 29⁶¹⁄₆₄ seconds, breaking Hutchens's record by a minuscule ³⁄₆₄ of a second. Many veteran followers of professional sprinting thought the performance was inferior to Hutchens's feat of nearly thirty years earlier. Hutchens had a clear-cut win and had been timed with a watch timing to ¹⁄₅ second. The *Sporting Chronicle*, however, was satisfied with the official time and paid Donaldson the £100 prize money.

At 5 feet 8 inches tall and weighing 146 pounds, Donaldson (figure 10.8) was not impressive physically. Yet he had a deep chest and long legs and ran with a stride of almost 9 feet. He raced Postle twenty-one times and won on fifteen occasions. Postle was Donaldson's equal over the shorter distances, but in their matches at 100 yards and longer, Donaldson almost always won. Because he was a pro, the American press never gave him his due. His time of 9%16 seconds for 100 yards, although aided by being run at altitude, was not beaten until Mel Patton ran 9.3 seconds in 1948.[25] In the 1920s, Charley Paddock tried many times to break Donaldson's 130-yard record of 12 seconds, but the best he could manage was 12⅖ at Pasadena, California, on June 18, 1920. Paddock gave up in disgust, saying 130 yards was an "unorthodox" distance.[26]

When war broke out in 1914, Donaldson enlisted in the British army. He was discharged in 1919 and, his running days over, moved to New York City, where he worked quietly, almost obscurely, in a big department store. In 1932 he ran a short distance to catch a streetcar. When he caught it and sat down, nearby passengers noticed that the once-mighty "Blue Streak's" lips were blue and his face white. A year later there was a brief notice in one of the New York newspapers that Jack Donaldson, employee at a local department store and a former professional runner, had died at age forty-seven. Although his death went nearly unnoticed in the United States, Australia was more kind to his memory. Stawell erected a fountainlike memorial at the approach to the grandstand in Central Park in honor of the great sprinter.

Professional sprinting in London ended when rioters destroyed the Lillie Bridge grounds in 1887 and the once-great Sheffield Handicaps ended in 1899 because the public no longer had confidence the races were being conducted honestly. As the nineteenth century ended, amateurism was the clear winner in the struggle for control of track and field. With a few exceptions, such as pros Postle, Donaldson, and Reggie Walker and amateurs Harold Abrahams and Percy Williams, American amateurs came to dominate sprinting in the early 1900s. Aided by former professional sprinters as coaches, American colleges and universities began turning out large numbers of world-class sprinters. Men such as Bernie Wefers, Arthur Duffey, and Charley Paddock and later the great black sprinters Eddie Tolan, Ralph Metcalfe, and Jesse Owens were faster than any of the pros running at the time. Professional sprinting lived on in Scotland, South Africa, and Australia, but none of the pros after Donaldson were able to run faster than the best amateurs.

American Eddie Tolan, winner of the 100 and 200 meters in the 1932 Olympics, was unable to find suitable employment after winning his two gold medals. In the midst of the Depression he went to Australia in 1934 to try to become the first man to win both the amateur and professional sprint

JACK DONALDSON, *Champion Sprinter of the World*

Figure 10.8. Jack Donaldson was Australia's greatest sprinter. From the program for "The Pedestrian Carnival" held at Salford Football Club, Weaste, Manchester, August 4, 1913.

championships of the world. With his good humor and wit, he proved to be an outstanding entertainer as well as runner and a crowd favorite. At the World Professional Sprint Championships, held in March 1935 in Melbourne, he won the 75-yard race in 7.5 seconds and the 100 yards in 9.75 seconds. Austin Robertson from Australia won the 130 yards in 12.38 seconds, but Tolan came back to win the last event, the 220 yards, in 21.5 seconds. Tolan's three victories gave him the professional sprint championship of the world but did not make him a wealthy man.[27]

Jesse Owens, America's greatest track and field star of the twentieth century, was forced into the pro ranks when he refused to continue an AAU tour shortly after the 1936 Olympics. Owens had trouble finding anyone to compete with as a professional. He sometimes ran against the women's 1936 Olympic champion Helen Stephens, who had also been banished to the pro ranks. Her offense was playing on a women's professional basketball team.[28]

Like Seward had done when he could find no human opponent, Owens sometimes competed against horses. He used a trick that Seward never thought of—he brought his own extra-loud starting pistol to these races that would usually spook the horse. In 1936 the Victoria Athletic League (VAL) in Australia invited Owens to compete there as a pro. Owens wanted to go but his manager, not satisfied with the small amount of money to be made, refused the offer.[29]

Australia's Stawell Gift, held in all but two years since 1878, developed into one of the world's most famous footraces. The "Gift" is still held every Easter in Stawell—a town of about 7,000 located three hours west of Melbourne. Today, the race attracts the cream of local and international athletes who compete for large prizes. The main sprint race is run over the Sheffield distance of 130 yards, which is considered a true test for professional sprinters. In the mid-1970s the distance was increased to 120 meters (131.2 yards). The participants in the Gift revere Stawell in an almost spiritual way. Central Park, where the Gift is run, has a cinder running track containing the spread ashes of many deceased runners.[30]

Jean-Louis Ravelomanantsoa from Madagascar is the fastest athlete to have won the Gift and the only athlete to win it from scratch—in 1975 he ran the race in 12 seconds from scratch. The fastest time recorded by a winner is 11.6 seconds, by W. I. Howard (off 5¾ yards in 1967) and I. A. Miller (off 9¾ yards in 1968).

The Stawell Gift is run on a grass track and the athletes run in lanes separated by ropes, much as Seward and his contemporaries did in the mid-nineteenth century. Stawell's status as the richest professional footrace has been superseded in recent years by the Botany Bay Gift Carnival that in 2000 gave total prize money (Australian dollars) of $120,000 with $70,000 for its main race ($50,000 first place). In 2000 Stawell gave $90,000 total prize money with the famous Gift being worth $54,000 ($32,000 first place).

Professional sprinting at Powderhall on New Year's Day continued into the 1990s, and the quality of running there was on a par with Stawell until the 1970s. The most famous winner at Powderhall was Willie McFarlane of Glasgow in the 1930s. He won the event in 1933 and a year later won again, this time from scratch—a feat never repeated. During the late 1940s, Albert Spence from Blyth dominated, running in five finals and winning in 1947. The star performers of the 1950s were Australia's Eric Cumming and Barnie Ewell of the United States. Ewell had finished second in the 1948 Olympic 100 meters and ran at both Stawell and Powderhall and was a great crowd pleaser. The 1960s and 1970s produced many top-flight sprinters, but Ricky Dunbar of Edinburgh, winner in 1963, and George McNeill of Tranent, winner in 1970 (11.61 seconds off 5.5 yards) and still the 120-yard record holder, stood out. In 1981, at age thirty-four, McNeill also won the Stawell Gift, becoming the only person to win at both places.

In recent years there were two notable performances when Kipper Bell and Bill Snoddy of the United States won in 1984 and 1987. But for the U.S. boycott in 1980, Snoddy would have represented the United States at the Moscow Olympics. Most recently, 1995 winner Doug Walker went on to become the European 200-meter champion. In December 1999, the 131st New Year Sprint was moved to Musselburgh Racecourse six miles east of Edinburgh. In 2005 the 110-meter New Year Sprint had a £4000 first prize.[31]

Sprinting by women for prizes or money dates from the "smock races" that were popular in the eighteenth century and before.[32] A few women ran professionally in the nineteenth century, but most of these "pedestriennes" concentrated on walking or running long distances. It was not until the early twentieth century that women began to make their presence felt in professional sprinting.

In June 1900 Ellen Lansing of Denver, Colorado, issued a challenge for a 100-yard race in the *St. Louis Republic*. She had moved to the United States in 1896 from her native Worcester, England. Although she had expected to race a woman, a well-known boxer, Kid Parker, answered her challenge. Dressed in bloomers and a sweater, Lansing defeated the "Kid" by 15 yards, much to his embarrassment.[33]

On April 1, 1908, Miss Ivy Evans ran three races at 50, 100, and 150 yards against Madame Isa Bell at the South Melbourne Cricket Grounds in Australia for a £50 bet. Evans won all three races, running 50 yards in 7⅕ seconds, 100 yards in 14⅕ seconds, and 150 yards in 22 seconds. In 1916 Bessie

Grandemange beat Hazel Meers by 6 inches in a 100-yard race at Mudgee in 11⅖ seconds. Grandemange remained unbeaten in nonhandicapped races from 50 yards to 220 yards during her professional career.

Ruby Baddock became Australia's professional champion in 1919 and took over Grandemange's title as the best sprinter in the country. During 1919 to 1923 women's professional sprinting was at its peak in Melbourne with Baddock the star performer. At Richmond, in 1919, she ran 60 yards in 7⅖ seconds, 75 yards in 9⅖ seconds, and 90 yards in 11 seconds and was undefeated when she retired in 1923. As the women professionals gained experience, they adopted some of the same tactics the men used to fatten their handicaps. The rising amateur movement as well as "not-trying" by some of the women to improve their handicaps led the VAL to drop women's professional sprinting in 1923.[34]

In 1973 the U.S.-based International Track Association (ITA) was formed and held its first meet on May 3. The ITA's mostly indoor track circuit included professional sprinting by both men and women. ITA meets were slickly packaged with twelve events "sequentially choreographed," cutting out the usual clutter caused when two or three events are taking place at the same time. Innovations included pacing lights, coed relays, celebrity races, and having the competitors interact with the fans.

Although several former Olympians competed for the ITA, many star amateur athletes refused to compete because of the modest amount of money to be made. They could earn more as amateurs by accepting "under-the-table" payments from meet promoters. Other athletes shunned the circuit because running for the ITA disqualified them from taking part in future Olympic Games. Lee Evans, winner of the 400 meters in the 1968 Olympics, was the most successful pro sprinter on the circuit and the leading ITA money winner in 1973. Although innovative and popular with fans, the ITA had trouble paying its bills and disbanded in 1976.

In 1975, Rowena Alsop, granddaughter of Arthur Postle, entered the Powderhall sprint, becoming the first woman to compete with men in a major professional sprint handicap. A year later, three-time Olympic champion Wyomia Tyus, who had been undefeated on the ITA circuit, considered running at Stawell. She asked for a handicap of 10 to 11 yards, but the most the VAL handicapper would offer was 8 yards, so she called off her trip to Australia.

It has often been claimed that professional sprinting failed to prosper because of innate corruption. Although the sport had its share of dishonest runners and promoters, a better reason for its failure was that it had no way to police itself. In January 1847, British distance runner Richard Manks wrote a letter to *Bell's Life* proposing an official governing body for pedestrians, but nothing ever came of it. Except for the VAL formed in 1895 in Australia, professional sprinting never had a worldwide or even national federation to regulate the sport and the betting associated with it. Runners who "sold" races or were otherwise dishonest were sometimes run out of town, but they just moved to a new location and repeated their offenses. There was no one in authority to punish or ban them from racing.

From the 1880s to the 1980s amateurism ruled and controlled access to the most prestigious races, including the Olympic Games. If a runner committed the "sin" of competing for money or against professionals, or even taking money for coaching, they were forever barred from the most important races.

An even greater problem for professional sprinting was that it was almost impossible for an elite sprinter who wanted to compete honestly to earn a good income. Seward's problem was repeated over and over. The top sprinters quickly ran out of people willing to compete with them in match races, and in handicaps they were often handicapped so severely they had little chance to win. Handicap races were most often won by less-talented runners who could more easily hide their ability and get favorable handicaps and betting odds.

In the 1980s, "shamateurism" ended and track and field became "open." Runners were allowed to compete for prize money as professionals and still be eligible for meets such as the Olympics and world championships. Sprinters no longer had to lie about the payments they received from meet promoters and it at last became possible for professional sprinters to earn incomes comparable to professional athletes in other sports. Little of this income was from winning match races or handicaps. It came from sponsors and ranged from free shoes and travel money to allowances and finally rich contracts from major athletic shoe companies.

Soon after track became "open" in the 1980s, professional sprinters became the most numerous of all professional runners. Today in the United States it is rare to see an Olympic Trials sprint finalist who is not a full-time professional or is a college athlete with a pro contract waiting for him or her after graduation. The best sprinters are also well paid. The world's fastest man or woman almost always becomes one of track and field's highest-paid athletes.

Professional sprinting now has a dark side the old-timers like Seward, Hutchens, and Donaldson never had to contend with. While professional sprinters were once distrusted because of fixed races, now they are regarded with suspicion because of drugs. In the 1970s and 1980s drug use among elite sprinters became widespread, and since then all the top sprinters have come under a cloud of suspicion. The use of steroids and human growth hormones have led many sports fans to assume that any track athlete running incredibly fast times must be cheating.

Although the use of performance-enhancing drugs is not unique to professional sprinting, it is especially devastating to the sport. A clean drug test does not prove one's innocence because cheaters have found many ways to beat the tests. Despite the warnings and deterrents, some elite sprinters are willing to risk their careers, their health, and their reputations to reach the top. Drug testing has improved in recent years. More cheaters are being caught and penalties have grown harsher, but currently it is impossible to say if drug testing will ever be able to insure that the top sprinters are drug free.

One wonders, if Seward were alive today, would he be able to compete with the best sprinters? Would he use drugs? There is no way to answer the first question. His 9¼-second 100-yard time would not get him a place at the Olympics or world championships. But the conditions have changed so much that a comparison of his time with those being run for 100 meters cannot be made with any certainty. The other question is easier. Like today's elite sprinters, he would be torn between his desire to reach the top and his sense of fair play. But based on what we know about him, if he could not win fairly he would have chosen another sport. Today's sprinters might do well to follow his example.

Notes

1. David S. Landes, *Revolution in Time: Clocks and the Making of the Modern World* (Cambridge, Mass.: Belknap Press, 1983).

2. "Timing of Athletics: Merits of the Fly-Back and Side-Movement Watches Discussed," *New York Times*, January 2, 1894, 6.

3. Edward S. Sears, *Running Through the Ages* (Jefferson, N.C.: McFarland, 2001), 51–52.

4. Information from personal correspondence with Peter Lovesey.

5. For a more complete description of Leach's career, see John Goulstone, *Turf, Turnpike and Track* (London: Author, 2003).

6. Llewellynn Frederick William Jewitt, *The Ballads & Songs of Derbyshire: With Illustrative Notes, and Examples of the Original Music, Etc.* (London: Bemrose and Lothian, 1867), 249–54.

7. Peter Lovesey, "1845: The Year of the Spike," *Track Stats* 43, no. 2 (2005): 66–67.

8. *Era*, November 21, 1847.

9. David A. Jamieson (a personal note, written in the 1940s). "Gaffer" is another word for backer. To keep the results of a sprinter's trials secret, the gaffer sometimes

had his runner's trials timed with watches that had paper pasted over the face of the watch. The watch was then delivered to the backer, who removed the paper so that only he could see the time.

10. David A. Jamieson, *Powderhall and Pedestrianism, the History of a Famous Sports Enclosure (1870–1943)* (Edinburgh and London: W. & A. K. Johnston, 1943), 59.

11. Joe Bull, *The Spiked Shoe* (Melbourne, Australia: National Press, 1959), 20.

12. Powderhall Stadium opened in 1870, and until the early 1900s various professional meetings from sprints to middle distance were held there. It was also used for athletics meetings in the 1950s and 1960s and for the New Year Powderhall Sprint until the 1990s. The ground was sold in 1995 and was demolished shortly after for housing. A more detailed history is in Jamieson, *Powderhall and Pedestrianism.*

13. "World's Best Sprinter: Some Stories of Harry Hutchens: Sheffield Handicap Memories by Joe Brinks," *News of the World*, 1926.

14. "Athletic Giants of the Past," *Outing*, June 1901, 269–71.

15. For a discussion of the origin of the crouch start, see Sears, *Running Through the Ages*, 96–98.

16. *National Police Gazette*, May 29, 1882.

17. "A Talk with the Champion Sprint Runner of America," *Chicago Daily Tribune*, July 26, 1886.

18. *National Police Gazette*, September 12, 1903, 3.

19. *Chicago Daily Tribune*, March 13, 1893, 12.

20. *New York Times*, December 23, 1948.

21. *Outing*, October 1905, 113.

22. Here is the record progression for 100 yards. Professional marks are denoted by an *. Only those who initially set the records are listed.

*George Seward (1844), 9¼ seconds (equivalent to 9½ seconds if started with a pistol)
*H. M. Johnson (1886), 9⅘ seconds
John Owen (1890), 9⅘ seconds
Arthur Duffey (1902), 9⅗ seconds
*Jack Donaldson (1910), 9⅜ seconds
Charley Paddock (1926), 9.5 seconds
Frank Wykoff (1930), 9.4 seconds
Mel Patton (1948), 9.3 seconds
Frank Budd (1961), 9.2 seconds
Bob Hayes (1963), 9.1 seconds
Ivory Crockett (1975), 9.0 seconds

Note 1. In an 1886 interview (note 17 above), Johnson said he believed Hutchens was faster than he.
Note 2. Donaldson's record was set at altitude.
Note 3. These records were all hand timed and the last two were set on synthetic-surface tracks.

In the 1970s the 100-yard sprint was superseded by the 100 meters and automatic timing became mandatory.

23. Donaldson's time was erroneously reported in the *New York Times*, October 13, 1910, as 9⅗ seconds. The time was actually 9%₆ seconds as taken on the ¹⁄₁₆-second-reading watches used to time the race. Johannesburg is 5,750 feet (1,753 meters) above sea level, which made the time about 0.08 seconds faster than it would have been had he run at sea level. He also benefited from the watch timing in ¹⁄₁₆-second increments. Had he run at sea level and been timed with a watch timing to ⅕ second, his time would have been about 9⅗ seconds.

24. Bull, *Spiked Shoe*, 92.

25. *New York Times*, May 30, 1948, S2.

26. Bull, *Spiked Shoe*, 224.

27. Bull, *Spiked Shoe*, 135–46.

28. *St. Louis Post Dispatch*, September 11, 1937.

29. Bull, *Spiked Shoe*, 145–46.

30. Peter G. Mewett, "Fragments of a Composite Identity: Aspects of Australian Nationalism in a Sports Setting," *The Australian Journal of Anthropology* 10, no. 3 (December 1999): 357.

31. John Franklin, *Gold at New Year* (Hawick, UK: Tweeddale Press, 1972).

32. John Goulstone, *Smock Racing* (Erith, UK: Author, 2005).

33. Eric L. Cowe, *Early Women's Athletics: Statistics and History*, vol. 2 (Bingley, UK: Author, 2005).

34. Bull, *Spiked Shoe*, 68–73.

APPENDIX

~

Known Performances
of George Seward

The following list of Seward's performances is from two primary sources. The *Sporting Times*, December 8, 1875, published a list that seems to have been extracted from earlier *Bell's Life* reporting. The *New York Clipper*, May 8, 1880, published a similar list with a few differences. The *Clipper* list is based on material Seward sent them and may have been compiled by him. These two lists, neither of which is complete, are the main sources for what follows. A few additional races from other newspaper reporting are included.

1838

Beaten by Lee in his first public race, 330 yards; Wallingford, Conn., 1838.

1840

Beat Henry Ainsworth, 100 yards, $50 a side; New Haven, Conn., October 18, 1840.

Beat Henry Ainsworth, 100 yards, $250 a side; near New York City, November 1840.

1841

Beat William Belden, 100 yards, $500 a side; Centerville Course, Long Island, December 7, 1841.

1843

Beat Jack Fowler, 100 yards, Seward having a 5-yard start, £4 a side; Liverpool, June 28, 1843.

Beaten in a foot hurdle race, 1,172 yards, over 16 hurdles; Bellevue, near Manchester, September 4, 1843.

Beat Samuel Wood of Levenshulme, 500 yards, £10 a side; Bellevue, near Manchester in early September 1843.

Beat John Jackson, 100 yards, £5 a side; Standrop, September 25, 1843.

Beat John Chapman, 120 yards, £3 a side (time, 13½ seconds); Cookton Hill, October 21, 1843.

Ran Charles Metcalfe a disputed 100-yard race, £8 a side; Darlington, November 13, 1843.

Beat James Routledge, 140 yards, £10 a side; place not stated, November 27, 1843.

Beat John Foster, 200 yards, £25 a side (time, 23 seconds); near Cockfield, December 21, 1843.

1844

Ran John Cooper a dead heat, 100 yards, £10 a side; Plawsworth Flats, January 1, 1844.

Beaten by Thomas Atkinson, 130 yards, £3 a side; near Shepherd's Inn, Durham, February 5, 1844.

Beat Joe Nixon, 120 yards, £15 a side; Low Fell, Gateshead, February 9, 1844.

Beat Richard Gowens, 150 yards, £25 a side (time, 16½ seconds); near Morpeth, February 10, 1844.

Fell at seventh hurdle and withdrew, 360 yards over 15 hurdles at Harlesdengreen, March 12, 1844.

Beaten by Frederick Scott, 120 yards, £10 a side; Hyde Park, London, March 23, 1844.

Beat Benjamin Badcock, 100 yards, £10 a side; Hampton, April 1, 1844.

Beaten by Benjamin Badcock, 250 yards over 15 hurdles, £10 a side; Beehive Cricket Ground, Walworth, April 9, 1844.

Won a silver cup, value 20 guineas, in a 440-yard race over six hurdles; Craven Course, Durham, April 18, 1844.

Unplaced in a 440-yard hurdle race; Beehive Cricket Ground, Walworth, July 9, 1844.

Beat John Smith ("the Regent-street Pet"), 100 yards, £50 a side (time, 10¼ seconds); Hammersmith, August 19, 1844.

Beat John Rush, who had a 2-yard start, 120 yards, £25 a side; Market Harborough, September 16, 1844.

Beat William Robinson of Newton Moor, 100 yards, £50 a side (time, 9¼ seconds); Seven Stars, Hammersmith, September 30, 1844.

Won a silver cup in four starts over hurdles; Northumberland cricket club ground, November 11, 1844.

Beat William Robinson of Newton Moor, 160 yards, £100 a side; Wimbledon Common, December 24, 1844.

1845

From scratch, won a silver cup in a 440-yard handicap over fifteen hurdles; Middle Deal, Kent, March 24, 1845.

Beaten by a pony (the Fox) belonging to George Leith of Liverpool House, Walmer, Kent, 400 yards, eight hurdles, heats, the pony carried 12½ stone and was ridden by the owner; Middle Deal, March 31, 1845.

Beat a horse, 440 yards over twelve hurdles; Beehive Cricket Ground, Walworth, April 14, 1845.

Won $50 in a 440-yard race over fifteen hurdles (times, first heat 1 min. 11 sec., second heat 1 min. 9 sec.); Beacon Course, Hoboken, N.J., July 9, 1845.

Won $50 in a 440-yard race over fifteen hurdles (times, first heat 1 min. 8 sec., second heat 1 min. 13 sec.); Beacon Course, Hoboken, N.J., July 28, 1845.

Forfeited $100 to Billy Barlow in a 1-mile race; Beacon Course, Hoboken, N.J., July 31, 1845.

Beaten by a horse named Hops, 440-yard hurdle race; Beacon Course, Hoboken, N.J., August 4, 1845.

Beaten by Edward Lamontagne, 250-yard hurdle race, £10 (time, 37 seconds); St. Pierre Course, Canada, October 22, 1845.

Received undisclosed forfeit for a $500-a-side match with Edward Lamontagne, who injured himself prior to the race; Montreal, Canada, October 25, 1845.

Beaten by Leakdigger, who had a 5-yard start, 150 yards, $50 a side; College Avenue, Toronto, November 4, 1845.

1846

Beat Cornelius Fitzgerald, 300 yards, over twelve hurdles, $50; Metairie Course, New Orleans, February 8, 1846.

Beat Collins, 100 yards, $500 a side; Metairie Course, New Orleans, February 15, 1846.

Ran unopposed, 440 yards, over 12 hurdles, $50; Canton Course, Baltimore, July 6, 1846.

Beat William Jackson and three others, 1,600 yards, over 50 hurdles 3 feet high, heats (times, 5 min. 48 sec. and 5 min. 58 sec.); near Washington, D.C., July 17, 1846.

Beat George Morgan, part Cherokee Indian, 100 yards, $500 a side; Washington, D.C., August 8, 1846.

From scratch, won £10 in a 500-yard handicap; Hyde Park, Sheffield, October 26, 1846.

Matched to give Charles Westhall a 2-yard start in 120 yards, £50 a side, but owing to the slippery state of roads Westhall was late and had to forfeit the stakes; Ganwick Corner, December 14, 1846.

1847

Beat Luke Furness, leaping twenty-five hurdles 4 yards apart, £10 a side; Hyde Park, Sheffield, February 1, 1847.

From scratch won £10 in a 508-yard handicap, over hurdles; Hyde Park, Sheffield, March 9, 1847.

Beat Charles Westhall, 200 yards, £50 a side (time, 19½ seconds); Duke of York Grounds near Ganwick Corner, March 22, 1847.

From scratch, won £10 in a 120-yard handicap; Bull's Head, Birchfield, near Birmingham, April 6, 1847.

Beat Charles Westhall, 120 yards, £25 a side, aids (time, 11½ seconds); Old Hat ground, Ealing, May 3, 1847.

From scratch, won £10 in a 440-yard handicap over ten hurdles; Sunderland Cricket Ground, Ealing, July 12, 1847.

Beat a horse, 200 yards over eight hurdles (heats); Bishopwearmouth Cricket Ground, July 26, 1847.

Won a purse of gold in a 1-mile race; near Darlington, August 9, 1847.

Won £10 in a 500-yard handicap, over ten hurdles; Victoria Cricket Ground, Leeds, September 30, 1847.

Beat Charles Westhall, who had a 5-yard start in 120 yards, for a £10 purse; Hyde Park, Sheffield, October 11, 1847.

From scratch, won £10 in a 100-yard handicap, over eight hurdles, and the same place and day beat separately John Handley, Joe Robinson, Charles Westhall, and Nutty Bodycoat, each of whom had 3-yard starts in 100 yards for £15 a side; Leicester Cricket Ground, November 1, 1847.

Beaten by William Birks, who had a 5-yard start in 100 yards, £5 a side (Seward fell lame during the race); Nottingham Cricket Ground, November 22, 1847.

1848

Won first prize, from scratch, in a one-lap handicap; Hyde Park, Sheffield, March 20, 1848. Beat W. Perrott, 300 yards for a purse, same place and day.

Undertook to run six men and give each a different start, 100 yards each, in one hour, for £10, but was beaten by the fifth runner, John Shaw, who had a 5-yard start; Hyde Park, Sheffield, April 17, 1848.

Won a £10 purse by beating four men separately, 100 yards each; Leeds, April 24, 1848.

Undertook to run six men 100 yards each, for a £20 purse, but after beating the first runner, Thomas Hopewell of Nottingham, gave up, having strained a back sinew of his right leg; Bellevue Gardens, May 8, 1848.

Beat six men separately, 100 yards each, for a £10 purse; Huddersfield Cricket Ground, May 22, 1848.

Beat six men separately, 100 yards within the hour, for £10; Aston Cross, June 12, 1848.

Beat six men separately, 100 yards; Aston Cross, June 16, 1848.

Beat eight men separately, 80 yards each, within 16½ minutes, for £10; Albion Tavern Enclosure, Wolverhampton, June 26, 1848.

Beat ten men separately, 80 yards each, in 29 minutes; Albion Tavern Enclosure, Wolverhampton, July 10, 1848.

Beat four men separately, 100 yards each, in 5 minutes, for £5; Albion Tavern Enclosure, Wolverhampton, July 12, 1848.

Beat six men separately, 100 yards each, for £10; Vauxhall Gardens, Manchester, July 31, 1848.

Beat six men separately, 100 yards each, in 30 minutes, for £10; Vauxhall Gardens, Manchester, August 25, 1848.

Beat six men separately, 100 yards each, in 30 minutes, for £20; Old Hat, Ealing, September 11, 1848.

Undertook to run ten men separately, 100 yards each, in 60 minutes, for £10, but was obstructed by the crowd, and the sixth beat him; Flora Grounds, Bayswater, October 2, 1848.

Forfeited £125, through ill health, to William Jackson, who was to have had a 15-yard start in 1 mile, £200 a side; October 30, 1848.

Forfeited £2 to H. A. Reed, in two matches, 200 and 440 yards, £50 a side each; December 28, 1848.

1849

From scratch won £5 in a 500-yard handicap; Hyde Park, Sheffield, April 19, 1849.

Received £1 forfeit from H. A. Reed, in a 200-yard match, for £1 a side; June 11, 1849.

Beaten by H. A. Reed, 440 yards, £100 a side (time, 48½ seconds); Harlington Corner, June 25, 1849.

Received £1 forfeit from George Martin, in a 100-yard match, over five hurdles, £25 a side; July 6, 1849.

Beaten by H. A. Reed, 120 yards, for £10; Flora Grounds, Bayswater, July 9, 1849.

Beat William Jones, 130 yards, for £10; Flora Grounds, Bayswater, July 9, 1849.

Beat H. A. Reed, one lap of Hyde Park, for a purse; Hyde Park, Sheffield, July 17, 1849.

Beat Mr. J. Harwood's mare Black Bess, 400 yards, over twenty hurdles (heats), £25 a side; Barrack Tavern Cricket Ground, Sheffield, August 6, 1849.

Beaten by Mr. Harwood's Black Bess, 200 yards, over ten hurdles, £25 a side; Pomona Gardens, Manchester, September 10, 1849.

Beaten by Mr. Nix's pony, Maid-of-all-work, 200 yards, ten hurdles, £20 a side; near Belper, September 17, 1849.

Beat Mr. Harwood's Black Bess, 100 yards, over eight hurdles; Walness, near Pendleton, October 1, 1849.

Beat Edward Roberts, 200 yards and 500 yards, at one start, £25 a side each event; Norfolk Cricket Ground, Sheffield, November 21, 1849.

From scratch, won a patent lever watch in a 500-yard handicap; Barrack Tavern Cricket Ground, Sheffield, December 24, 1849.

1850

From scratch, won a watch, valued at £5, in a 440-yard handicap, over hurdles; Huddersfield Cricket Ground, March 4, 1850.

From scratch, won £10 in a 440-yard handicap, over fifteen hurdles; Trent Bridge Cricket Ground, Nottingham, May 6, 1850.

From scratch, won £7 in a 440-yard handicap; Croft, near Newark, May 15, 1850.

Beat Richard Conway, three-quarters of a mile, £25 a side (time, 3 min. 22 sec.); Hyde Park, Sheffield, June 3, 1850.

Beat John Howard, of Bradford, 100 yards, £50 a side (time, 10 seconds); Flora Grounds, Bayswater, June 10, 1850.

Beat H. A. Reed, 440 yards, £50 a side (time, 51 sec.); Boxmoor, November 18, 1850.

From scratch, divided £10 with Charles Westhall in a 120-yard handicap; Copenhagen Grounds, November 25, 1850.

1851

Beaten by Alfred Simpson, who had a 40-yard start in an 880-yard handicap; Barrack Tavern Cricket Ground, Sheffield, January 20, 1851.

Beaten by Mark Parramore, who had a 4½-yard start in 50 yards, for £5 a side and a bet of £2; Hyde Park, Sheffield, January 22, 1851.

Beat Joe Pinder, who had a 10-yard start in 506 yards; Hyde Park, Sheffield, January 27, 1851.

Beaten by a horse, 350 yards; Barrack Tavern Cricket Ground, Sheffield, March 3, 1851.

From scratch, won a purse, in a 350-yard handicap; Barrack Tavern Cricket Ground, Sheffield, March 10, 1851.

Beat John Howard, of Bradford, 200 yards, over eight hurdles for a silver cup; Retford Cricket Ground, March 31, 1851.

Ran a quarter of a mile and jumped four hurdles in 57 seconds; Vauxhall Grounds, March 31, 1851.

Beat William Matthews, 1,100 yards, £25 a side (time, 2 min. 45 sec.); Hyde Park, Sheffield, June 23, 1851.

Forfeited £1 to Joe Pinder in a match to run once around Hyde Park, for £25 a side; Hyde Park, Sheffield, July 1, 1851.

Beaten by George Grantham, 1 mile, £25 a side; Slough, July 29, 1851.

From scratch, won £10 in an 880-yard handicap; Victoria Tavern, Agrove road, Stepney.

Beat six men separately, J. Mayne, W. Jones, Perch, Langsdale, Delaney, and W. Richards, in 24 minutes, for £10; Flora Grounds, September 25, 1851.

Beat H. A. Reed, who had a 2-yard start in 120 yards, £5 a side; Flora Grounds, Bayswater, September 29, 1851.

Ran H. A. Reed a dead heat (Reed had a 2-yard start in 150 yards), £20 a side; Copenhagen Grounds, October 8, 1851.

Undertook to run four men separately, 100 yards, over four hurdles, for £10, but fell and withdrew; Sunderland Cricket Ground, December 15, 1851.

1852

Beat James Patterson, 200 yards, over ten hurdles, £25 a side; Copenhagen Grounds, June 7, 1852.

Beaten by L. Bardsley, who had a 4-yard start in 100 yards, £5 a side; Copenhagen Grounds, June 14, 1852.

Won first prize, £20, in a handicap race, beating H. A. Reed, Charles Westhall, J. Lovell, and J. Mayne; Copenhagen Grounds, July 12, 1852.

Beaten by Charles Westhall in a 1-mile sweepstakes, £25 each; Copenhagen Grounds, July 26, 1852.

Beat William Jackson, who had a 10-yard start in 1 mile, £25 a side (time, 4 min. 53 sec.); Copenhagen Grounds, September 20, 1852.

Forfeited £25 through illness to William Jackson, who was to have given a 10-yard start in 2 miles, £25 a side; October 11, 1852.

1853

Won £5 in a 220-yard race over hurdles; Flora Grounds, Bayswater, May 16, 1853.

Beaten by John Howard, of Bradford, who had a 10-yard start in 440 yards, £15 a side; Hove, June 6, 1853.

Beaten by H. A. Reed, 440 yards, £50 a side (time, 54 seconds); Garratt Corner, August 8, 1853.

Won a 500-yard race; Flora Grounds, Bayswater, September 5, 1853.

1854

Beat Benjamin Badcock, B. Groves, and Ellis of Halesowen, 100 yards each, in 15 minutes; Aston Cross Grounds, January 27, 1854.

Beat a horse, the best of three heats, 160 yards, over eight hurdles, £10 a side; Aston Cross Grounds, February 6, 1854.

From scratch, won £10 in a 200-yard handicap, over four hurdles, Lea Brook Grounds, Birmingham, February 27, 1854; same place and day, from a 4-inch block of wood leaped 6 feet in height; cleared two hurdles, 6 feet apart and 4 feet high; cleared two hurdles 3 feet high, 12 feet apart; stood and jumped 12 feet clear, over a 2-foot hurdle, £20.

1855

Beat William Thomas, 200 yards, £10 a side; Newbridge, October 29, 1855.

1858

Beaten by an amateur, who had an 8-yard start in 150 yards, over six hurdles; Stalybridge Recreation Grounds, February 20, 1858.

With a 50-yard start, won a belt, value £20, in a 400-yard handicap; Copenhagen Grounds, Newton Heath, near Manchester, March 15, 1858.

1866

Beat Joe Horrocks, 100 yards, £25; Stalybridge Recreation Grounds, February 24, 1866.

~

Bibliography

Autolycus. *Life and Performances of William Gale*. London: J. A. Brooks, 1877.

Bartholomew, George Wells. *Record of the Bartholomew Family: Historical, Genealogical and Biographical*. Austin, Tex.: G. W. Bartholomew, 1885.

Blake, Jim. *Official History Commemorating the Centenary of the Stawell Athletic Club, Victoria, Australia, April 9, 10, 11, 1977*. Maryborough, Victoria: Stawell Athletic Club, 1981.

Bull, Joe. *The Spiked Shoe*. Melbourne, Australia: National Press, 1959.

Camp, Walter. *Rowing and Track Athletic*. London: Macmillan & Co., 1905.

Cowe, Eric L. *Early Women's Athletics, Statistics and History*. Vol. 2. Bingley, UK: Author, 2005.

Crowther, Samuel, and Arthur Ruhl. *Rowing and Track Athletics*. New York: Macmillan, 1905.

Cuddon, J. A. *The Macmillan Dictionary of Sports and Games*. London: Macmillan, 1980.

Cumming, John. *Runners & Walkers: A Nineteenth Century Sports Chronicle*. Chicago: Regnery Gateway, 1981.

Downer, A. R. *Running Recollections and How to Train*. London and Aldershot: Gale & Polden, 1902.

Duncanson, Neil. *The Fastest Men on Earth*. London: Collins, 1988.

Egan, Pierce. *Pierce Egan's Book of Sports, and Mirror of Life: Embracing the Turf, the Chase, the Ring, and the Stage*. London: T. Tegg and Son, 1832.

Egan, Pierce. *Sporting Anecdotes, Original and Selected: Including Numerous Characteristic Portraits of Persons in Every Walk of Life . . . The Whole Forming a Complete Delineation of the Sporting World*. London: Sherwood, 1825.

Franklin, John. *Gold at New Year*. Hawick, UK: Tweeddale Press, 1972.

Franklin, John. *The Professionals*. London: Tweeddale Press, 1964.

Goulstone, John. "George Seward, the American Wonder." *Sports Quarterly Magazine No. 2* (1977).

Goulstone, John. "George Seward, the Cockfield Putter." *British Society of Sports History Newsletter No. 9* (Spring, 1999): 37–42.

Goulstone, John. "The Running Career of James Wantling." *Sports Quarterly Magazine No. 13* (1980).

Goulstone, John. *Smock Racing*. Erith, UK: Author, 2005.

Goulstone, John. *Turf, Turnpike and Track*. London: Author, 2003.

Hahn, Archie. *How to Sprint: The Theory of Sprint Racing, Being a Compilation of the Best Methods of Competition and Training*. New York: American Sports Publishing, 1923.

Hone, Philip, and Allan Nevins. *The Diary of Philip Hone, 1828–1851*. New York: Dodd, Mead and Co., 1927.

James, Ed. *Practical Training for Running, Walking, Rowing, Wrestling, Boxing, Jumping and All Kinds of Athletic Feats*. New York: Author, 1877.

Jamieson, David A. "The Golden Age of Pedestrianism." Unpublished manuscript, c. 1940.

Jamieson, David A. *Powderhall and Pedestrianism, the History of a Famous Sports Enclosure (1870–1943)*. Edinburgh and London: W. & A. K. Johnston, 1943.

Jewitt, Llewellynn Frederick William. *The Ballads & Songs of Derbyshire: With Illustrative Notes, and Examples of the Original Music, Etc.* London: Bemrose and Lothian, 1867.

Lagerstrom, Ulf. *The Sprinters, Volume I, 1876/1914*. Rio de Janeiro, Brazil: Grafline Editora, 1993.

Landes, David S. *Revolution in Time: Clocks and the Making of the Modern World*. Cambridge, Mass.: Belknap Press, 1983.

Lee, Brian. *The Great Welsh Sprint: The Story of the Welsh Powderhall Handicap, 1903–1934*. Pontypridd: Gwyn Thomas, 1999.

Levett, John. *How to Train*. London: Newbold, 1862.

Lovesey, Peter. "The Beginnings of Indoor Athletics." *Track Stats* 43, no. 3 (August 2005): 40–44.

Lovesey, Peter. "1845: The Year of the Spike." *Track Stats* 43, no. 2 (2005): 66–67.

Lovesey, Peter. "Flash Harry." *Athletics Weekly*, December 25, 1982.

Lovesey, Peter. "Harry Hutchens—Finest Sprinter of Them All?" *Athletics Weekly*, May 17, 1982, 18, 45.

Lovesey, Peter. *The Official Centenary History of the Amateur Athletic Association*. Enfield, England: Guinness Superlatives, 1979.

Lupton, James I., and James M. K. Lupton. *The Pedestrian's Record; to Which Is Added a Description of the External Human Form*. London: Allen, 1890.

Lynch, Arthur. *Religio Athletae*. London: Remington, 1895.

Mallon, Bill. "The Race to Break Evens." *ATFI Annual* (1991): 119–22.

Mason, Percy. *Professional Athletics in Australia*. Adelaide: Rigby, 1985.

McNab, Tom. *The Fast Men*. New York: Simon and Schuster, 1988.

McNab, Tom, Peter Lovesey, and Andrew Huxtable. *An Athletics Compendium: An Annotated Guide to the UK Literature of Track and Field*. London: British Library, 2001.

Mewett, Peter G. "Fragments of a Composite Identity: Aspects of Australian Nationalism in a Sports Setting." *The Australian Journal of Anthropology* 10, no. 3 (December 1999): 357.

Pattern, James M. *Pattern's New Haven Directory for the Year 1840*. New Haven, Conn.: Author, 1840.

Quercetani, Roberto. *Athletics: A History of Modern Track and Field Athletics (1860–1990), Men and Women*. Milan: Vallardi, 1991.

Radford, Peter. *The Celebrated Captain Barclay: Sport, Money and Fame in Regency Britain*. London: Headline, 2001.

Radford, Peter. "Women's Foot-Races in the 18th and 19th Centuries." *Canadian Journal of the History of Sport* 25 (May 1994): 37–68.

Roe, Warren. *Front Runners: The First Athletic Track Champions*. Sussex, England: Book Guild, 2002.

Scoville, S., Jr. "Athletic Records, Past and Present." *Outing*, June 1893, 206–8.

Sears, Edward S. *Running Through the Ages*. Jefferson, N.C.: McFarland, 2001.

Shearman, Montague. *Athletics and Football*. 3rd ed. London: Longmans, Green, 1889.

Sheedy, Kieran. *Peerless Tom Malone*. Cleveragh, Cahercalla Hill, Ennis, Co. Clare, Ireland: Bauroe Publications, 2000.

Stothers, Richard B. "The Great Tambora Eruption of 1815 and Its Aftermath." *Science* 224, no. 4654 (1984): 1191–98.

Terry, Dave. "Britain's First Great Sprinter—James Jem Wantling." *Athletics Weekly*, January 2, 1965.

Thom, Walter. *Pedestrianism; or, an Account of the Performances of Celebrated Pedestrians During the Last and Present Century; with a Full Narrative of Captain Barclay's Public and Private Matches; and an Essay on Training*. Aberdeen, Scotland: A. Brown and F. Frost, 1813.

Walker, R. E. *Text Book on Sprinting*. London: Health & Strength, 1910.

Wheeler, C. A. *Sportascrapiana by Celebrated Sportsmen*. London: Simpkin, Marshall & Co., 1867.

Wilkinson, H. F. *Modern Athletics*. 2nd ed. London: "The Field" Office, 1875.

Zarnowski, Frank. *All-Around Men: Heroes of a Forgotten Sport*. Lanham, Md.: Scarecrow Press, 2005.

Zarnowski, Frank. *The Decathlon: A Colorful History of Track and Field's Most Challenging Event*. Champaign, Ill.: Leisure Press, 1989.

Index

217

~

About the Author

Edward S. Sears, a retired aerospace engineer living in Shawsville, Virginia, is also a longtime runner and track coach. He is the author of *Running Through the Ages* (2001).

DIVERSITY AND DECOMPOSITION IN THE LABOUR MARKET

Explorations in Sociology, Volume 16

Diversity and Decomposition in the Labour Market

Edited by
GRAHAM DAY
The University College of Wales, Aberystwyth
with
LESLEY CALDWELL, KAREN JONES,
DAVID ROBBINS and HILARY ROSE

Gower

Published by Gower Publishing Company Limited,
Gower House, Croft Road, Aldershot, Hampshire, England

British Library Cataloguing in Publication Data

   Diversity and decomposition in the labour market.
     1. Industrial sociology - Great Britain
     I. Day, Graham
     306'.3   HD6957.G7

     ISBN 0-566-00556-5

Printed and Bound in Great Britain by
Robert Hartnoll Limited, Bodmin, Cornwall.

Contents

Acknowledgements

We would like to acknowledge the enormous assistance given to us by Anne Dix and Mike Milotte in the preparation of this volume and in the organisation of the BSA 1981 Conference on Inequality which gave rise to it. We would also like to thank all those who contributed to the conference and those students at the University College of Wales, Aberystwyth who helped to run it. Finally, we would like to thank Adrienne Lee and Jane Watts for their good-humoured and efficient efforts in typing barely readable manuscripts, often at short notice.

Lesley Caldwell
Graham Day
Karen Jones
David Robbins
Hilary Rose

March 1982

1 Introduction: Diversity and Decomposition in the Labour Market

Few would dispute the centrality of the labour market as a feature of capitalist society. The selling of labour power, the variation in the terms on which it can be sold, and the social regulations surrounding the contract of employment define a large part of the field of industrial sociology (Brown, 1980). These issues have assumed a growing importance within what has been termed the 'new' industrial sociology (Hill, 1981) as sociologists have belatedly begun to give sustained attention to the operation of the labour market, and to the linkages between career and employment patterns and class formation. This reflects an awareness that more general theories and concepts of stratification in contemporary capitalism need to be tested and refined through the examination of detailed and often local variations. This volume brings together a number of contributions to the 1981 British Sociological Association annual conference, on the theme of inequality, which continue this emphasis. The papers provide a range of insights into the empirical reality of particular labour market sectors and the complexity of different employment situations. At the same time, their authors share a concern with theoretical relevance that leads them to enter into several of the important debates which have been taking place, often without sufficient reference to one another, around the central question of how sociology can best capture the differentiation of the various classes, and the composition of the working class in particular.

A great variety of positions now exist which stress the existence of a fragmented working class; they assign differing weights to the impact of a number of sociological fault lines which are said to split the class, inhibiting the development of a unified class consciousness and preventing mobilisation for action around supposedly shared interests. Opinions differ as to the depth and permanence of these fractures, as well as to the extent to which differentiation and diversity in the labour market is to be seen as the major element producing such divisions. The tendency has been to seek to handle diversity through a set of simplifying assumptions or categories which can be accepted as having universal validity, within at least the capitalist mode of production; characteristically, one

1

recent text, drawing its empirical material from Britain, maintains that 'although our argument takes its specificity from this instance, its general theme is universally applicable to trends in advanced capitalist societies, notwithstanding local variations' (Clegg and Dunkerley, 1980, p.402). This belief, which is widely prevalent, had encouraged a readiness to transfer models developed in one society to others with relatively little alteration. There are however considerable dangers in this: as Parkin has commented, analyses formulated too specifically for one society can resemble theories of 'capitalism in one country'; so, he contends,

> in the sociology of the working class, the terminology of affluent and traditional, old and new, rough and respectable, secular and deferential, and so forth, sets up distinctions that appear to derive more from the peculiarities of British society than from the universal, systemic features of capitalism (Parkin, 1979, p.29).

In practice, lately, the temptation has been to import American models into Britain, without always scrutinising them carefully enough to assess their applicability. This is something called into question by several of the papers which follow.

Where systemic properties of capitalism have been indicated, they have often been oversimplified to provide excessively generalised explanations both for the internal divisions in the working class, and for processes which might be expected ultimately to transcend them; examples of such one dimensional, single process accounts would include the notion of 'embourgeoisement', widely discussed in the 1960s and (as the other side of the coin) some accounts of proletarianisation, and the more recent deskilling thesis, as formulated by Braverman, in which a more or less constant, uniform thrust towards the homogenisation of work by the elimination of skills is asserted (Braverman, 1974). The closer the attention paid to specifying actual, historical class fractions, or the more detailed the investigation of market processes and work organisation, the more critically either abstract <u>a priori</u> categorisations or simplified empirical descriptions tend to be viewed: the market is more complex and less orderly, and the differentiation within the class less easily constituted, than the models tend to suggest.

In some respects, British sociology has a healthy pedigree with regard to the empirical study of labour market situations (see, for example, Lockwood, 1958; Lupton, 1963; Cunnison, 1966; Mann, 1973). But criticisms levelled at market centred approaches by Marxists and feminists highlight two major areas of difficulty which they encounter. The first concerns their ability to specify the distinct positions or places to be filled by the labour force; the second has to do with the processes through which workers are recruited into these positions.

The basic problem for students of the labour market is how to reduce a potentially infinite variety of market situations to a manageable and theoretically grounded set of categories (Crompton and Gubbay, 1977, p.34): in other words, that moving from a conception of market 'inequalities' to an account of how the market is structured. This entails locating salient discontinuities or boundaries: hence the significance given to concepts of 'structuration' and 'closure' in recent Weberian sociology, in which the method employed is to seek to define distributive groupings which share the same broad market situation by virtue of similar market capacities, such as skills, qualifications, or organisational strength. Market situation then essentially defines 'class' in terms of a stable pattern of inequalities generated by the market mechanisms: the classic example is the boundary said to exist between manual and nonmanual employees.

The alternative approach has been to treat the market as 'merely' distributive, and therefore secondary: to see market institutions and practices as concerned only with access, with assigning workers to positions which are defined elsewhere, in 'production', through the division of labour in the workplace and the relations of control and domination surrounding the process of value creation. Some analyses in this Marxist tradition are quite dismissive of the relevance of variations in market conditions and rewards which are allowed at best a derivative significance: differentiation in the labour market is held to be relatively marginal in relation to the truly fundamental class divisions between capital and labour.

In reality it is difficult to sustain a sharp distinction between 'production' and 'distribution' as determinants of class, since both the opportunities typically encountered in the market, and the functions performed in work enter into the formation of class identity and affect the potentialities for action. Therefore some attempt to bridge the two is usual. David Lockwood in his pioneering effort brought both 'market' and 'work' situations into his attempt to define the class position of clerical labour; subsequent writers have tried to relate market differentiation more closely to the exigencies of production, either in terms of patterns of control, or of the imperatives of valorisation and accumulation. Some kind of correspondence is looked for between productive functions and market situations. According to Blackburn and Mann, in the most thorough study so far of a segment of the British labour market, this presents no particular problem, given that 'workers with a common position in production relate similarly to the market, and vice versa' (1979, p.3). However, this would by no means be generally accepted, and it is those instances where the two appear not to coincide which give rise to some fairly intractable boundary disputes, and produce inconsistencies and ambiguities in attempts to resolve them.

Further difficulties arise when it comes to locating the

origins of market capacity or the conditions for success and failure in the market. This requires clarification of the processes which in fact allocate workers to positions in one or other section of the job market. The possibilities are indicated by a comment of Barron and Norris (1976, p.53) that the attributes which link social groups to labour market positions are simultaneously 'a product of the social relationship between employer and worker ... (and) qualities which are to some extent shaped elsewhere in the social structure and brought to the employment market'. Most accounts would accept that the formation of market segments depends upon an interaction between factors 'within' production and those outside it, but there is considerable dispute as to their relative priority. At one pole, the key to labour market differentiation is said to lie in practices and structures beyond the strictly economic sphere, which are 'found' but not created by the social relations of production. Thus capitalism is held to appropriate, and possibly modify or reinforce, a variety of pre-existing structures.

This case has been argued most forcefully and thoroughly with regard to sexual differentiation in the labour market. Not only does a particularly sharp split exist between jobs available to men and to women but in certain respects it even appears to be increasing (Hakim, 1978). Indeed it is partly because there has been so little interchangeability of work between men and women that it has been possible for industrial sociologists to pay hardly any attention to the specific market situation and experiences of women. The feminist critique of the inadequate understanding of women's role in production and in the occupational structure which results has so far made only limited inroads into mainstream sociology of industry: research continues to be done which either leaves women out entirely, or perpetuates the discredited practice (see West, 1978; Garnsey, 1978) of simply assigning women to the class position of their husbands or fathers. This effectively means that a crucial dimension of labour market structure is taken for granted, as given outside analysis: treating women as peripheral to the class structure allows the question how and why men occupy the positions they do to go unanswered.

In some interpretations the basis of this labour market segregation has to be traced to conditions external to production itself. It arises as a consequence of prejudice and discrimination which is possible only because other economic activities co-exist with the particular organisation of domestic production. Capitalist relations interact with the structures of patriarchy (Beechey, 1978). A number of other divisions of labour, racial, ethnic and cultural, can be regarded as broadly analogous, although less deeply rooted (Hartmann, 1979). For this reason, one will find a close fit between the sectioning of the labour market, and other poocesses of group formation; such divisions, which are used within production but established elsewhere, can only be fully analysed in terms of the 'separate dialectics'

4

(Edwards, 1979, p.195) of sexism and racism, or the operation of 'sexual and racial divisions of labour' (Friend
and Metcalf, 1981).

Others would attach primacy to developments within production and the labour process, viewing it as 'accidental',
but convenient for dominant interests, that visible criteria
of ascription - age, sex, race - become markers for selection into places that have their origin in economic
necessities such as the need to cope with variability, or
the different requirements of capital and labour intensive
technologies. Such factors can be held for example to bring
about market separations between those whose labour is used
in positions where the premium is on stability, reliability,
and responsibility, and those whose commitment is not
needed, since they form part of disposable or marginal
labour. From these basic contrasts is generated a whole
range of features attributed to 'dualism' in the labour
market.

There has been a proliferation of models which claim to
detect dualism either in the segmentation of the market, or
within the structure of production itself and the associated
organisation of labour. The basic outlines of the approach
are now reasonably familiar (Barron and Norris, 1976;
McNabb, 1980) but there are considerable unresolved problems, some of which are tackled in the paper by Morgan and
Hooper.

The notion of the dual labour market sets up a distinction between those workers who occupy places in a 'primary'
market, where work is secure, relatively well paid, afford-
ing some prospects for mobility, chiefly through administrative arrangements within the employing firm, and protected by strong unionisation and/or by managerial policy,
and a 'secondary' market for low paid, insecure, dead end
jobs where labour organisation is weak or nonexistent. These
are seen as more or less self contained labour force
segments, engendering a division within the modern working
class similar to, and perhaps as fundamental as that which
others have detected historically between the mass of
ordinary workers and a relatively privileged 'labour aristocracy'. Indeed, Edwards accommodates the latter in his
version of contemporary labour market segmentation in the
USA when he constructs a three tier framework comprising an
'independent' primary sector which includes mobile skilled
craft workers, a 'subordinate' primary sector of the
routine, semiskilled working class, and the secondary
sector. These he regards as roughly equal in size, and held
apart by deep structural barriers into 'separate groups,
each with its distinct job experiences, distinct community
cultures, and distinct consciousness' (1979, p.184).

The same tendency for an initial duality to be broken
down into further subdivisions occurs elsewhere in the
literature (Berger and Piore, 1980, p.18). The scope for
disagreement as to how many layers within the working class

5

should be accorded significance reflects the problem already mentioned, of making break lines within a continuum of market situations. While some regard the divisions as marking qualitative discontinuities, others are prepared to see them as matters of degree. Moreover, some regard dualism as existing in certain labour markets, but not all, whereas others (such as Berger and Piore) view dual arrangements as universal. Barron and Norris adopt an agnostic position, saying that

> dualism is a matter of degree. Some labour markets are more dualistic than others, but probably most labour markets are neither wholly dualistic nor entirely unsegmented (1976, p.49).

Further complications arise as soon as we ask where precisely the boundaries of the segments are to be drawn. Among possibilities suggested we find the following:

(i)   dual institutions that correspond to sectoral divisions within the economy, such as those between the 'monopoly' and 'competitive' sectors, or between the 'core' economy and its 'periphery'. The basis of this separation is seen to depend on possession or lack of possession of the ability to regulate demand and guard against economic fluctuations, since it is this which affords scope to create primary jobs.

(ii)   Differences between firms - between large corporations and small business, or between 'traditional' and 'modern' enterprises (Berger and Piore, 1980). Here dual arrangements may cut through industries, as in the interdependent relationship of mass manufacturers and small component suppliers.

(iii) Boundaries within firms, for example between central and peripheral labour (Friedman, 1977) where the occupants of different jobs are treated in radically dissimilar ways according to whether their labour is believed to be essential or dispensable.

(iv)   Contrasts between spatial units and regions, where it is possible to draw upon theories of development to link developed and underdeveloped areas; the secondary labour market, for example, being typical of the inner city or geographical periphery.

(v)   Distinctions between whole sections of the population, as when one finds suggestions of 'a marked tendency towards the maintenance of a dual labour market in which women are routinely underprivileged by being consigned to a secondary sector' (Clegg and Dunkerley, 1980, p.405; Barron and Norris, 1976). Alternatively blacks or ethnic minorities may be considered to provide the secondary labour force or a reserve population: the idea of labour market dualism was originally developed to characterise the work and market situations of blacks in the USA.

It is clear that the relative balance of class fractions will differ very considerably depending on how these various distinctions are used to slice up the workforce. Secondary labour may be seen as a marginal minority, or as a sub-

6

stantial element in the working class. Giddens, for
instance, believes the emergence of a 'massive' and 'quite
highly structurated' underclass (the secondary workforce)
to be 'a fundamentally important phenomenon now conditioning the American experience' (1973, p.216). Similar assertions can be made about the British situation, particularly
where specific local class structures are concerned (Friend
and Metcalf, 1980; Gilroy, 1980). However the overlapping
nature of the divisions referred to, and the scope this
affords for shifting between levels of analysis, makes the
'theory' of dualism elusive and difficult to test.

Morgan and Hooper subject dual labour market approaches
to critical review in their paper; while applauding them
for allowing a way into sociological analyses of the labour
market which have been lacking in the past, they are
sceptical as to the mileage to be got from them. Their
criticisms bear on both the theoretical and empirical content of models of dualism. Thus, it would seem that theoretical ambiguities and disagreements indicate that the
dual framework is really at best a descriptive formulation,
since whatever explanatory content it has rests either with
conceptualisations of the production process or with claims
about the market capacities of different groups and col-
lectivities. In any case, the authors show, British uses of
the framework have tended to become detached from the
theoretical context, explicit or implicit, within which
the original American formulations were produced.

Furthermore, Morgan and Hooper point out that as descriptions, dual models are quite poor; either the relevant
evidence is lacking altogether, or the data which are available fail to match up to the theoretical categories employed, as is the case with the heavy reliance placed upon
average aggregate data. As they suggest, this encourages
the central ambiguity as to whether dualism is indeed a
discontinuity or a matter of degree, and allows a certain
selectivity in the use of data, a concentration on those
measures which highlight extreme situations extracted from
what might in reality be continuous distributions. Such
arguments lead the authors to reject the dual labour market
model as lacking any distinctive explanatory power, and to
recommend instead the development of alternative forms of
analysis.

Their case study of what might, at first sight, seem a
prime candidate within Britain for a 'secondary sector'
industry, woollen and worsted manufacture, bears out the
limited usefulness of the dualistic model. Despite the
presence in this industry of low wages, highly competitive
market relations, declining economic status, and probably
the highest concentration of black workers to be found in
British industry, no simple dichotomous framework can do
justice to the actual complexity they find. For instance,
while the industry is relatively low paid, it proves to be
male employees who are most disadvantaged by comparison
with conditions elsewhere; occupations within the industry

are not strongly sexually segregated; skill levels are relatively high; and some firms enjoy a strong market situation and so provide stable employment against a back-ground of the rapid rundown of the industry in recent years. Since it is impossible to place the industry straight-forwardly into either the 'primary' or 'secondary' category, the authors suggest that rather than imposing a dualistic model it would be fruitful to adopt a more concrete mode of analysis, involving historically specific research into the capital-labour relation in the industry.

The paper is valuable for the careful examination of the kind of empirical data required to provide rigorous tests of the dual labour market approach. The problems of devising appropriate measures, and the limited availability of evidence make this difficult to execute, and the inquiry remains relatively confined to external economic indicators such as wage levels, occupational classifications, and investment ratios. Dual labour market models do, of course, seek to move beyond such basic economic features to deal with the total situation of workers in different branches of industry; the arguments refer to the overall configur-ation made by economic determinants, job structures, and modes of selection for employment. Morgan and Hooper make a serious start towards analysing this total complex, and their contribution should ensure that future research will have greater clarity as to what features of different industrial situations merit attention. A complete test of dualistic theories would require detailed study of the interaction of 'variables' such as skill, pay, career pros-pects, type of employing organisation, and worker character-istics; as the authors say, this would certainly imply close historical investigation.

It might in fact transpire as the analysis of this industry was taken further, that other formulations of dual-ism could become relevant. The empirical section of the paper relies on a version of dualism in which particular industries are expected to fall categorically into one or other segment of the duality. But the evidence provided points to a process of continuing monopolisation in the woollen and worsted industry, with certain large firms prospering (up to the time of the study) while the more 'competitive' small firms face being squeezed out: in other words, a hint of dualism appears at the level of the firm, and to see whether this is indeed so would require a study of inter-firm relations, and of relations to other branches of the economy.

The theme of the complexity, or indistinctiveness, of boundaries between labour market segments is further addressed in the two papers by Cousins and Curran, and Smith. Cousins and Curran question a particular aspect of the 'fragmented' working class thesis, the conception which became widespread during the era of 'full employment' that the unemployed were a definite, clearly demarcated sub-section of the working class distinguished by particular experiences and 'qualified' for deprivation by their special circumstances. This view of the unemployed as a residual minority could, they suggest, in common with other notions of working class fractionalism, lead towards attitudinal and subcultural types of explanation. The burden of their paper, drawing on data collected even before the traumatic experience of mass unemployment returned to Britain, is that unemployment and its associated labour market deprivations has not been confined to a sharply segregated subgroup.

Unfortunately, Cousins and Curran do not examine the extent to which the experiences of female workers differ significantly from those of men; they can therefore throw no light on the vital question whether divisions in the modern working class crystallise about the sex of the worker. The contention that women are peculiarly marked out, by the sexual division of labour, as members of the reserve army of labour (Beechey, 1978) would imply that their experience of unemployment and underemployment is distinctive, and should not be set to one side.

The evidence is drawn from survey work undertaken in selected areas of Newcastle on Tyne, among a population of working class men living in predominantly council housing. It shows that the experience of unemployment is quite general, in that between 40 per cent and 70 per cent met it during a ten year period, while a substantial minority (12 to 40 per cent) had either prolonged or recurrent unemployment. A related conclusion is that working class men in these districts were not, for the most part, stratified by rigid differences in skill; many workers over the period studied had moved between jobs and industries which would be officially classified as differing significantly in the skill required. For example, among the workers in unskilled jobs at the time of study, only a tenth had had exclusively unskilled work during the preceding decade. The exception, where there were comparatively rigid skill boundaries, involved those classic sites of the labour aristocracy, the engineering and shipbuilding industries.

Cousins and Curran conclude that present unemployment is a reflection of a wider and deeper package of disadvantages, each of which carries certain penalties. They define five such disadvantages, and show that there are substantial overlaps between those workers who suffer from them, without any dominant common thread; that is, large proportions of this type of core working class population are vulnerable to one or more of a cluster of disadvantages, which is loosely arranged so that it is difficult to draw a boundary around the 'disadvantaged' which would effectively distinguish them from others who manage to avoid deprivation. It is a matter of degree, therefore, how widely the working class is represented as disadvantaged, since its members are caught up in a process that means, over time, a probability of meeting deprivation. No less than 42 per cent of the sample were victims of multiple economic deprivation.

The 'underclass', according to this account, is neither a small, residual subgroup, nor a clearly perceptible and large section of the working class. Instead, unemployment and deprivation remain normal features of working class life. Rising levels of unemployment will of course have contributed to the further breaking down of any separation between workers likely to meet job loss, and those who feel safe from it. The political implications are intriguing, since on the one hand many will experience unemployment as a transitory state that does not encourage identification with a distinctive collectivity; but on the other hand, the generality of the experience is a reminder of the over-whelming unity of the working class as providers of labour, subject to the whims of the market. It emerges from Cousins and Curran's analysis that the compartmentalisation of skills and occupations is <u>less</u> among younger workers than it is among the old, while the experience of unemployment is more general; hence among young workers, the undifferenti-ated nature of labour should be more readily perceived.

In her paper, Diana Smith provides a detailed illustration of the scope for formation and reconstitution of a sexual division of labour over time. The growth of Croydon as a commuter town in the early years of this century, assembling white collar and middle class residents in quite new concentrations, provided the basis for novel kinds of commercial development. Smith deals with the expansion of the retail trades, in the course of which organisational innovations such as the department store and the multiple chain store transformed the occupational structure of the industry. Women came to dominate employment at the level of the shop assistant in the larger stores, but were sys-tematically excluded from managerial and proprietorial positions. In fact Smith states that as the economy grew, and a more complex division of labour evolved, women found a narrowing range of positions open to them, as their employment was increasingly concentrated into domestic service, sales, clerical and typing jobs; it was a phase of 'ghettoisation', during which the subordination of women was intensified.

Smith regards it as too simple to assert that such developments merely reflect the already existing relations between the sexes constituted by patriarchal domination, superimposed onto capitalist productive relations from the outside. Instead she advances a unitary conception of the social relations of production, stressing the totality of the economic subordination of women: the participation of women in the economy is vitally affected by the articulation of 'public' and domestic production, of wage with familial labour. The particular status of women in paid employment reflects their assumed dependence as members of family units, and the responsibility ideologically assigned to them for the home. No matter whether women were employed as shop assistants, or provided unpaid family labour to small retail businesses, says Smith, 'In each case their labour was ex-ploited directly or indirectly according to their familial status as women'. This presumed dependence, which was by no means a real condition for all women, made them vulnerable to low paid work without career prospects. Hence, in Croydon as everywhere else, and in the retail trade in particular, we find a workforce 'stratified fundamentally by sex'; these differences presenting only an aspect of a deeper differentiation between male and female labour power.

Yet even here there is no simple relation such that shop assistants in retail businesses are always women; the differentiations uncovered by Smith are more subtle. Women predominate in the larger stores, while men do basically the same work in smaller shops; and different branches of the retail trade are constituted differently. The closer the commodities dealt in match the home responsibilities of women, the more women are represented: clothing, textiles, bread, footwear, for example. Yet men are found more prominently in groceries, meat, fish and ironmongery. In part, this reflects the extent to which new forms of ownership and organisation penetrate the different branches, but it also has to do with the skills practised. Smith's preliminary sketch of the situation, and her arguments concerning the interaction of family structure and economic organisation, provide some useful pointers to the work which has to be done to uncover the full range of determinations which enter into the kind of division of labour by sex which so often presents itself as part of everyday experience. It is however clear that a good deal of detailed research is necessary to clarify the extent of free play that exists between patriarchal principles of subordination, and the capitalist organisation of work, and that this will have to take the form of examining the processes within which particular job hierarchies and market patterns are formed over time. (1)

The contribution by Roger Penn revolves around a critique of the efforts of R.C. Edwards to integrate discussions of labour market segmentation in which he has been a leading protagonist, with Marxist conceptions of class, or at least industrial, conflict: the defects in his work are taken to provide a general test of the adequacy of such a synthesis. The merits of Edwards' analysis in Contested Terrain are seen to lie with the move he makes from an understanding of labour markets as simply empirical clusterings of various characteristics towards a more structural account. Typically, so far as radical labour market theory in the United States goes, Edwards assigns the leading role to managerial strategies for control. He claims that each significant labour market segment corresponds to one of three major modes of control within capitalist enterprises; the working class is split accordingly, as an effect of the operation of the market. Penn's contention is that there is no such simple correspondence: the degree of variation within and between the working class fractions identified by Edwards is far greater than the model allows, and the typology he offers fails to pinpoint the actually existing divisions in the working class.

Edwards is accused of sharing a number of failings with other American 'radical' or neo-Marxist labour market theorists. These include an overly voluntaristic account of capitalists and their managerial agents, who are seen as selecting those forms of technology and systems of control which will most weaken working class opposition, in a process of divide and rule which confers relative benefits on certain sections of the labour force at the expense of others; a markedly contrasting conception of the working class itself as passive and reactive; and a blindness to important findings of 'orthodox' industrial sociology. In particular, the extensive literature on workers' orientations and normative commitments to work, which has been more fruitfully developed in Britain than it has, so far, in the USA, shows that workers have their own expectations which they actively struggle to maintain and pursue. Penn's demolition of the one-sided, managerialist, focus on systems of control leads him to emphasise instead the active part played by the working class in its own fragmentation. Even within the manual working class, a class far more narrowly defined than Edwards' own extensive concept of the working class (which includes all but the highest managerial labour), one finds, as Penn puts it,

> a whole series of practices and institutions created and sustained through struggles between sections of the manual working class and capitalist management that serves to actively stratify this class and which are embodied in the rules and norms that govern workplace interaction.

These are the practices which Parkin would refer to as 'dual closure'.

For Penn, it is essentially within the 'dialectics of skill', whereby different groups and levels within the working class compete over the definition, maintenance, reproduction and possession of skills that the key to fragmentation is to be found: the fundamental distinction in Britain is between a skilled and an unskilled manual working class. Penn relates the 'dialectics' surrounding skill to their expression in the ideology and political practices of the working class. The ambivalent response of skilled manual workers in Britain to socialist programmes is explained as the outcome of the structurally contradictory position they occupy at the point of intersection between systems of 'craft' and 'mass' production. They are simultaneously engaged in the defence of their skills against periodic managerial thrusts to wrest control via technological change, which leads skilled workers to respond favourably to anti-capitalist sentiments, but also in the preservation of their relative privileges over against ordinary workers. For this reason, skilled workers can, at different times, act both as conservative labour aristocrats and as labour militants. It should be added that a similar ambiguity arises from the fact that skill is generally the preserve of male workers, and skill definitions themselves 'saturated with sexual bias' (Phillips and Taylor, 1980, p.79). The norms and practices of workplace stratification include those intended to protect this state of affairs. The tendency to equate the working class with male workers alone conceals this.

Penn's framework brings the argument closer to the organisation of production, and the politics of the workplace. While it is developed on the basis of the British experience, Penn notes indications that it has wider relevance, whereas the review of Edwards' work shows how often he incautiously universalises a limited American pattern. It may well be however that Penn's own model suffers from some of the problems he identifies with Edwards': a readiness to adopt bifurcated categorisation of class positions (skilled/nonskilled) which does not do justice to the complexity of skill differentiation, and a tendency to dismiss altogether the significance of control and managerial policy, replacing it with the notion of a self-stratified working class. This goes too far, since in the dialectics of skill, both managerial interventions and workers' projects are interdependent; both are implicated in the process of struggle. Edwards makes more allowance for this than Penn concedes and there are other approaches which would also attach greater importance to variations in managerial initiatives in sectionalising the working class, and eliciting differing responses from different parts of the labour force (Friedman, 1977; Nichols and Beynon, 1977).

Among the criticisms Penn makes of Edwards' analysis is the over-simple classification he provides of control systems. For example, 'paternalism' is subsumed as just an aspect of the entrepreneurial strategy of 'simple control'. A substantial body of British work has clarified the relationships involved in paternalistic control, and shown that the links between it and organisational size and structure can be quite complicated: not all paternalistic organisations are small; neither are all small firms paternalistic. Goffee and Scase in their paper insist on the way in which control strategies are constrained by the material conditions of production in particular industries. Among the constraints, we must include the institutions and practices of the relevant labour market.

The paper by Goffee and Scase displays some of the strengths of the 'orthodox' industrial sociology mentioned by Penn in the way it gets to grips with the variability and specificity of different employment situations with some precision. The authors note the tendency to treat the 'small business' sector as a residual, as if all small firms were alike in their essential features, whereas significant variations exist. If a 'secondary' sector does exist, it is by no means coextensive with the sphere of small business.

In line with what has been said about the vital interaction of employers' strategies and workers' responses, Goffee and Scase argue that it is a congruence between the 'orientations' of employers and employees that makes for a

13

relatively smooth and effective system of control. The exchange of paternalism and deference which has been shown to typify relationships in certain agricultural settings, and to exist in a number of other industrial contexts, depends for its existence upon restricted prospects of mobility, and a degree of monopolistic control over employment opportunities (Norris, 1978; Newby, 1977). These preconditions are lacking in the construction industry, where one finds small firms faced with highly competitive market relations, with easy access to, and high risks of exit from, business; labour which is very mobile not only between employers, but also between employment and self-employment, ownership and non-ownership; and the absence of state protection. Lack of decisive market control combined with a tradition of labour 'autonomy' renders paternalistic domination problematic.

Goffee and Scase provide a brief and lucid description of an alternative form of control more suited to the industry, which they term 'fraternalism'. Among the small, but they believe, typical sample of employers in the industry which they have examined, they find a strong propensity to deny the importance of hierarchy within their firms. Instead, the manner in which work is organised retains powerful elements of 'craft' production (or what Offe would refer to as 'task continuous' structures; Offe, 1976). The employer lays stress on the skills which he shares with his employees, and works alongside them in a condition of apparent equality. Readiness to share work activities, combined with a flexible attitude to time and the use of materials, is used to secure trust and commitment from the workers. Small employers in an unstable product market, within which workers retain quite extensive control over the immediate process of production, are heavily dependent on their employees. This occasions considerable selectivity in recruitment, and despite the unavoidable insecurity of the industry, employers will seek to provide some stability of employment in exchange for reliability of performance.

It would be difficult to describe the market situation of building workers employed by such small concerns as either 'primary', since they lack career prospects, organisational strength and protection against business fluctuations, or as 'secondary', since employers would lose by treating them as readily dispensable labour. Goffee and Scase examine some of the contradictions which stem from the ambiguous position of small builders as both employers and workers: the pull of market rationality, towards profit and exploitation of opportunities for growth, conflicts with the preservation of craft conditions for 'fraternalism', setting limits to the expansion, and business-like operation of small firms. There are important connections to be made here between treatment accorded to labour within a particular market, and the forms of control which remain in the hands of employees. Goffee and Scase say little about the sanctions which workers could bring to bear should their employers deviate from the expectations involved in 'fraternalism', but we

14

would expect them to be quite substantial. In line with Newby's analysis of paternalism as a form of interaction (Newby, 1975), the origins of the fraternal control structure has to be traced to both employers' and workers' adaptations to situational constraints.

Small employers in the building industry might be said to occupy a marginal class position, among the petit bourgeoisie, while their employees are a rather distinctive element in the contemporary working class. The subjects of Crompton and Jones' research have a more central place in debates about the composition of the working class. One of the main lines of argument among British students of class has been preoccupied with the meaningfulness of the distinction between manual and nonmanual labour. As the authors show in the course of their examination of the state of the 'proletarianisation' debate, the status of clerical labour has been interpreted as a crucial test of the claim that all, or most, who perform wage labour occupy a common proletarian class position. In this debate, the class situation of manual (male) workers has generally been held to epitomise the proletarian position, and the question has then been raised as to whether or not nonmanual labour differs from that condition in significant ways. Crompton and Jones argue that too much attention has been given to the measurement and comparison of condition - wages, hours, promotion prospects and so on - and too little to the roles filled by different kinds of labour within a social division of labour. Their preference is to define the class place of nonmanual labour according to an analysis of the labour process in which it is involved, and the distribution of functions of control within it; possession or lack of possession of significant control becomes the criterion of class.

Their empirical results, part of a study of a variety of organisations employing nonmanual workers, shows that the class boundary, so defined, is indeed problematic. In the past, clerical labour was highly heterogeneous. Recent change has simplified this, by bringing into being a sizeable layer of routine nonmanual employees; but as part of the same process, administrative and managerial levels have become more mixed. To a large extent, all that has happened is that a shift of labels has taken place, with some nominal 'upgrading' of jobs to provide an element of promotion without any redistribution of control; as a consequence many so-called 'managers' are in reality skilled or experienced employees. But Crompton and Jones also allow that some substantive change has been occurring, as managerial positions have been deskilled or stripped of control through processes of centralisation, computerisation and bureaucratisation. 'Manager', they suggest, is now one of the least meaningful of job descriptions, and many managers lack significant powers of control.

The other issue they face arises from recent questioning in the work of Goldthorpe and Stewart, and their associates

15

(Goldthorpe et al,1980; Stewart et al, 1980), of the validity of making comparisons between the conditions of clerical
and manual labour, not because clerical work is heterogeneous, but because lower nonmanual positions cannot be
looked at separately from the career trajectories of the
individuals or groups occupying the positions at a
particular time. This relates to concepts of lower white
collar strata as 'buffer zones' or 'transmission belts'
between major social classes. It is a point which has been
particularly stressed with regard to male mobility through
such positions. Crompton and Jones accept the importance of
looking at proletarianisation as a process, but not one
conceived in terms of individual careers, since this poses
the recurrent problem of confusing the 'place' of jobs or
occupations within the class structure, and the social
background of their incumbents. They would argue that
mobility of individuals between different occupational
categories matters less in class terms when the positions
themselves are being reconstituted, and often pushed down
into a more clearly proletarian location where their
holders are excluded from control. The situation is further
complicated by the extensive feminisation of lower white
collar work, and hence the intervention of the sexual division of labour into the formation of classes at this level
(West, 1978; Phillips and Taylor, 1980). Crompton and Jones
point to the same effects of family organisation as Smith
in accounting for how women have been brought in to fill the
'deskilled' clerical jobs. While this again suggests the
possibility of a dual market for clerical labour, with men
taking the career route and women filling the ranks of
permanently subordinated routine clerks, Crompton and Jones
believe there is sufficient overlap, and pressure for
change from the Women's Movement, for this to break down in
the long run. On present evidence, it must be said that it
is likely to be a very long run indeed!

   Crompton and Jones develop their arguments within basically Marxist assumptions. Philip Cooke draws extensively on
Marxist class categories in his ambitious survey of the
reconstitution of the industrial working class of one
specific region, South Wales, over a long period. His
central insistence, which echoes points already made in
connection with the papers by Penn, and Goffee and Scase, is
that class is a relational concept, the outcomes of which
are therefore 'doubly determined'. Neither a reconstructed
'logic of capital' based on the imperatives of capital
accumulation, nor the action and practices of the working
class in isolation, is decisive; rather, it is the interaction of the two, in a process of struggle, which is
crucial. This, of course, is very easily lost sight of in
the pursuit of watertight systems of classification of class
positions. The codification of positions into a static
typology is never adequate to the complexity and dynamic
nature of class formation, the outcomes of which, while
constrained, are always indeterminate. For the same reason,
Cooke rejects certain fashionable concepts of Marxist
analysis (formal and real subordination) as too stark and

16

simplistic to give purchase on the 'dualistic' relations of class.

Cooke concentrates on the spatial, or regional, conse-quences of successive phases of capitalist production during this century. He stresses the extremely important interrelations of production and reproduction, between work-place and community, which are central to any examination of class structuration at the local level. From his account it is very clear that the shape of the working class is a product of processes of combined and uneven development which do not yield easily to a set of limited class cate-gories. Thus the industrial base of the South Wales working class is seen as laid down by two dominant industries, coal and steel, which share certain organisational features but develop very differently, and in a manner that is hardly ever synchronised. Such fragmentation by industry is a fundamental consideration in working class consciousness, and for Welsh workers the two industries have constituted the foundations of quite distinct experiences. Whereas in coalmining extensive control over direct production was won, and retained, by 'unskilled' face workers, the steel industry was a prime example of the separate, and dominant organisation of a labour aristocracy. In coal, the history is one of a succession of explosive wage-centred conflicts set within a decaying export industry; steel had a long record of exceptional industrial peace, with relatively undisturbed craft controls, generally buoyant employment prospects, and rising wages.

Cooke provides the outlines of a general account of the transformation of the regional structure of the British economy, framed within a changing world economy in which Britain was in relative decline, and America, until recent-ly, ascendant. The penetration into Britain of foreign capital, stimulating the growth of new consumer industries, and bringing about large shifts of population, can be seen in part as a strategy to weaken the working class by cutting the ground from beneath the organised labour move-ment while pulling in new and inexperienced sections of the population: Cooke notes examples of quite conscious action against Welsh workers because of their militancy. The resolution of this interwar phase of development was a 'settlement' around the combination of Labourism and incor-poration, economically based on the new mass consumer industries, which provided the grounds for the post-1945 debates about the 'affluence' of the British working class. Returning to Wales, Cooke describes how in the postwar period a wholesale reconstruction of the working class has been taking place, in which the community bases of earlier solidarity and a militant reputation have been destroyed; coalmining has been displaced from the centre by new types of manufacturing and service employment, male labour has been replaced, often, by work for women, and steelworkers have experienced the destruction of their skill controls through technological change. In all of these changes, he notes, the state has played a central role; at least within

Wales, the formation and transformation of the working class happens almost wholly through the mediation of state agencies of one sort and another.

The analysis of South Wales makes it evident that changes in the British labour market are fully comprehensible only within a much wider, international, context. The awareness of this may come more readily to those whose concern is the economic and social development of relatively peripheral areas. Some of the threads of Cooke's discussion are picked up in Murray and Wickham's paper on some leading developments in the Irish economy. By placing the recent growth of electronics manufacturing within an evolving international division of labour, they establish the critical standpoint from which to challenge prevalent ideological legitimations fostered by agencies of the Irish state. They show how assertions about the technological content of electronics have been used to bring about the expansion of this sector, which has been interpreted as peculiarly suited to the needs of Irish national development, economically desirable for its growth potential, and above all seen as providing the basis for an advanced production sector requiring a highly skilled labour force. Murray and Wickham trace the way in which recent educational policy in the Republic has been oriented towards the alleged needs of the industry, to aid in the reconstruction of the Irish labour force, to the exclusion or subordination of other social objectives, such as equalisation; similar effects are being felt elsewhere, for example in health care.

Yet it can be shown that the claims made for skilled labour requirements are unrealistic, since Ireland - along with other comparable peripheral regions — attracts basically the assembly and routine research functions within a spatially constituted division of labour. Once the ambiguities of skill classification are penetrated, most of the new jobs prove to be semiskilled assembly work, carried out by female labour. A convergence of interests and ideologies between Irish development agencies and transnational electronics corporations helps fix the Irish working class in a condition of dependent industrialisation, in which national economic development is so defined that it coincides closely with the consolidation of externally dominated private enterprise. It is only when development in Ireland is divorced from the realities of what Murray and Wickham refer to as the 'interlocking class, sexual and national state hierarchies of the division of labour' that this ideological construction can seem convincing. By reuniting the contemporary formation of the working class in Ireland with these multiple determinations and situating it within an <u>international</u> decomposition of the labour process, the authors underline that there are indeed universal processes at work, but that the exact way in which they express themselves in particular situations remains, in the end, a matter for empirical examination.

This is a lesson that could be taken from all the papers

presented here. They display a sensitivity to complexity and an awareness of the need to locate particular relationships fully in their context, including historically. Possibly this results in a certain untidiness, but the authors would agree that this is preferable to excessively neat but empirically misleading simplification. The work included here shows that a lengthy phase of intensely theoretical debate within British sociology has produced a greater conceptual and methodological sophistication, which is now being combined with a more traditional concern for the empirical adequacy of particular models and frameworks. The close attention that has been given to the problems of defining and specifying class locations has been absorbed into research programmes. As yet, feminist theorising has had a more limited impact, but it is becoming harder for studies to be done as if a sexual, as well as a class, division of labour did not exist.

NOTE

(1) This is the point of departure for a paper presented at the Conference which regrettably could not be included in this volume, Cynthia Cockburn's 'The Material of Male Power', which has been published in <u>Feminist Review</u>, 9, Autumn 1981, pp.41-58.

REFERENCES

Barker, D. and Allen, S, (1976), <u>Dependence and Exploitation in Work and Marriage</u>, Longman, London.

Barron, R.D. and Norris, G.M, (1976), 'Sexual Divisions and the Dual Labour Market' in Barker, D. and Allen, S, (eds.) <u>op.cit</u>, pp.47-69.

Beechey, V, (1978), 'Women and Production: a critical analysis of some sociological theories of women's work' in A. Kuhn and A. Wolpe (eds.), pp.155-97.

Berger, S. and Piore, N.J, (1980), <u>Dualism and Discontinuity in Industrial Societies</u>, Cambridge University Press, Cambridge.

Blackburn, R.M. and Mann, M, (1979), <u>The Working Class in the Labour Market</u>, Macmillan, London.

Braverman, H, (1974), <u>Labour and Monopoly Capital</u>, Monthly Review Press, New York.

Brown, R.K. (1980), 'Sociologists and Industry - in search of a distinctive competence', BSA Conference Paper.

Clegg, S. and Dunkerley, D, (1980), <u>Organisation, Class and Control</u>, Routledge and Kegan Paul, London.

Crompton, R. and Gubbay, J, (1977) <u>Economy and Class Structure</u>, Macmillan, London.

Cunnison, S, (1966), <u>Wages and Work Allocation</u>, Tavistock, London.

Edwards, R.C, (1979), <u>Contested Terrain</u>, Heinemann, London.

Friedman, A.L, (1977), <u>Industry and Labour</u>, Macmillan, London.

Friend, A. and Metcalf, A, (1981), <u>Slump City: the Politics of Mass Unemployment</u>, Pluto, London.

Garnsey, E, (1978), 'Women's Work and Theories of Class Stratification, <u>Sociology</u>, 12, 2, pp.223-43.

Giddens, A, (1973), <u>The Class Structure of Advanced Societies</u>, Hutchinson, London.

Gilroy, P, (1980), 'Managing the Underclass', <u>Race and Class</u>, 21, 4.

Goldthorpe, J, Llewellyn, C. and Payne, C, (1980), <u>Social Mobility and Class Structure in Modern Britain</u>, Clarendon Press, Oxford.

Hakim, C, (1978), 'Sexual Divisions within the Labour Force: Occupational Segregation', <u>Department of Employment Gazette</u>, pp.1264-79.

Hartmann, H, (1979), 'The Unhappy Marriage of Marxism and Feminism: towards a more progressive union', <u>Capital and Class</u>, 8, pp.1-33.

Hill, S, (1981), <u>Competition and Control at Work</u>, Heinemann, London.

Kuhn, A. and Wolpe, A, (1978), <u>Feminism and Materialism: Women and Modes of Production</u>, Routledge and Kegan Paul, London.

Lockwood, D, (1958), <u>The Blackcoated Worker</u>, Allen and Unwin, London.

Lupton, T, (1963), <u>On the Shop Floor</u>, Pergamon, Oxford.

McNabb, R, (1980), 'Segmented Labour Markets, Female Employment and Poverty in Wales' in G. Rees and T.L. Rees, (eds.), <u>Poverty and Social Inequality in Wales</u>, Croom Helm, London.

Mann, M, (1973), <u>Workers on the Move</u>, Cambridge University Press, Cambridge.

Newby, H, (1975), 'The Deferential Dialectic', <u>Comparative Studies in Society and History</u>, 17, pp.139-64.

Newby, H, (1977), <u>The Deferential Worker</u>, Allen Lane.

Nichols, T. and Beynon, H, (1977), <u>Living with Capitalism</u>, Routledge and Kegan Paul, London.

Norris G.M, (1978), 'Industrial Paternalist Capitalism and Local Labour Markets', <u>Sociology</u>, 12, 3, pp.469-89.

Offe, C, (1976), <u>Industry and Inequality</u>, Edward Arnold, London.

Parkin, F, (1979), <u>Marxism and Class Theory: a Bourgeois Critique</u>, Tavistock, London.

Phillips, A. and Taylor, B, (1980), 'Sex and Skill: Notes Towards a Feminist Economics', <u>Feminist Review</u>, 6, pp.79-88.

Stewart, A, Prandy, K. and Blackburn, R.M, (1980), <u>Social Stratification and Occupations</u>, Macmillan, London.

West, J, (1978), 'Women, Sex and Class', in A. Kuhn and A. Wolpe (eds.), pp.220-253.

2 Labour in the Woollen and Worsted Industry: a critical analysis of dual labour market theory

GLENN MORGAN AND DAVID HOOPER

During the last decade the concept of the dual labour market has gained widespread currency in British Sociology as central to the analysis of the employment positions of certain groups of workers, particularly women and black people. In this paper we wish to critically examine the usefulness of this concept. Our starting point is to note that the notion of the dual labour market has been used in a number of ways, both in Britain and America. In Britain there seems to have been an attempt to use the term without establishing a relevant theoretical or methodological framework, while in the USA, although there have been moves towards a systematic development of the concept, we will try to show that the level of its theoretical explication does not provide it with the powers of explanation attributed to it by its authors. Our argument is that although the notion of a dual labour market may describe certain differences in employment conditions between some groups of workers it does not provide an explanation of such differences, and that, in any case, the description is only adequate if a selective observation of employment conditions is made. Through an analysis of the British woollen and worsted industry we will try to point to weaknesses in the dual labour market theory that undermine its ability to account for the complexity of employment positions within this industry.

DUAL LABOUR MARKET THEORY IN THE USA

Two factors can be seen to be of significance in the emergence of dual labour market theories in the USA. Firstly, there has developed a conception of the modern US economy as being differentiated into a monopoly sector and a competitive sector, with it being possible to locate firms in one or other of these sectors. Secondly, there has been a measured disparity between the earnings of white male workers on the one hand and of female or black workers on the other.

Certain authors argued that orthodox economic approaches were unable to account for these newly conceptualised phenomena during the 1960s at a time when American society was undergoing considerable political and racial conflict. This led a number of authors to develop their theorising beyond the bounds of the framework established in orthodox perspectives. The outcome was a 'radical' consensus that the American economy had developed a fundamentally dualistic structure in which white male workers were predominantly represented in the monopoly sector and reaped all the advantages therefrom, of relatively stable employment, high wages and strong trade unions, whilst the competitive sector's workforce was predominantly female or black and suffered from unstable employment, low wages and a low level of trade union organisation. It should be noted that these discontinuities, both in the structure of industry and in employment conditions are asserted rather than demonstrated; after all, even continuities have their extremes. By focussing upon the extremes, the possibility that there may be continuities is ignored.

Anyway, if this was the consensus about the existing state of affairs, explanations for this have varied widely. Three of the most influential formulations are outlined below.

(a) Doeringer and Piore in a series of books and articles (1) give importance to the development of internal labour markets in certain industries in the formation of a dual-istic structure in the economy as a whole. Their argument essentially concerns the necessity for on-the-job training in highly capital intensive industries. It is held that the skills needed to work on or with machines worth millions are only developed by experience on the particular machine, and that firms utilising such machinery need to encourage labour stability which they do by developing an internal labour market in which rewards, both in terms of wages and employment conditions, are allocated on the basis of seniority and duration of employment. Other firms however, are less in need of employment stability: skills are easily learned, breakages are less expensive, and anyway the market for the actual product may vary so widely that employment instability, rather than stability, is a defining factor of the employment situation of the workers. The conditions of work in these two sectors reflect the differential sig-nificance given to labour in the production process; the primary sector looks for stable employees, the secondary sector demands unstable employees. By unstable employees Doeringer and Piore are referring to women and black people. The creation of these groups as 'unstable' is a two-way process. On the one hand they are denied employment in the primary sector by racism and sexism, and on the other, according to Doeringer and Piore, there are elements in the workers themselves that make unstable employment more suited to them. In the case of women, the socially ascribed primary responsibility for child rearing is seen by Doeringer and Piore to be congruent with unstable employ-ment. For black people they relate the rejection of stable employment to the coexistence of a preindustrial culture (derived from conditions of agricultural production in the south or Puerto Rico or wherever in the pre-migration

24

period) and a modern 'street' culture that interact to generate antipathy amongst certain groups to the dominant work ethic. They see blacks as preferring to seek employment only in times of temporary monetary crisis.

(b) R.C. Edwards et al. (2) build on the existing Marxist analysis of Baran and Sweezy in <u>Monopoly Capital</u> and place central emphasis on the issue of control within the firm. In their view, as the American economy became divided into a primary sector and a secondary sector the problem of control changed its form. Whereas previously managers could replace workers easily if they became too demanding, now, because the skills needed were learned only on the job, the cost of labour turnover would be too high. The problem for the monopoly sector managers was how to maintain control of a workforce that was potentially strong and unified by its central role in the production process. The answer, according to Edwards et al. was found in the creation of internal labour markets:

> Job ladders were created with definite entry level jobs and patterns of promotion ... The central thrust of the new strategies was to break down the increasingly unified worker interests that grew out of both the proletarianisation of work and the concentration of workers in urban areas ... This effort aimed to divide the labour force into various segments so that the actual experiences of workers would be different and the basis of their common opposition to capitalism would be undermined ... At the same time as firms were structuring their internal labour processes, they undertook similar efforts to divide the groups they faced in the external markets. Employers quite consciously exploited race, ethnic and sex antagonism in order to undercut unionism and break strikes. (3)

The dualistic structure of the economy, then, is reflected in the different forms of control used by managers over the workforce; in the primary sector workers are rewarded according to seniority and loyalty - thus control is via a form of sophisticated bribery. This bribery, i.e. paying workers above the value of their labour power, is possible because these employers are in a monopoly position and are able to channel part of their monopoly profits to make up the bribery payment. In the secondary sector workers are controlled by threat of the sack. These two forms of control are legitimated by reference to sexual and racial stereotypes of the work orientation of black people and women.

(c) E. Bonacich is one of a number of authors (4) who have been critical of the failure of both these approaches to see the central role played in the process of dualism by white male workers. In her discussion of black-white relations she argues that

> what fits the evidence better is a picture of a capitalist class faced with (rather than creating) a

labour market differentiated in terms of bargaining
power (or price). Capital turns towards the cheaper
labour pool as a more desirable workforce, a choice
consistent with the simple pursuit of higher profits.
Higher priced labour resists being displaced and the
racist structures they erect to protect themselves are
antagonistic to the interests of capital. (5)

Thus, according to Bonacich, white male trade unionists
force capitalists into discriminating against black
workers and women thereby keeping white male wages higher
than they otherwise would be in a situation of free
competition for labour. (6) Bonacich therefore puts major
emphasis on the role of trade unions rather than either
capital intensity or the problems of control in the formation of the dual labour market. This means that the
structure of Bonacich's argument is rather different from
those considered earlier. Both Doeringer and Piore, and
Edwards et al. give primary explanatory weight to the
differentiation between firms according to the nature of the
production process, with particular reference to levels of
skill and experience required by the worker to perform the
work tasks. This differentiation is asserted as a dualism
that can be expressed in terms of either the monopoly/
competitive or primary/secondary distinction. It is then
argued that there are differentiations within the total
pool of available labour that are transformed into a dual
labour market structure by the mechanisms previously
described. With Bonacich it is the other way round, the
differentiations in the pool of labour are asserted as a
dualism, albeit a dualism that has developed alongside the
development of capitalism; through the activities and
organisation of workers, this dualism presses itself on
the industrial structure.

Criticisms of the dual labour market theories

There are a number of general comments that can be made
about these theories. Firstly, as Blackburn and Mann note,
there are problems in trying to apply the theory in a
British or West European context; but even with regard to
the USA, they comment, with particular reference to the
work of Doeringer and Piore, 'We should note at once that
they have produced very little hard data to support their
arguments, which are really interesting hypotheses rather
than established fact.' (7)

We would go further and argue that the hypotheses themselves are ambiguous and, as such, not easy to support
with hard data. Thus if we consider the authors' failure
to clarify the supposed breakpoint between primary and
secondary sectors, we can see that there are a number of
possibilities as to where the breakpoint could come:
(a) between industries, e.g. is the chemical industry in
the primary sector whilst clothing is in the secondary?
(b) Between firms in the same industry, e.g. between large
firms which maintain a stable production and dominate a

major part of the market and small firms competing for the variable section of demand.
(c) Within firms, e.g. between either (i) occupations - skilled/unskilled or (ii) contracts of employment - full time/part time.

Just stating alternatives such as these suggest that the imposition of a dualist structure may be a gross over-simplification. The problem is that even to seek to locate the breakpoint is both to assume its existence and to adopt a dubious methodological procedure. The distinction between primary and secondary, or between monopoly and competitive, sectors is a matter of theoretical concern that cannot be settled by reference to any amount of data. The mode in which firms and/or industries are analysed demands a theoretical orientation that is constituted in the analysis. Thus, to use average wages data in a demonstration of dualism not only fails to show the degree of overlap between the groups under consideration but confuses the whole issue of what is being looked at, since it turns attention away from the particulars of the theoretical explanations. Not only do average wage rates not give any help in understanding the factors responsible for the differences that are found, but also in their very form they point to discontinuities that could, in alternative analyses, be represented as continuous.

IS THERE A DUAL LABOUR MARKET THEORY IN GREAT BRITAIN?

One of the earliest explicit discussions of dual labour market theory in Britain was an article by Doeringer and Bosanquet that appeared in the Economic Journal in 1973. These authors argued that

A basic distinction can usefully be made, in Britain as well as the United States, between the primary and secondary sectors. In the primary sectors, workers, on average show relatively low levels of turnover, have higher earnings and relatively good advancement and on-the-job training opportunities. In the second-ary sector, workers have low levels of skill and on-the-job training, earnings are low, promotion opportunities are infrequent and turnover is relatively high. Women and coloured workers, with the exception of the better educated, find access to on-the-job training and promotion severely limited. (8)

Whilst the authors recognise the difficulty of applying the theory primarily because of the difficulty of finding relevant data, they argue that 'It is possible to examine circumstantial evidence on age-earnings profiles, job tenure, internal labour markets and discrimination in order to arrive at some judgement concerning the existence and degree of market duality in Great Britain.' (9)

In spite of this, however, the main evidence that they present relates to earnings data; the other categories that they refer to are taken up only in a piecemeal way on the basis of evidence collected for other research and rather inadequate for lending support to the authors' endorsement of the dual labour market in its Doeringer and Bosanquet version. We also find interesting their use of the term 'degree of market duality'. Strictly, we would suggest that there exists either a duality, or some alternative to it. However, being less pedantic, the term could be admissible as referring to a movement which is a tendency towards duality. In which case, it would seem to us that it is necessary to articulate theoretically the nature of this tendency. Without such articulation the phrase can easily be used to avoid specifying an alternative to this 'duality' which does not quite exist in its own right. Such an alternative would need to account for the complexities of both the industrial structure and employment situations that we have described earlier.

A second important discussion of dual labour market theory in the British context is the paper by Barron and Norris entitled 'Sexual Divisions and the Dual Labour Market'. They state:

> In our view, dualism in a labour market can cut through firms, industries and industrial sectors ... dualism is essentially a matter of degree. (10)

This view presents us with great difficulty. If dualism can cut through firms, industries and industrial sectors then it would seem to be unambiguous, and certainly not a matter of degree. On the other hand, if dualism, as a matter of degree, has this ability to 'cut through' then it would appear to us that it is not dualism at all but merely a device that avoids the specification of a more adequate conceptualisation. Either interpretation we find unsatisfactory.

Looking at the evidence that Barron and Norris present does not clarify the situation. This evidence is based both on wage rate differences between men and women and on actual segregation between men and women in jobs. They identify the growth of the primary sector 'as the result of the various strategies adopted by firms to reduce the level of voluntary and involuntary turnover amongst certain groups of employees; and as a response to the demands of certain sections of the labour force'; employers select recruits on the basis of their perceptions of the differing qualities of workers: black and female workers, stereotyped as an unreliable, unstable workforce, enter the secondary sector; white males, their stability taken for granted - particularly those with children and a mortgage - enter the primary sector. The main problem, as we see it, is that this almost defines the distinction between the primary and the secondary sectors in terms of the workforce they employ. There is no attempt made to identify dualism with either industry, firm or occupational differences. The result is that nothing more is being said than that groups in the workplace possess differential amounts of power, dependent partially on internal technological and economic factors and partially on external factors such as the social positions of black and female workers. In fact, as has already been suggested, we are taking this position here in rejecting the dual labour market concept as lacking any distinctive explanatory power in the analysis of labour market processes.

This is important because it may be suggested that recently there has been a tendency to invoke the concept in a way that makes little reference to the theoretical framework of dualism. As an example John Rex has made cautious reference to this theory, arguing that:

> Our figures may not confirm that there is a completely dual labour market situation with whites gaining internal appointments and promotion in protected jobs and the immigrants getting what jobs they can in the open market. But they are consistent with the notion of two kinds of job situations with whites pre-dominant in one and blacks in the other. (11)

It is unclear which of the various dual labour market theories Rex and Tomlinson are espousing. Whichever it is, one has to be sceptical about any attempt to see industry in Birmingham as protected by its monopoly status from the competitive pressures of the market and thereby needing to buy the loyalty of its workforce. Even at the time of Rex and Tomlinson's research in Birmingham this view would surely have been undermined by the experience of British Leyland and Chrysler. One could add to this the argument that Rex and Tomlinson have no data about internal labour markets (except for one table on promotion), capital intensity, managerial or trade union policies at a level necessary to substantiate their claims about the possible existence of a dual labour market. In fact their argument depends mainly on differences in average earnings, a measure which, as mentioned earlier, masks overlap and overemphasises difference, and also on the differential offers of promotion to their black sample as compared to their white sample, where again overlap is significant.

In answer to our question, 'is there a dual labour market theory in Great Britain?' the answer is that there certainly is something of this ilk floating round but it has not yet been very well developed to overcome the weaknesses of the American versions, nor has any real judgement been made on these versions; so far it seems that Doeringer and Piore's framework has been dominant by default rather than anything more positive.

In many ways the difficulties of dual labour market theory, whichever version, are self-inflicted. The complex interaction of elements to be accounted for by the theory really requires macro and micro analysis, historical and contemporary evidence, qualitative and quantitative data. This may not be a disqualification in itself, indeed it may be a positive encouragement to some ambitious researche with a lifetime to spare. If however, that effort seems unlikely to succeed anyway, then why not abandon the concept altogether and get back to a more workable analysis of labour market processes? For the remainder of this paper we will examine the woollen and worsted industry of West Yorkshire and we will attempt to show that, in spite of having many characteristics that may seem to be supportive of a dual labour market theory, such a view of the woollen and worsted industry would be very misleading.

THE WOOLLEN AND WORSTED INDUSTRY

This sector of the textiles industry is concerned with all the processes involved in the making of woollen and worsted cloth from the preparation of the wool through the spinning and weaving of the cloth to its final dyeing and finishing. The industry has been predominantly concentrated in West Yorkshire since its development during the industrial revolution wiped out the wool industries of East Anglia and the South West. In 1967 74 per cent of total employment was concentrated in the Yorkshire and Humberside region, a figure that has remained stable despite the massive overall shrinkage in the industry since then. (12) In 1967 there were 110,569 workers employed in direct production of woollen and worsted; (13) by 1979 the number had fallen to 48,390, and at present is declining even more rapidly.

At first sight the industry would seem an ideal candidate for a secondary industry: wages are low; high numbers of women and black workers are employed; there are a large number of competing firms in the industry; there is not security of employment in the industry as a whole. In this paper we examine each of these areas separately to show what light they throw on dual labour market theory.

Wages in the Woollen and Worsted Industry

This industry has traditionally been known as a low pay industry. For each of the years since 1967, when current survey records began, the average earnings for men in woollen and worsted were lower than the average of any of the standard industrial classifications for manufacturing. (14) In fact, so low are men's wages in this sector that they are just below the average hourly earnings for women in the vehicles industry group: 183.1 pence per hour for men in woollen and worsted in 1979, compared to 184.39 pence per hour for women in vehicles; (15) this is one of a few examples where one can see men getting lower hourly earnings than women, and as such warns us that even were we to identify dualism with the male/female divide, there are overlaps. So as not to seem partisan, though, we must state that because of the number of hours worked, men's weekly wages in woollen and worsted were £81.68 in 1979 for an average week of 44.6 hours compared to an average for women in vehicles of £69.52 for a 37.6-hour working week.

Within the woollen and worsted industry itself, however, there is the usual differential between men and women, though interestingly, not to the same extent as in other manufacturing industries. The effect of the Equal Pay Act seems to have been as found in previous research, (16) i.e. an initial increase in women's wages followed by the re-establishment of a stable differential between men and women.

Table 1
Women's earnings as a percentage of men's

	Woollen and Worsted		All Manufacturing	
	per week	hourly	per week	hourly
1967	54.1	67.5	48.1	57.4
1974	60.9	74.1	55.1	65.1
1979	66.7	80.6	59.5	69.1

If we break down the categories of wage earners amongst manual workers in woollen and worsted further we find that while average earnings for men over 21 years were in general below the average of all industries in manufacturing, the situation was different for other groups. In particular, the industry is relatively high-paying for boys and girls, and this means that the spread of earnings in woollen and worsted is smaller than in most other industries;

Table 2
Hourly earnings in woollen and worsted ranked*
in relation to other manufacturing industries

	Men (21 or over)	Boys (under 21)	Women (over 18) full-time	part-time	Girls (under 18)
1967	15	9	15	14	1
1974	17	8	16	15	6
1979	18	12	15	17	2

*For 1967, the ranking of all groups is out of 15; for 1974 and 1979 the ranking is out of 18 with the exception of girls where it is out of 16.

thus in 1979 the average hourly earnings of girls in woollen and worsted was 63 per cent of that of men's, whereas in manufacturing industries as a whole girls earned only 46 per cent of men's average hourly earnings. Similarly, boys' average hourly earnings in woollen and worsted were 67 per cent of men's whereas in all manufacturing industries, the corresponding figure was 61.7 per cent. One interpretation could be that this is prima facie evidence that internal labour markets are not very highly developed in the woollen and worsted industry since such a small spread of earnings would militate against employers having the room to develop the complex wage structure concomitant with internal labour markets. To this extent it lends support to the view that woollen and worsted is a secondary industry. What complicates this, however, is that relative to the position of workers in other industries, it is men who comparatively are most disadvantaged in terms of low wages. Therefore the simplistic equation of secondary industry with predominant female employment must necessarily be in question.

We reach this conclusion from an analysis of average wage rates derived from aggregate data for industries as a whole. We have already suggested that using this type of data is conducive to finding support for dualist theories in that it lays emphasis on discontinuities. However, when we try to break down aggregate data for the industry as a whole on a firm by firm basis our doubts about the concept of dualism are heightened even further.

Information on employment and wages for 93 companies in the industry is available from a Wool Textile EDC report. Together these companies accounted for 53,800 employees out of a total employment in the industry of about 78,000. Table 3 shows the wages and salaries bill, average remuneration and employment in those 93 companies. (17)

Table 3
Wages and salaries bill and average remuneration

Asset size	No. of companies filing 1976/7	Wages and Salaries 1976/7 £000	Average remuneration			No. of employees 1976/7
			1976/7 £	1975/6 £	1974/5 £	
£0.5-£2m	50	21,252	2,335	1,973	1,614	9,100
£2m-£5m	25	25,496	2,512	2,130	1,727	10,151
Over £5m	18	85,384	2,473	2,061	1,639	34,528
Total	93	132,133	2,457	2,059	1,653	53,779

These figures cover all employees and not just those in manual work but it should be noted that in 1977 78 per cent of all employees were in direct production. These figures suggest not only a considerable disparity in wage levels between firms within the industry, but particularly that medium and large firms have significantly higher levels of remuneration than small firms and, perhaps surprisingly, that it is the medium sized firms that pay the best rates on average. Although no final judgements can be made from figures such as these they do tend to give support to our view that a dualist structure is over-simplistic.

Our argument gets more support if the same data are broken down in a different fashion. From Table 4 we see that on a firm by firm basis there is a very great range in average remuneration. In fact the lowest average remuneration was £1,611 p.a. and the highest was £3,750. Now although these figures cannot prove anything they do bear out our contention that gross averages tend to exaggerate discontinuity. In order to take our analysis further we need to look at the nature of occupational concentration in the industry.

Table 4
Average remuneration and number of firms

Average remuneration £000/annum	Number of firms
1.50-1.75	4
1.75-2.00	7
2.00-2.25	19
2.25-2.50	30
2.50-2.75	18
2.75-3.00	14
3.00-3.25	7
3.25 and above	5

It should be noted that as far as we are able to ascertain low pay in the industry cannot be explained on the basis of the low skill content of the work. (18) The most easily available data we have derives from the census classifications. From these Routh has calculated that the ratio of skilled workers to all manual workers in various occupational groups in 1971 was in textiles 48 per cent while in coalmining it was 37 per cent. At first sight then there is certainly not a low proportion of workers being classified as skilled according to the census in the textile industry as a whole. More detailed analysis of the 1971 census through the Economic Activity Group Leaflet for Yorkshire; West Riding confirms this picture. Textile workers (census occupational units 064-073, 110) in this area will invariably be woollen and worsted (rather than cotton) workers. (19) Examining the 10 per cent sample for the area as a whole we find the following breakdown for workers in these occupational units.

Table 5

	Male	Female	All
1. Socioeconomic group 9 Skilled manual workers: employees engaged in manual occupations which require considerable and specific skills	2,160	1,952	4,112
2. Socioeconomic group 10 Semi-skilled manual workers: employees engaged in manual occupations which require slight but specific skills	1,790	1,826	3,616
3. Socioeconomic group 11 Unskilled manual workers: other employees engaged in manual occupations	1,006	335	1,341

From this we can calculate two further tables for textile workers in West Yorkshire:

Table 6
Percentage of socioeconomic group by sex

	Male	Female
SEG 9	53	47
SEG 10	49.5	50.5
SEG 11	75	25

Table 7
Socioeconomic groups as percentage of all workers in occupational groups 064-073, 110

(figures in brackets refer to Great Britain as a whole)

	Male	Female	All
SEG 9	43 (59)	47 (24)	45 (51)
SEG 10	36 (25)	44 (48)	40 (30)
SEG 11	21 (16)	9 (28)	15 (19)
	100	100	100

While we would be reluctant to make any very definite claims on the basis of these figures, we do feel that they show that woollen and worsted cannot be considered to be a particularly low skill industry in the terms of the census. What is peculiar to the industry is the proportion of women workers who occupy a skilled position, over half of them in occupational group 072, 'Textile Fabrics and related produce makers and examiners n.e.c.', i.e. mainly persons examining textile yarn and cloth for defects and rectifying them. As has already been said, the concept of skill is highly problematic, but as far as can be ascertained from the census, the woollen and worsted industry is not an especially low skill industry. Moreover, the skilled jobs that are available are not monopolised by men (20) and, in fact, unskilled textile operations are predominantly male.

Employee concentration in woollen and worsted

It is sometimes argued that where a large proportion of the workforce has the characteristics of secondary labour the wages of other workers in the industry will be pulled down. In woollen and worsted there are two relevant factors here. The first is the proportion of black workers in the industry. Figures are available to us from the Wool Industry Bureau of Statistics, and they indicate, firstly that black workers (a category which is made up of two other categories in the WIBS census of production: (a) Indians or Pakistanis (b) other Commonwealth or Foreign workers) are predominantly male, and secondly that as a percentage of production workers their proportion is probably higher than in any other industry, and in fact is continuing to grow. We have calculated this percentage on two bases: firstly, the numbers as a proportion of all those in production in the industry (Table 8); and secondly, black workers as a proportion of all workers in West Yorkshire (Table 9). The second calculation is based upon

34

two assumptions: (a) that the ratio of direct production
workers to non-direct production workers is not significantly different outside and inside West Yorkshire. There is no
evidence to suggest to us that this is a false assumption;
(b) that very few black workers are employed in woollen
and worsted outside West Yorkshire. We have been able to
locate geographically firms employing over 90 per cent of
all workers in the industry and have found that almost all
firms outside West Yorkshire are in areas unlikely to have
many black workers (e.g. places in Scotland such as Kinross,
Selkirk and Renfrew, and in England in areas such as
Devon and Somerset). Given that a few West Yorkshire firms
are located outside the metropolitan districts and less
likely to employ black workers we feel that this assumption
is most defensible. Whilst it is possible that these figures
(Table 9) are an overestimate, it is our opinion that they
nevertheless closely represent the actual proportion of
black workers in direct production in the West Yorkshire
wool textile industry.

Table 8
Indians, Pakistanis and other Commonwealth or Foreign
Workers* in direct production in the woollen
and worsted industry as a per cent of all direct
production workers

Year	Men	Women	Both
1969	21.44	1.99	11.98
1970	21.00	2.02	11.99
1971	22.38	2.15	12.98
1972	23.69	2.40	13.93
1973	23.80	2.70	14.22
1974	23.35	2.70	13.85
1975	23.36	2.55	14.17
1976	23.32	2.92	14.41
1977	23.46	3.18	14.52
1978	23.52	3.17	14.66
1979	24.01	3.23	15.01

*This specifically excludes Austrians, Italians, Poles and
Ukrainians who made up 2.9 per cent of workers in direct
production in 1979.

While we have yet to come across any figures as comprehensive as this for other industries, from all previous
research it seems that there is no other industry which
could claim as high a concentration of black male workers
either at regional level or at industry level. An immediate
interpretation could be that of the evidence presented so
far this does give considerable support to a dualist
hypothesis. Here we have a very high concentration of black
workers in an industry that it is claimed could be classed
as secondary. However, we must be cautious about reading
more into these figures than is, in fact, justifiable.
After all, if labour is judged to be appropriate by
employers because of characteristics that are attributed to
it through the application of criteria of race or

35

nationality, then it must be emphasised that 70 per cent of
male workers in direct production industry are white, as are
80 per cent of all direct production workers, and if sex
criteria are also applied then 43 per cent of all direct
production workers are white males.

Table 9
Indians, Pakistanis and other Commonwealth or Foreign
Workers* in direct production in woollen and worsted
industry in West Yorkshire as a per cent of all West
Yorkshire direct production workers

Year	Men	Women	Both
1969	28.98	2.69	16.20
1970	28.38	2.72	16.21
1971	30.24	2.91	17.45
1972	32.00	3.29	18.83
1973	32.16	3.67	19.21
1974	31.55	3.67	18.72
1975	31.57	3.44	19.15
1976	31.51	3.95	19.48
1977	31.71	4.29	19.63
1978	31.80	4.28	19.81
1979	32.45	4.37	20.29

*As in Table 8

This caution on our part is reinforced if we analyse the
wage figures that we have looked at earlier in this paper,
together with these concentration figures. We have already
pointed out that there are considerable problems in
attempting to demarcate unambiguously the woollen and
worsted industry as being in the secondary sector. Nevertheless, one expectation that we might have is that wages
paid in West Yorkshire firms where there is this high
concentration of black labour would, on average, be lower
than outside West Yorkshire where the labour is, in our
estimate, almost wholly white. Our analysis of remuneration
paid in 1977 is shown in Table 10.

Table 10
Remuneration inside and outside West Yorkshire

	Total remuneration	Number of employees	Average remuneration
West Yorkshire	£120.757m	47,725	£2,530 p.a.
Outside W. Yorkshire	£ 19.781m	7,994	£2,474 p.a.

Remembering that these figures are based on all workers and
not just direct production workers then we have, contrary
to our expectations, a slightly higher level of remuneration in West Yorkshire firms: £48.53 in West Yorkshire
compared to £47.46 elsewhere when the figures are
converted to weekly earnings.

Through an examination of the census of production figures
we have also looked at the proportion of women workers in

industry which allows us to see their importance to the
industry as a whole. As we see in Table 11 women's
employment has declined as a proportion of the total by
roughly 5 per cent, but this seems to have made no
difference to the proportion of women employed part-time,
which has remained roughly constant at around 20 per cent,
a figure which is relatively representative of most women's
employment in manufacturing industry (e.g. 20.07 in 1979
in electrical engineering; 17.2 in vehicles; 21.4 in
textiles as a whole).

Table 11
Men and women in direct production
(part-time and full-time)

	Men	Women	part-time as % of all workers	part-time W as % of all women	part-time M as % of men
1969	51.4	48.6	10.8	19.3	2.7
1970	52.7	47.3	9.4	16.8	2.7
1971	53.6	46.4	8.6	15.7	2.4
1972	54.1	45.9	9.6	18.1	2.4
1973	54.6	45.4	10.4	20.4	2.1
1974	54.0	46.0	10.8	20.0	2.9
1975	55.9	44.1	9.8	18.9	2.6
1976	65.4	43.6	9.9	19.6	2.4
1977	55.9	44.1	19.6	21.3	2.1
1978	56.4	43.6	10.1	20.5	2.1
1979	56.7	43.3	9.2	19.2	1.6

In terms of the actual job position of women in the
industry we are able to make use of the census of production
again. There are thirty-nine activities in production
identified in the censuses (see Appendix A for full list)
and so it is possible to determine the degree of concentration, and compare it with data such as Hakim's for
concentration in all occupations. (21) While the categories
of the census are not discrete occupations, they can
approximate to such. From Tables 12 and 13 we can see in
particular that occupations in woollen and worsted are not
as sexually segregated as in most other occupations. We
also find evidence to confirm findings elsewhere, such as
Snell (1979), that legislation on equal opportunities during
the 1970s had led to men entering women's occupations rather
than vice versa. Indeed women may, to some extent, be
forced out of male-dominated occupations, as shown by the
slight increase in concentration shown in male-dominated
occupations in Table 13. It is of interest to note that
the largest occupational group for women, in terms of
numbers, is 'Perching, burling, knotting and mending',
processes which refer to the delicate sewing-type tasks
necessary to ensure that cloth is ready for the final
finishing processes: a fairly clear example of a home-
based definition of women's work being translated into the
factory situation.

Table 12
Proportions of all occupations which have:

	No women workers	70% or more women workers	above average* % women workers	above average*% men workers
All occupa-tions**				
1971	2	12	26	74
Wool & Worsted				
1971	3	15	26	74
Wool & Worsted				
1979	5	12	23	77

* above average here means higher % than in labour force as a whole.
** from C. Hakim: Occupational Segregation. Other figures from WIBS

Table 13

	% men working in occupations which had male percentage of:						% women in occupation which had female percentage of:					
	100	90+	80+	70+	60+	50+	100	90+	80+	70+	60+	50+
All occupations 1971	16	55	69	77	85	86	0	24	33	45	73	76
Wool and Worsted 1971	0	31	35	65	66	67	0	20	24	47	47	86
Wool and Worsted 1979	0	33	41	69	76	88	0	18	23	35	48	69

Structure of the industry

In terms of dualist arguments it would seem a straight-forward matter to classify the woollen and worsted industry as being in the competitive sector. Thus in 1976 there were 802 enterprises in the industry that operated 973 establish ments. However, in line with our earlier arguments we hold that a closer analysis of available data indicates that there are problems in attempting to impose a simple dual structure upon industry as a whole, locating any particular industry, such as woollen and worsted, unambiguously in one of the sectors.

The latest report of the Wool Textile EDC examines 161 firms which it estimates accounts for at least 92 per cent of the industry's total assets, and according to our calculation these firms employ over 90 per cent of all workers in the industry. A further breakdown of these figures shows the five largest companies in 1977 accounted for 33 per cent of assets, 31 per cent of sales, and 30 per cent of all employment. Of these five companies the second and third largest are both wholly-owned subsidiaries of the same parent company, representing their woollen and worsted interests. Summarising this data, it seems that four corporations share about 30 per cent of the industry while the smallest 600 or more firms (those outside the EDC survey) are responsible for something under 8 per cent of the industry's business. Table 15 shows the companies with assets over £0.5 million invested over £26 million in plant and property. Companies with assets over £5 million accounted for 61 per cent of this capital expenditure, and also for 68 per cent of the total £17 million of future commitments. It is noticeable that the ratio of plant to property is twice as high in large firms compared to small firms.

Table 14
Financial structure of wool textile industry

Asset size £m	Number of companies	Total assets £m	%
0.5-2.0	103	99	17.8
2.0-5.0	33	103	18.6
Over 5.0	25	353	63.6

Table 15
Capital expenditure and commitments 1976/77 (£000)

Asset size £m	Capital expenditure Property	Plant	Capital commitments
0.5-2.0	1,180	5,083	2,955
2.0-5.0	1,166	5,134	2,519
Over 5.0	1,516	12,219	11,814
Total	3,862	22,436	17,288

This brief analysis of the financial structure of the industry suggests, in accordance with our general analysis that the dualist model is likely to disguise the complexity of the situation in its imposition of an over-simple structure.

Finally in this section we have brought together some of the financial data with our analysis of concentration in the industry. According to dual labour market theories it would be expected that levels of capital intensity are lower where there is a high concentration of black workers. From all the data available we have taken the ratio of capital employed to remuneration, comparing industry inside with that out-side West Yorkshire. The results are given in Table 16, and would seem contrary to the expectations of dual labour market theorists.

Table 16
Capital intensity inside and outside West Yorkshire

	West Yorks.	Outside West Yorks.
Total value of capital employed (£m)	283.437	38.678
Total remuneration paid (£m)	124.129	18.069
Capital/Remuneration ratio	2.28:1	2.14:1

Stability of employment

A major role is played by the notion of job security in all versions of the dual labour market theory; in the secondary sector, it is agreed by all, that there is low job security. Now although we are not able to give a detailed analysis on the basis of information available to us at the present time we are able to note some interesting points.

During the period from 1973 to 1977 total employment in the industry fell from about 107,000 to about 78,000. On the basis of Wool Textile EDC data we are able to examine whether this decline was uniformly distributed through the industry. For 93 firms for which we have data we find that in 32 of them the total number of employees rose during this five-year period of substantial decline. If we look at the ten largest employees we find that the total number of persons in their employ fell only from 31,997 to 29,099, while their proportion of total employment in the industry rose from about 30 per cent to about 37 per cent.

Although, at present, we do not have any data on rates of labour turnover we would speculate that these figures do not point to low job security as being a characteristic of the employment conditions of a large number of workers in the woollen and worsted industry. It must be stressed, of course, that we are referring to notions of security in the sense used by dual labour market theorists. After all, it is not part of their account that unstable labour is employed in order that the firm can close down. What we are able to point out is that there are a certain number of firms in the industry that are adopting expansionist policies both with respect to employment of labour and of capital, even during this time of massive decline.

CONCLUSION

The primary purpose of this paper has been to assess whether dual labour market theory can adequately account for the structure of a particular industry, woollen and worsted. We would argue that it is impossible to impose a dualistic structure on our data. Whilst it is undoubtedly the case that the industry is relatively low paying, and has a high proportion of black and female workers, there are other characteristics that complicate the picture and lead us to reject any simple designation of woollen and worsted as a secondary industry.

In the area of wages we have seen in our comparative analysis that the relative disadvantage of working in the industry is greatest for men; wages for women, whilst low, are not the lowest for women's work in manufacturing industry as a whole. Wages for young people, particularly girls, are comparatively high. In the area of skill, we would argue on the basis of the census classifications that woollen and worsted is not a low skill industry, and to that extent employers are likely to be interested in the retention of skilled labour, a point which our analysis of the stability of employment in the industry supports. Also, our data seems to support the notion of the industry as gradually undergoing a process of concentration, such that by 1977, the ten largest employers, whether measured in terms of assets, sales or employment, employed 37 per cent of all workers in the industry.

The coexistence of these factors undermines the dualist argument which leads us to expect either the characteristics of the primary sector, or those of the secondary sector.

It is clear to us that in any analysis of labour in the woollen and worsted industry, the division of labour between men and women is very important. Our data seems to indicate that this division is not as strong here as it is in other industries. In terms of hourly wages, women earned 80.6 per cent of men's wages compared with 69.1 per cent in all manufacturing industry. Also, whilst there is considerable segregation between the sexes in occupational terms, it is not as great as in other industries, a finding which the 1971 census results support. Furthermore, given the finding that some women in other industries have higher hourly earnings than men in woollen and worsted, we feel that the intricacies of the sexual division of labour require further investigation outside of the dualistic framework.

This paper has had a limited objective: utilising data from the woollen and worsted industry, we have shown the difficulties of imposing a simple dualistic structure on the results. However, allowing for this, what positive suggestions can we make? Certainly dual labour market theory has pointed us in the right direction, by trying to move beyond the models of neo-classical economics into the area of sociology. However, the implications of such a move are only gradually being understood. In particular we would insist that the solution is not to be found in attempts merely to introduce social institutional determinants into the theory, either to supplement the determining effects of market forces, or to explain deviations from them. We have not been arguing simply that dual labour market theory presents an oversimplified picture, but also that it is cast in an inadequate mode of theorising.

It is this inadequacy that has given rise to our response which has been predominantly concerned with aggregate data, and wide-ranging trends. This rather static approach, for us, indicates the need to locate the analysis within the dynamic of the capital-labour relation that admits labour as a social relation and does not isolate the labour market as an object to be explained. In other words, to make sense of the position of labour in an industry such as woollen and worsted one must look at capital and the historical development of the capital-labour relation within the competitive conditions of the particular sector of industry under analysis. If we are interested in questions concerning the structure of wages, skills, occupations and sexual or ethnic segregation in the industry then we should not prejudge that structure by analysing it as consisting of some form of dualism. The problem with dual labour market theories seems to be that they have been reluctant to move into such concrete analyses which involve looking at the historical development of relations between capital and labour, between capitalists, and within the working class. (22)

In conclusion we would argue that the importation of dual labour market theory into British Sociology has borne fruit, in that it has prompted sociologists to enter the previously forbidden domain of the labour market. The time is now ripe to enter into a critical debate with that approach. In this paper, through an analysis of the woollen and worsted industry, we have tried to show the fundamental weaknesses of the theory and the necessity of moving towards a more concrete analysis of the capital-labour relation. It is then to a thorough reexamination of this in particular contexts that we must turn, rather than to the uncritical importation of terms such as 'dual' labour market.

NOTES

(1) See in particular P.B. Doeringer and M.J. Piore, <u>Internal Labour Markets and Manpower Analysis</u> (1971) and M.J. Piore, <u>Birds of Passage</u> (1979).
(2) R.C. Edwards, M. Reich and D.M. Gordon, <u>Labour Market Segmentation</u> (1975). Edwards has reformulated his ideas somewhat in <u>Contested Terrain</u> (1979) away from dualism to a slightly more complex analysis of labour, though retaining similar emphases.
(3) Edwards et al, <u>op.cit</u>, pp.x, xi, v.
(4) Besides the main articles by Bonacich: 'A Theory of Ethnic Antagonism: the Split Labour Market' <u>ASR</u> (1972) and 'Advanced Capitalism and Black/White relations in the US: A Split Labour Market Interpretation' in <u>ASR</u> (1976), see also J. Rubery, 'Structured Labour Markets, Worker Organisation and Low Pay', <u>Cambridge Journal of Economics</u>, 1978.
(5) Bonacich, 1976, p.44.
(6) C.f. R.M. Blackburn and M. Mann, <u>The Working Class in the Labour Market</u> (1979). 'It is not clear that it is

42

in the interests of capitalists to preserve women or indeed any other group as a separate segment of the labour force. If women, blacks, adolescents or any other secondary groups were suddenly interchangeable with white adult males might not the latter's average wages fall, just as the former's might rise. It is not clear at all that to retain segmentation keeps down the general level of wages and there is no evidence to show that employers believe this.' (p.31)

(7) Ibid, p.23.
(8) P.B. Doeringer and N. Bosanquet, 'Is There a Dual Labour Market in Britain?' Economic Journal 1973, p.432.
(9) Ibid, p.426.
(10) In D. Barker and S. Allen (eds.) Dependence and Exploitation in Work and Marriage (1974).
(11) J. Rex and S. Tomlinson, Colonial Immigrants in a British City (1979) p.279.
(12) Figures derived from the Wool Textile EDC Report entitled 'Finance and Profitability in Wool Textile Industry 1972/3-1976/7' (1979).
(13) All figures on production personnel are derived from the Census of Production conducted annually since 1969 by the Wool Industry Bureau of Statistics.
(14) The source for the wages statistics quoted here, unless otherwise stated, is from the Annual Survey of the Earnings of Manual Workers collected since 1967 and published each year in what is now the Department of Employment Gazette.
(15) In general we shall use the indicator of hourly earnings in our discussion of wages. Weekly earnings are slightly misleading because men nearly always work more hours a week than women and this explains the greater disparity between their weekly earnings than exists in relation to their hourly earnings.
(16) For example, M..Snell, 'The Equal Pay and Sex Discrimination Acts', Feminist Review 1, 1979.
(17) Figures derived from Wool Textile EDC, op.cit.
(18) A central question concerns whether there is such a thing as an objective skill; certainly one may doubt the Census classifications but whether one should doubt the whole idea of skill is another matter. See C. More, Skill and the English Working Class (1980) for a useful recent discussion.
(19) See Appendix A for a full list derived from the Classification of Occupations, 1970.
(20) Within the Census occupational groups for Yorkshire: West Riding, however, we can discern a degree of occupational segregation:

SEG 9	Per cent males	Per cent females
067	51	49
068	55	45
069	40	60
070	84	16
071	95	5

	Per cent males	Per cent females
SEG 9		
072	31	69
	53	47
SEG 10		
064	74	26
065	51	49
066	13	87
073	62	38
	49.5	50.5
SEG 11	75	25

(21) C. Hakim, 'Occupational Segregation' (Dept. of Employ-
     ment, 1979).
(22) For some interesting approaches that open up these
     problems in a way that looks fertile for the
     analysis of labour in woollen and worsted, see the
     articles in the Cambridge Journal of Economics 1979, 3.

Acknowledgements: We would like to acknowledge our thanks
to the staff of the Wool Industry Bureau of Statistics for
allowing us to examine the Annual Census of Production in
the Wool Industry.

APPENDIX A

Occupational Unit Group

X Textile Workers

064 <u>Fibre preparers</u>: persons preparing
fibres for spinning etc, including
openers, rag-grinders, wool sorters,
carders, combers, drawers and wool
washers. Persons setting up and
doing minor repairs and maintenance
and card grinders are included. Rag
and wool carbonisers are excluded
and classified in 070   10   IV

065 <u>Spinners, Doublers, Twisters</u>: persons
operating spinning and doubling
(twisting) machines in the manufacture
of yarn and thread. Persons setting
up, adjusting and doing minor repairs
and maintenance are included.   10   IV

066 <u>Winders, reelers</u>: Persons operating
machines which wind yarn and thread
from one package to another.
Persons setting up, adjusting and
doing minor repairs and maintenance
are included.   10   IV

067 <u>Warpers, sizers, drawers-in</u>: persons
operating machines which wind yarn
to weaver's beam: sizing yarn and
drawing threads into loom harness.
Persons setting up, adjusting and
doing minor repairs and maintenance
are included.   9   IIIM

068 <u>Weavers</u>: persons operating weaving
machines of all types; lace-makers.
Persons setting up, adjusting and
doing minor repairs and maintenance
are included.   9   IIIM

069 <u>Knitters</u>: persons operating knitting
machines or knitting by hand. Persons
setting up, adjusting and doing
minor repairs and maintenance are
included.   9   IIIM

070 <u>Bleachers and Finishers of Textiles</u>:
persons bleaching and otherwise
treating textile fibres, yarn, cloth
and goods including gassers, fullers,
calenderers, stenterers, rag and
wool carbonisers.   9   IIIM

071 <u>Dyers of textiles</u>: persons dyeing
textile fibres, yarn, cloth and goods. 9   IIIM

072 <u>Textile fabrics and related product</u>

45

makers and examiners n.e.c: persons examining textile yarn and cloth for defects and rectifying them (including minders and hosiery menders); making net, rope and twine; clipping lace; operating braiding machines; making bullion cord; preparing jacquard pattern cards; operating machines mixing and purifying fur fibre; forming hat forms from fur fibres and wool felt; hardening and shrinking hat forms; making wool felt sheeting. Self employed textile manufacturers are included.   9   IIIM

073 Textile fabrics etc. production process workers n.e.c: persons feeding or unloading textile machinery; piecing yarn; assisting jobbers (as banders, oilers and cleaners); guillotining and turning felt; winding and plaiting cloth; pressing yarn or waste; operating lace bobbin pressing, hydro-extracting, hosepipe brushing and turning, dust shaking machines; acting as assistant to rope-makers, dyers, harness builders, warpers, croppers, singers; employed in other textile fabric etc; production occupations not elsewhere classified.   10   IV

110 Labourers and unskilled workers n.e.c. Textiles: textile operators, cotton operators, and textile workers.   11   V

APPENDIX B

Production activities listed in WIBS Census

MERCHANTING, TOPMAKING, COMBING, etc.
1. Wool, hair, tops or noils warehouse
2. Wool sorting or grading
3. Wool carbonising
4. Wool scouring
5. Wool recombing only
6. Wool combing and/or recombing
7. Man made fibres combing
8. Machine blender or willeyers

WORSTED SPINNING
9. Tops and roving warehouse
10. Yarn warehouse and despatch
11. All operations up to and including folding
12. Winding reeling and warping
13. Making up, etc.

RAG WASTE MERCHANTING AND PROCESSING
14. Rag and waste, etc. warehouse
15. Rag waste sorters
16. Rag and waste pullers
17. Machine blender and willeyers
18. Carbonisers and dyers

WOOLLEN SPINNING
19. Warehouse and raw material
20. Wool sorters and graders
21. Rag and waste sorters
22. Rag and waste pullers
23. Carbonisers and dyers
24. Machine Wenders, willeyers, scourers, Carders, Fetters,
    Spinners, pieceners
25. Winding reeling and warping
26. Yarn warehouse
27. Making up

MANUFACTURING
28. Yarn warehouse
29. Winding, reeling and warping
30. Twisting in, healding
31. Weaving, turning, etc.
32. Perching, bailing, knotting, mending
33. Pattern room and piece warehouse

DYEING (OTHER THAN RAG DYEING).
34. Yarn dyeing, slubbing dyeing
35. Piece dying

FINISHING
36. Milling and scouring
37. All other finishing processes

MISCELLANEOUS
38. Miscellaneous occupations

FELLMONGERING
39. All occupations

3 Patterns of Disadvantage in a City Labour Market

JIM COUSINS AND MARGARET CURRAN

INTRODUCTION

The study of inequality is nearly always conducted by
reference to the possession of a disadvantaged status (such
as being out of work) at a point in time, or by reference
to distributions along a scale (such as family incomes) at
a single point in time:

> The spotlight picks out the variety of particular
> circumstances - old age, sickness, large family size,
> single parenthood, unemployment, especially low pay
> which push working-class people under an arbitrarily
> defined poverty line. It leaves only dimly lit the
> wider structure of inequality, and the overall
> condition of dependence which exposes workers at large
> to the risk of 'poverty' in such circumstances. (1)

The inequality revealed, or assumed, by scale distributions suffers from definitional problems and the political
weakness of being ineradicable. (2) The lowest decile <u>will</u>
always be with us. It also builds the minority status of
the disadvantaged into the definition, and encourages
interpretations based on personal, cultural or ethnic
attributes. (3) To study inequality or deprivation by
reference to current unemployment is similarly limited.
Until the last five years unemployment seemed to be a
locally, or regionally concentrated problem. The traditional
analytical division of unemployment into frictional,
cyclical and structural components assisted in breaking
down the unemployed of any one time into sub-minorities.
The most numerous of these were unemployed only for short,
transition periods between jobs. Amongst the unemployed
only small minorities were unemployed repeatedly, or for
long continuous periods (though no one was sure how these
two groups overlapped). These minorities could be held to
account for a large share of the total quantity of unemployment measured in man-weeks, (4) and a large proportion of
the total number of unemployment incidents, measured in
separate spells. (5) Even though the total numbers of
unemployed are now at high levels the 'real problem' of
unemployment can still be seen as long term or recurrent
unemployment which is an experience of only very small

numbers in the workforce, with very particular personal, family or locational attributes. (6)

It is, of course, possible to combine the analysis of status disadvantage and scale inequality to see the long term unemployed as the 'core of a lumpenproletariat' separate from the rest of a 'cohesive and homogeneous' working class; (7) or to see labour market inequality being particularly concentrated on those few who are the victims of a 'severe package of disadvantages'. (8)

In this way inequality becomes a problem related to the existence of a number of small, specified, residual groups - 'separated subsets facing a particular difficulty' (9) - separated from each other and from society at large. Nor does the currently fashionable preoccupation with the dual labour market necessarily help. It is true that the 'primary' and 'secondary' labour markets can be related to structural features of the economy. But, when it is so related, the secondary labour market almost immediately decomposes into different sorts of secondary labour market. (10)

Attempts to define, rather than describe the secondary labour market are operationally inchoate, and there is a general readiness to switch into discussion in terms of 'sub-cultures' or personal attributes, or phases in people's work careers, typically before settling down. (11) If it starts by dividing the labour force into sharply differentiated sectors, the call to investigate employment inequality in terms of 'structures' rather than individuals risks ending where it began: with culturally defined and divided residual groups, clearly differentiated from the workforce at large.

It is by looking at the experience of individuals through time that we can see whether the labour market is so clearly segmented, and the experience of inequality so focussed on a congeries of small, sharply defined minorities, as these approaches suggest. It may instead be that:

the poor are not a separate and relatively fixed section of society. At any particular time there are households who, because of demotion, unemployment, sickness, disablement, retirement or increase in dependency, have recently fallen into poverty, just as there are households who, because of promotion, engagement or re-engagement at work, recovery from sickness or decrease in dependency, have just emerged from poverty. (12)

There are now a number of indications of a longer term assessment of the impact and extent of employment inequality being adopted. It is this approach which can test whether those experiencing employment disadvantage are as diverse, as few in number, and as sharply differentiated from the mass of the labour force as previously implied.

The longer term assessment of work careers was an approach

favoured many years ago by students of labour mobility. (13) Their conclusions are also not without interest, though the context of their work (the return to a peacetime labour market) was entirely different. They found that though the experience of <u>frequent</u> job changing was a characteristic of a minority of the labour force (usually around 15 per cent), job changing was a very widespread experience. The longitudinal studies of Glasgow boys in the labour market drew similar conclusions: 25 per cent of boys were frequent job changers; and 11 per cent experienced unemployment of over three months in length over a two year period of virtually complete full employment. (14)

A number of more recent studies argue for, or provide evidence of, the existence of widespread 'underemployment' or 'subemployment'. (15) These indicate that many of the unemployed are recurrently unemployed, whether for long or short periods: thus Hill (1974) noted that 60 per cent of the unemployed in Newcastle had been unemployed twice or more in the last three years, while Daniel (1977) found that less than 20 per cent of the 1973 unemployed had stable employment between 1973 and 1976. Also, over a period of years many men in the labour force will experience unemployment. According to Norris (1978) 25 per cent of men in Sunderland had suffered unemployment over a five year period, and 15.6 per cent were to be regarded as 'subemployed'; 38 per cent of a sample of currently employed men in North Shields had experienced some form of unemployment over a ten year period (Turner, 1978).

In the analysis of low pay the Low Pay Unit have reworked the earnings survey figures for April, 1976 to show that, if PBR supplements and overtime and shift pay are excluded, over 40 per cent of manual men have basic pay less than the lowest decile cut-off point for all earnings combined. (16) The Department of Employment reworked the earnings surveys for 1970-74 to examine those individuals who were in the survey in all years: 21.5 per cent of the male workforce were in the lowest decile of earners in at least one of the five years. (17)

Almost all the studies mentioned refer to the period before the much higher levels of unemployment of the last five years. Much of the detailed survey work relates only to a sample that starts with the currently unemployed (though Turner has a matched sample of currently employed men and Norris draws his samples of unemployed and subemployed men from a much larger household survey. It is for this reason that Norris' study casts most doubt on the assumed atypicality of the subemployed). Nor do these studies tell us as much as we should wish about the <u>employ-ment</u> as well as <u>unemployment</u> histories of respondents. For this reason it becomes easy to equate the low skills of their most recent jobs with their underemployment. Nonetheless these studies clearly do confirm that the types and the extent of employment disadvantage, as well as the sharpness of the dividing line between those currently so disadvantaged and those not, are real issues.

THE LABOUR MARKET IN NEWCASTLE ON TYNE

Newcastle is, in a sense, a dual economy. It has a concentration of service industry appropriate to a 'regional capital', drawing in a large nonresident commuter labour force. It is a regional capital not only for commerce, finance and distribution, but also for central government (regional headquarters offices and the large DHSS complex at Longbenton); local government (not only the City Council but also two local County Councils); public services (law courts; the regional water and regional health authority headquarters); education (Newcastle University and Polytechnic); and health services (three major hospitals which contain virtually all the regional specialisms).

Second, it is part of industrial Tyneside with its base still in shipbuilding, ship-repairing, heavy engineering and heavy electrical engineering. Perhaps to these a third element should be added: a large construction labour force which existed in the 1970s on central area redevelopments and several large infrastructure projects such as roads, the Tyneside interceptor sewerage scheme and the Tyne and Wear 'metro' rapid transit railway. (18)

The data used in this paper were drawn from a comparison of three areas of Newcastle upon Tyne: two 'inner' areas and one 'outer'. (19) These areas were chosen to reflect both sides of the city's economy outlined above. The inner city area with a manufacturing base ('Walker') comprised five enumeration districts in Walker and Walkergate wards, two miles and more to the east of the centre of Newcastle. The other inner city area ('Elswick') consisted of five 1971 census enumeration districts in Benwell and West City wards less than one and a half miles to the west of the city centre. The outer city area ('Denton') was composed of three enumeration districts in the Denton and Westerhope wards about four miles to the west of the centre of the city. All three areas are similar in their socioeconomic and tenure base: all are areas of rented, overwhelmingly municipally-owned housing (Walker less so than the rest), and overwhelmingly working class (Denton less so than the rest).

The areas were chosen after discussion with Newcastle City Council officials and after consulting 1971 Census Enumeration District data and other more recent Ward level survey data. We knew from research carried out in 1977 in a different, but adjacent, area of Elswick that there was a heavy dependence on employment in the service sector (transport, distribution, public sector services, etc.) in that area. (20) Available information suggested that in Walker there was still considerable male employment in shipbuilding and marine engineering, and heavy electrical engineering. Employment in Denton was likely to be varied and to involve considerable journeys to work as there were few sources of employment close to the area. We also knew that the areas were different both in their housing stock, and the degree of housing change that they had experienced since the 1971 Census. In both the inner city areas, and especially in Elswick, considerable changes have taken place during the last decade.

The results of a household survey to half the households in the chosen enumeration districts, and a follow-up, more detailed survey to all the economically active members of these households confirmed this general picture of employment. The occupational and industrial structure of these three areas was different, as expected. Denton had the greatest numbers of clerical and related workers: 23 per cent of male fulltime workers were in clerical, sales or professional work, compared with 17 per cent in Walker and 14 per cent in Elswick. Employment in Elswick was dominated by services (especially transport and distribution for men) though, by contrast, it had the highest proportion of manufacturing workers amongst women. Walker's employment was dominated by heavy manufacturing industry employment for men.

However, there was little difference between the areas in training or qualifications, which were everywhere at low levels. The most significant source of training was apprenticeship for men but only about 30 per cent of men had been apprentices in Walker and Denton, and even fewer in Elswick.

About a quarter of male, and 30 per cent of female employment, was in the city centre. Residents of inner city areas worked mostly in the inner city of Newcastle, though about 20 per cent of men in Walker and about 10 per cent in Elswick worked in adjacent Districts' inner areas. Outer area residents' employment was split about half and half between inner and outer areas. Significantly the use of a car to get to work was highest for Denton men, though even there it did not exceed use of public transport. Walking and cycling remained significant modes of travel, and in inner areas exceeded the use of cars.

Earnings were everywhere low, though there are reasons to suppose that the extremely low earnings figures we found may be exaggerated. Car and telephone ownership was about the city average or above in Denton, but much lower in Walker and Elswick, where less than 20 per cent of households had access to a car.

In other words, the three areas we studied were representative of the labour market for workers in Newcastle. They were characterised by manual work and council housing. Jobs were drawn from a very confined area and the dominant mode of travel to work was public transport (bus). The data which follow concern patterns of male employment in these areas.

THE INCIDENCE OF EMPLOYMENT DISADVANTAGE

The detailed surveys on the employment patterns of economically active men were completed in Spring 1979. Therefore, the data do not reflect the recent intensification
of employment problems. Even so, the men we interviewed
were experiencing, or had experienced a considerable degree
of employment disadvantage. We summarise this experience
here under three headings: lack of employment, lack of
skill and lack of stability or security.

Lack of employment

Male unemployment was high by the national level current at
the time of the survey in 1979 (which was about 6.5 per
cent). Unemployment in Denton was slightly above the regional and city levels of the time (10 per cent). Unemployment
in Walker was much higher (14 per cent for men); and higher
still in Elswick (20 per cent plus). Half the unemployed
had been out of work for over six months. But the experience of unemployment was more widespread than these
figures suggest. Forty per cent of men in Walker and
Denton had experienced at least one period of unemployment
in the last ten years. In Elswick 70 per cent of men had
experienced at least one period of unemployment.

Recurrent unemployment was also not an uncommon experience. A third of men in Elswick, a fifth of men in
Walker and an eighth in Denton had had two or more spells
of unemployment within the last ten years. Recurrent unemployment seems particularly to be a feature of men under
the age of thirty, in all three areas. In Walker nearly
30 per cent of men under thirty had been unemployed at
least twice; in Elswick, 40 per cent. Experience of a single
period of unemployment over a year in length within the
last ten years was less common: about 13 per cent in Walker
and Elswick, and 7 per cent in Denton. However, when the
periods of unemployment were added up to see if they
totalled more than a year and assessed together with recurrent unemployment, it once again seemed that large
numbers of men had experienced either two or more spells
or periods which cumulated to a year: 22 per cent in
Walker, 17 per cent in Denton and 38 per cent in Elswick.

Experience of unemployment was, therefore, widespread as
at May 1979. About a fifth of men had experienced either
recurrent or intense unemployment.

Lack of skill

Few male workers, less than an eighth, were currently
employed in unskilled work, although this is itself a
large figure compared with the overall Newcastle figure of
seven per cent. Fewer workers still had been entirely
dependent on unskilled work over ten years. However, the
numbers of workers with at least some experience of unskilled work are not spread evenly in our three areas, and

are much larger than the current figures. Nearly 40 per cent of Elswick's workers had some experience of unskilled work, 24 per cent of Walker's, but only 14 per cent of Denton's. Experience of unskilled work rises for men in their twenties to almost half of Elswick men, 30 per cent in Walker and 20 per cent in Denton.

A high level of experience of unemployment is also a feature that is very strongly associated with experience of unskilled work. Eighty per cent of workers who had experienced unskilled work had also experienced unemployment. Once again Elswick had the highest figure (89 per cent) and Denton the lowest (67 per cent). More than half of men with experience of unskilled work had been made redundant at least once; and their current unemployment rates were 25 per cent in Denton, 20 per cent in Walker and 37 per cent in Elswick. The same applies to recurrent unemployment (two or more spells): 60 per cent of unskilled in Elswick, 40 per cent in Walker and 30 per cent in Denton had had recurrent unemployment.

If semiskilled work is included with unskilled then over a third of currently employed men in Walker and Elswick are 'nonskilled' workers, about double the city average; and 22 per cent in Denton. Almost half of Walker men had experienced nonskilled work over ten years; 35 per cent in Denton and 64 per cent in Elswick. The experience of semiskilled work is associated with the experience of unemployment at least once over ten years, though not nearly as strongly as in the case of unskilled workers; over half of those with semiskilled experience in Walker and Denton and over 80 per cent in Elswick had been unemployed.

Yet there must be a note of caution about the equation of lack of skill with employment disadvantage. The degree of stratification of the workforce into skill groups can be exaggerated. For example, 'skill' is defined here as census Socioeconomic group 9. This includes a great many workers who are not skilled in the sense that a Tyneside heavy engineering worker would recognise, such as van drivers and bus drivers. Only half of the workers with experience of skilled manual work had worked at skilled manual jobs continuously over ten years (though this figure was much higher in the shipyard and engineering employment area of Walker where skill boundaries were more rigid). Of those with experience of other work as well as skilled manual work, over half had experience of semiskilled work and about a third of unskilled work. Less than 70 per cent of those who had ever had skilled manual work were currently employed in that sort of work: 18 per cent were in other sorts of work (mostly less skilled) and 13 per cent were unemployed.

The work experience of those with experience of semiskilled and unskilled work was much less 'stratified' (or more 'diluted') even than this. Little more than a quarter of those with experience of semiskilled manual work had

worked only in jobs of that kind. Of those with experience
of other sorts of job 60 per cent had experience of skilled
work, and a third of unskilled. Only 10 per cent of those
with experience of unskilled manual work had had no
experience of other sorts of work. Of those who had done
other types of work, all had some experience of semiskilled
work, and about half of skilled manual work.

The degree of stratification is also clearly lessening.
Only 27 per cent of men over forty with experience of
skilled manual work had ever worked in any other sort of
work in the last ten years. Amongst men under 40 nearly 60
per cent had experience of other sorts of work. Therefore,
there seems to be an association of the experience of nonskilled work with the experience of unemployment, and the
number of those with experience of nonskilled manual work
is both large, and likely to become larger: 42 per cent of
those under forty had experience of semiskilled manual
work, and only 22 per cent of those over forty; 31 per cent
under forty experienced unskilled manual work, and only 10
per cent of those over forty.

Lack of stability and security

About 30 per cent of workers had only had one job within the
last ten years (though 16 per cent of these men had been
unemployed). At the other extreme about a quarter of the
men (nearly half of those in Elswick) had had four or more
jobs in the last ten years. The mean number of jobs per man
was 2.8 in Walker and Denton, and 4 in Elswick. Thirty per
cent of those who had left jobs at all had had at least one
experience of redundancy; 50 per cent of those with experience of unskilled manual work had experienced
redundancy.

Many of these job changes were 'complex', that is, they
involved a change of occupation, type of work or industry
as well as a change of employer. Of those who had experienced any job change at all in the last ten years, 71
per cent had experienced a change of CODOT occupation major
group; 73 per cent a change of OPCS occupational order;
71 per cent a change of Socioeconomic group and 80 per
cent a change of industry (as defined by SIC industry
order). Nor were those workers who had skilled manual work
experience much less likely to have complex job changes.
Among the skilled men 68 per cent had changed CODOT group,
69 per cent OPCS group, 65 per cent socioeconomic group and
83 per cent industry. (21)

However, frequency of job change does seem related to
unskilled work and age (particularly among the under-
forties). Eighty per cent of those who had changed jobs
four or more times in the last ten years were under forty
at the date of interview. Eighty per cent of those with
experience of unskilled jobs had had more than three jobs
in ten years. All but a handful of these were under forty
at the date of interview: 29 per cent were currently

unemployed; and 31 per cent had been unemployed three times
or more over ten years (though 20 per cent were currently
working in jobs that were either nonmanual or skilled
manual). These men were not an insignificant number and
comprised 19 per cent of all economically active male respondents. But they accounted for less than half of the men
with three or more jobs (who comprised 44 per cent of all
male respondents). Indeed, half the men with even skilled
manual experience had had three or more jobs: 80 per cent
of these were also under forty; 16 per cent of them were
currently unemployed; 19 per cent had been unemployed three
or more times in ten years; 24 per cent were currently
working in semi or unskilled manual jobs; and a third were
working in construction, transport or distribution. So, the
association of frequent job changing with various kinds of
labour market penalty seems widespread. It is particularly
striking in the case of those who have experience of unskilled manual work, but certainly not confined to them.

If the experience of recurrent unemployment (two spells or
more) is taken together with frequent job changing (three or
more jobs) 16 per cent of all workers appear in both categories. But while Walker and Denton are very similar (14
per cent and 11 per cent respectively of all male workers
appear in this group), Elswick is clearly different (29 per
cent appear).

To conclude, the high unemployment rates which are
apparent in the areas we studied are only the starting point
to considering the labour market disadvantages of workers
there. When work histories are assessed over a period of
years a much wider (in the sense of the numbers of men
affected), and a much deeper (in the sense that there is a
range of recurring problems) package of disadvantage
appears. Yet it is possible that while the base of disadvantage is a broad one, distinct and separate types of
economic disadvantage might exist.

TYPES OF ECONOMIC DISADVANTAGE

In order to test the existence of distinct groups of the
economically disadvantaged, we defined five possible types
of employment disadvantage: two by reference to current
jobs, two by reference to experience of unemployment, and
one by reference to employment history. These groups were
then analysed to see how far their memberships overlapped,
and how far they had attributes of employment disadvantage
other than the defining ones.

The first group we called those in 'poor jobs'. These
were currently employed in jobs classified under census
social classes 4 and 5 (broadly semi and unskilled manual
work) and also in the lowest earnings band (which was an
estimate of the lowest decile of regional earners as at
the previous year's earnings survey and revised for inflation). Fifteen per cent of currently employed men came into

this group. Next we identified a group of 'new entrants into poor prospect jobs'. These were aged between sixteen and twenty-one and were employed in construction, labouring n.e.c, transport, junior clerical, sales, service, sport and recreation workers (OPCS occupation groups 15 to 23). This group comprised half the employed men of the appropriate age group. Next was a group of men, 'the long-term unemployed', who had experienced a period of unemployment over a year in length at any time since 1969. This included 13 per cent of all men, but a quarter of men in Elswick. Then there were 'the recurrently unemployed' who had had at least two periods of unemployment in their working lives. Almost a quarter of the men we interviewed were included. Finally there were the 'unstably employed' who had had an average length of job of less than a year since 1969. This group was 15 per cent of all men. Of all the men we interviewed, 44 per cent came into one or other of the five groups, of whom half were in at least two groups.

'Poor Jobs'

Members of this group were some of the least overlapped with other groups. It was not particularly strongly linked to any one other group. The strongest links were with recurrent unemployment (29 per cent); the weakest with long term unemployment (18 per cent). The main source of employment for these men was in construction, transport, professional services, and, in Walker, other manufacturing. Their employers were likely to be small, or in the public sector. The men were mostly very young but with a group of men in their forties in Walker, and forties and fifties in Denton as well. In Denton (but only there) this group tended to be a group of poor but respectable workers - less likely to have promotion prospects, but less likely to have been unemployed than other workers in Denton. These men were less likely to have worked in skilled manual work, or have any qualifications, But they were much more likely to have changed job, and changed it in 'complex' ways.

New entrants in poor prospect jobs

This group was small, but very closely overlapped with other groups. It was strongly linked to the poor jobs group (50 per cent) and to the 'unstably employed' (46 per cent) but less well to the unemployed groups. Their work was non-skilled, though there was an element of routine clerical work. Their level of trade union membership was low. They had an above average tendency to have school qualifications in Walker and Denton, but a well below average tendency in Elswick. They were rather more likely to have been unemployed and to have had job changes than their age group.

The long term unemployed

This was a group nearly all of whose members were members of other groups. Two-thirds were also members of the recurrently unemployed group, and 39 per cent were members of

the unstably employed group, though other connections were
weak. They were highly geographically concentrated into
Elswick and one small part of Walker. They were much less
likely to be car owners, and more likely to be under forty
in Walker and Denton and under thirty in Elswick. About half
were currently unemployed, though only in the case of less
than a half of the group was it their present unemployment
that had caused them to be defined in the group. In other
words, this group was chronically unemployed. Their jobs
were likely to be in foundries, construction and transport.
They were very much more likely to have had unskilled work,
and to have experienced redundancy. They were three times
more likely to have had an average job length of under two
years, and twice as likely to have had complex job changes.
In summary, the long term unemployed did not have a different
sort of employment from the recurrently unemployed but a
less skilled, and more chronically unemployed version of it.

The recurrently unemployed

This group was a large one and one of the least well
connected to other groups: 42 per cent were nonmembers of
any other group; 35 per cent of its members were also in
the long term unemployed group and 33 per cent in the
unstably employed group. It was very much a group of inner
city area residents. Forty per cent of its members were
currently unemployed, and those of its members who did have
jobs were rather less likely to be skilled manual workers.
There was less of an industrial concentration than in the
case of the long term unemployed; they were rather less
likely to have experience of skilled manual, and rather more
likely to have had nonskilled manual work. Their work experience was much less different from the sample as a whole
than that of the long term unemployed, though they were
almost as likely to have had an average job length of under
two years as the long-term unemployed.

The unstably employed

Two-thirds of this group were members of other groups, the
strongest connection being with recurrent unemployment (53
per cent) and long term unemployment (33 per cent). Three-
quarters of its members were under thirty, but over two-
thirds were currently working. The number working in skilled
manual work was not very different from that for men taken
as a whole. Nearly all worked for smaller employers. Over
80 per cent had been unemployed at some time. The employment history of this group shows them not less likely to
have been skilled manuals, but much more likely to have been
nonskilled manual workers. They were more likely to have had
two periods of unemployment, and more likely to have
accumulated more than a year of unemployment in their
working life (though not necessarily as a single period),
despite being much younger than men as a whole. They were
obviously more likely to have had complex changes of job
than the sample as a whole, though less so, especially in
the case of changes of industry, than other deprived groups.

The unstably employed show up as a group of younger men working for small employers; not necessarily less skilled but moving around from job to job. They were gradually accumulating a substantial experience of unemployment.

In conclusion, the groups showing least overlap with membership of other groups were those in poor jobs and those recurrently unemployed. But there were reasonably strong links between all three groups constructed by reference to work history. It becomes possible to see different patterns of employment disadvantage. For example, those in poor jobs in 1979 seem relatively distinct from those with experience of unemployment. But, while they are no more likely to have had two or more spells of unemployment than men as a whole, yet still 30 per cent of them had done so. There are no distinct boundaries between these groups. There is neither distinct membership nor any common basis of membership across the groups.

MULTIPLE ECONOMIC DEPRIVATION

Since it was not readily possible to define distinct groups with employment disadvantage, we then explored the possibility of devising a portmanteau category of employment disadvantage which could discriminate between those who were disadvantaged and those who were not. We scored our respondents on seven indicators: (i) having a current job in census social classes 4 and 5; (ii) being in the lowest earnings band; (iii) having an average job length of a year or less since 1969; (iv) having had work experience of unskilled manual work; (v) having experienced redundancy since 1969; (vi) having had at least two periods of unemployment since 1969 and (vii) having at least one period of unemployment longer than six months.

When a score of three was selected, the best fit was found with membership of the five previous groups. Only 26 cases were left out and only 17 more included: 42 per cent of men were included as 'multiply economically deprived' on this definition; 35 per cent of the economically active men of the outer area, Denton, were included, 41 per cent of Walker men and 57 per cent of Elswick men.

It is important to realise how internally inchoate the multiply economically deprived were. Three-quarters of the lowest earnings group were included, three-quarters of those experiencing redundancy, 80 per cent of those experiencing unskilled manual work, and 90 per cent of those with two plus periods of unemployment or any period of long unemployment. Yet barely half, at best, of the group had any one of these attributes. Though the group were less likely to be in skilled work, nearly 30 per cent of those with a current job were in skilled manual work. Again, though this group was particularly strongly represented in a small range of current occupations (food, drink; general labourers; warehouse workers; miscellaneous services); and in a small range of current industries (food, construction, professional and scientific services) this range accounted for only 40 per cent of all the current occupations, and a third of the current industries of the group. The group was much more likely to have had complex job changes than those not in the group, but no particular sort of complex change affected more than a third of the group. They were far more likely to have had first jobs in nonskilled manual work but only 43 per cent of the group had started out in such jobs.

In an attempt to distinguish clearly between the multiply deprived and the non-multiply deprived we applied dis- criminant analysis to the two groups. When compared with the nondeprived, multiply economically deprived men tend to be: younger, and _more likely_ to have worked in the public sector after 1969; to have worked outside Tyne and Wear; to be the sole economically active person in the household; to be single; to choose a self determination statement in a forced choice question; and to give pay as the most important feature in a job. They are _less likely_ to: have a first job in SEG 8 and 9; to have completed an apprentice- ship; to be able to specify a main line of work; to specify a main line of work in SEG 8 or 9; to have a 'skilled' father; to have had training in jobs after 1969 (after a correction for the number of jobs); to think job prospects are good; and to give security or interest or prospects as a 'most important job feature'.

Discriminant analysis was used in an attempt to find a linear combination of those factors which will 'predict' whether a given individual is or is not deprived. Using this method the factors which discriminated between the multiply deprived and the nondeprived are as follows (in order of importance as reflected by standardised coefficients):
1. not having a skilled main line of work
2. not having had training in jobs since 1969
3. being under thirty
4. not rating job security first as a job feature
5. not rating 'interest of job' first
6. not rating job prospects first.

However, this discriminant function is overall not very successful (canonical correlation = 0.415). When used to predict group membership (i.e. deprived/nondeprived) of the men in the sample it is fairly efficient in identifying the nondeprived (81 per cent correctly classified with a prior of 58 per cent based on sample size) but much less good at identifying the deprived (55 per cent correctly classified with a prior of 42 per cent). But, if an add- itional dummy variable for area is included in the function, its inclusion only adds very marginally to the explanatory power. Hence, although these factors do not constitute an entirely adequate method of predicting group membership, the 'deprived' are distinguished from the 'nondeprived' by their lack of skill and training, their youth, and their relative lack of interest in job security, interest and prospects. But note that the latter factors do not necessarily reflect

a 'money-seeking' insecure labour market strategy. It may
simply be that the important feature of a job for the
deprived is that it exists and gives income. There is no
statistical evidence of a very strong 'Elswick effect'.

The factors that discriminate best between the deprived
and the nondeprived, relate, as we have seen elsewhere in
this paper, to being young. But are these differences an
attribute of youth itself (in which case the young can be
expected to 'mature')? Or are they caused by recent changes
in the labour market which the young have particularly
experienced? In the latter case the young will not mature;
and gradually the labour market characteristics of the
deprived will become general to the labour force as a whole.
The answer to this question will perhaps be clearer when the
analysis of a second round of interviews carried out a year
and a half later in the autumn of 1980, becomes available.

CONCLUSION

We have attempted to outline the extent and nature of
employment disadvantage; to explore the possibility that
there are different kinds of disadvantage; and to seek out
the factors that separate the disadvantaged from the not-
so-disadvantaged. It does not seem to us that, in the areas
where our study was done, disadvantaged men in the labour
market can be seen as a small, tightly-defined residual
group.

If the disadvantaged formed a large group, but one with
distinct subgroups, then it would be possible to mount
subgroup-specific ameliorative policy programmes. The
political consequences of widespread economic disadvantage
would be limited by sectionalism amongst the disadvantaged.
On the other hand, if the disadvantaged were a large group
that could be readily distinguished from the nondeprived,
the policy problems of dealing with disadvantage would be
much more intractable; and the political consequences of a
large definite disadvantaged group could well be far-
reaching. However, neither of these possibilities seem to
apply to those we studied. It is possible to see some
difference in the pattern of disadvantage, but the differences are not such as to create very distinct groups. There
is a large overlap between the groups, and a number of
indicators and attributes which members of the different
groups can have in common. Nor is it easy to discriminate
between the disadvantaged and the not-so-disadvantaged.

It seems that large numbers of men in the kind of
northern, working-class, council estate areas we studied
experience disadvantage in the labour market at some point
in their working lives; and that those who do not are not
very different from those who do. As recent writers on
unemployment have pointed out (22), it is for most a transitory status with which men do not identify even as they
experience it. Even in a community with a very high level of

chronic employment problems these problems will only affect a minority at any one time. The young, though, have a higher level of exposure to disadvantage, possibly because they are affected more by recent changes in the labour market. If so, then employment disadvantage may well for them, and their successors, become a normal and general experience. But, even if the degree of employment disadvantage we can see in our study in 1979 worsens, and continues for several years, inurement and isolation may be as likely an outcome as protest and change.

NOTES

The data on the urban labour market of Newcastle which are drawn on in this paper form part of a wider study supported by the Department of the Environment's Inner City Research Programme. This study investigated the work situation, careers and attitudes of the economically active members of a sample of households in three areas of the City of Newcastle. The views expressed are those of the authors and not necessarily those of the Department itself.

(1) J. Westergaard and H. Resler, Class in a Capitalist Society, Penguin, Harmondsworth, 1975, p.19.
(2) R. Berthoud, The Disadvantages of Inequality, a PEP Report, Macdonald and James, London, 1976, p.27.
(3) M. Castells, The Economic Crisis and American Society, Blackwell, Oxford, 1980, pp.186-7.
(4) R. Disney, 'Recurrent spells and the concentration of unemployment in Great Britain', Economic Journal, March, 1979.
(5) J. Stern, 'Who Bears the Burden of Unemployment?' in W. Beckerman (ed.), Slow Growth in Britain, OUP, Oxford, 1978.
(6) S. Brittan, Second Thoughts on Full Employment Policy, Policy Studies Institute, London, 1975.
(7) D. Metcalf, 'Unemployment: History, Incidence and Prospects', Policy and Politics, vol.8, no.1, 1980, pp.21-37, p.27.
(8) M.J. Hill, evidence to Royal Commission on Income and Wealth Distribution in Select Evidence to Report No.6, HMSO, London, 1978.
(9) G. Norris, 'Defining urban deprivation', in C. Jones (ed.), Urban Deprivation and the Inner City, Croom Helm, London, 1979, p.28. Norris argues vigorously against this approach.
(10) R. Kreckel, 'Unequal opportunity structure and labour market segmentation', Sociology, 1980, pp.525-49; R. Loveridge and A. Mok, 'Theoretical approaches to segmented labour markets', International Journal of Social Economics, 1981, pp.376-411.
(11) P.B. Doeringer and M.J. Piore, Internal Labour Markets and Manpower Analysis, Heath, Lexington, 1971, esp. ch.8; N. Bosanquet and P.B. Doeringer, 'Is there a Dual Labour Market in Britain?', Economic Journal, 1973, pp.421-35; R.C. Edwards, M. Reich and D.M.Gordon

(ed.), Labour Market Segmentation, Heath, Lexington, 1975, esp. introduction, and papers, by H.M. Wachtel and M.J. Piore.

(12) P. Townsend, ch.19 in A.B. Atkinson (ed.), Wealth, Income and Inequality, Second Edition, OUP, Oxford, 1980.

(13) M. Jefferys, Mobility in the Labour Market, Routledge and Kegan Paul, London, 1954; G.L. Palmer, Labour Mobility in Six Cities, SSRC, New York, 1954; H.S. Parnes, Research into Labour Mobility, SSRC, New York, 1954.

(14) Ferguson and Cunnison, The Young Wage Earner: a study of Glasgow Boys, Nuffield, OUP, Oxford, 1951, and In Their Early Twenties, Nuffield, OUP, Oxford, 1956.

(15) For example, A. Sinfield, 'Poor and out of work in Shields', ch.13 of P. Townsend (ed.), The Concept of Poverty, Heinemann, London, 1970 (data relates to 1963-4); D.M. Gordon, (ed.), Problems in Political Economy - an Urban Perspective, D.C. Heath, Lexington, 1971; D.M. Gordon, Theories of Poverty and Under-Employment, D.C. Heath, Lexington, 1972 (data refers for the most part to 1967-9); M.J. Hill, 'Unstable employment in the histories of unemployed men', IMS Monitor, December, 1974, pp.70-84 (data refers to 1971-2); G.M. Norris, 'Unemployment, Sub employment and personal characteristics, I and II', Sociological Review, 1978 (data refers to 1972-3); W.W. Daniel, 'A National Survey of the Unemployed', PEP Broadsheet no.546, 1974, (data refers to 1973); and the follow-up W.W. Daniel and E. Stilgoe, 'Where are they now?', PEP 1977, (data refers to 1976); Department of the Environment, Inner London, policies for dispersal and balance, HMSO, London, 1977 (report of employment survey, pp.78-9 (data refers to 1972-3); S. Turner and F. Dickinson, In and out of work, North Tyneside CDP, 1978, (data refers to 1976); and P. Townsend, Poverty in the United Kingdom, Penguin, Harmondsworth, 1979 (data refers to 1968-9).

(16) Evidence of the Low Pay Unit to the Royal Commission on the Distribution of Income and Wealth, Select Evidence for Report no.6, HMSO, London, 1978.

(17) Department of Employment, 'How Individual Earnings Change', D.E. Gazette, January, 1977.

(18) For a readable polemical review of the City's economy and prospects see Permanent Unemployment, Final Report Series, Benwell Community Development Project, 1978.

(19) A full description of the research on which this is based is contained in Urban Employment Study, First Report: Households, Individuals and the Economically Active in three areas of Newcastle upon Tyne (1980) and Second Report: Characteristics and Attitudes of the Economically Active (1980), both obtainable from Urban Employment Study, Department of Sociology and Social Policy, University of Durham.

(20) J.M. Cousins and R.K. Brown, Transmitted Deprivation and the Local Labour Market, 1979 (unpublished: the Final Report of SSRC research project RB/2/5/47).

(21) SIC: Standard Industrial Classification; OPCS: Office of Population Censuses and Surveys; CODOT: Classification of Occupations and Directory of Occupational Titles.

(22) For example, B. Pimlott, 'The North East: Back to the 1930s?', _The Political Quarterly_, 1981, pp.51-63.

4 Women in the Local Labour Market: a case study with particular reference to the retail trades in Britain 1900-1930

DIANA J. SMITH

INTRODUCTION

The local labour market provides us with specific examples of the more generalised divisions existing between male and female workers in Britain's labour force. These divisions of labour can be seen to operate between and within the various industries located in a particular geographical area.

The occupational status of women, their wage levels and working conditions are features of both the labour process and the sexual divisions within waged labour. The conditions under which women sell their labour power are directly related to the incorporation of sexual divisions by the labour process itself. In taking this approach it will be argued that the specific nature of women's wage labour does not rest simply on the type of work women are engaged in; the way in which capitalism continues to distinguish between male and female labour must also be confronted. (1) In looking at the sexual divisions of labour within the labour market during a thirty year period, my aim is to show the formation of these divisions as the labour force of particular industries was restructured.

A MATERIALIST ANALYSIS OF WOMEN'S WAGE LABOUR

The formation of sexual divisions in different industries and occupations constitutes part of a social and historical process. The example of the retail trades suggests that the formation of these divisions is not determined purely by predefined categories of labour by sex. It is evident that the retail trades reconstituted their own sexual divisions of labour continuously throughout the late 19th century and early 20th century.

The division between the family and work increasingly altered the relationship of women to production, and particularly to wage labour. Yet in both economic and ideological terms, this division remained indistinct for many women. This was due in part to the number of women who were employed in personal and domestic service well into the

20th century. Yet the emergence of the idea of the male breadwinner rested on a restriction of women's participation in production outside the home. (2) The idea of women's economic dependency did not correspond with the reality of many women's material existence. Writing on women's economic status in the early 20th century, Barbara Hutchins dispels this time honoured supposition.

> It will be seen that, even on the assumption that all wives are provided for by their husbands, which is by no means universally true, a very large proportion of women before 35 and after 55 are not thus provided for, and that an unknown but not inconsiderable proportion never marry at all... The adoption of occupations by women may in a few cases indicate a preference for independence and single blessedness; but it is much more often due to economic necessity. It is perfectly plain that not all women can be maintained by men, even if this were desirable. The women who have evolved a theory of 'economic independence' are few compared with the many who have economic self-dependence forced upon them. (Hutchins, 1978, pp.79-81)

This conflict between the supposed economic status of women and the material circumstances in which many found themselves has continued to have a major effect upon the nature of women's participation in the labour market. The separation of production from the family has strengthened further this relationship of dependency which women are expected to enter.

This condition, being placed on women as wage workers, bears a fundamental contradiction which has largely been overlooked in socialist thought. The family is defined as external to the capitalist mode of production. Labour, on the other hand, is recognisable in the wage form only because it can be seen to have a specific value and its exploitation can therefore be traced. (3) All work which is carried out by men and women outside the wage sphere, without remuneration, is not so defined. It is precisely this distinction between different forms of labour, albeit a real one, which serves as a contradiction for women wage workers in particular. This contradiction is embodied in the idea of the free wage labourer who is also supposed to represent an individual unit. Women's domestic labour is incongruous with both aspects of wage labour under capitalism. (4)

> Alice Clark records how as the seventeenth century pro-gressed the advance of capitalism and the development of the state diminished the value and worth of women as it diminished the value of the family and elevated the importance of the individual. (Stacey and Price, 1981, p.33)

It is insufficient to present the work which women do in the family in the form of housework, child care and the general care of others as totally separate from the 'public' domain of work in capitalist society. (5) Such an approach ignores the relationship between the 'public' and 'private' domains which is crucial to women's participation in both forms of production. A static notion of the family must be avoided if we are to investigate the sexual divisions of labour which exist in the labour market and in the family itself. The division between work (the 'public' domain) and the family (the 'private' domain) in both an ideological and economic sense, obscures the analysis of women's position in the labour market. It is therefore necessary to adopt an approach to this area which places both family and work into an historical context.

By concentrating my attention on the conditions operating in the local labour market at a particular time, it is hoped that the formation of sexual divisions of labour can be illustrated. As previously stated, the division between the family and work continues to have a fundamental influence upon women's wage labour. It is important to look at this division more closely. Attempts to theorise the relationship between these two spheres have tended to use a mechanistic approach which does not transcend the appearance of this division. (6) Such an approach has given rise to the following problematic: are we to locate the sexual divisions within wage labour purely within the context of social production, as separate from, yet parallel to, those divisions within the family? Or, as suggested by Bland et al. (1978), has capital developed its own divisions of labour from sexual divisions which existed prior to its own structures? Likewise, are these divisions within the wage sphere simply a more complex organisation of male and female labour power than existed in pre-capitalist production? This particular approach to the determination of the sexual divisions within wage labour accepts the separation between domestic and social production as inevitable for capitalist society whilst recognising that contradictory forms of human labour coexist. It is impossible to investigate the nature of these sexual divisions without first confronting the major problematic arising from the separation of production from the family.

The specific concern of this paper is women's wage labour. Beechey has suggested that both Marx and Marxists have failed to provide a materialist analysis of the form which the family has taken historically. (7) She also comments on the failure of functionalist sociology to provide a theory of the relationship between women as domestic labourers and as wage labourers. She recommends that an integration of the analysis of the labour process with an analysis of the family is required for an adequate investigation of women's wage labour. It is from this position that I wish to look at the emerging sexual divisions of labour in the early 20th century.

SEXUAL SEGREGATION IN THE LABOUR MARKET FROM 1900

The increasing participation of women in the labour force

69

from the 19th century did not result in a less sexually segregated workforce between different occupations and industries. In fact, labour markets existing during the early part of the 20th century indicate an intensification of sexual divisions within wage labour. In C. Hakim's survey of the changing pattern of women's employment from 1900 to 1970, the intensification of these divisions is shown to have taken two forms: vertical and horizontal job segregation. (8) The overrepresentation of women in particular industries and occupations is combined with a preponderance of women in unskilled and semiskilled jobs. The former is referred to as horizontal segregation, the latter as vertical segregation. Hakim maintains that these two forms of segregation are logically separate as the first refers to all female sectors of the workforce while the second refers to segregation between men and women within the same area of employment in a clearly hierarchical form.

This dual model of sex segregation in the labour market however does not appear to correspond with the incidence of sexual divisions in quite so clear a manner. In looking at the specific conditions within the labour market for women at any particular time, it appears that these forms of segregation are not as distinct from each other as Hakim suggests. If we adopt Hakim's model it becomes difficult to assess the significance of differences between women workers. Even though they appear to congregate in certain occupations and industries, women are nevertheless stratified by variable conditions of employment.

The survey does reveal some important features of women's position in the labour market despite these shortcomings in the model. Hakim concludes that there has been little overall change in the degree of occupational segregation between men and women since the turn of the century. Although the proportions of exclusively 'male' and 'female' occupations (horizontal segregation) have declined, the patterns of employment indicate a greater degree of vertical segregation. This would suggest that the gradual increase in the division of labour within most areas of the labour market, during the earlier part of this century, has altered the complexity of sexual divisions. Certain industries and occupational groups, which now employ a large majority of the female labour force in Britain, have adopted this pattern of segregation with increasing intensity throughout the last seven or eight decades i.e. retailing, clerical and service workers.

A further observation is made in this survey regarding the increasing division between male and female workers. Hakim . refers to Oppenheimer's study of the labour force in the USA in which it is argued that sharp divisions exist between men and women. Oppenheimer concludes from her research that there has been an increasing demand for specifically female labour power since the turn of the century which has meant an increase in the employment of married women in particular and the growth of a separate

70

female labour force in general.

I wish to illustrate the formation of both processes operating within the local labour market over a thirty year period. In general many new areas of employment developed during this period, from 1900 to 1930, in particular, the tertiary and service sectors. The concentration of women into these occupations and industries set a pattern for the future. This ghettoisation of female labour took place remarkably quickly in relation to the almost static pattern of job segregation by sex in Britain since the end of the second world war. It is necessary to locate these changes in the sexual division of wage labour within a given labour market. The regional variations within the British labour force as a whole necessitate this degree of specification. It will be seen from my analysis of the Croydon labour market that its industrial makeup is by no means typical. However the composition of Croydon's female labour force and the rates of female participation in the labour market are representative of the population as a whole. Furthermore the incidence of both horizontal and vertical segregation is clearly evident. The full effects of both types of segregation or division are best understood within the structure of the local labour market. From this we can obtain a better picture of the sexual divisions of labour between industries and occupations and the complexity of both vertical and horizontal segregation can be fully appreciated.

This study of Croydon looks first at the overall structure of the labour market from 1900 to 1930. I will then consider the role which women played within this structure. Finally I have chosen to describe the ways in which retail trades incorporated their own particular sexual divisions of labour both vertically and horizontally.

CROYDON: SOCIAL AND HISTORICAL BACKGROUND

The commercial development of Croydon began to accelerate during the 19th century. Up until then it was principally a Surrey market town ten miles south of London. The town is now the centre of a large London Borough, Britain's tenth largest town, containing the eighth largest shopping centre. Prior to Croydon's development as a major London suburb, in the latter half of the 19th century, the market (aptly named Surrey Street market) was the prime attraction for traders and farmers from the surrounding rural estates. By 1800 the town had become a centre for trade and an important stopping place for coaches going to and from London.

The town's population grew dramatically from 1850. Between 1801 and 1851 it had increased by approximately one-third during each decade, from 5,743 to 20,343. By 1900 the population had reached 134,037. (8) The opening of the first London to Croydon railway in 1839 marked the beginning of its development as a desirable residential location for

London's migrating population. The vast majority of Croydon's 'new' population can be attributed to this exodus out of London throughout the latter half of the 19th century. The Croydon Census for 1901 gives a total population of 133,895, of whom 29,527 (22 per cent) had been born in London. More than half of this 22 per cent were women. Given the vast numbers of private indoor domestic servants in Croydon, it is quite probable that this form of employment had attracted young, single, working class women from the city as well as from the surrounding rural areas. Fifty-eight per cent of Croydon's population in total had been born outside the county of Surrey.

The town centre formed only a small proportion of the municipal area. The larger shops became concentrated in this small area surrounding the street market. The three principal streets were developed to accomodate many of these large retail shops. During the period from 1850 to 1880 three large drapers opened in the main street through the centre of town, all of which grew into departmental stores by the turn of the century. These shops served the growing middle class population who were congregating in the new prosperous dwellings, recently built conveniently close to the two central railway stations. The majority of shops throughout the town were much smaller, employing no more than one or two assistants. This preponderance of small shops remained until after the second world war.

Shopkeepers established a significant voice in the local community from the 18th century and were influential in local politics along with other prominent tradespeople. A group of these individuals campaigned for the incorporation of the town during the second half of the 19th century and shopkeepers had founded the first of Croydon's banks prior to this. The owner of the town's largest drapers became a JP and magistrate; he was also the first chairperson of Croydon's Chamber of Commerce. Small traders on the outskirts of the area were opposed to the incorporation of Croydon according to P. Saunders in Urban Politics: A Sociological Interpretation (1979).

The complex of Croydon's shops resembled that of a prosperous rural town up until 1900. Commercial development followed the growth of Croydon as a large urban area in the latter half of the 19th century. New localised shopping areas grew from this period, situated outside the town centre. This meant a restructuring of Croydon as a centre for trade. Small family businesses survived, and in some areas became more numerous, whilst many individual traders gradually became replaced by specialist shops, multiple stores and department stores within the town's centre.

THE LOCAL LABOUR MARKET 1900-1930

The predominant trend during this thirty-year period was a gradual decline in small scale manufacturing run by

individual tradespeople and the growth of the tertiary
sector. Throughout this period Croydon's labour market
developed a much larger proportion of white collar occupational groups. The sexual divisions within the labour
market took both horizontal and vertical forms between
certain occupational groups and industries. Despite this
rapid shift towards a predominantly white collar labour
force the overall status of women in the labour market
remained consistently low. The sexual divisions within the
new sections of the labour market in particular intensified
this inferior position in relation to the male labour force
as a whole. The retail trades represent a prime example of
the intensification of both vertical and horizontal
divisions of labour.

The following analysis of Croydon's labour market has been
derived from the 1901, 1911, 1921 and 1931 censuses. (10) By
1901 the employed population numbered 56,659. Women represented 34 per cent of this population (32 per cent of the
total female population aged ten and over). These proportions for women altered slightly during the following thirty
years. If we compare these figures with national figures
there exists a marginal deviation only. (11) The participation rates for Croydon women were just below this national
average. Women made up slightly less than one-third of the
Croydon labour force until an increase in the late 1960s.

Trades and industries

The building and construction industry employed a large
proportion of the male population throughout the period. In
1901 approximately 20 per cent (7,329 men) worked in one of
several trades within the industry. By 1911 this proportion
had fallen to 16 per cent. The reclassification of
occupations for the 1921 and 1931 censuses means that only
a rough approximation of the increase in these trades can
be made. The 1931 census shows that a total of 22.2 per cent
of the male labour force was so employed. The majority
worked as carpenters, joiners, bricklayers, painters and
decorators. Women were almost entirely absent from all these
occupations within the building trades.

By 1901 another major industry was transport, employing
12 per cent of all male workers as carmen, railway employees
and general messengers. This proportion had dropped only
fractionally to 11 per cent by 1931. Very few women were
employed in either road or rail transport. By 1931 the only
women working in this sector were concentrated into a
limited range of occupations as telegraph operators, telephone operators and messengers.

The number of persons employed in the growing areas of
commerce and distribution is difficult to determine until
the reclassification of occupations in the 1921 census.
Nevertheless it is apparent that this vast category of
occupations came to include a large proportion of the

73

Croydon labour force. By 1921 the two industrial orders which included the majority of these occupations (the Commercial, Finance and Insurance Occupations; Clerks and Draughtsmen), accounted for almost 30 per cent of the labour force. By 1931 this proportion had grown to 33 per cent. This increase can be attributed almost entirely to the growth in the number of people working in retail and clerical occupations. In the area of personal service, indoor domestic service had remained a chief source of employment for the majority of single women throughout the thirty-year period. However this section of the labour force later included a larger proportion of women working in laundries and elsewhere as charwomen and office cleaners. This sector, in total, accounted for no less than 38 per cent of the entire labour force by 1931. Male workers in this sector were employed almost exclusively in public houses and hotels. Men had previously been included in this category as private domestic servants, mainly in the form of gardeners and chauffeurs.

The occupational structure within each of these industries and trades can give a much more accurate picture of the sexual divisions in the labour market. The extent to which one can speak of male and female occupations is clearly demonstrated by this structure which placed women into an increasingly limited range of occupations. As the divisions within new industrial and occupational structures grew more complex the range of occupations employing women declined. It is therefore necessary to deal with female occupations separately from male occupations.

The female labour force 1900-1930

Before the expansion in commercial occupations the majority of Croydon's female workforce were employed either as domestic servants, or in one of the dressmaking trades, or in laundry and washing services. An ever-increasing number were employed in, or were associated in some way with trading (both wholesale and retail). Even so a total of 50 per cent remained in the occupation of indoor domestic service. Teaching was the only professional occupation in which they formed the majority of employees.

In 1901 only 18 per cent of employed women were either married or divorced. The areas in which married women pre-dominated were the 'Domestic Offices or Services'. Married women were concentrated in charring and laundry work. They were also overrepresented in food dealing in the retail trade. The 1901 Census states that 11.8 per cent of all married women were in some form of employment. By 1911 they made up a slightly lower proportion of 11 per cent. These figures for 1921 and 1931 are not given so we are unable to assess the rates of labour force participation for married women beyond 1911.

Although the 1911 Census indicates little change in the

occupational distribution of women the proportion working
in clerical occupations doubled between 1901 and 1911. In
the retailing and wholesaling trades the proportion of
female employees had increased from 6 per cent to 11 per
cent. Women were concentrated in the bakery and confectionery, drapery, dress and grocery trades. Virtually no women
worked in the fish, ironware, wood and furniture and meat
trades. By 1921 the numbers of women employed in retailing
and clerical occupations had increased further, and by 1931
these occupations accounted for nearly 40 per cent of the
female labour force. By the end of this thirty-year period
the number of occupations employing women had actually declined despite the expansion in the occupational structure
as a whole. Fifty-nine per cent of women workers were by
now employed in one of four occupations: domestic service,
clerical work, or as sales assistants and typists:

Occupations Employing Women (Croydon Census 1931)

1.	Domestic Servants (Indoor)	9,027
2.	Clerks	4,502
3.	Sales Assistants	3,451
4.	Typists	3,286
	Total	20,266

The remainder of all female employees worked in the
traditional 'female' occupations (laundry and cleaning,
dressmaking and teaching), apart from the influx of women
into the subsidiary sections of the communications industry
as telephone and telegraph operators.

The male labour force 1900-1930

Two of the major areas of the Croydon labour market, the
building and construction and transport industries, were
almost exclusively dominated by men. By 1900 there existed
a substantial number of local tradespeople in food,
tobacco, drink and lodging; 11 per cent of the male labour
force, which included proprietors. A further 7.5 per cent
were employed as commercial or business clerks. Those
employed in the dress trades were predominantly tailors.
The boot and shoe trade, which is included in this category,
was another 'male' trade and one which had excluded women
from both the production and distribution of such goods from
the 19th century. An increasing number of men in the grocery
and general foods trade is evident from the 1911 Census. The
most noticeable increase came in the clerical and commercial
occupations as a whole, employing one third of the total
male workforce by 1931.

This general description of the sexual divisions within
the Croydon labour market provides more than simply
divisions between male and female workers. While some of the
new areas of employment excluded women almost entirely
(transport, building and construction) a more significant
trend was the mobilisation of a large proportion of the
female workforce into distinct job categories. These jobs

were concentrated overwhelmingly in the expanding service and tertiary sectors which were either new forms of employment to meet the industry's labour requirements (sales assistants and typists) or were jobs previously done by men (clerks). New occupations such as telephone and telegraph operators had begun to employ more women; in particular the first of these became a female occupation as the numbers of telephone operators increased. The formation of these sexual divisions of labour added a more complex dimension to a labour market which already contained a distinctly horizontally segregated workforce.

The vertical divisions of labour within a particular industry were always much more difficult to demonstrate at such a generalised level and especially within a historical context, given the relative nature of job status and social class. For these reasons it is necessary to examine one particular section of the workforce where both men and women are represented to show the workings of vertical as well as horizontal job segregation. For Croydon retailing represented an industry which permeated every part of the local economy and which placed a high premium upon its continuous development.

SEXUAL DIVISIONS AND THE RETAIL TRADE

The sexual divisions of labour within the retail trades took on new forms as the organisation of retail distribution itself changed. The largest group of workers to emerge during the late 19th century and early 20th century within retailing in Britain was the shop assistants. Shopworkers as a whole did not form a cohesive group and this is equally true for shop assistants in particular. The problems encountered in attempting to identify shopworkers as an emerging occupational category are reflected in the census itself. (12) It is possible that the reason for poor enumeration and classification before 1911 can be attributed to the predominance of small retailing outlets. Prior to this census the status of people working in retail and wholesale distribution was indeterminate given the emphasis on industrial classification rather than on occupation. The class known as 'dealers' included anybody working, in whatever capacity, in a retail establishment. The clarification of status was hindered by this form of classification and also by the structure of the retail trades.

In 1981 the shopworkers union, the Amalgamated Union of Co-operative Employees, had estimated that distributive workers totalled between 700,000 and 750,000. L. Holcombe's estimations of the number of shopworkers are taken from the census for England and Wales from 1861-1911. She states that by 1914 the number of shop assistants was estimated at about one million. According to the 1911 Census, 1,606,514 people were working as 'dealers'. Therefore nearly two-thirds were employed as shop assistants. It is clear from later census reports that women formed a disproportionate number of these assistants, although men and women were employed in equal numbers. It is also interesting to note that the heterogeneous nature of the retail trades had resulted in the submergence of shop assistants as a distinct category of workers. Holcombe observes, from the 1895 Select Committee on Shops (Early Closing) Bill, that the majority of assistants were employed in medium sized shops where there were ten or more assistants; while a few employers had many more employees. Only a minority of assistants worked for the smaller independent employer.

The revisions to the 1921 Census for Croydon placed 'salesmen and shop assistants' under the general classification of Commercial, Finance and Insurance Occupations, along with the other categories of retail workers and employers. (13) It is evident from this census that sales assistants had become a sizeable proportion of those working in all forms of distribution. Women were highly concentrated in retailing at this level, yet were under-represented in the class of managers and employers. The preponderance of small shops in Croydon is evident from the number of proprietors and managers who had maintained a relatively high ratio to the number of assistants (3,473 proprietors and managers to 5,087 sales assistants). The 1921 Census is of limited use within the context of this paper. Its most obvious limitation in relation to retailing is that it is occupationally based. The vertical divisions between men and women are partially evident but without knowledge of the particular trades in which these people worked it is impossible to say where men and women were employed or were employers.

Another shortcoming with the census in general is the exclusion of family workers. Although it is clear that women were concentrated into the class of shop assistants in 1921, this figure would certainly have been an under-estimation of the total number of women working in shops in their capacity as relatives of the proprietor (as wives, mothers, daughters etc.). This hidden labour force presents a major problem when assessing the part which women play in small scale retailing in particular. A woman whose husband owned a small shop but who was herself managing the day-to-day business would not have been classified as either sales assistant or as manager. If a husband was also employed elsewhere it is uncertain to which occupational group he would have been assigned. The wife would rarely have received much in the way of financial reward for herself. A survey of London retail shops in the 1920s had this to say:

> The man who uses the shop as a second or third string to his bow may be the owner of a small general shop in a working-class district, who puts his wife in charge, while he himself a factory worker, or perhaps an insurance agent or traveller. He serves in the shop

in the evening. He does not expect to make much out of
the concern; his takings may be only £5 or £10 per
week and his makings only enough to cover rent and
other contingencies, but it gives the wife an interest
and is a considerable help in times of low commission
or unemployment, and they will be sure of house-room
and will probably also be able to let one or more of
the rooms. (14)

R. Roberts' account of his own mother's contribution
to the family income as manager of her husband's small
general shop, describes her thirty-two years of work as
'a life sentence' in which she also bore seven children.
After twenty years her reward was a twelve hour day
compared to her previous sixteen hour day. She had managed
to open a bank account after this period of twenty years
and was determined to move away from the shop to a comfortable house with a garden; a promise which her husband
had been making ever since she first moved into the shop
a year after their marriage. When she had finally accumulated enough money to fulfil her ambition, after thirty-
two years, he refused to leave 'his' shop which he referred to as 'his little bank'. She left him and died
shortly after. (15)

The rising population of female shop assistants was
not evident in the majority of Croydon's retail outlets
but was mainly confined to the largest of the town's
drapers and textile retailers. This factor, which divided
the majority of female shop assistants from their male
counterparts, can be clearly traced from the 1931 Census.
The 1921 Census indicates that few women were employed in
the more enterprising occupations within distribution,
i.e. commercial travelling and buying. A combination of
the information in both censuses suggests that the high
proportion of women working as shop assistants is partly
attributable to the concentration of women in specific
trades where employers tended to require a large number of
assistants, i.e. drapery and clothing. Although women
were to be found in all types of shops the growth in
large scale retailing tended to accelerate during the
1900-1930 period precisely in those trades where women
were already employed in large numbers. In the clothing
and footwear trades large scale retailers' share of the
total sales for this main commodity group rose from 14-16
per cent in 1900 to 34-38.5 per cent in 1930 for the UK
as a whole. Not only was the size of clothing and footwear
outlets growing but also the type of large scale organisation was changing. During this period the multiple shop
retailers (firms possessing ten or more outlets) began
to take the lead in the proportions of total retail
sales, replacing the department store as the large retailer
in the clothing and footwear trades. At the same time the
Co-operative Societies failed to compete with either forms
of large scale retailer. The multiple clothing retailer became typical in the trade by the late 1930s, commanding
about twenty-six per cent of total retail sales. (16) Women

comprised almost the total number of sales assistants in
this type of shop. It is interesting to note that in the
food and household trades which remained predominantly
within small and medium sized retail distribution right up
until the 1950s, men continued to outnumber women as shop
assistants with the exception of sugar confectionery
(sweets) and bread and flour confectionery.

The 1931 Census provides a much more comprehensive picture
of the divisions within the retail trades in Croydon. (17)
Here the vertical and horizontal divisions between the
sexes can be demonstrated, firstly according to status and
secondly according to trade; although I do not consider
that these two forms of division can be simply categorised
as either horizontal or vertical, as the two are not
distinctly separate. It becomes impossible to separate the
vertical divisions from the horizontal divisions because
trade may determine the size of shop and possibly the
number of shops under the same ownership. This is complicated further by the wage disparities for shop assistants
working in different trades and those existing between
males and females within the same trade.

The 1931 Census for Croydon indicates a segregation
between men and women as both employers and employees in
the retail trades. Women proprietors or managers are
concentrated in the sale of sweets, tobacco, textiles and
clothing. Men are concentrated in grocery and provisions,
meat and greengrocery; although they also owned the
majority of drapery and clothing shops. From a total of
ninety druggists only six were women, although the number
of assistants in this trade was almost equal between the
sexes. Druggists were gradually becoming reorganised from
small scale retailing to multiple shop retailing, i.e.
Boots Ltd and Timothy Whites. Meat retailing, on the other
hand, continued to be dominated by the independent small
scale retailer. Ten female shop assistants were employed
in this trade at the time of the census compared to five
hundred and seventy-one males, many of whom would be
apprentices; the females would have been mainly cashiers.

Female shop assistants were again concentrated in the
textiles and clothing trades. Over one third of Croydon's
female assistants worked in these shops, a total of 1,309
women. They also represented the vast majority of assistants in the sale of bread and flour confectionery, sweets,
tobacco and footwear. The employers and managers in the
bread trades are not classified under commercial occupation
but under food manufacture. It is impossible to ascertain
from the 1931 Census how many men, compared to women, were
employers in this trade. However it is clear that men were
concentrated in the production side of this industry
(432 male bakers and pastry cooks compared to 24 women).

Male assistants tended to be concentrated in trades where
the majority of employers were also male, i.e. grocery and
provisions, meat, fish and poultry, ironmongery, green-

grocery and furniture. Most of these trades are also dominated by men in wholesale and production. It would be impossible to investigate each of these trades in detail in this paper. There exist important differences between all of these trades especially in terms of the sexual division of labour. The most noticeable feature which was common to all the trades mentioned here was the wage differentials between men and women.

A survey of London trades carried out in the 1920s, the New Survey of London Life and Labour, gives these differentials for specific trades. One large drapery firm had published its wage levels for different age groups and is referred to in the survey.

> From this it appeared that out of a total of 650 men and boys, the income of 358, that is, of appreciably more than half, ranged from £3 9s. to £6 6s. per week, and the greatest number at any one rate of income was 49 at £5 2s. weekly. The average age of these 49 men was 40. In the case of women and girls, out of the total (1,663) the income of 641 (38 per cent) was from 36s. to 51s. weekly, and the greatest number at any one rate of income 145 at £2 8s. and an average age of 28. This firm makes a deliberate endeavour to see that increased wages are received by its staff as they advance in years. (p.179, vol.V).

The survey's own figures for wages in three trades give similar discrepancies in the weekly earnings between males and females. The average adult male and female wages in these trades were for grocery and provisions, 65s. 6d. and 35s; in the drapery trade, 73s. 6d. and 40s.; and in the meat trade, 79s. and 37s. (18) These wage rates were similar to those agreed by the union, the National Union of Distributive and Allied Workers (known as the Amalgamated Union of Co-operative Employees until 1921), for the co-operative employees.

The wage differentials between men and women, as mentioned above, were dependent upon age. This affected women differently from men. In the grocery trades boys and girls were paid similar, if not equal, levels of pay up until the age of eighteen. The London Survey mentions that the 'boy's rate' would be expected to pass the 'woman's rate' by the age of eighteen to twenty years.

Despite the important variations between different trades several conclusions can be drawn from this brief overview of the sexual divisions within retailing in the local labour market. There coexisted the women who worked in shops as members of a family business, and who would probably have been married with children, with other distinct groups of predominantly young, single women working as shop assistants for very low wages who would have been dependent on their parents or other relatives for basic requirements such as housing and food. Indeed many employers were reluctant to employ a single woman unless she was living at home with her parents.

The working conditions for these two groups of women differed according to the size and type of shop but although they were employed under very different circumstances their status remained comparably low in both situations. In each case their labour was exploited directly or indirectly according to their familial status as women.

The job prospects for female assistants were extremely limited. Trades in which women were given training tended to be organised by employers in medium sized shops (with about ten employees) where male assistants would have opportunities for management positions, and would be replaced by women temporarily during the First World War. This form of replacement took place in the grocery and provisions trade and was to have an impact upon the previous sexual division of labour within that particular trade. The position for the majority of female assistants working in both small independent outlets or in very large shops was far worse. Restrictions upon age meant that, in the drapery trade in particular, twenty-five would often be the age limit for women entering retailing and once having left a job it would be very difficult for a woman to obtain another. This restriction did not operate in small shops to the same extent.

The trades in which men predominated both as employers and as assistants tended to be categorised as crafts and a closer relationship existed between production of goods and selling, i.e. the meat and furniture trades. The training given in these trades would have helped young men to become familiar with all aspects of retailing a particular range of goods.

One factor which appears to have increased the employment of female assistants throughout the retail trades was the growth in large scale retailing and the emergence of multiple shop trading. Large scale retailing first took place in trades where a female workforce already predominated. This trend continued once large scale retailing began to control a large proportion of sales for a particular commodity group. The multiple form of retail organisation chose a distinctly female workforce from the beginning. The reasons for this deserve closer attention than is given here. It is nevertheless significant for the central theme of this paper insofar as the reorganisation of retail distribution from the late 19th century, continuing to the present day, stratified its workforce fundamentally by sex.

CONCLUSION

Feminist approaches to the analysis of women's employment have raised specific problems concerning the comparison

between male and female workers. Certain fundamental
conditions which exist for workers entering the labour
market indicate that a distinction between men and women
must be made when assessing the position of females alone.
These conditions are summed up by Barrett in the following
passage.

> In assessing the factors which might account for the
> position of women as wage labourers it is impossible
> to escape the conclusion that family structure and the
> ideology of domestic responsibility play an important
> part. (19)

The attribution of this 'position' to factors which lie
outside the sphere of social production itself implies that
a straightforward comparison between male and female workers
cannot be made. In an article entitled 'The Unhappy
Marriage of Marxism and Feminism: towards a more progressive
union' Heidi Hartmann argues that the distribution of wage
labourers between particular places in a hierarchy
determined by sex represents the organisation of patriarchy. This hierarchy she sees as complementing that which
already exists within capitalist relations of production.
Hartmann defines the material basis of patriarchy as 'men's
control over women's labour power'. She stresses that the
hierarchy of sex under capitalism is far from inevitable
and that the interests of capitalism and those of patriarchy have often conflicted particularly over the control of
women's labour power. If we can locate this conflict we will
be able to identify the material base of patriarchal
relations in capitalist society according to Hartmann.

This dualistic model used by Hartmann to account for the
position of women in waged labour fails to confront the
peculiarities of the capitalist labour market. Hartmann
takes the distribution of women within particular places in
the labour market as a hierarchy which is pre-structured
according to sex. How women come to occupy these 'places'
in the first instance and what the implications of these
positionings are do not figure in her analysis. In this
paper I have attempted to demonstrate the formation of
sexual divisions of labour within the capitalist labour
market from a historical perspective. This brief analysis
of the Croydon labour market from 1900 to 1930 draws
attention to the necessity for detailed investigations of
the formation of sexual divisions of labour as a historical
process. This form of research raises questions regarding
the significance of sexual divisions. Fundamentally, do
these divisions constitute the basis of women's inferior
position in the labour market? I would suggest that actual
job segregation between men and women is only one factor
contributing to the position of women as wage labourers.

Hartmann states that the dominant position of men in the
labour market has been maintained by sex-ordered job
segregation and that such segregation represents a key to
the basis of women's subordinate position in relation to men

per se. Ultimately male domination is seen to rest on the sexual division of labour in its entirety and therefore this must be eliminated in order to overthrow such domination. In attempting to develop an analysis of capitalism in which a system of patriarchy is maintained, Hartmann forces a categorical leap from one source of domination to another. The idea of capitalism as 'sex-blind' thus remains intact. (20)

The sexual divisions which exist within the capitalist labour market are directly related to other forms of sexual division; both constitute a power struggle between men and women. In this paper I have attempted to show how these power relations rest, on one level, upon women's overall economic status. The material and ideological conditions under which women sell their labour power are clearly influenced by their economic status outside the sphere of wage labour insofar as they are continuously classified as dependents of either men or the state. As wage labourers women are also subject to the social relations of production. They therefore occupy a relation to capital which has hitherto been regarded as indistinguishable from wage labour as a whole. However the proposition that women's low economic status within the labour market is directly related to their low status as dependents also suggests that a concept of undifferentiated labour power has to be rejected. The relations through which women sell their labour power appear to contain this aspect of material dependency.

The history of female wage labour indicates that the labour process itself is central to the analysis of women's specific relation to capital. Sexual divisions of labour do not constitute the major barrier to equality between men and women in the labour market. D. Elson and R. Pearson make this point in relation to the employment of women in the Third World. They add:

> We do not accept that the problem is one of women being left out of the development process. Rather, it is precisely the relations through which women are 'integrated' into the development process that need to be problematised and investigated. For such relations may well be part of the problem rather than part of the solution. (21)

This argument can also be applied to the analysis of women's participation in the British labour force as capitalism has developed its own divisions of labour. Here the social relations of production involve an economic distinction between men and women which is not restricted to the sphere of wage labour alone. These relations must therefore be confronted in terms of women's labour in total and not as distinct forms of control which are categorically separate from all other forms of labour.

NOTES

(1)   In her critique of dual labour market theory Veronica
        Beechey argues that the sexual division of labour is
        integral to the position of women in the labour
        market. She rejects the argument of Barron and Norris
        which depicts sexual divisions as external to this
        position. V. Beechey 'Women and Production: a critical
        analysis of some sociological theories of women's
        work', in <u>Feminism and and Materialism</u> edited by
        A. Kuhn and A. Wolpe, pp.155-197, 1978.

(2)   Ivy Pinchbeck notes that in the field of business and
        crafts women's activity decreased during the period of
        the industrial revolution (I. Pinchbeck, <u>Women Workers
        and the Industrial Revolution 1750-1850</u>, p.282). This
        she attributes to the withdrawal of commercial act-
        ivities from within the home and to the concentration
        of capital into large scale businesses. The economic
        partnership which certain women undertook, within
        their capacity as wives, began to decline. Lee Davidoff
        argues however that the separation of work from the
        home was not simply the result of technological de-
        velopments. It was within the urban middle classes in
        particular that the idea of the male breadwinner first
        emerged as a desirable state for family support. This
        powerful ideological influence upon women's economic
        status within the family is interesting given the
        continuing contribution which married women were
        expected to make, for example, in small retail outlets.
        The submergence of this form of labour is just as much
        a reflection of the ideological influences which
        helped to redefine work, as the changes in women's
        productive role in general. L. Davidoff, 'The Separation
        of Home and Work? Landladies and Lodgers in Nineteenth-
        and Twentieth-Century England', p.64, S. Burman (ed.)
        <u>Fit Work for Women</u>, 1979.

(3)   The necessary link between capitalist exploitation and
        the theory of value is open to question within
        Marxism, according to D. Elson. She rejects the idea of
        labour as distributed within a pre-given structure of
        production:

                It is a fluidity, a potential which in any society
                has to be socially 'fixed' or objectified in the
                production of particular goods, by particular
                people in particular ways. Human beings are not
                pre-programmed biologically to perform particular
                tasks. Unlike ants or bees, there is a potentially
                vast range in the tasks that any human being can
                undertake... This fluidity of labour is not simply
                an attribute of growing industrial economies:
                human labour is fluid, requiring determination, in
                all states of society. But it is true that only
                with industrialisation does the fluidity of labour
                become immediately <u>apparent</u>, because the jobs that
                individuals do are obviously <u>not</u> completely
                determined by 'tradition', religion, family ties
                etc., and individuals do quite frequently change

the job they do.
D. Elson, 'The Value Theory of Labour', p.128, D. Elson
(ed.), <u>Value: The Representation of Labour in
Capitalism</u>. In a footnote to this passage, Elson
gives the sexual division of labour as an exception
to this tendency within industrial economies,
suggesting that 'natural' biological factors retain
a certain autonomy in this respect. Yet the sexual
division of labour itself is also fluid and is not
pre-determined entirely by tradition, in terms of
these 'natural' differences. It is possible for these
differences to become reinterpreted, as sexual
divisions of labour do not operate within a vacuum,
separate from the social organisation of labour as a
whole. However, the sexual division of labour does
take specific forms which are neither arbitrary nor
pre-determined, but are created socially.

(4)   M. Stacey and M. Price, in their book <u>Women, Power and
Politics</u> (1981), observe that the role of housewife
emerged long before the industrial revolution; however
the significance of this role altered under capitalism
when wage labour became predominant.

(5)   M. Stacey and M. Price (<u>ibid.</u>) stress the need for
more detailed investigations into the relationship
between domestic and social production, particularly
in terms of both social class and gender:
> We are dubious whether the theoretical case for
> the disappearance of sexual oppression when the
> involvement of personal relationships in a wage
> economy has been broken has been adequately made.
> The theory in our view is not yet sufficiently
> conclusively developed and the ways in which the
> mode of production and the relations of production
> of the wider society relate to the production
> and social relations in the domestic sphere still
> remain to be satisfactorily worked out. It is
> clear to us, however, that there are important
> connections between these arenas. (<u>Ibid.</u>, pp.185-
> 186.)

(6)   In a paper entitled 'Women "inside and outside" the
relations of production', Bland, Brunsdon, Hobson
and Winship incorporate the division between the
'industrial' and 'domestic' spheres in their analysis
of the position of women in contemporary capitalist
society. They argue that both the relations of capital
and the relations of production in the family
represent a bifurcatory structure in which women's
subordination can be located. The separation between
these two spheres is presented here as part of an
historical process but their argument fails to develop
beyond the appearance of this division and therefore
fails to question the concept of labour as defined
according to its exchange value:
> The nature of the 'domestic unit', concerned
> with the reproduction and maintenance of the
> labour force, which <u>always</u> remains a precondition
> of the reproduction of capital, is partly

determined by the absolute separation capital sets
up between the worker's individual consumption
and her/his productive consumption, and the
necessity for the worker to sell her/his labour
power to obtain the means of subsistence. (P.39,
Women Take Issue, aspects of women's subordination,
Women's Studies Group, Centre for Contemporary
Cultural Studies, 1978.)

This argument contributes little to the analysis of
women's labour. The separation to which they refer is
only 'absolute' in appearance and it is precisely this
determination of different forms of labour which must
be seen as part of the analysis of sexual divisions
of labour.

(7) See V. Beechey, ibid., pp.194-5.
(8) C. Hakim, Occupational Segregation, Research Paper
     no.9, Department of Employment, November 1979, p.34.
(9) These figures are taken from R.C.W. Cox, Some Aspects
     of the Urban Development of Croydon, 1870-1940. M.A.
     thesis, University of Leicester, 1966.
(10) The census provides only a limited picture of the exact
     structure of the local labour market. It is regretted
     that more specific information on individual trades
     and occupations has been difficult to obtain given the
     poor availability of suitable documentation. However,
     for the purposes of this paper, such detailed
     information would require greater space than is avail-
     able here. It should be emphasised that the variations
     between all four censuses serve as a further restrict-
     ion to the accuracy of my analysis. These differences
     will be referred to briefly in relation to retailing
     in particular.
(11) I have compared the Croydon figures with those given
     by C. Hakim (ibid.) for England and Wales. It can be
     seen from these comparisons that in Croydon women's
     contribution to the local labour force, between 1901
     and 1931, was consistently greater than for England
     and Wales as a whole. Conversely the percentage of
     women employed was parallel with national participation
     rates:

Women's contribution to the labour force 1901-1931

	Percentage of women employed:		Women as percentage of total labour force:	
	England & Wales	Croydon	England & Wales	Croydon
1901	31.6	32	29.1	34
1911	32.5	32	29.7	32
1921	32.3	31	29.5	31
1931	34.2	34	29.7	31

(The minimum ages are identical for both sets of
figures:
1901 - persons aged 10 or over.
1911 - persons aged 10 or over.
1921 - persons aged 12 or over.
1931 - persons aged 14 or over.)

(12) The first attempt to classify occupations into
specific orders or classes (1851 Census) had been
devised to take in all occupations in the form of
sub-orders. Little consideration was given to the
expanding divisions between the production of goods
and their distribution. The food industry, for example,
was classified under the general heading: Food,
Tobacco, Drink and Lodging, up until 1921 when each
class or order was listed in terms such as 'Makers
of...' or 'Workers in...'. Another industry which was
expanding its methods of distribution throughout the
latter half of the 19th century was the clothing
industry, yet the only concession given by the census
was to list the class of 'dealer (drapers and others)'
under order of 'Textile Fabrics' or 'Dress'. Other
occupational groups which were comparable to shop
workers had long since been given separate status,
external to their specific trades and industries.
W.A. Armstrong notes an important change from the 1881
Census, in which clerks, porters, engine drivers,
stokers, carmen etc. were classified by occupation
thus: 'commercial clerk', 'messenger' and 'porter'.
Formerly they would have been classified according to
their particular trade (W.A. Armstrong, 'The Use of
Information about Occupation, Part I: A Basis for
Social Stratification, Part II: An Industrial
Classification 1841-1891', in E.A. Wrigley (ed.) 1973,
Nineteenth Century Society: Essays in the Use of
Quantitive Methods for the Study of Social Data).

(13) Given below is the occupational category: Commercial,
Finance, and Insurance Occupations. Sub-order 1) is
Commercial Occupations, in which all distributive
workers and employers are included, irrespective of
trade. This table is taken from the 1921 Census for
Croydon.

Commercial, Finance and Insurance Occupations (other than Clerical)

1) Commercial Occupations	Males	Females
Total	8,190	3,305
Proprietors, Managers of Wholesale or Retail Businesses	2,854	619
Brokers, Agents, Factors	332	19
Buyers	198	43
Commercial Travellers	1,080	18
Canvassers	46	20
Salesmen and Shop Assistants	2,623	2,464
Roundsmen and Van Salesmen	473	2
Costermongers and Hawkers	308	86
Newspaper Sellers	39	5
Advertising	71	3
Other Commercial Occupations	166	26

(Table 16, Occupations by Sex of Persons Aged 12 Years
and over, Croydon County Borough, 1921)

N.B. The distinction between 'salesmen' and 'sales
assistants' appears to denote sex rather than status.

This distinction was rarely used in the contemporan-
eous literature on retail employees. The most
commonly used names were 'shop workers' and 'shop
assistants'. The name 'salesmen' was generally used
within the context of selling skills; hence
'salesmanship'.

(14) This extract is taken from The New Survey of London
Life and Labour, Volume 5, London Industries 2,
directed by Sir Hubert Llewellyn Smith in 1928. The
chapter entitled 'Retail Shops and Shop Assistants',
from which this quote is taken, is based upon an
inquiry conducted by Miss F.A.F. Livingstone but was
written under composite authorship. The survey itself
was designed as a sequel to C. Booth's Life and Labour
of the People in London.

(15) R. Roberts, The Classic Slum: Salford Life in the First
Quarter of the Century.

(16) These estimates are taken from J.B. Jefferys, Retail
Trading in Britain 1850-1950, p.78, Table 22.

(17) 1931 Census, Croydon County Borough.

Commercial, Finance and Insurance Occupations
(Excluding Clerks)

1) Commercial Occupations

Total   Males: 12,585   Females: 4,709

Trade	Proprietors, Managers of Retail Businesses		Salesmen and Shop Assistants retailing	
	Males	Females	Males	Females
Coal	77	5	4	0
Sugar Confectionery	101	111	10	146
Bread & Flour Confectionery	–	–	10	222
Grocery and Provisions	437	47	739	279
Milk & Dairy Products	93	21	40	100
Meat	243	8	571	10
Fish & Poultry	106	10	179	15
Greengrocery	359	29	210	81
Tobacco	93	56	48	84
Drugs & Druggists' Sundries	84	6	97	87
Ironmongery	61	10	121	41
Boots & Shoes	80	12	67	130
Textiles & Other Clothing	336	207	527	1,309
Paper, Stationery, Books & Periodicals	206	52	114	137
Furniture	109	8	199	13
General & Mixed Businesses	102	49	70	118
Other Retail Businesses	517	126	485	679
Wholesale Businesses	843	16	492	104
Wholesale & Retail Businesses	54	3	23	3
Brokers, Agents, Factors (Misc. not elsewhere enumerated)	419	22	–	–
Buyers	252	68	–	–
Commercial Travellers	1,797	27	–	–

	Males	Females	Males	Females
Canvassers (not Dock, Insurance or Railway)	244	50	–	–
Roundsmen & Van Salesmen	–	–	988	3
Costermongers & Hawkers	–	–	458	104
Newspaper Sellers	–	–	36	–
Advertising	–	–	150	13
Other Commercial Occupations	–	–	334	88
TOTAL	3,004	757	3,491	3,451

(18) The wage rates given here were for the Greater London area and therefore did not include Croydon which remained a County Borough until 1965. According to the survey, however, these rates were typical of the urban retail trades.

(19) M. Barrett, Women's Oppression Today, Problems in Marxist Feminist Analysis, (1980), p.157.

(20) This argument is used by Hartmann in her paper 'Capitalism, Patriarchy and Job Segregation by Sex', Z.R. Eisenstein, ed., Capitalist Patriarchy and the Case for Socialist Feminism.

(21) D. Elson and R. Pearson, '"Nimble Fingers Make Cheap Workers": An analysis of women's employment in the Third World export manufacturing', Feminist Review, Spring 1981, p.87.

BIBLIOGRAPHY

Armstrong, W.A, (1972), 'The Use of Information about
    Occupation', in E.A. Wrigley (ed.), Nineteenth-Century
    Society: Essays in the Use of Quantitative Methods for the
    Study of Social Data, Cambridge University Press.
Alexander, S, (1978), 'Women's Work in Nineteenth-Century
    London: a study of the years 1820-50', in J. Mitchell and
    A. Oakley (eds.), The Rights and Wrongs of Women, Penguin.
Barrett, M, (1980), Women's Oppression Today: Problems in
    Marxist Feminist Analysis, New Left Books.
Beechey, V, (1978), 'Women and Production: a critical
    analysis of some sociological theories of women's work',
    in A. Kuhn and A. Wolpe (eds.), Feminism and Materialism,
    Routledge and Kegan Paul.
Bland, L, Brunsdon, C, Hobson, D. and Winship, J, (1978),
    'Women "inside and outside" the relations of production'
    in Women's Studies Group, Centre for Contemporary Cultural
    Studies, Women Take Issue: Aspects of Women's Subordin-
    ation, Hutchinson.
Cox, R.C.W, (1966), Some Aspects of the Urban Development of
    Croydon 1870-1940, M.A. Thesis, University of Leicester.
Conference of Socialist Economists, Sex and Class Group,
    (1981), 'Exploitation and Oppression: Rethinking Socialist
    Strategy', Unpublished Conference Paper.
Davidoff, L, (1979), 'The Separation of Home and Work? Land-
    ladies and Lodgers in Nineteenth and Twentieth Century
    England', in S. Burman (ed.), Fit Work for Women, Croom
    Helm.
Elson, D, (ed.), (1979), Value: The Representation of Labour
    in Capitalism, CSE Books.
Elson, D. and Pearson, R, (1981), '"Nimble Fingers Make
    Cheap Workers": an analysis of women's employment in third
    world export manufacturing', Feminist Review, Spring.
Gent, J.B, (ed.), (1977), Croydon: The Story of a Hundred
    Years, The Croydon Natural History and Scientific
    Society, Ltd.
Godelier, M, (1981), 'The Origins of Male Domination', New
    Left Review, 127, May-June.
Hartmann, H, (1979a), 'The Unhappy Marriage of Marxism and
    Feminism: towards a more progressive union', Capital and
    Class, 8.
Hartmann, H, (1979b), 'Capitalism, Patriarchy and Job Segre-
    gation by Sex', in Z. Eisenstein (ed.), Capitalist Patri-
    archy and the Case for Socialist Feminism, Monthly Review
    Press.
Hakim, C, (1979), 'Occupational Segregation', Research
    Paper 9, Department of Employment.
Harrison, J, (1978), Marxist Economics for Socialists: a
    critique of reformism, Pluto Press.
Holcombe, L, (1973), Victorian Ladies at Work, David and
    Charles.
Hutchins, B.L, (1978), Women in Modern Industry (1915),
    E.P. Publishing.
Jefferys, J.B, (1954), Retail Trading in Britain 1850-1950,
    Cambridge University Press.
Llewellyn Smith, H, (1933), The New Survey of London Life

and Labour, Volume 5, London Industries 2, P. King and
     Son, Orchard House.
Pinchbeck, I, (1981), Women Workers and the Industrial
     Revolution 1750-1850, Virago Press.
Roberts, R, (1971), The Classic Slum, Penguin.
Saunders, P, (1979), Urban Politics: a Sociological Inter-
     pretation, Hutchinson.
Stacey, M. and Price, M, (1981), Women, Power and Politics,
     Tavistock.

ACKNOWLEDGEMENTS

I should like to thank Michele Barrett and Miriam Glucksmann
for their comments on an earlier draft of this paper.

5 'The Contest Terrain': a critique of R. C. Edwards' theory of working class fractions and politics

ROGER PENN

R.C. Edwards' recent work, <u>The Contested Terrain: The Transformation of the Workplace in the Twentieth Century</u> (1979) involves an attempt to integrate works on American labour markets such as Doeringer and Piore (1971) and Edwards <u>et al.</u> (1975) with contemporary sociological models that characterise class conflict in advanced capitalist societies in terms of an interaction between 'managerial strategies' and 'workers' resistance'. These sociological models have been premised upon a set of distinct but not unrelated economic theories. In the case of writers like Friedman (1977a and 1977b) and the Brighton Labour Process Group (1977), the underlying framework is Marxist, whereas for 'neo-Ricardians' like Glyn and Sutcliffe (1972), Wood (1981) and Elbaum <u>et al.</u> in the <u>Cambridge Journal of Economics</u>' Symposium on 'The Labour Process, Market Structure and Marxist Theory'(1979), a less deterministic model is in evidence. Edwards himself opts unambiguously for an attempt to link labour market analyses with Marxist theory and his text represents, therefore, a test of the adequacy of such a synthesis.

Unlike Braverman (1974), who argues that the working class in advanced capitalist societies has become increasingly homogeneous, Edwards argues that these working classes are increasingly riven by a series of structural 'faults'. These 'divides' actively weaken working class opposition to capitalist hegemony and provide the explanation of why the United States has failed to throw up either a serious socialist political movement or a socialist system. Edwards' concern can be seen as one central both to Marxism and academic sociology in Britain since 1945, namely 'the revolutionary potential of the western working class'.

Edwards' thesis, based upon evidence culled exclusively from the United States, is that the working class is divided into three fractions. His definition of the 'working class' includes all wage earners and most salaried employees, thereby incorporating technicians, professionals, supervisors and middle management: indeed all non-capitalists who are not in the 'echelons of upper management'. Clearly this is not the working class of everyday discourse, or of conventional sociology, but a category premised upon the neo-Marxist belief that the working class is synonymous with the category 'labour'. Nevertheless, although there is a danger of terminological confusion over the definition of the 'working class', there can be no <u>a priori</u> objection to such usage. The crucial issue is whether such a definition enhances social scientific understanding. As will become apparent, Edwards' use of the term simply serves to increase confusion.

Edwards argues that the tripartite structure of the contemporary working class is the direct consequence of the three kinds of labour control system that underpin the three major labour markets that characterise advanced capitalist societies. For Edwards, capitalism is defined by the commodity form of labour or, more precisely, the purchase of labour <u>power</u>. Consequently, the crucial problem for the purchaser of this labour power is not its cost but the question of how to ensure that work actually gets done. The problem of control can be separated into three aspects: direction, evaluation and monitoring and finally, discipline. Historically, three different combinations of these elements of 'forms of control' have evolved to deal with the problems of coordination in the capitalist enterprise: 'simple', 'technical' and 'bureaucratic'.

'Simple' control occurs in small firms with little internal division of functions, operating within competitive markets. Employers exercise power in an arbitrary, 'idiosyncratic', 'unsystematic' way. The central image invokes a picture of the classic nineteenth century capitalist enterprise. However, with the increasing concentration and scale of industrial capitalist firms, there is strong internal pressure towards structural differentiation and an increasing impracticality of the traditional, 'simple' form of control. New formalised types of control emerge which take two forms. The first, historically, is 'technical', where control over the labour force is achieved by embedding systems of coordination in the physical structure of the labour process or, in other words, in the machinery. Under this system workers become mere machine attendants, dominated at work by the rhythms and exigencies of the physical plant which envelops them. However, according to Edwards this system produces its own problems of control, particularly in the form of trade unionisation, and ultimately this leads to the 'mutual administration' of production by 'management and (as a junior partner) unions'. (Edwards 1979, p.20)

Nevertheless, it does not appear as if the internal logic of technical control systems actually <u>produces</u> bureaucratic forms of control. 'Bureaucratic' control is a different way of organising the workforces of large firms, particularly the growing proportion of nonmanual workers. 'Bureaucratic' control involves control embedded in the social relations of the workplace. For Edwards, 'rule of (company) law replaces rule by supervisors' (Edwards 1979, p.21). The introduction of bureaucratic control systems in the twentieth century involves a process of the 'redivision of labour' and the working class becomes splintered into three distinct fractions: the 'working poor', the 'traditional proletariat' and the 'middle layers'. Each fraction of the working class is located in a different labour market - the 'secondary' (the working poor), the 'subordinate primary' (the traditional proletariat) and the 'independent primary' (the middle layers). To summarise, the three types of control are embodied in the three main kinds of labour markets identified by Doeringer and Piore (1971) and Edwards et al. (1975). However, unlike these previous authors who have merely characterised labour markets as bundles of contingently related empirical variables, Edwards sees them as structured by distinct, underlying modes of control.

It would appear reasonable to ask three questions in response to these bold formulations. Firstly, is Edwards' notion of working class fractions useful sociologically? Does Edwards capture the real relations between labour market structuration and control? Finally, can one explain political phenomena - in this case the dynamics and rhythms of socialist politics - in the way suggested?

However, there are clear difficulties in adopting Edwards' scheme in a British context. Firstly, trade unions operate in all three categories of manual work and ipso facto in relation to all three labour markets and within each kind of control system. Consequently, Edwards' emphasis on the role of trade unions in relation to technical control systems alone is misleading in a comparative context: it might be true in the United States but this is a contingent feature of trade unionism there rather than a necessary part of trade unionism per se. Secondly, formal rules are present in all three labour markets in Britain. The competitive, low-paid, unskilled arena is subject to formal regulation both by the state and by collective bargaining and it is mistaken to see it as arbitrary or lacking in formal regulation. Furthermore, paternalist forms of management are neither separate from formal regulation of work practice nor present only or typically in small scale, nonskilled working environments. Paternalist forms of management may exist in large factories like the one in Lancaster analysed by Martin and Fryer (1973) or at Pilkingtons in St. Helens as described by Lane and Roberts (1971). Paternalist forms of management also exist in agriculture where the labour market is administered by quasi-state institutions as has been shown by Newby (1977). Clearly, this evidence suggests that some of Edwards' key empirical relationships are mis-conceived. They do not apply in Britain, which is a serious problem for his position since none of his neo-Marxist explanatory categories presume specifically American relationships. It is a common fallacy of arguments like Edwards' that they assume that one historical example can demonstrate the empirical validity of a general model.

Indeed, if we wish to explain why workers actually work in

advanced capitalist societies, it is inadequate to start
from Edwards' assumption that without control in the workplace nothing would be done. This is a point of view highly
'managerial' in its overtones and based upon a complete
failure by radical labour market analysts and neo-Marxists
to incorporate the findings of orthodox industrial sociology
into their accounts. In reality, the 'effort bargain' is a
function of normative expectations which include those of
workers themselves. Eldridge (1968), Behrend (1957 and
1961), Baldamus (1951 and 1961) and Brown and Sisson (1975)
amongst others have shown how normative expectations are
central to a series of different aspects of industrial
relations and concomitant work practices. If Gouldner's
work in the 1950s is anything to go by (1955), there is no
reason to assume that the United States is radically
different. Indeed, it would appear more plausible to suggest
that workers in advanced capitalist societies are prepared
to work for primarily instrumental reasons and that much
industrial conflict centres not on this basic motivation
but upon two variables within the basic orientation: pace
of work and wages. Nevertheless, it should not be assumed,
as so many appear to do, that an instrumental orientation to
work precludes normative expectations about the organisation
and remuneration of work. As Maitland (1980) has shown in
his comparative research in a British and a West German tyre
factory, there is no pervasive anomie that characterises
British industrial relations. Arguing against Fox and
Flanders (1969) and Goldthorpe (1969, 1974a, 1974b) Maitland
reveals that British industry possesses weak management,
powerful sectional bargaining and a general disapproval by
manual workers of the disorderly outcomes of such an
industrial relations system. British manual workers do
appear to have strong normative commitments both to the
overall capitalist system and to traditional differentials
as embodied in notions of 'comparability' and 'fair pay'.
What they object to most is not the overall structure of
rewards but the anarchic conditions brought about by management and 'other workers'.

It is also necessary to reject as unproven Edwards'
general view that capitalists choose their technology with
control systems in mind and that they or their managerial
representatives can choose technology more or less at will.
Edwards' view is stated clearly: '... considerable choice
surrounds the selection of any productive technique. In
most industries, a range of techniques is already
available.' (Edwards 1979, p.179) Such a viewpoint is
popular amongst radical American social scientists but the
empirical evidence for such an assertion appears slight.
The most notable discussion is by David Noble (1978) and
rests upon the example of social choice in the area of
automatic machine tools but Edwards does not cite this
source and refers only to an unpublished Harvard Ph.D. which
he claims is 'persuasive'. Evidence about the role of
technological constraints on the forms of work practices
from the Chinese People's Republic (Lockett, 1980) suggests
that the idea that capitalists (or industrialists) have a

range of productive systems available, from which they choose the one which maximises their control over labour, is both overly voluntaristic and factually implausible. Edwards' example of the steel industry where he claims that a choice is possible between labour-intensive and capital-intensive forms of production ignores the crucial point that the different systems produce _different_ commodities. If these choices really existed it is very hard to see why countries with vast supplies of labour like India, China and Russia have been so perverse as to adopt capital-intensive systems of steel production. There are, of course, variations within the general determinants associated with steel production but they are not of the kind suggested by Edwards.

This leads directly to the central conceptual weakness within Edwards' account. His version of managerial strategies and workers' resistance portrays the working class as passive, defensive and reactive, thereby ignoring the role of workers and particularly workers' organisations in the self-stratification of labour. This lacuna is the result of Edwards' reliance on a non-interactive model of industrial relations and his 'managerial' bias which portrays the structuration of work practices as dictated by an omnipotent management. This in turn is a result of his mistaken _general_ assumption that only management is engaged in strategies of control.

Workers and workers' representatives in Britain also engage in active strategies of control over machinery. The primary rules on manning and demarcation in wide areas of British industry and the panoply of secondary strategies used to buttress these exclusive practices are all rule-governed, and negotiated, and their continuation a function of the relative power of management and labour. Indeed, a great deal of industrial conflict in the metal industries (engineering and shipbuilding), printing and construction has focussed around the exclusive practices of skilled trade unions. The significance of these practices (apprenticeship rules, manning arrangements, demarcation and 'priority' rules) for the nature of working class unity or sectional-ism is that the strategies of exclusion embodied in the skilled/nonskilled distinction actively _divide_ the British manual working class. Relative differentials in wages and relative status are zero-sum rewards: one section's gains are another's loss. (1)

There is considerable evidence that shows that many machines can be made idiosyncratic by workers themselves. Catling (1969) has shown this to be true historically in the cotton spinning industry and Jones (1981), Green (1978) and Noble (1978) all suggest that this is true for the engineering industry. The model of the assembly line is in many ways atypical of the normal relationship of men to machines but even assembly lines, which embody the highest form of physical control, can vary within certain limits, as is evidenced by comparisons of British and Belgian Ford plants or by the differences between the British Leyland TR7 plants at Speke and Canley. The latter comparison makes the point well. Management at Speke was not able to alter work practices significantly in the 1970s despite their 'evident' irrationality. They were unable to get maintenance men to engage in forward maintenance (a general feature of the British car industry) (2) nor could they prevent the evolution of informal work groups on the shopfloor which were able to allocate work periods and rest periods according to group norms. Of course, this is not to suggest a complete indeterminacy: clearly, control over labour is built into the physical plant and embedded in the division of labour. Nevertheless, any model which assumes either that trade unions are the only form of resistance or, more startlingly, that trade unions are management's poodles must be very far from the mark.

It is now possible to answer the question as to the utility of Edwards' notion of working class fractions. The idea of attempting to produce a theoretically informed division of the working class is a move forward. However, Edwards subscribes to a romantic view of the underlying, pristine unity of all elements of labour. This is naive and unjustified even with regard to the manual working class. There are a whole series of practices and institutions created and sustained through struggles between sections of the manual working class and capitalist management that serve to actively stratify this class and which are embodied in the rules and norms that govern workplace interaction. Edwards' project is superior to the a priori exercises in definition so popular with structuralist Marxists like Poulantzas (1975), Carchedi (1975) and Wright (1976), but in practice he ignores the degree of variance both within and between his three 'working class' fractions. His passive model of industrial relations means that his approach cannot capture the essential forms of working class structuration as they exist. Clearly, social science is in need of improved class categorisations but it would appear that Edwards' use of labour market theory cannot solve the problems involved.

What then is the relationship between working class fractions and socialism? If we examine the problem initially by taking Edwards' version of working class fractionalisation, it is clear that his failure to locate his theories in a comparative perspective renders them impotent. Clearly, it depends what is meant by socialism. If he intends the term to refer to socialist movements it should be clear that such movements have developed in situations where the kinds of labour market structuration which he describes have existed. The failure of American socialist movements is a political phenomenon not to be understood in terms of control systems or labour markets that are universal in their nature. Furthermore, it is possible to turn Edwards' formulations on their head and suggest that in certain contexts, such as France and Italy, the bifurcated structure of the socialist movement, coupled with the form of trade unionism, has served to 'fractionalise' the manual working class at the point of production. If, on the other hand, socialism is meant to refer to successful socialist revolutions, then given that there have been none in advanced capitalist societies and given that Edwards' labour market theories suggest a pervasive fractionalisation of labour, it would appear as if either there is nothing to explain or, if there is, it is not a case of American exceptionalism but one of the many general features of advanced capitalism.

However, if we abandon Edwards' passive, non-interactive model, it is possible to suggest that the active self-stratification of the manual working class around the axis of 'skill' is connected with the development, and particularly the rhythms of socialism in Britain. At present there would appear to be two schools of thought concerning the relationship of changes in work situation, industrial relations and technology with the rhythms of politics; and in particular with the evolution of workers' militancy and socialist movements. One school, represented by Scott (1974) and Sewell (1971) emphasises the signifi-cance of material changes focussed in the work situation as the most salient set of causal factors. Moss (1977) and Stein (1978), on the other hand, argue that such writers have tended to ignore the autonomous importance of political and ideological changes in the structuration of workers' responses to changes enforced by capitalist management in the sphere of work.

If we examine the relationship of skilled manual workers to militancy in Britain historically, it would appear that they have been in the vanguard at three periods. These three periods, the 1890s 'employers offensive', the First World War labour disputes and the ensuing period until 1923, and the 'state's offensive' beginning in the late 1960s and continuing during the 1970s were all periods which also saw a growth of socialism and its articulation with and by skilled manual workers, particularly those in the metal industries. Yet the very mechanisms of exclusion, outlined earlier, used to reproduce 'skill' in the labour process meant that these same workers were suspicious of other elements in the labour force and were often involved in workplace practices that maintained their relative power at the expense of the less skilled. Manning arrangements whereby skilled union negotiators acquired the right for craftsmen to operate machinery that could have been worked by the nonskilled are a clear example of this. The paradox of skilled manual workers' simultaneous espousal of socialist politics and their strong reliance upon exclusive practices at the point of production has been captured in the debate between the two dominant social historical theories about the internal structuration of the British manual working class around the axis of skill - the 'militant craftsman' tradition and the theory of the 'labour aristocracy'. Advocates of the 'labour aristocracy' like Hobsbawm (1964), Foster (1974) and Gray (1976) argue that

British skilled manual workers are intrinsically conservative since their exclusive practices at work and their
strong sectional trade union organisations have misdirected
the working class from its appointed revolutionary path.
In contrast to this Marxist problematic, theorists of the
'militant craftsman' like Hinton (1973), Montgomery (1976)
and Lucas (1976) demonstrate that skilled workers have, at
times, been highly militant in advanced capitalist societies
and, on occasion, have even constituted the revolutionary
vanguard. Both theories contain elements of the truth but
neither is sufficiently complex to incorporate the
historical realities of skilled manual workers in Britain.
The most important point to be made is that British skilled
manual workers are located in a <u>contradictory structural
location</u> and that this contradiction is derived from the
articulation of craft and mass production in Britain.

Craft forms of production allow considerable scope for
workers' controls over manning and the mode of producing,
while craft factory production denies capitalist management
full control over the mode and forms of work. The fullest
'rationality' of production, according to the 'logic' of
capitalism, requires that labour be predictable, uniform
and controllable. It demands the establishment of complete
managerial authority. Craft factory production stands
diametrically opposed to such a value system with its
emphases on self-direction and autonomy. For skilled craftsmen, the nonskilled act as a permanent mirror to the future
if managerial 'prerogatives' are uncontested, and craftsmen
stand opposed to modern capitalist management and its
utilisation of technical change to increase social control
over producing. Yet here lies the dilemma for skilled
manual workers; they are highly organised but defensive,
requiring an ideology with which to combat capitalist
management. Socialism, with its explicit rejection of
capitalism and its ideological commitment to more humanised
forms of production offers such a value system. Socialism
also stands for the unity of labour and for a belief in
equality. Clearly, there are contradictory pressures for
skilled craftsmen involved in a commitment to socialism.
Furthermore, the functional congruence of certain elements
in socialist ideology for skilled manual workers does not
necessitate either their adoption or the particular type
of socialism taken up. Any notion of simple technological
determination of workers' ideology must be rejected.

Nevertheless, it is possible to hypothesise a relationship between the dialectics of skill and socialism which is
less deterministic than Scott and Sewell's model but nonetheless emphasises 'material factors'. It would seem that
it is in periods when widespread technical change is en-
visaged and being implemented by capitalist management in
Britain that socialism has appeared most attractive. The
anti-capitalist ideological elements would appear at such
times to outweigh, or facilitate a 'selecting out' of the
negative egalitarian implications of socialism. Such a
process finds its expression in the 'militant craftsman'

tradition and it would seem that in such situations the image of a powerful common capitalist enemy 'masks' the difficulties associated with egalitarianism for the skilled. At other periods, those of relative 'technological stasis', the image of the labour aristocracy is more pertinent.

This is not to deny the autonomous character of politics, nor to hide behind vague notions of 'relative autonomy' but to suggest a possible set of relationships between socialism and technological change in Britain mediated by the organisations of skilled labour built up during the craft period of industrial capitalist factory production. Other more directly political factors must also be taken into account apart from the dialectic of 'managerial strategies' and 'workers' militancy'. If, for example, we examine the massive swing in support by skilled manual workers towards the Conservative Party manifest in the 1979 British General Election (3) it would appear that Labour Government incomes policies, particularly as they affected the engineering industry, were a highly significant pre-cipitating factor. Systematic analyses of such phenomena are, as yet, lacking but it would appear from the evidence reported by Brown (1976) as if these incomes policies, devised as they were by representatives of the general, non-skilled unions, made significant inroads into established relativities within the manual workforce. The success of the skilled in preserving or widening differentials in the 1920s and 1930s was related in turn to the organisational weakness of the general unions in the period after the collapse of the 1926 General Strike and the passing of the 1927 Trade Disputes Act and the ensuing mass unemployment. Nevertheless, it would appear as if, despite other significant variables like the relative power of skilled versus nonskilled unions, there is a strong positive correlation in the period between 1890 and 1979 between espousal of socialist ideology and managerial assaults on the exclusive controls sustained by skilled manual workers. During the 1890s, socialism gained ground rapidly amongst engineering workers (particularly their District Officials) (4) in the period of 'the employers offensive'. The First World War revealed a similar, if stronger, set of develop-ments. The resurgence of militancy and the rise in strength of the left within the AUEW in the late 1960s was also parallelled by managerial attacks on the power of the skilled worker under the aegis of productivity bargaining. We may hypothesise that the very same skilled elements who supported the rise of Thatcherism in 1979 will shift rapidly leftwards if the long-heralded micro-chip revolution begins to change significantly the established working practices of Britain's skilled engineering workers, most of whom work in relatively small workshops. (5)

The central point about this admittedly schematic, dis-cussion of the 'dialectics of skill' in Britain is that it provides clear answers to the three questions posed earlier about the validity of Edwards' arguments. Firstly, it is clear that sociology needs to theorise and explain the

internal structure of the working class. However, even
when the focus was narrowed to the _manual_ working class (a
conception far narrower than Edwards' romantic Marxist one),
it became clear that Edwards' highly schematic labour market
typology was inadequate.

If the internal structuration of the manual working class
around the axis of skill is examined it becomes clear that
Edwards' concepts fail to capture the real divisions within the manual working class at the point of production.
When coupled with his passive model of working-class action
(or inaction) it became clear that Edwards failed to grasp
the essential relations within the manual working class
between labour market structuration and strategies of
control. _A fortiori_, it becomes clear that Edwards' specific
notions about working class fractionalisation are not
helpful and must be rejected.

It is clearly far more relevant to examine the internal
bifurcation of the manual working class around the axis of
skill rather than to focus analysis of the structuration of
the working class in terms of labour control systems
imposed by capitalist management. Such an orientation has
the double advantage of being closer to the viewpoints and
self-understandings of actual entities in the labour market
in Britain and to traditional sociological images of the
manual working class in terms of a skilled 'divide', eg.
Glass (1954), OPCS (1970) and Goldthorpe _et al_.(1980). No
doubt different systems of labour control exist but there
appears little evidence to suggest that such categories
provide an improved model of social stratification.

Finally, the example of the relationship of British
skilled manual workers and socialist politics in the period
between 1890 and today suggested strongly that Edwards'
mode of explanation is inadeqate. The reality is far more
complex than can be encapsulated within his technicist
formulations. Even the example analysed above suffers from
being focussed exclusively on Britain. This was done in
order to cast doubt upon Edwards' universalistic arguments.
However, the model of structural contradiction used to
explain the rhythms of socialist politics in relation to
skilled manual workers may have more general validity.
Recent work by Fridenson in France (1978), Geary in Germany
(1978) and Spriano in Italy (1975) all suggest that if one
wishes to examine the dynamics of socialism in relation to
the 'contested terrain' at work, then the model outlined
(in particular the emphasis on the mode of articulation
between craft and mass forms of production) is the way
forward rather than the application of contemporary
American labour market theories.

NOTES

(1) These issues are dealt with in my Ph.D. dissertation
    and also in R. Penn, 'Skilled Manual Workers in the

Labour Process, 1856-1964' in S. Wood (ed.), <u>The Deskilling Debate</u> (1981).

(2) As of British industry as a whole. D. Gallie, <u>In Search of the New Working Class</u> (1978, p.112) describes how refinery workers were highly critical of the autonomy enjoyed by maintenance workers and wanted management to regain control in the interests of greater efficiency. I. Maitland, 'Disorder in the British Workplace: The Limits of Consensus', <u>British Journal of Industrial Relations</u>, XVIII, 3, 1980, shows that production workers in a tyre factory wanted machine setters to work on weekends to enhance productivity (p.359).

(3) According to opinion poll data reported by K. Coates (ed.), <u>What Went Wrong: Explaining the Fall of the Labour Government</u> (Nottingham, 1979), p.31, the proportion of skilled manual workers voting for the Conservative Party in the 1979 General Election was virtually the same as that voting Labour (around 40 per cent).

(4) There is a lack of systematic research into this area. My evidence is taken from research reported to the N.W. Labour History Group at its meeting of October 15th, 1975. Also, my own research in Rochdale confirmed the increasing influence of socialism amongst District officials in the Engineering Union. See R. Penn, 'Skilled Manual Workers in British Class Structure, 1856-1964', Ph.D dissertation, Cambridge University, 1980; chapter VII.

(5) There is clearly a need to examine the interaction between the rhythms of socialist politics and developments in the sphere of production. Even in France, where social historians have investigated this problem, there is a lack of systematic research or any set of clear-cut conclusions.

REFERENCES

Baldamus, W, (1951), 'Type of Work and Motivation', British Journal of Sociology, 2.
Baldamus, W, (1961), Efficiency and Effort, London.
Behrend, H, (1957), 'The Effort Bargain', Industrial and Labour Relations Review, 10.
Behrend, H, (1961), 'A Fair Day's Work', Scottish Journal of Political Economy, 8.
Braverman, H, (1974), Labour and Monopoly Capital: The Degradation of Work in the Twentieth Century, New York.
Brighton Labour Process Group, (1977), 'The Capitalist Labour Process', Capital and Class, 1.
Brown, W, (1976), 'Incomes Policy and Pay Differentials', Oxford Bulletin of Economics and Statistics, 58, 1, February.
Brown, W and Sisson, K, (1975) 'The Use of Comparisons in Workplace Wage Determination', British Journal of Industrial Relations, 13, 1, March.
Catling, H, (1967), The Spinning Mule, Newton Abbot.
Carchedi, G, (1975), 'On the economic identification of the new middle class', Economy and Society, 4, 1.
Coates, K (ed.), (1979), What Went Wrong: Explaining The Fall of the Labour Government, Nottingham.
Doeringer, P and Piore, M, (1971), Internal Labour Markets and Manpower Analysis, Lexington, Massachusetts.
Edwards, R.C, Reich, M and Gordon, D (eds), (1975), Labour Market Segmentation, Lexington, Massachusetts.
Edwards, R.C., (1979), The Contested Terrain: The Transformation of the Workplace in the Twentieth Century, New York.
Elbaum, B, Lazonick, W, Wilkinson, F and Zeitlin, J, (1979), 'The Labour Process, Market Structure and Marxist Theory', Cambridge Journal of Economics, 3.
Eldridge, J.E.T, (1968), Industrial Disputes: Essays in the Sociology of Industrial Relations, London.
Foster, J, (1974), Class Struggle and the Industrial Revolution, London.
Fox, A and Flanders, A, (1969), 'The Reform of Collective Bargaining: From Donovan to Durkheim', British Journal of Industrial Relations, 7.
Fridenson, P, (1978), 'The Coming of the Assembly-Line to Europe' in Krohn, Layton and Weingart (eds), 'The Dynamics of Science and Technology', Sociology of the Sciences, 2.
Friedman, A, (1977a), Industry and Labour: Class Struggle at Work and Monopoly Capitalism, London.
Friedman, A, (1977b), 'Responsible Autonomy versus Direct Control over the Labour Process', Capital and Class, 1.
Gallie, D, (1978), In Search of the New Working Class, Cambridge.
Geary, R, (1978), 'Radicalism and the Worker: Metalworkers and Revolution, 1914-23', in Richard J. Evans (ed), Society and Politics in Wilhelmine Germany, London.
Glass, D, (ed) (1954), Social Mobility in Britain, London.
Glyn, A and Sutcliffe, B, (1972), British Capitalism, Workers and the Profits Squeeze, Harmondsworth.

Goldthorpe, J.H, (1969), 'Social Inequality and Social
Integration in Modern Britain', The Advancement of
Science, 26, 127, September.
Goldthorpe, J.H, (1974), 'Social Inequality and Social
Integration in Modern Britain' in D. Wedderburn (ed),
Poverty, Inequality and Class Structure, Cambridge.
Goldthorpe, J.H, (1974), 'Industrial Relations in Great
Britain: A Critique of Reformism', Politics and Society,
4.
Goldthorpe, J.H and Hope, K, (1974), The Social Grading of
Occupations: A New Approach and Scale, Oxford.
Goldthorpe, J.H, (in collaboration with Llewellyn, G, and
Payne, C) (1980), Social Mobility and Class Structure in
Modern Britain, Oxford.
Gouldner, A, (1955), Wildcat Strike, London.
Gray, R.Q, (1976), The Labour Aristocracy in Victorian
Edinburgh, Oxford.
Green, K, (1978), 'Group Technology and Small-Batch
Engineering', paper presented to Windsor SSRC Conference,
on 'Deskilling'. (Mimeo.)
Hinton, J, (1973), The First Shop Stewards' Movement,
London.
Hobsbawm, E, (1964), Labouring Men, London.
Jones, B, (1981, forthcoming), 'Destruction or re-distribu-
tion of engineering skills? The case of numerical control'
in Wood, S, (ed), The Deskilling Debate, Hutchinson.
Lane, T and Roberts, K, (1971), Strike at Pilkingtons,
London.
Lockett, M, (1979), 'China: Industrial Management and the
Division of Labour', paper presented to the British
Association for Chinese Studies, November. (Mimeo.)
Lucas, E, (1976), Arbeiterradikalismus: Zwei Formen von
Radikalismus in der deutschen Arbeiterbewegung,
Frankfurt.
Maitland, I, (1980), 'Disorder in the British Workplace:
The Limits of Consensus', British Journal of Industrial
Relations, 18, 3.
Martin, R and Fryer, R, (1973), Redundancy and Paternalist
Capitalism, London.
Montgomery, D, (1976), 'Workers' Control of Machine
Production in the Nineteenth Century', Labour History,
17, 4.
Moss, B, (1977), 'Workers' Ideology and French Social
History', International Labour and Working Class History,
11, May.
Newby, H, (1977), The Deferential Worker, Harmondsworth.
Noble, D.F, (1978), 'Social Choice in Machine Design: The
Case of Automatically Controlled Machine Tools, and a
Challenge for Labour', Politics and Society, 8, 3-4.
OPCS, (1970), Classification of Occupations: 1970, London.
Penn, R, (1981), 'Skilled Manual Workers in the Labour
Process: 1856-1964', in S. Wood (ed).
Poulantzas, N, (1975), Classes in Contemporary Capitalism,
London.
Scott, J.W, (1974), The Glassworkers of Carmaux, Cambridge.
Spriano, S, (1975), The Occupation of the Factories,
London.

Stein, M.B, (1978), 'The Meaning of Skill: The Case of
  French Engine-Drivers, 1837-1917', <u>Politics and Society</u>,
  8, 3-4.
Sewell, W, Jnr, (1971) 'La Classe ouvriere de Marseille
  sous la Seconde Republique', <u>Le Mouvement Social</u>, 76,
  July-September.
Wood, S, (ed), (1981), <u>The Deskilling Debate</u>, Hutchinson.
Wright, E.O, (1976), 'Class Boundaries in Advanced Capital-
  ist Societies', <u>New Left Review</u>, 98.

6 'Fraternalism' and 'Paternalism' as Employer Strategies in Small Firms

ROBERT GOFFEE AND RICHARD SCASE

It has often been argued that small employers maintain the identification of their workers through the cultivation of paternalistic relationships. Further, it is generally accepted that the exercise of paternalism is, to some extent, determined by the size of the enterprise. <u>Above</u> a certain limit the personal and particularistic elements of the paternal mode of control break down and give way to more bureaucratic organisational structures which 'separate' employers and workers. However, we would argue that <u>below</u> this limit paternalism is but one employer strategy which may not be appropriate in every context. This paper suggests, on the basis of an empirical study, that small employers in the building industry adopt a <u>fraternal</u> attitude towards their employees which lacks the hierarchical elements commonly associated with paternalism. (1) As with paternalism, the relationship is subject to inherent strains and conflicts. However, given the material conditions of production in the building industry, <u>fraternalism</u> represents the most appropriate managerial strategy for small-scale employers.

THE EMPLOYMENT RELATIONSHIP IN SMALL BUSINESSES

The development of industrial capitalism has brought about the growth of large scale units of production. This growth, and its impact upon social relationships in industrial society, has attracted the attention of social commentators since the earliest stages of industrialisation. (2) The interest continues today in more general discussions of the characteristics of contemporary 'monopoly capitalism' at one extreme and the more narrowly defined debates concerning the nature of the 'size effect' at the other. Overall, most attention has been devoted to large scale industrial organisations since these are frequently seen to be symptomatic of the growing concentration of industrial, commercial and financial resources accompanying the development of modern capitalism. By contrast, small scale organisations are frequently interpreted as 'relics' from a previous stage of capitalism which are in inevitable decline. (3) Whilst these trends cannot be denied, it must be recognised that small scale enterprises continue to play a significant role in certain sectors of the modern economy. (4) However, the nature of the employment relationship within such enterprises has been relatively unexplored.

Some writers have claimed that social relations in smaller units of production display a number of distinctive features. It is often suggested, for example, that the relationship between workers and employers is particularistic and structured on the basis of personal attributes. Face-to-face interaction fosters 'affective' ties and leads to the greater identification of employees with their employers. (5) This declines, however, with growth in scale since the emergence of more specialised, bureaucratic forms of control reduces the ability of employers to exercise interpersonal control through face-to-face contact. (6)

Such a view has been subject to numerous criticisms since it tends to confuse the effect of size per se with other variables which influence social relationships within small firms. There is, for example, no reason why high levels of personal interaction should necessarily increase the intensity of employee identification with an employer; on the contrary, it is conceivable that such 'close proximity' can, in some cases, increase employee antagonism by emphasising feelings of relative deprivation. (7) What is often more important than size is, as Newby has recently pointed out, the congruence or the degree of fit between employees' orientations and employers' control strategies. (8) The extent to which subordinates identify with superordinates may, then, be more powerfully influenced by the nature of the employment relationship than solely by 'size' factors.

Further, the relationship between employers and workers in small scale enterprises may vary considerably between different sectors of the economy. Curran and Stanworth, for example, in their analysis of small firms in the printing and electronics industries emphasise the significance of the industrial subculture ('the technology and other meanings, definitions and institutionalised social practices peculiar to an industry') in influencing vertical social relationships. (9) However, most investigations fail to distinguish between small scale enterprises in terms of the socio-technical features which are often the basis of comparison for the study of larger enterprises. Indeed, there is a tendency to regard 'small firms' as a generic category which may then then be simply contrasted with their larger counterparts. (10) Consequently, it is often assumed that one particular type of employment relationship, characterised by employer paternalism and employee deference, predominates in smaller enterprises. Lockwood, for example, includes those employed in small scale 'family enterprises' amongst those workers 'most exposed to paternalistic forms of industrial authority'. (11) For him, paternalism may be defined in the following manner:

The essence of this work situation is that the

relationship between employer and worker is personal
and particularistic. The worker has a unique position
in a functional job hierarchy and he is tied to his
employer by a 'special relationship' between them
and not only by considerations of economic gain. (12)

Probably the most recent and systematic examination of
the content and form of paternalism is that undertaken by
Newby and his colleagues in their study of agricultural
capitalism in East Anglia. (13) Despite a high level of
capital investment, East Anglian farmers are small scale
employers who maintain a personal relationship with their
workers through the exercise of paternalism. (14) Thus,
according to Newby et al., paternalism legitimates an
inegalitarian and hierarchical social order because,

> On the one hand its interest is to maintain a degree
> of hierarchical differentiation from those over whom
> it rules; on the other hand it wishes to cultivate
> their identification by defining the relationship as
> an organic partnership in a co-operative enterprise.
> (15)

Consequently, on the basis of their evidence, the authors
conclude,

> Most farmers are quite prepared to construct an
> intricate web of paternalistic labour relations in
> order to obtain the identification of their workers;
> on the smaller farms this will occur spontaneously
> out of the much closer involvement of employers and
> employees in the work situation, whereas on the larger
> farms it is often a matter of conscious or unconscious
> policy. (16)

This statement has, however, to be set against the fact
that the smaller farmers in their sample (those with an
average of 3.5 non-family workers) tended to lack 'the
wherewithal to exercise paternalism - for example, a large
tied housing stock, the ability to offer various per-
quisites, the time and resources to engage in home visits,
charity etc.' (17) Indeed, Newby emphasises that the
employers' ability to treat their employees in a paternalistic manner depends upon favourable market conditions; a
shift in consumer preference or a radical change in
technology, for example, may force paternalistic employers
to drastically restructure or, indeed, make redundant
sections of their labour force in order to maintain market
competitiveness. (18) Such actions are likely to destroy
social obligations which have been cultivated within
paternalist employment relationships. The choice of
strategies available to employers is, therefore, severely
constrained by prevailing market conditions such that even
when enterprises are predominantly small scale and
characterised by a high level of personal employer-employee
contact, paternalism may be an inappropriate employer
strategy. Given the variability of market conditions in
different sectors of a capitalist economy, it is reasonable

to assume that paternalism will be but one of a number of possible employer strategies. Thus, if market conditions within agriculture encourage paternalism, the contrasting circumstances of the building industry, for example, compel small employers to adopt a more _fraternal_ approach.

MARKET CONDITIONS IN THE AGRICULTURAL AND BUILDING INDUSTRIES: A COMPARISON

Small employers in the building industry cultivate a fraternal relationship with their employees which differs significantly from that between farmers and farmworkers as described by Newby and his associates. This, we would argue, is primarily because of the strongly contrasting product and labour market conditions evident within the two industries.

In both the agricultural and building industries, small businesses produce commodities for a market which is heavily conditioned by state intervention. But whereas in agriculture the state acts to protect the industry from the 'free play' of market forces and, therefore, to stabilise conditions, its attitude towards building is quite the reverse. Indeed, the construction industry is consistently used by the state as a means of regulating the aggregate level of demand within the economy and, consequently, it bears the brunt of market fluctuations. (19) Severe variations in building demand resulting from 'stop-go' policies exacerbate market conditions which are already unstable. In addition, for small businesses in the industry, market uncertainty is compounded by the considerable risks of competitive tendering and the pitfalls of the sub-contracting system. (20) These conditions, combined with the industry's susceptibility to climatic and geological conditions, are conducive to high rates of business form-ation and dissolution, particularly amongst smaller enterprises. Indeed, The Royal Commission on the Distrib-ution of Income and Wealth observed the considerable variation in the rate of bankruptcy amongst the proprietors of unincorporated companies, 'the risk being particularly low in agriculture and the professions, and highest in transport, retailing and construction'.(21) (our emphasis.) In fact, the ratio of receiving orders to number of self-employed businesses in 1975 was 1:335 in construction by comparison with 1:1,492 in agriculture. (22)

These fluctuations are matched by similar instabilities in the labour market. The construction industry is characterised by high rates of labour mobility; employees are prone to switch employers, move in and out of the industry and indeed, to become employers or self-employed. A recent survey of carpenters and bricklayers found,

> In addition to movement between other occupations and industries ... very significant movement within con-struction carpentry/joinery; between firms, between

firms and public authorities, between bench and site
... between shuttering and other carpentry on site.
For bricklayers, there is considerable movement
between contractors and also between employment and
self-employment. (23)

These patterns of mobility are both a response to market
uncertainty <u>and</u> a reflection of a strong tradition of
worker autonomy and 'self-reliance'. (24) This tendency to
'play the market', both in and beyond the building industry,
contrasts strongly with the labour market behaviour of
agricultural workers. Thus, although Newby found some evidence of geographical mobility among farm workers this
tended to be 'over very short distances indeed, certainly
over a range within which the choice of occupation and of
employer was extremely limited'. (25) Such a particularistic
market situation led him to the conclusion that the agricultural workers' position was 'one of considerable power-
lessness compared with urban industrial workers'. (26)
Further, farmers' dominance over their employees was
reinforced by their control over accommodation and the high
average age of agricultural workers. (27)

If there is little opportunity for agricultural workers
to change employers, their chances of becoming small
farmers are almost non-existent. Earnings of agricultural
workers are among the lowest in Britain and the range of
inequalities within farming finds no parallel in the
construction industry. To quote, once again, the <u>Royal
Commission</u>:

> In the agriculture trade group ... very few employees
> reach the level of the top twenty per cent of the self-
> employed in the same trade group ... (In building) it
> is noticeable that ... employees tend to have greater
> incomes than their self-employed counterparts, and
> their mean earnings are also greater. (28)

Despite the limitations of these statistics (they do not,
for example, measure the material 'perks' of self-employment), they do indicate an equality of earnings between
employees and small employers in the building industry
which is conspicuously absent in agriculture. These figures
also suggest that, given the low level of fixed capital
required, building workers have greater opportunities to
become self-employed and to start their own business.

Differences in the product and labour markets of the
building and agricultural industries have repercussions for
the nature of the employment relationship. While conditions
in agriculture are conducive to the adoption of paternalism
as an employer strategy, this is not the case in building
where market and employment instabilities render the
domination of employers over employees problematic. Thus,
small employers in the building industry cope with these
by adopting a <u>fraternal</u> strategy which is quite distinct
from the paternalism of agriculture. More specifically, we
would argue that <u>fraternalism</u> represents a way of organising

work largely without resort to clearly-defined hierarchical control. Within the context of relatively equal earnings, the conflicting interests of employers and employees are partially resolved through the task at hand. This determines a technical division of labour within which employers and employees perform their tasks with a high degree of personal autonomy. In this way, small employers are able to emphasise their role as 'fellow workers' and to 'conceal' their role as employers. This functions to reduce tension in the employment relationship and enables employers to secure the commitment of skilled tradesmen whose work is not susceptible to more <u>direct</u> forms of supervisory control.

THE FRATERNALISM OF SMALL EMPLOYERS

Our evidence is drawn from interviews with twenty-five small employers as part of a larger study of business enter-prises in the building industry. (29) These small employers worked alongside their employees in addition to being responsible for all the administrative and financial aspects of their businesses. (30) They had all begun their working lives as tradesmen; twelve were carpenters and joiners and the rest had been apprenticed in the plumbing, electrical, plastering, bricklaying, painting and decorating trades.(31) In terms of social background, seventeen had fathers who were or had been manual employees, while a further six had been self-employed or owned small businesses. (32) The average age of the respondents was forty-nine, with ten in their forties and six in their fifties. On average, they employed six workers, although many of them supplemented this through the use of subcontracted labour at various times. Their annual turnover ranged between £10,000 and £125,000 and they were all based in the South of England and predominantly engaged in general building work for private customers. (33) 'Labour-only' subcontractors were deliberately excluded from the sample. (34) The respondents were selected in a non-random fashion from trade directories, local advertisements and through personal contacts. The interviews were loosely structured, tape recorded and then fully transcribed.(33) Although, then, the data cannot pro-vide support for statistical generalisation they give some insight into the strategies adopted by small employers towards their staff. These, we would argue, are fairly typical of those adopted by small employers in the building industry in general.

Among those we studied the essence of the employment strategy can best be described as <u>fraternal</u>. In effect, small employers continue to see themselves as tradesmen working <u>with</u> and <u>alongside</u> their employees. In this sense their work situation bears a close resemblance to their prior experience as employees and as self-employed, and it continues to influence their present behaviour as <u>employers</u>. The following statements illustrate these points:

I try to be fair with them. I don't know if, after a few

years, whether you get biased to an employer's outlook, but I try and look back over the years when I was employed and see what my reaction would have been and use that as a guide. I feel that in a small business if you can't do it on a friendly relationship then you should go. When there's just the three of you in close proximity, if you've got to have a heavy boss-worker relationship then you might just as well not bother. (Interview no.220)

The best way to handle men is to be straight with them for a start. Be straight, and treat them as if you're work mates ...The way I look at it is if you've been brought up in the trade, then you are a tradesman. These men treat me like I was when I was working as an ordinary tradesman. Whether I'm a boss now or not, they talk to me the same as they do to their mates. (Interview no.203)

You've got to know what you are talking about. The men have got to have confidence in you ...If they've got any problems I go on site and they can always speak to me. They all know that they'll always be treated fairly and, obviously, they know that I, being in the game all my life, know what it's all about. (Interview no.224)

If during the 'normal' working day they work alongside their employees, they also cost their own labour in the same manner. (36) It is primarily through end-of-year profits and fiscal 'perks' of self-employment that they are able to benefit from their position as business proprietors:

My accountant always tells me I am paying the men too much money ...They earn more than me - they take home more than me. Thrice as much sometimes. They always do, but that's a fact of life. Obviously, with things like the car, the van and petrol and telephones - I get my perks that way. But in actual cash, they're better off. (Interview no.214)

I pay myself a weekly wage ... costed as an ordinary bricklayer ...It wasn't many years ago we were still paying ourselves eleven pounds a week... Obviously, we draw from the bank or from the firm according to our requirements, but this probably doesn't exceed a bricklayer's wage anyway. (Interview no.207)

Their reluctance to become devoted to full-time administration is linked to the view that such work is 'unproductive'. Further, for them to cease manual work would not only increase costs but also introduce a hierarchical dimension into the employment relationship which could generate resentment and seriously reduce the productivity of their employees. They cannot, then, afford to be seen as 'living off' the profits created by others and as such they feel obliged to work as competent and productive tradesmen.

My men appreciate me in as much as they know they don't keep me. I can keep myself. So, therefore, they don't get all bolshy and they don't turn round and say, 'Look

at him riding around in a big car. He's got this and
he's got that'. Because they know that I do earn it.
They don't support me. (Interview no.213)

The more work you take on and the more employees you
have, the more paperwork you get. You get snowed under
with it. But if I'm in the office doing all the paperwork and not doing any manual work ... my charges
would have to go up a lot and I wouldn't get the work.
(Interview no.219)

Small employers maintain a close, day-to-day, personal
contact with their employees. Despite this, they leave
their workers to 'get on with the job'. The technical
division of labour enables their employees to work with a
considerable degree of personal autonomy. Being themselves
tradesmen, they realise the need to grant their workers the
freedom to exercise their skills. This, in turn, maintains
a high level of job satisfaction and reinforces their
employees' identification with the business.

I've found that if you give a man a little bit of
responsibility he'll do a better job for you and he's
got something to work at, hasn't he?...If you were
building an extension and you sent a couple of blokes
round and said, 'I want the base done' and they get on
and do the base and you don't tell them anything about
what's going on top, they're not interested. And if a
man is not interested in his work, he's not going to
work so hard and let's face it, they're there to make
a profit for you, aren't they? (Interview no.204)

From the beginning, if you give men a job to do, you
must explain exactly what's got to be done and let them
get on with it ... it doesn't matter how long they take
... as long as they make a reasonable job of it and if
they do, tell them they've made a reasonable job ...If
you treat people as though you've got a bit of confidence in them, they probably won't let you down,
whereas the ones you keep on to, have a sort of 'I
don't care' attitude. (Interview no.210)

Because skilled employees are 'expensive' they must be
'kept working' and it is a common practice for small
employers to 'relegate' themselves to various subsidiary
tasks or 'service' functions. (37) This emphasises the
fraternal nature of the employment relationship whilst
allowing small employers to periodically check on the progress of work. More overt forms of employer control are
difficult to impose and, in any case, are likely to trigger
an antagonistic response from workers who value their work
autonomy:

I supervise them with great difficulty ... it's almost
impossible. I can only look at the job at the end and
see that it's come out reasonably well within my
expectations. If I call at the job too many times then
they obviously get the idea that I'm checking up on
them ... then they have two hours for lunch ... I mean,

I can't win! So I can only look at the job at the end and think, 'Well, that's turned out within my expectations so we'll discard half a day - they've still got the job out on time ...I try not to push too much and hope ... that I get a reasonable amount ...All I expect is a reasonable day's work. I don't expect them to break their necks. (Interview no.220)

I want someone that I don't have to run after. I'd rather pay the money and know that the work is going to be done right than get someone who'd do it as a cheap Jack ... so I need someone reliable ...Take the one I've got now, I know I can leave him ... because he'll tell me what he wants and I'm confident I can leave him. I know it will be done. I rely on him a lot and he revels in it... I find if you ask them to do something that's better than brow-beating. I don't brow-beat. You can't say, 'You will do this, you will do that'. I get more done for me by buttering them up as it were, 'That's a good job' or 'Do you think that you could get that done by Friday?' Put it in that manner and invariably you find that it gets done. (Interview no.219)

Most people in the building trade are prickly types - they don't like to be treated as serfs, as one might say. They like to be asked... They're very independent - builders... You can't supervise workers on a site like you can in a factory. (Interview no.224)

The dependence of small employers on their workers is heightened by the fact that they typically employ only six or seven men. Consequently, the poor performance - or absence - of one man can have a disproportionately large impact on productivity. This vulnerability emphasises small employers' reliance upon their men working together as equals in a team which 'pulls together'. If this all-round effort is not achieved the consequences can be disastrous:

One bloke we've got is deteriorating ... you put him on a job and it goes into debt. Every day is a head-ache - what can we give him today?... With a bigger firm they can afford to carry him, but a small firm can't. (Interview no.201)

For their part, small employers reciprocate this commit-ment by giving their employees special privileges. In doing so, they cultivate personal relationships which are characterised by well-established patterns of mutual obligation.

Well, with employing a small amount of people you find that you know them all personally. I can go to any one of my fellows and say to him 'Look George, we're in trouble'... Last week one chappy was on holiday, we had one fellow go sick and another one break his thumb. That means to say that myself and my partner were virtually the only ones left in the firm. I said to the chap who's on holiday, 'We could do with you back on Monday'. 'Okay, no problem', he said. This is the sort of reaction you get. But on the reverse side of the coin, if that chap said, 'Look Governor, I need £100', I'd find him £100 and I'd let him pay me back when he could. This is it - it's a personal relationship. Let's put it this way, we're working with them eight hours a day and you're only with your spouse about another eight so this is the sort of relationship that you get. (Interview no.208)

'Fringe benefits' such as these are generally used as a means to retain good employees but in some cases they also give them the opportunity to 'experiment' on their own. Perhaps the major fringe benefit is the use of the employers' equipment and materials for the purposes of spare-time work. Small employers recognise the importance of this as a source of supplementary, cash income and a means whereby pressure for wage increases can be reduced. (38) The implications of this practice are, however, far-reaching since it allows employees to 'trade' auto-nomously and thereby obtain experience of a quasi-form of self-employment,

This is the great thing with me, if somebody wants something - a can of paint or something because they've got a job to do - as far as I'm concerned, they can have it. If they ask for anything, nine times out of ten, they will get it ... you get little bits and pieces over and you don't mind (letting them have it) ...If a bloke wants to work, say the afternoon himself, then as far as I'm concerned, it's alright as long as he doesn't work on my patch. (Interview no.219)

One chap takes the van home evenings and weekends... I wouldn't object if they do odd jobs. In fact, I let them have the materials. (Interview no.212)

They do work on their own ... as long as it's not one of my customers I'm not worried ... if they want the van for their own use, fair enough, it doesn't worry me. I mean, I don't even charge them petrol. (Interview no.210)

If these spare-time practices prove to be successful, some employees may decide to start their own businesses on a full-time basis. (39) Thus, the fraternalism of small employers demands the extension of fringe benefits which can eventually lead to employees becoming self-employed. Perhaps the most extreme instance of this practice is when small employers make the necessary legal arrangements for their employees to eventually take over the ownership of their businesses. The assets involved in such a transfer may not be particularly extensive but the implications for the employment relationship are significant,

We've got a limited company in the offing and we are going to pass the business over to the lads. We'll be in an advisory capacity or, perhaps, I shall be doing a bit of work for them. As long as I can earn a bit of money. (Interview no.225)

116

I made two of my blokes into directors... I hope that in perhaps ten years' time I can consider getting out of it altogether... The reason I made it a company and two of my fellow employees into directors is that they've both got children and eventually they should have sufficient capital to buy me out. If not, they've got shares and I will climb into the background and still take an income from it. (Interview no.211)

Clearly, the bond between small employers and their employees extends beyond the 'cash-nexus'. A working relationship is established which allows employees considerable job satisfaction and provides them with the personal skills and assets necessary for them to 'go it alone' should they so wish. Because small employers put considerable 'trust' in their workers and expect them to behave in a responsible and conscientious manner, they are careful in their recruitment procedures. (40) Workers are expected to meet criteria of acceptability as employees who can be relied upon to do a 'reasonable day's work' and as people who will be able to establish satisfactory relationships with customers. Thus, employers' perceptions of customers' preferences often determine the personal qualities of the workers they are prepared to employ.

I've got to have someone that I can leave on the job to keep my customers happy. Someone who will look after my interests and generally see to it that we keep the customers happy. (Interview no.219)

I try to find somebody who has got a reasonable personality because when you are going into private houses and dealing personally with mostly women you feel you've got some responsibility to send somebody who is a bit respectable looking ...Customers are entitled to expect something for what they pay for ... so it's a question of finding someone who can handle these situations. (Interview no.220)

You'd want him (a new employee) on a trial period to see that the type of work he does is really neat. I think also the appearance of him is important; neat and tidy, a pleasant sort of chap. Somebody who could deal with customers - talk to customers as well as I can, really. (Interview no.212)

Careful recruitment further enables small employers to partially relinquish the responsibilities of supervision and control. In effect, notions of customer obligation operate as a form of employee control since workers feel it is their 'duty' to complete a reasonable and fair-priced job. 'Unreasonable' and 'expensive' work has to be paid for, it seems, by the customer rather than the employer.

My men are working for a private person and they have got to satisfy that person. That is why I'll never have a job number; the time is always booked to Mr and Mrs So-and-So. If you book it to a job number, any

117

amount of time can go on a number. When they're
charging an hour's time, they're charging Mrs So-and-
So and she's got to pay it. I like them to realise that.
(Interview no.209)

The heavy emphasis upon the 'personality' of workers
partly accounts for small employer claims that there is
a general shortage of suitable, skilled labour. But
'suitable' in this sense normally refers to general personal
characteristics as well as to technical competence. Hence,
many small employers are reluctant to recruit from Job
Centres on the grounds that those available may not be
'reliable', 'conscientious' or 'trustworthy':

(My workers) are all skilled men in their own right...
If they were to leave I could never replace them. I
would just have to go back to being a one-man band...
Tradesmen are so hard to get ... I do private work and
when they go into people's homes I don't mean they've
got to touch their forelock or call them sir, but
they've got to be a little bit respectful ... you want
a person who's got a bit of respect for people... You
cannot take somebody off the Labour Exchange or Job
Centre and bring them in... I think a lot of them are
virtually unemployable. (Interview no.213)

If, by virtue of their recruitment and work practices,
small employers establish personal relationships with their
employees, this rarely extends into non-work life. Contact
outside work is limited if only because of the long
working day consisting as it does, of 'productive' manual
work and 'non-productive' administration in the evenings
and at weekends. (41)

Our leisure time is normally taken up with running the
business and the day is filled quite comfortably
without joining any clubs. (Interview no.217)

I haven't got any free time... I've got bits and pieces
to do. Occasionally, I might nip up the local and have
a jar. I get up there at ten and they close at eleven.
But just an hour away from booking at times, you feel
you need it. (Interview no.223)

One of the small employers' wives put her point of view in
strong terms:

I would like to see my husband not work so hard... I
can't remember when he's had a free Saturday or a free
Sunday for a very long time. When you take the staff
home on a Friday they're finished. They don't know how
lucky they are... They've got peace of mind Saturday
and Sunday which we haven't got still ...We are so busy
trying to make a go of it that you don't think of
leisure time so much... So we don't make a habit of
seeing any of the customers ... and we don't go out
with the employees. (Interview no.218w)

In the limited leisure time which is available, small

employers sometimes meet their workers on an informal basis. This is typified by having an occasional drink with their employees, either at home or in the pub,

> Some of the chaps who work for me started at school the same day as me and I go out and have a drink with them on Friday or Saturday night, the same as I did before I took over the business. That doesn't worry me as long as I enjoy someone's company. (Interview no.210)

> If the men are doing a very dirty job or a late job on a Saturday or Sunday we take them home and give them a drink and what have you... I make them a meal as well - it might be breakfast, lunch or evening meal. But we always make something - make sure they have something to eat. I think they do appreciate it... My husband looks after them. Although it's an employer-employee relationship, he's one of the boys and this helps an awful lot... When I'm here it's just the same. I'm just another employee as far as everybody else is concerned ... there's no barrier. (Interview no.207w)

These, then, are the central features of the _fraternal_ strategy. The dependence of small employers upon 'indispensable' workers, the nature of the work tasks and the unstable and competitive conditions of the market compel the structuring of egalitarianism between employers and employees. Given the conditions under which these businesses operate, _fraternalism_ represents the most feasible means by which proprietors can control and manage labour. Small employers, then, define the relationship with their employees as 'an organic partnership in a co-operative enterprise'. (42) However, _hierarchical differentiation_, which represents the other key element in Newby's definition of paternalism, is largely absent. Fraternalism represents a means whereby small employers can overcome the tension deriving from their role as both employers _and_ workers. Although they may own various physical assets, their businesses are primarily dependent upon theirs' and others' _labour_. Small farmers may also work alongside their employees but, we would suggest, the larger capital assets which they possess - often through inheritance - fundamentally affects the relationship with employees in two major ways. (43) First, it makes the contribution of their own manual labour to the success of the business relatively less important than that of the productive assets which they own. Secondly, it ensures a difference in material wealth between themselves and their employees which makes the exercise of paternalistic authority a more appropriate form of managerial control.

As with paternalism, however, _fraternalism_ has its own contradictions which lead to strain, conflict and perpetual 'redefinition'. In a variety of ways the employment of labour demands that small employers behave in a reasonably 'rational' and 'calculative' manner. In order to retain their employees they must ensure a regular flow of work, possess sufficient assets for cash flow purposes, adopt reliable bookkeeping systems and negotiate credit with banks. These market pressures conflict with their self-identity as tradesmen. Consequently, they are frequently torn between their role as employer and as productive worker. Recent attempts to 'formalise' and 'regulate' employment relationships have heightened this conflict. The legislative measures of the mid-1970s, for example, assume that the participants in the employment relationship are either employers or employees. (44) They fail to recognise the dual role of small employers and the nature of employment relationships within these enterprises.

> The paper work and the rules these days are really colossal for a small businessman. The rules were made looking at big business ... but when you are running your own business you don't get round to doing it... It's also more difficult in a small business because you're in a more personal relationship and there's more friction if you reprimand somebody than there is in a big firm. (Interview no.220)

Small employers object to this legislation because it restricts their prerogatives as employers and also challenges their fraternal relationship with employees. (45) This, in turn, damages the operating efficiency of their enterprises and their ability to maximise profits. There are, then, forces which inevitably compel small employers to exercise their authority as business proprietors. These necessarily differentiate them from their employees despite the operation of fraternal strategies. Small employers cope with these tensions largely by reference to the risks which they have incurred in establishing their businesses. The instabilities of the market are as evident to employees as they are to small employers; indeed, many now working for others will have experimented with their own businesses in the past. It is this which mitigates tensions in the employment relationship; dissatisfied workers can, with a minimum of capital, set up on their own and trade largely on their skills. Once established, they too can employ others and, if successful, can legitimate their material benefits and workplace authority by reference to risks taken in an unstable market. Some may even 'break through' to a size of enterprise which removes them entirely from direct involvement in manual work and makes the fraternal strategy less appropriate. Many more, we suspect, revert to working entirely on their own or, indeed, become once again, employees.

CONCLUSION

A central problem for any employer within a capitalist economy concerns the acquisition and maintenance of at least a minimum degree of employee 'commitment'. In small-scale enterprises employee identification may be achieved through face-to-face interaction between owner-managers and workers. One 'congruent' form of such interaction is characterised by employer paternalism and employee deference. Although this relationship has received some attention over recent years it would be wrong to assume that it necessarily represents the predominant form in small scale enterprises generally.

Employer strategies are strongly influenced by material conditions of production and labour and product market constraints. These are subject to considerable variation as our comparison between the agricultural and building industries indicates. Whereas paternalism represents an appropriate mode of control for small scale employers in agriculture it is inappropriate for employers of a similar size in building. Our sketch of the _fraternal_ strategy pursued by small employers is no more than a preliminary outline which we hope to refine and substantiate as our research progresses. Nevertheless, we may, at this point, tentatively suggest that, beyond the well researched confines of farming, employment relationships in small scale enterprises may be structured along rather less 'traditional' lines than those in agriculture. More specifically, in those sectors of the economy where there is a less 'rigid' distinction between owner-managers and their workers in small scale enterprises, employment strategies may more closely resemble _fraternalism_ rather than paternalism.

NOTES

(1) We are grateful to our colleagues in the SSRC Social Stratification Group (in particular, Howard Newby, Gary Runciman and Mike Rose) for their helpful comments on an earlier draft of this article. After discussions with them we altered the term originally chosen to describe the small employers' strategy - _egalitarianism_ - to _fraternalism_. This term better recognises the imbalance of power which, in the final analysis, exists between employer and employee.

(2) An insightful review is provided in H. Newby, 'Paternalism and Capitalism', in R. Scase (ed.), _Industrial Society: Class, Cleavage and Control_, London, 1977.

(3) Their decline is frequently linked with that of an entire social class: the 'traditional' petite bourgeoisie. See, for example, K. Marx and F. Engels, _The Communist Manifesto_, 1848 in K. Marx and F. Engels, _Selected Works_, London, 1968; N. Poulantzas, _Classes in Contemporary Capitalism_, London, 1975.

(4) For a detailed analysis of their contribution in different sectors of the economy see _The Report of the Committee of Inquiry on Small Firms_ (The Bolton Report), Cmnd 4811, London, 1971 and, more recently, _The Financing of Small Firms_, (The Wilson Report), Cmnd 7503, London, 1979. Explanations of this persistence are offered in J. Boswell, _The Rise and Decline of Small Firms_, London, 1973; A. Friedman, _Industry and Labour_, London, 1977 and R. Scase and R. Goffee, _The Real World of the Small Business Owner_, London 1980.

(5)   See, for example, G.K. Ingham, Size of Industrial
      Organisation and Worker Behaviour, Cambridge, 1970.
(6)   H. Newby, op.cit.
(7)   The evidence is discussed in D. Lockwood, 'Sources of
      Variation in Working Class Images of Society' and
      subject to critical review in, for example, C. Bell
      and H. Newby, 'The Sources of Variation in Agricultural
      Workers' Images of Society', both in M. Bulmer (ed.),
      Working Class Images of Society, London, 1975. See also
      J. Curran and J. Stanworth, 'Worker Involvement and
      Social Relations in The Small Firm' Sociological
      Review, 27, 1979.
(8)   H. Newby, op.cit.
(9)   J. Curran and J. Stanworth, op.cit., p.338.
(10) For recent attempts to differentiate this category see,
      for example, J. Boswell, op.cit. and R. Scase and
      R. Goffee, op.cit.
(11) D. Lockwood op.cit., p.19.
(12) Ibid., p.20.
(13) H. Newby, C. Bell, D. Rose and P. Saunders, Property,
      Paternalism and Power, London, 1978.
(14) Even in the sample with the largest farmers the
      average number of employees was only twenty.
(15) H. Newby, et al., op. cit., p.29.
(16) Ibid., p.189.
(17) Ibid., p.172.
(18) H. Newby, op.cit., p.71.
(19) The experience of the building industry in the current
      recession fits in with a well-established pattern. For
      recent discussions see Direct Labour Collective,
      Building with Direct Labour, London, 1978; How
      Flexible is Construction? (National Economic Develop-
      ment Office), London, 1978.
(20) See, for example, C. Foster, Building with Men, London,
      1969; P. Stone, Building Economy, London, 1966;
      Tavistock Institute of Human Relations, Interdepend-
      ence and Uncertainty: A Study of the Building
      Industry, London, 1966.
(21) Royal Commission on The Distribution of Income and
      Wealth, Report Number 8, Cmnd, 7679, London, 1979,
      p.207.
(22) Ibid., Table 12.2.
(23) How Flexible is Construction?, op.cit., p.42.
(24) For an insightful account of this pattern amongst
      'unskilled' construction workers see A.J. Sykes,
      'Navvies: their work attitudes' and 'Navvies: their
      social relations' in Sociology, vol.3, 1969.
(25) H. Newby et al., op.cit., p.156.
(26) H. Newby, The Deferential Worker, London, 1977, p.165.
(27) Over fifty per cent of agricultural workers in East
      Anglia are above forty-five years of age. H. Newby
      et al., op.cit., p.159.
(28) Royal Commission on The Distribution of Income and
      Wealth, Report Number 8, op.cit., p.190.
(29) This research is financed by the SSRC and we are
      grateful for their support. A lengthier analysis is
      available in R. Scase and R. Goffee, The Entrepreneur-

ial Middle Class, London, 1982.

(30) 'Paperwork' is, however, largely undertaken in the evenings or at weekends; the greater part of the working day being devoted to manual labour.

(31) We include in this group those who had completed formal apprenticeships as well as those who had under- gone more short-term government-sponsored training courses. The predominance of carpenters reflects an industry-wide pattern. Carpentry is still a central trade in the building process and carpenters are often responsible for co-ordinating the tasks of other tradesmen. This serves as a useful training for potential proprietors. See How Flexible is Construct- ion?, op.cit., and B. Reckmann, 'Carpentry: The Craft and Trade' in A. Zimbalist (ed.), Case Studies on the Labour Process, New York, 1979.

(32) The remaining two fathers were employed as 'middle' level managers.

(33) The research was limited to this area in order to save costs. We acknowledge that in other areas - and in the North of England in particular - union representation amongst building workers is stronger and that this affects the nature of employment relationships.

(34) For an analysis of the distinct situation of 'labour- only' subcontractors see, for example, Direct Labour Collective, op.cit., and T. Austrin, 'The Lump in the UK Construction Industry' in T. Nichols (ed.), Capital and Labour, Glasgow, 1980.

(35) The evidence presented in this paper is drawn selectively from these transcripts. Where parts of the first-hand account have been omitted this is indicated by (...).

(36) Labour-time devoted to administration is largely uncosted by our respondents.

(37) In the building industry such tasks might involve, for example, mixing concrete, fetching appropriate tools, collecting materials and so on.

(38) In this sense, small employers encourage their employees to operate in the 'black' economy.

(39) The practice of 'moonlighting' has recently been described as 'one of the single biggest spurs to setting up one's own business'. P. Stothard, 'Trapped - Why Our Small Businesses are Still Struggling', Sunday Times, 10.2.1980. For further evidence see R. Scase and R. Goffee, op.cit. (1980).

(40) We use this term, following Fox, to refer not to personal 'liking' or 'disliking' but to the trust relationship that emerges where work roles are not rigidly defined and formally-prescribed measures of work performance are unnecessary. See A. Fox, Beyond Contract, London, 1977.

(41) This severely limits the ability of small employers to regularly engage in any type of 'formal' recreational activity; membership of clubs and associations is low.

(42) Cf. note 15.

(43) For evidence concerning the material assets owned by small farmers see H. Newby et al., op.cit.

(44) We refer specifically to the provisions contained in the Trade Union and Labour Relations Acts of 1974 and 1976 and The Employment Protection Act of 1975.

(45) For a survey of small-employer attitudes towards this legislation see R. Clifton and C. Tatton-Brown, _Impact of Employment Legislation on Small Firms_, Research Paper no.6, Department of Employment, 1979. The 1980 Employment Act has exempted small businesses from some of the requirements stipulated under earlier legislation.

7 Clerical 'Proletarianisation': Myth or Reality?

ROSEMARY CROMPTON AND GARETH JONES

Although the word is of ancient origin, the concept of 'proletarianisation' is invariably associated with Marx and Engels' account of the development of industrial capitalism. In the <u>Communist Manifesto</u>, they describe the proletariat as 'the modern working class ... <u>a class of labourers who live only so long as they find work, and who find work only so long as their labour increases capital</u>'. Inseparable from the notion of the 'proletariat' is that of the 'bourgeoisie': 'In proportion as the bourgeoisie, i.e. capital, is developed, in the same proportion is the proletariat ... developed'. As Marx and Engels' simple definition makes clear, an essential element of the proletarian condition is wage labourer status. However, if the 'proletariat' is simply taken to include those of wage labour (or employment) status, it is immediately apparent that there exist (and indeed, have always existed), considerable variations in condition within the heterogeneous group so identified. These variations in condition (e.g. income, working conditions, etc.) produce empirically a hierarchy of 'employment consequences'. Rather than a dichotomy of 'bourgeois' and 'proletarian', the investigation of condition reveals 'upper', 'middle' and 'lower' levels of employment, and it is in the 'middle levels' that clerical workers have traditionally been located.

Not surprisingly, the emergence and persistence of the 'middle layers' has been a persistent focus of debate in class theory. Those unsympathetic to Marx have been able to claim that the existence of the 'middle classes' 'disproves' Marx's analysis; whilst those more sympathetic have endlessly debated the precise manner in which they should be 'located' within a Marxist framework. Much of the debate has been explicitly concerned with 'condition', with a description of incomes, attitudes, working conditions, and so on. Writing in the 1930s, Klingender, for example, argued that clerks, both in terms of their income and status as propertyless employees, were properly to be identified with the industrial proletariat. To the extent that clerks denied their 'true' class situation - for example, by not joining trade unions - they suffered from false consciousness. On the other hand, Lockwood's influential work (published at the end of the 1950s) concluded that, despite their common employment status, the class situation of the clerk differed significantly from that of the manual worker. In terms of their 'work' and 'market' situations, the benefits enjoyed by the clerks both at work and in the market were such as to differentiate them from manual workers, and clerks were not therefore falsely conscious of their class situation if they failed to join trade unions or seek common cause with manual workers.

As a useful heuristic device, Lockwood and Klingender's common strategy may be described as being to examine the conditions of clerical work and compare them with those of manual work - the latter being assumed to represent the 'ideal' proletarian condition. (This representation is, in fact, somewhat unfair to both authors.) This examination is both interesting and useful. Nevertheless, it can be argued that such a strategy, whilst documenting inequalities of condition, does not explain them. (Nichols, 1979, p.153.)

We would suggest that this is because, in the 'proletarianisation' debate the examination of the proletarian condition has become separated from the analysis of the proletarianisation process. We want to argue that static descriptions of conditions cannot, on their own, adequately test a thesis about process and social dynamics. Braverman's Labour and Monopoly Capitalism attempts to bring together both process and condition. Briefly, Braverman, following Marx, argues that the initial subjection of labour to capital was 'formal' - that is, although the craftsman sold his labour to the capitalist (and therefore did not control the material means of production) he retained control over his own labour power and thus over important aspects of the labour process. The real control of capital over labour (and the labour process) was only achieved via the 'deskilling' of labour, the separation of 'conception' from 'execution' rendering work into a series of simple, fragmented tasks and removing any control by the workers over the labour process. Deskilling is seen by Braverman as the inevitable outcome of the internal dynamics of the capitalist mode of production, in which by (i) reducing labour costs and (ii) enhancing the productivity of labour, the 'degradation of work' serves to maximise accumulation. (1)

As with manual work, Braverman argues that non-manual work has, with the development of monopoly capitalism, been similarly deskilled and thereby rendered truly 'proletarian'. To quote directly: to ascribe 'middle class' or 'semi-managerial' functions to the 'millions of present-day clerical workers' is a 'drastic misconception of modern society', yet this is 'exactly the practice of academic sociology' (p.293). On the contrary, clerical work has become the province of 'an immense mass of wage-workers. The apparent trend to a large non-proletarian "middle class" has resolved itself into the creation of a large proletariat in a new form. In its conditions of employment, the working population has lost all former superiorities over workers

126

in industry, and in its scales of pay has sunk almost to the
very bottom.' (Braverman, 1974, pp.355-6.)

It is clear that Braverman, like Klingender and Lockwood,
makes his case for clerical proletarianisation by pointing
to the similarities between routine clerical and manual
work. Although Braverman was working within an explicitly
Marxist framework, and his position apparently rejects that
of Lockwood, the argument he presents is by no means incom-
patible. The empirical data presented in his chapter on
clerical workers chart the impact of 'scientific management'
on the office and the decline of clerical salaries -
clearly important aspects of 'work' and 'market' situations.
What separates Braverman and Lockwood, we would suggest, is
not a fundamental difference of approach, but twenty years
of social development. Although writing from differing
perspectives and reaching varying conclusions, one feature
common to all three authors discussed above is the
assumption that it is the manual worker who exemplifies the
proletarian condition. That is, to be a 'proletarian', it
is not sufficient to be employed, in addition the worker
must also be subject to control, work discipline and
generally 'less favourable' conditions of employment. Such
an analysis of inequalities of 'condition' has been contrasted by Nichols with the analysis of '<u>place</u>' where this
term refers to place within the social division of labour
as a whole.

In common with many other recent authors (e.g. Poulantzas,
1975; Carchedi, 1975; Wright, 1976), we would emphasise
that 'place' in the social division of labour characteristic
of contemporary capitalism is not 'given' simply by virtue
of individual ownership or non-ownership of the means of
production, but also by the extent of <u>control</u> of productive
forces. Therefore, for example, a senior manager who
effectively controls production, investment and/or labour is
clearly carrying out the function of capital even in the
absence of legal ownership, and the 'place' of such an
individual in the social division of labour is identified
with that of the bourgeoisie. We would take this argument
further by suggesting that, historically, the 'middleness'
of the 'middle classes' may have reflected not only their
relatively superior condition vis-a-vis the mass of manual
workers, but also the fact that, within the social
division of labour, many carried out both capital and
labour functions. (Crompton and Gubbay, 1979; Crompton,
1976; Wright, 1976.) Clearly, the extent to which the
conditions of non-manual employment approximate to the
conditions of manual employment is an important issue which
should not be ignored; we would emphasise, however, that
this analysis of 'condition' should not be divorced from
the analysis of 'place'. In other words, 'place' may prove
as important a test of proletarianisation as 'condition'.
Proletarianisation has been described as 'the complex
historical process which produces a working class' (Larson,
1980, p.132). That is, proletarianisation is a process
which generates proletarians - a class which not only lives

by the sale of its labour but also does not exercise control in respect of capitalist functions - in short, is hired simply <u>as</u> labour and is itself controlled and directed accordingly.

Braverman brings together the analysis of condition with the analysis of social dynamics and process by focussing on the removal of 'skill' from clerical work. This is essentially concerned with the <u>individual's</u> control of his or her own labour. Whether or not an individual's control in this respect renders their place in the social division of labour significantly different (in class terms) from those who do not is not an issue that we can resolve here (Wright, 1976; Crompton and Gubbay, 1979). However, we would suggest that, by focussing on the possession of skill by individuals and the implications this has for the control of their own labour Braverman has ignored the question of other aspects of control. As we have argued above, 'work' can involve carrying out not only skilled or unskilled activities regarding the labour process, but also the exercise of control and authority over both the work of others and/or the material means of production. Changes in the organisation and content of clerical work may affect not just the 'skill' of the clerk but also the extent of the clerk's control in these respects, and thus their position in the social division of labour (Crompton and Reid, 1981). However, despite these critical comments, we would emphasise that both Braverman and Lockwood (and to a lesser extent Klingender), place the nature of the clerical work process at the centre of their enquiry. We would agree that such an examination remains important for both the analysis of proletarian condition and the proletarianisation process.

Two recent contributions to British sociology have strongly rejected the thesis of clerical 'proletarianis- ation' (Goldthorpe, 1980; Stewart <u>et al</u>, 1980. Although the bases of the rejections are apparently similar, there are in fact important differences between the two approaches which we shall attempt to identify in our account.

Goldthorpe's rejection is brief. Firstly, notions of the '"proletarianisation" of lower-level non-manual employment, and in particular ... that of the emerging "office-factory"' are dismissed as '<u>facile</u>'. We interpret this statement as being largely concerned with the <u>empirical</u> question about the nature of lower level white-collar work. If we are correct, we would simply note that the authorities cited by Goldthorpe in support of his case (Mercer and Weir, 1972, Lockwood, 1958 and Dale, 1962) can hardly bear the weight of the rejection, which would itself be contradicted by a number of more recent empirical studies (Mann and Williams, 1960; Jaeggi and Weidemann, 1965; Hoos, 1961; Stymne; Whisler; Braverman, 1974).

Secondly, Goldthorpe questions the 'proletarianisation'

thesis by pointing to the fact (revealed by the Nuffield mobility studies) that the social groupings in which routine clerical workers are commonly located 'are known to be ones with highly fluctuating memberships even over a relatively short-run period' (Goldthorpe, 1980, p.258), thus undermining 'the potentialities for class-based socio-political action' amongst these groups. More particularly,

> Even if one were to accept (and the point is debatable) that the market and work situation of the employees in question have tended overall to move closer to those of manual wage-workers, the import of such a shift is not all that apparent if, as we have shown for males at least, there is a high frequency of work-life mobility from routine non manual positions to both manual and higher-level white-collar ones. (ibid, p.259)

That is, male clerks have not been 'proletarianised' because proletarian status - if it exists at all - is left behind in the move to higher-level white collar positions. Women have been removed from class analysis, as, for the decades covered by the Nuffield study, their class position (or rather, the class position of the family unit) was effectively 'mediated' through that of men (ibid, p.288).

Stewart et al.'s rejection of the 'myth' of clerical proletarianisation is more substantial but, we would argue, in certain important respects resembles that of Goldthorpe. (Indeed, Goldthorpe cites their evidence in his own critical comments on the thesis.) Again, a central point of their argument is the empirical finding that men do not usually remain in occupations classified as 'clerical': 'Careers starting out in clerical work and moving on to better things remain the dominant feature of (male) clerical employment' (p.193). Thus the apparent status discrepancy - identified by writers such as Lockwood - of the well-educated but lowly paid clerk disappears when it is appreciated that such an individual will no longer be a clerk by his mid-thirties. Today, clerical work is carried out by women, younger men and older, ex-manual men. With respect to 'proletarianisation', Stewart et al. summarise the position of these three groups as follows:

> Certainly the ex-manual workers are not proletarianised; they are, by both past and current experience, proletarian. Those (men) who entered at an early age, for the most part, are not proletarianised. The vast majority leave clerical work, mostly in an upward direction... Whether the women are proletarianised raises complex questions ... but it seems the answer must be no. They have always been employed in routine positions, mainly in specifically female jobs. (1980, p.193)

These criticisms of the thesis of clerical proletarianisation by both Goldthorpe and Stewart et al. therefore, centre on the empirical finding that men who begin their careers as clerks do not remain clerks for the whole of their working lives. In the latter case, however, it must be appreciated that their rejection of clerical 'proletarianisation' reflects a theoretical perspective more generally critical of conventional stratification theory. A common misconception of such theory, they argue, is to assume that it is the nature of the job which locates an occupation in a particular class. Although some occupations which encompass a career (for example, the professions) may give a reasonably accurate indication of the class situation of the incumbent, this is not true for many others. The present occupation of a male clerk, viewed strictly in terms of work content, gives no indication of future career development, which will almost inevitably ensue. Clerical workers, therefore, do not belong to a single class (as is assumed, for example by the Registrar General), and 'the very question(s) "What is the class position of clerks?" is invalid, because "clerks" does not define a meaningful reality in stratification terms.' (Stewart et al, 1980, p.113)

Clearly, this argument has important implications. For the moment, however, we would frankly admit that serious consideration lies outside the scope of this paper, which focusses more narrowly on the thesis of clerical 'proletarianisation'.

In evaluating these arguments, we would emphasise that both rest on the fact that few, if any, individuals have been 'proletarianised' (Stewart et al, 1980, p.194). We would certainly agree that this fact, if correct, has important consequences. We would also agree that it has received insufficient attention from exponents of the 'proletarianisation' thesis. However, does it constitute a sufficient basis on which to reject it? To put the question another way, is there anything in the original thesis which indicates that 'proletarianisation' only occurs when it happens to somebody? A moment's reflection should be sufficient to realise that this cannot be so. We have earlier described proletarianisation as a process which generates proletarians; it is essentially a concept about the social division of labour. To write of 'the growth of the industrial proletariat', for example, does not commit the author to the assertion that every person so identified had once worked on the land. To be sure, individuals may be 'proletarianised', but it would be placing impossible restrictions on the concept if this was the only sense in which it could be applied.

It becomes apparent, therefore, that the two sides in the proletarianisation 'debate' are arguing from different premises, different conceptions of the theory and different accounts of the data appropriate to it. We would only note that the contributions of Stewart et al. and Goldthorpe et al. do have some features in common. They locate their 'refutations' of clerical proletarianisation at the level of class formation. Both Goldthorpe et al.'s observations about social mobility and Stewart et al.'s arguments about the problematic relation between occupation and class raise problems concerned with the structuration of classes. The points they raise may have considerable relevance for such questions but they do not strictly bear on the question of class _location_. As a consequence their analyses have moved away from a consideration of the social division of labour and have emphasised the individual's experience of his (never her) occupation. Stewart et al. regard this move as crucial with regard to the proletarianisation thesis, indeed they remark that 'we enter this debate not in the hope of final settlement, but to seek to transform it' (p.91).

Our objectives are more modest. At the present time, we would suggest, the proletarianisation debate has effectively been rendered sterile by recent interventions. Given the different bases of the argument assumed by the two 'sides', the only course open is to 'choose' one interpretation or the other. In the discussion that follows, therefore, we shall look more closely at two substantive areas highlighted by recent exchanges - male mobility and female participation in the non-manual labour force. In so doing, we hope to emphasise that, although the protagonists of the thesis of clerical 'proletarianisation' may certainly be criticised for their failure to consider these problems, their detractors, in failing to take account of recent developments in the non-manual labour process, may equally be subject to criticism.

MALE MOBILITY

Although the empirical fact of male mobility is crucial to the refutation of the 'proletarianisation' thesis by both Goldthorpe and Stewart et al, they differ in their interpretation of the processes involved. Goldthorpe's account retains an assumption, conventional in stratification theory, that occupations can be utilised as reasonable indicators of class position. Therefore, a move from 'clerical' to 'managerial' work would be a move from Class III to Class II (Goldthorpe, 1980, pp.40-1); that is, the class position of the individual is actually changed by such a move.

Stewart et al, as we have seen, make an explicit break with conventional stratification theory by denying that (except in particular cases) occupations give an unproblematic account of the class position of the individual. Rather they suggest that it is misconceived to think that 'the significance of occupation in determining class resides in the nature of job', while ignoring the relations between jobs and their occupants (p.93). With respect to clerical proletarianisation they argue that

> If clerical work has been in any sense proletarianised
> it is only in the limited sense that proletarians now
> undertake clerical work which was previously the

131

preserve of those middle-class careers. No actual groups of individuals or type of employee has been proletarianised (p.194).

What is suggested in this statement is that 'proletarian' (or 'non-proletarian') status is given not by place in the social division of labour, but rather, by the characteristics of the individuals who occupy these places. That is, what may be termed the 'mobility potential' of the men effectively renders them 'non-proletarian'. Yet, as is made equally clear, some people who do clerical work are proletarians.

In this paper we are not concerned to adjudicate on the relative merits of these two approaches. What we would emphasise is that both approaches treat the boundary between 'clerical' and 'managerial and administrative' work as unproblematic. Goldthorpe, because such a move is a common move across a class boundary which inhibits class formation. Stewart et al. because they want to stress that reasonably well-qualified men do not stay in clerical work but are promoted out of it fairly quickly. Therefore, to be 'a clerk' does not, in this case, indicate a stratification position. If the 'non-proletarian' status of the male clerk is given by their capacity to 'move on', then, logically, their destination - managerial work - must be non-proletarian.

Our research, which was designed to focus on the non-manual labour process, gave us ample opportunity to examine the nature of this boundary. As our discussion will show, we found it to be highly contentious. (2) In the first place, the use of 'clerk' as an occupational title has undergone a considerable transformation. Although, since the middle of the nineteenth century, the 'clerical' category has always included individuals performing routine clerical functions on low pay (Anderson, 1976), the category of 'clerk' also included many (if not the majority - at least until the early years of this century) whose work role - and corresponding rewards - could more properly be described as 'managerial' (Pollard, 1968; Lockwood, 1958). The heterogeneity of the 'clerical' category is reflected in the apparent difficulties in the social class allocation of this occupation in the census. In 1911 clerks were allocated to Social Class I, by 1921 they were demoted to Social Class II, and in 1931 to Social Class III, which is where they remain at the last census (Hakim, 1980).

Although the 'clerical' category is still heterogeneous, it is reasonable to suggest that the occupational title has shown a long-run tendency to be increasingly reserved for only the lowest levels of non-manual employment. This assumption is reflected in, for example, Goldthorpe's description of Class III, as including 'routine non-manual - largely clerical - employees in administration and commerce' (Goldthorpe, p.40). As one personnel manager put it to us: 'Nobody wants to be known as a clerk'.

However, although there is perhaps now a greater consistency in the use of 'clerk' as an occupational title, the changing manner of its use does raise problems with regard to empirical evidence in considering the historical development of the occupation. For example, earlier census classifications will have included in the 'clerical' category occupaticns which today would be considered 'managerial'; therefore to compare, say, the 'clerical' category of 1911 with the 'clerical' category of 1971 - a practice which is common to many longitudinal represent-ations of the occupational structure - is to run the risk of simply not comparing like with like. (Comparisons after 1931 would be valid if one assumes, along with the census, that the Social Class/SEG of clerks has not changed since then!) Similarly if our assumptions about the use of the occupational title are correct, then the 'growth' of the clerical category during this century will have been increasingly a 'growth' of routine non-manual occupations. That is, the decline in status of the occupational title has been paralleled by a change in clerical work content.

We have stressed that these changes have been long-term, and our own research revealed several examples of the progressive specificity of the title as an occupational label. For example, in a major clearing bank, a 'second clerk' became, on job evaluation in the mid '60s, a 'branch accountant', and a 'chief clerk' a 'sub-manager'. Similarly, in an insurance company, a 'chief clerk' became a 'departmental manager' (Executive Grade 4), and a 'section clerk' an Executive Grade 2 on job evaluation at the end of the 1960s. In all of the examples we have quoted above, these changes in occupational labels were not accompanied by any change in job content. (3)

Although the progressive removal of 'managerial' occupations from the clerical category may have had the effect of rendering 'clerical' status less contentious in respect of the occupational hierarchy, we would point out that, as a consequence, the 'administrative and managerial' category is rendered more contentious. That is, 'adminis-trative and managerial' grades appear at lower levels in the hierarchy than hitherto. Further evidence in support of this assertion is suggested by the fact that the 'manager-ial' category is getting younger (Stewart et al, 1980, p.181). We are not suggesting, by any means, that the whole of the increase in 'administrative and managerial' grades is to be explained by this 'labelling shift'; clearly, the growth of administrative and managerial employment is part of a wider development of the occupational structure which also includes the growth in routine clerical employment mentioned earlier.

In summary, we would argue that the changes in the use of the occupational title of 'clerk' should make one sensitive to the possibility that the 'administrative and managerial' category might be more heterogeneous than hitherto. This possibility is further explored in the second issue we will examine in this section; that is the nature of the non-manual labour process and its implications for male mobility.

Not surprisingly, the 'clerical proletarianisation' debate has tended to focus rather narrowly on <u>clerical</u> work. Although there are those who would challenge this assertion (Shepard, 1979; Goldthorpe, 1980), the balance of evidence seems to indicate that much clerical work has been effectively 'deskilled'. Viewing non-manual work as a whole, therefore, one possible scenario is of a mass of routine clerks controlled by 'management'. From this perspective, the gulf between 'clerical' and 'managerial' work would be considerable, and unambiguously express a 'class' boundary (Becker, 1973). In reality, however, our preliminary research findings indicate that the situation is not nearly so simple. Our discussion has already indicated that there exists a considerable 'grey area' between 'clerical' and 'managerial' work. In particular, many of the jobs we examined which were described as 'administrative' or 'managerial' proved to be largely clerical in terms of actual work content - that is, the 'manager' did the same work as his or her subordinates.

Few social scientists would locate managers and their subordinates in the same class. However, does it follow that all <u>managers</u> are therefore in the same class situation? For the 'managerial' category is, without exaggeration, the most heterogeneous of those with which the class/social stratification theorist has to grapple. A 'manager' may be an effective controller within a large organisation, perhaps with a considerable ownership interest, or, as we have intimated above, a relatively subordinate employee. The heterogeneity of managerial employment has increasingly led to the suggestion that the class position of many managers is highly ambiguous (Westergaard and Resler, 1975; Carchedi, 1975, Wright, 1976). These ambiguities, we would suggest, make it. increasingly difficult to represent with any confidence the transition from 'clerical' to 'managerial' work as a 'class' move.

In abstract terms, a manager may be said to be carrying out capital functions when he or she effectively controls either labour power or the material means of production. (4) Such criteria may be too rigid to act as infallible fieldwork guides but they are useful to situate the work of many of the managers in our study. As we have already noted, many 'managers' did the same work as their subordinates. (5) A typical case would be, say, a Team Leader in a Local Authority (AP 4/5), or an Executive Grade 2 in the Insurance Company (still widely referred to as a 'section clerk'). Invariably, such individuals, although doing the same work as their subordinates, would also deal with or give advice on the difficult or unusual cases or problems which arose in the course of the work. Here, we would suggest, the manager was effectively acting

134

as a 'skilled worker' - as opposed to the relatively less
experienced, semi or unskilled clerk.

It is true that the vast majority of these managers did
have a formal supervisory role. However, 'supervision' was
defined by both the managers and their subordinates as
'helping out with problems' rather than 'policing', serving
further to emphasise the view of the manager as 'skilled
worker'. In any case, it would have been extremely
difficult for such managers to <u>directly</u> control their
subordinates, even had they wished to do so. Hiring, firing,
staff evaluation and discipline were all carried out by the
Departmental Manager (or his assistant) in co-operation
with a Central Personnel Department. Even timekeeping,
traditionally an area where first-line supervision
exercises direct control, had been effectively centralised
through the introduction of 'flexitime'.

Even if these managers did not have effective personal
control over their subordinates, it is still possible that
they exercised control in other respects - over the organisation of the work, decision-taking on resources, etc. As
far as the organisation of the work was concerned, this
again seemed an area in which lower-level managers had very
little control. With the widespread computerisation of non-
manual work, both work organisation and pace are effectively
shaped by the computerised system. These managers may
possibly allow, for example, informal job rotation, but
even this was more usually arranged at the discretion and
initiative of the Departmental Manager or his assistant.
One area in which many of these managers <u>could</u> be said to
exercise a degree of control, however, was in the author-
ising of decisions concerned with various payments. For
example, it might be possible for a salaries Team Leader
to authorise an interim payment to someone whose medical
condition was not fully clear; or, in insurance, the payment of a claim, up to a certain limit could be authorised.
Even here, however, the criteria governing such decisions
tended to be explicit and rule-bounded; unusual cases or
large amounts would be dealt with by the Departmental
Manager.

In summary, our evidence suggests that many middle to lower
level 'managers' spend very little, if any, of their time
at work exercising what would be thought of as 'managerial'
functions. Rather, they act as skilled and/or experienced
workers. This view seems to be endorsed by the attitudes
of their subordinates. When asked to say who they thought
of as 'management', the lowest level identified by the
vast majority of clerks was the Departmental Manager or his
assistant, or, in the case of the Bank, the Branch Manager.
In making this point, we would emphasise that intermediate
positions were clearly seen as <u>promotion</u>, but not,
apparently, as a move to 'management'.

Although the empirical evidence we can produce at this
stage of the project is rather sketchy, we have been able

to show that, apparently, the 'deskilling' of non-manual work has not been confined to the clerical section of the non-manual labour force. Much lower-level managerial work has also been routinised, control functions have been effectively centralised leaving the 'manager' more like a skilled employee. Additionally, we would suggest that, on the basis of our evidence, Braverman's assertion of the 'polarisation of office employment and the growth at one pole of an immense mass of wage workers' (1974, p.355) is not entirely correct. Although the growth of non-manual employment has been in large part that of routine employees, between these workers and the more senior levels of management there exists a substantial portion of the non-manual workforce.

In the terms in which occupational categories are conventionally employed, therefore, we would suggest that the move from 'clerical' to 'managerial' work should not invariably be assumed to be a move across class boundaries. Although it is true that most men are promoted out of clerical work, the work to which they are (initially) promoted in many cases differs only marginally from that of ordinary clerks. If this represents the full extent of male mobility, then the significance of this mobility in undermining the 'proletarianisation' thesis must be weakened. This must be the case whether male mobility is taken to indicate a move across a class boundary (Goldthorpe), or male 'mobility potential' seen as determining class position (Stewart et al.).

THE CLASS POSITION OF WOMEN

Again, the position of the two authors under discussion would seem, apparently, to differ on this issue. For Goldthorpe, women are effectively excluded from the debate:

> it is the class position of males which has been the overwhelmingly direct determinant of the class 'fate' of the large majority of families and households: in other words, the way in which women have been located in the class structure has tended to reflect their general situation of dependency. (Goldthorpe, 1980, p.67).

Stewart et al. would seem to regard female clerks as 'proletarians'. This seems to be implied by their statement that 'proletarians now undertake clerical work'. These 'proletarians' clearly cannot be the younger men, for they are promoted out of clerical work. Therefore they must be the women and ex-manual men who they have identified elsewhere as major components of the clerical workforce (Stewart et al, 1980, p.93, pp.136ff.). However the proletarian status of women is largely irrelevant as women have not personally experienced 'proletarianisation'. This latter interpretation gives rise to an intriguing paradox. If the development of non-manual work has drawn increasing numbers of women, as proletarians, into the non-manual labour force, then surely a process of 'proletarianisation' is occurring? Alternatively, is it being suggested that women are invariably proletarian by virtue of their gender and therefore cannot possibly be 'proletarianised'? Yet another possible interpretation of this assumption is that the female component of the routine non-manual labour force is exclusively drawn from women whose families of origin are 'proletarian'. Neither of these latter possibilities seems reasonable, and we would endorse West's statement that:

> Although the proletarianisation of white-collar work is far from an undisputed reality, analysis of it is hindered, not helped by a refusal to consider it just because women happen to be the occupants of the jobs in question. (West, 1978, p.229)

Nevertheless, Goldthorpe's assumption that class position is effectively given by the location of the family, which in turn means the class position of the male breadwinner has, until recently, been widespread in sociology. We would not claim any originality in challenging this view, and indeed, the major points we would make in countering this argument have already been summarised elsewhere (West, 1978).

Firstly, there is the problem of locating those un-attached and/or non-dependent women whose social position is not derived from either their families or male head of household. In the UK, it has been recently estimated that at least one in six households are substantially or solely supported by women (West, 1978, p.225). Do such households not have a class position, or, alternatively, should they be automatically categorised as reflecting the 'general situation of dependency' of women as a whole? Alternatively, should independent women/female heads of households be 'granted' a class position in the same terms as male heads of households?

Secondly, with the increasing employment of women (particularly married women) it is clear that women's earnings have a considerable impact on family 'life-chances' even where the woman is not the 'main' bread-winner. To the extent that women's employment becomes the norm, then clearly, the life chances of the family will be crucially affected by a woman's capacity to work. To make a final point: in excluding women from consider-ation as proper subjects of stratification theory, it is being implicitly asserted that the class position of particular occupations depends, not on the occupation per se, but on the gender of the occupant. That is: 'the character of certain jobs in (the) market depends on who occupies them' (West, 1978, p.233).

However, although we would reject the view that gender excludes women from consideration in class and stratification theory, it is obvious that women are, on the whole, considerably disadvantaged in the non-manual labour market by virtue of their gender. In all of the three organisations we studied, women predominated at the lowest levels of the organisational hierarchy, and few had risen to 'managerial' positions - even the somewhat attenuated managerial positions described in the previous section. Although we did find some evidence of overt discrimination, far more important in the explanation of the women's lowly position in the non-manual hierarchy were the difficulties they encountered in displaying 'promotion qualities' given the constraints of their domestic roles. In a previous paper based on just one of our case studies (Crompton, Jones and Reid, forthcoming), we have shown that promotion depended on a combination of factors including (i) long, unbroken service, (ii) the acquisition of formal post-entry qualifications, and (iii) a willing-ness to be geographically mobile. Breaks in service due to childrearing, the conflicting demands of family and work, and a perceived inability to move because of the husband's job, all conspired to severely handicap women as far as promotion was concerned. However, to recognise that women who enter employment may be encumbered by serious handicaps with regard to promotion does not, logically, lead to the conclusion that they have no place in the class or stratification system. For example, it has never been seriously suggested that an unqualified male school leaver is similarly 'declassed' by the very real problems he would face.

If a wider perspective is taken on non-manual employment as a whole, the position of women appears less problematic. Our own position is very simple. As non-manual employment has grown, non-manual labour costs have become an ever increasing proportion of total costs. (The exact reasons for the growth of non-manual employment need not concern us here.) Faced with ever-rising labour costs, employers have been under pressure to (a) increase the productivity of labour and/or (b) reduce the costs of labour. (We would point out that there is nothing particularly radical in this assertion; from the employers' point of view, it is just sensible 'management' of resources.) One conse-quence of these pressures is that much non-manual work has been routinised and broken down into its constituent elements. As Braverman so graphically demonstrates - and his assertion is not contradicted by our research findings - Taylorism is applied in the office as it has been in the factory. This process has been facilitated by the introduction of a machine, the computer, that can mani-pulate symbols as earlier machines manipulated wood, iron and cotton. As non-manual work has been routinised and simplified, employers have found it possible to hire less skilled and cheaper labour than hitherto. In this particular case, women were highly suitable. We would emphasise that there is _nothing_ particularly unusual in this. For example, women were brought into the textile industry in the nine-teenth century for very similar reasons.

138

Although the reasons for the increasing participation of women in the labour force have been often examined (Amsden, 1980; Bowen and Finegan, 1969; Greenhalgh, 1980) we can briefly review here some which are particularly relevant to the recruitment of women to clerical work:

(i)   both rising demand for, and routinisation of clerical labour occurred during a period of full employment (the decades following the Second World War). Additionally, changes in family patterns and control of fertility 'released' women for employment for longer periods than hitherto.

(ii)   Women's labour, as _relatively_ short term, unskilled, and immobile, was cheap. Additionally, women's traditionally dependent status has always been associated with lower wages (Beechey, 1977).

(iii)   The work available (routine clerical) was highly suitable for women - i.e. light, not shift work, etc. (Computer operators, who often work shifts, are usually male.) There are also positive advantages to employers in employing women in socially visible work; as one Bank Manager put it, 'customers like to see a pretty face behind the counter'.

(iv)   There was little or no resistance to the increasing employment of women by the existing work force, unlike, for example, the Engineers' resistance to 'dilution' (Hinton, 1973). In part, this was probably due to the fact that the existing workforce was only weakly unionised, but more important must have been the fact that women were (on the whole correctly) not seen as a threat to male prospects.

With the increasing recruitment of women into clerical work, it has been suggested that the non-manual labour force has been effectively structured into two tiers which broadly correspond to gender (see Stewart _et al_, 1980, pp.93-4 and Giddens, 1973, p.288). In the lower tier are those in routine clerical jobs with few promotion opportunities (mainly women), in the upper tier those (mainly men) who will make a career in non-manual work. (These two tiers are neatly encapsulated in Bank argot as 'jobbers' and 'careerists'.) Presented in this light, the structure appears extremely stable. There are a number of reasons, however, for believing that this apparently stable two-tier structure may not be smoothly reproduced in the future.

Not all jobs in the lower tier are entirely devoid of opportunities. This clearly cannot be the case, as men pass through the lower tier on their way upwards. It is also probable that a substantial part of the growth of female clerical employment has been in occupations from which upward mobility is possible. For example, in insurance, clerks in branch offices have _always_ been women. No promotion is possible from clerical jobs in branch offices, because branch office managers are always re-cruited from (male) agents. It follows, therefore, that the increase in female employment in insurance has been concentrated in the larger head offices of insurance companies, where promotion from routine clerical grades is a real possibility. It was in the large office, rather than the smaller branches, that we found women expressing discontent with their lack of promotion. In the smaller offices, the women's response was resigned - as promotion was clearly impossible, no strong feelings were expressed on the issue.

Much of the expansion of female clerical employment has been 'in the most menial clerical tasks with limited opportunities for promotion' (Stewart et al, 1980, p.94). We would include here the secretarial ghetto, data preparation and small administrative units whether these are offshoots of larger organisations or, for example, a solicitor's office, or the office of a small manufacturing company. The extent to which women are confined in such clerical occupations, however, can be exaggerated, and many women, perhaps even the majority, will be in clerical occupations in which promotion possibilities exist. In some of these cases, women will effectively be 'forced' into the lower tier by, for example, organisational demands for geographical mobility such as exist in banking (Heritage, 1977; Graham and Llewellyn, 1976).

However, where these constraints are absent, there are a number of factors that suggest that women may not necessarily continue to accept extended service in lower-grade jobs. In the first place, more women are working for longer periods, and this includes women with dependent children. As women's earnings are increasingly accepted as a regular source of family income (rather than as a supplement or 'pin money') it would be unusual if women did not seek to maintain or increase this source of in-come. Secondly, the change in attitudes brought about by such things as the activities of the women's movement and Equal Opportunities legislation may be difficult to quantify, but they cannot be entirely ignored. Initial results from our study suggest that it is the younger women who are most concerned about their promotion pros-pects, and, more importantly, there are some indications that they are beginning to acquire the post-entry qualifi-cations so necessary to career development. Lastly, as we have indicated, lower level managerial jobs have been considerably routinised and are well within the capacities of most women (we are not suggesting that they are in-capable of undertaking higher-level posts, however), a fact which many women in our study were not slow to appreciate. As a twenty-one-year-old clerk said in ex-plaining her desire for promotion: 'Just to learn a different job - to get in with different people. (There's) no power attached - no more responsibility to being an E1 than a C4!'

In summary, we would not dismiss the increasing employment of women in clerical jobs as irrelevant, rather, we would cite it as evidence for the proletarianisation of non-manual work. As non-manual work has been 'de-skilled', and as control has been centralised, so many women have been recruited (amongst others) to fill the essentially 'proletarian' positions so created. However, many of these 'proletarian' jobs still provide opportunities for upward mobility - although the <u>extent</u> of mobility must be called into question because of the routinisation of much 'administrative and managerial' work. Women's mobility chances are certainly severely constrained by their domestic roles. Nevertheless, we are somewhat sceptical of the assumption that women will be content to remain in low-level clerical positions in those circumstances where opportunities for upward mobility exist.

SUMMARY AND CONCLUSIONS

In this paper, we have suggested that the debate on clerical proletarianisation as presented by Klingender, Lockwood and to a lesser degree Braverman, has focussed on the proletarian <u>condition</u> at the expense of the proletarianisation <u>process</u>. That is, the argument has been presented somewhat statically, and the major question to be answered has been whether or not clerical work approximates to the proletarian condition. In the case of all three authors, manual work is taken to be the exemplar of the proletarian condition. Recent critics of the proletarianisation thesis (Goldthorpe, Stewart <u>et al</u>.), have, on the other hand, tended to disregard (or treat as relatively unimportant) the question of proletarian condition. An important consequence of this shift in emphasis is their claim that, because men do not remain in clerical work throughout their careers, clerical proletarianisation has not occurred and is in fact a 'myth'.

Our position is that a proper examination of the debate on clerical proletarianisation must include both condition and process. That is, although earlier theorists may be criticised for their lack of attention to process, their critics may be criticised equally for their treatment of the proletarian condition. In particular, it is our contention that a sustained examination of what may be loosely described as the 'non-manual labour process' provides a mechanism whereby both condition and process may be examined. To be sure, a detailed examination of non-manual work is, at first sight, largely a characteristic of the first approach we have described. However, we would emphasise that an examination of the non-manual labour process does not imply a static approach. Rather, it forces the consideration of processes which change and restructure non-manual work, and which are closely associated with proletarianisation.

To illustrate our position, we examined two substantive

areas highlighted by the recent debate - male mobility and female participation in the clerical labour force. The importance of male mobility to the critics of the proletarianisation thesis rests on the assumption that managers are non-'proletarian'. This would seem to be an entirely reasonable assumption. However, on examining the non-manual labour process (rather than just clerical work), our research indicates that many lower-level 'managerial' jobs are, in fact, almost entirely devoid of what would usually be thought of as 'managerial' content. Therefore, although progression to lower management certainly consti- tutes promotion, it is questionable whether the <u>class</u> position of these lower-level managers differs signifi- cantly from that of the 'clerks'.

Unfortunately, the mobility data available does not give us a clear indication of how much 'upward' male clerical mobility is eventually to what are unambiguously 'managerial' positions, and how much is to what we have described as 'skilled clerical' managerial positions. However, we would suggest that our findings should give rise to some scepticism as to the nature and extent of male mobility.

Female participation in the non-manual labour force (and indeed, more generally) is an important topic which has received insufficient sociological attention in the past. Our position here is very different from that of the critics of clerical proletarianisation. We would regard the extensive recruitment of women, as proletarians, to clerical work as evidence <u>for</u> clerical proletarianisation, not against.

Women's employment in non-manual work has always been concentrated at the lower end of the job hierarchy, and this feature is amply confirmed by our own research. However, this does not mean that women are confined to clerical occupations from which promotion is impossible. To the extent that women are in jobs where promotion opportunities exist, then the longer they are established in these positions, the more likely they may be to regard promotion as a real possibility. Recent figures indicate that women are delaying both marriage and childbearing; as a consequence, the (realistic) possibilities for at least short-range promotion must improve (<u>Social Trends</u> II, pp.35-7). If even only a minority of women do actively seek promotion, then male mobility - and its significance - will be further attenuated.

Our strategy in this paper has been to positively confront the complex issues raised by the clerical proletarianisa- tion debate. In particular, we recognise that critics of the proletarianisation thesis are entirely correct in emphasising the heterogeneity of the clerical workforce - it is indeed the case that:

This curiously ageless, abstract creature, 'the clerical

worker', serves to simplify the relationships between individuals and occupations by creating a false identity between them. (Stewart et al, p.112)

Nevertheless, it is equally the case that occupations cannot simply be characterised in terms of their occupants - as is implicitly suggested, for example, when female employment is treated as irrelevant to the 'proletarianis-ation' debate simply because it _is_ female.

Besides the heterogeneity of the clerical workforce, we would also emphasise the heterogeneity of clerical work. In fact, we would prefer to speak of the 'non-manual' work-force and 'non-manual' work. The terms 'clerical' and 'managerial' suggest more or less clearly defined work tasks and more or less identifiable personnel; in reality, as we have suggested, similar work content may be spread over a range of occupational labels.

Finally, we would re-affirm our belief that an examination of the labour process is central to both class theory and the more general understanding of the stratification system. In particular, this approach enables us to overcome some of the limitations of theorising in this area imposed by the legacy of occupational classifications. As such, it may have important consequences for the analysis of the con-temporary class structure.

NOTES

The authors would wish to acknowledge the support of the SSRC who funded the research cited in this paper.

(1) It has been argued that new skilled occupations such as computer programming and systems analysis emerge as a consequence of clerical deskilling thus undermining the overall thrust of the deskilling thesis. It falls outside the scope of this paper to examine the validity of this position.
(2) We would point out that we are only in the final stages of completing the fieldwork on this project. As we have not yet completed our data analysis, the evidence we offer in this paper will tend to be suggestive, rather than conclusive. We anticipate being able to offer more substantial evidence once data analysis has been completed.
(3) We are, of course, aware that chief clerks would not have been coded with routine clerical employees. Our present point is concerned with the instability of occupational titles.
(4) Such distinctions have been given consideration by Gorz (1972), Marglin (1976) and others.
(5) Many of these positions could plausibly be described as 'foreman clerical'. However, given their occupational titles, it is worth pondering where they would appear in occupational classifications.

REFERENCES

Amsden, A.H, (ed.), (1980), The Economics of Women and Work.
Anderson, G, (1980), Victorian Clerks (MUP), Penguin.
Becker, J.F, (1973), 'Class Structure and Conflict in the
    Managerial Phase', I and II, in Science and Society,
    vol.37, nos.3, 4.
Beechey, V, (1977), 'Some Notes on Female Wage Labour in
    Capitalist Production', Capital and Class, no.3, Autumn.
Bowen, W.G. and Finegan, T.A, (1969), The Economics of
    Labour Force Participation. Princeton University Press.
Braverman, H, (1974), Labour and Monopoly Capital, New York,
    MRP.
Carchedi, G, (1975), 'On Economic Identification of the New
    Middle Class', Economy and Society, vol.4.
Crompton, R, (1976), 'Approaches to the Study of White
    Collar Unionism', Sociology, vol.10, 3.
Crompton, R. and Gubbay, J, (1979), Economy and Class
    Structure, Macmillan.
Crompton, R, Jones, G. and Reid, S, (1982), in J. West (ed.),
    Women in the Labour Force, Routledge and Kegan Paul.
Crompton, R. and Reid, S,'The Deskilling of Clerical Work', in
    S. Wood (ed.), (1982), Degradation of Work?, Hutchinson.
Dale, J.R, (1962), The Clerk in Industry, Liverpool
    University Press.
Giddens, A, (1973), The Class Structure of the Advanced
    Societies, Hutchinson.
Goldthorpe, J.H. et al, (1980), Social Mobility and Class
    Structure in Modern Britain, Clarendon Press.
Greenhalgh, C, (1980), 'Participation and Hours of Work for
    Married Women in Great Britain', Oxford Economic Papers.
Graham, S. and Llewellyn, C, (1976), 'Women in the Occupa-
    tional Structure: A Case Study of Banking', Nuffield
    College Paper.
Gorz, A, (1972), 'Technical Intelligence and the Capitalist
    Division of Labour', Telos, no.12.
Hakim, C, (1980), 'Census Reports as Documentary Evidence:
    The Census Commentaries 1801-1951', Sociological Review,
    vol.28, no.3, August.
Heritage, J.C, (1977), 'The Growth of Trade Unionism in the
    London Clearing Banks, 1960-1970: A Sociological
    Interpretation', University of Leeds Ph.d. thesis.
Hoos, I.R, (1961), Automation in the Office, Washington.
Hinton, J, (1973), The First Shop Stewards Movement, Allen
    and Unwin.
Jaeggi, U. and Weidemann, H, (1965), 'The Impact on Managers
    and Clerks in West German Industry and Commerce' in W.H.
    Scott (ed.), Office Automation: Administrative and Human
    Problems, OECD, Paris.
Klingender, F.D, (1935), The Condition of Clerical Labour
    in Britain, Martin Lawrence.
Larson, M.S, (1980), 'Proletarianisation and Educated
    Labour', Theory and Society, no.9.
Lockwood, D, (1958), The Blackcoated Worker, Allen and
    Unwin.
Marx, K. and Engels, F, (1967), The Communist Manifesto,
    Penguin.

Mann, F. and Williams, L, (1960), 'Observations on the Dynamics of a Change to EDP', <u>Administrative Science Quarterly</u>, vol.5, September.

Marglin, S.A, (1976), 'What do bosses do?' in <u>The Division of Labour</u>, (ed. A. Gorz), Harvester Press.

Mercer, D.E. and Weir, D.T.H, (1972), 'Attitudes to Work and Trade Unionism among White-Collar Workers', <u>Industrial Relations Journal</u>, vol.3, Summer.

Nichols, T, (1979), 'Social Class: Official, Sociological and Marxist', in I. Miles and J. Evans (eds.), <u>Demystifying Social Statistics</u>, Pluto.

Pollard, S, (1968), <u>The Genesis of Modern Management</u>, Penguin.

Poulantzas, N, (1975), <u>Classes in Contemporary Capitalism</u>, New Left Books.

Routh, G, (1980), <u>Occupation and Pay in Great Britain 1906-79</u>, Macmillan.

Shepard, J.M, (1971), <u>Automation and Alienation</u>, Cambridge, Mass.

Stewart, A, Prandy, K. and Blackburn, R.M, (1980), <u>Social Stratification and Occupations</u>, Macmillan.

Stymne, B, (1966), 'EDP and Organisational Structure: A Case Study of an Insurance Company', <u>The Swedish Journal of Economics</u>.

West, J, (1978), 'Women, Sex and Class', in <u>Feminism and Materialism</u>, eds. A. Kuhn and A. Wolpe, RKP.

Westergaard, J. and Resler, H, (1975), <u>Class in Capitalist Society: a Study of Contemporary Britain</u>, London, Heinemann.

Whisler, T.L, (1970), <u>The Impact of Computers on Organisations</u>, Praeger, New York.

Wood, S, (ed.), (1982), <u>Degradation of Work? Deskilling and the Labour Process</u>, Hutchinson.

Wright, E.O, (1976), 'Class Boundaries in Advanced Capitalist Societies', <u>New Left Review</u>, no.98.

8 Class Relations and Uneven Development in Wales

PHILIP COOKE

INTRODUCTION

In the aftermath of the Ford strike of 1969 over regrading and the New Wages Structure, regional differences in class cohesiveness and organisation emerged as a potent issue in the subsequent Campaign for Parity. Conflict was with both the Ford management and what was seen as an 'incorporated' union leadership centred on Dagenham. In the period leading up to the long, nine-week strike for parity with Midlands and Southern workers in 1971, when an interim deal was accepted by some plants but not others, the issue was put as follows by a shop steward:

> It's not the fault of the Dagenham lads. All working class blokes are the same basically. It's the leadership that's at fault. They can't have been reporting back to those Dagenham lads. They hardly ever see the lads.
> We've got a whole history of working class militancy behind us in Liverpool and South Wales. We've got the tradition, the equipment ... everything. And we're cashing in on it too. We're going to take over this show. We're off. We've got to tell them that we're going, and if they want to get on board they're welcome but we're driving from now on.
> Obviously we can't think of leaving the combine but we've got to sort this one out. We've got to be hard with them. (Beynon, 1975)

This expression of frustrated intent raises important issues in the analysis of processes of regional uneven development, and especially of the relationships between class composition, class consciousness and class organisation and the imperatives of valorisation, capital accumulation, and the production and reproduction of capitalist social relations. In what follows three of the many questions worthy of examination will be discussed, and related to concrete instances of the formation of inter-regional uneven development. (1)

The first issue to be addressed is that of incorporation and, in particular, the underlying historical, sectoral variations in its incidence, and reasons for these. Here the development of work control in different industries, the centrality of craft unionism and the role of the labour aristocracy are important. The second issue raised involves the extent to which industrial location decisions are affected or determined by perceived or actual regional variations in the habituation of workers to capitalist control of the labour process. Here the importance of sectoral unevenness in regional development will be assessed, and the relationships between spheres of production and reproduction in constituting class relations will be considered. The third concern will be to seek to identify major reasons for the essential dualism of class action and inaction based upon workplace issues. That is, to pay attention to the contradictory and hence, indeterminate outcomes of conjunctures in which class responses might be expected to be predictable, captured in the tension between 'movement' and 'position' in the shop steward's conclusion quoted above. In discussing each of these issues there will be a questioning of the assumption that, once established, class militancy is necessarily a constant factor in areas with which it is traditionally associated. Of some concern here is the interaction of class interests and capitalist development as observed at a regional level, either directly, through corporate decision-making, or indirectly as mediated through the shock-absorbers of the state.

The whole of this analysis will be predicated upon the axiom that while in capitalist societies the imperatives of accumulation must determine the ultimate uses made of space by capitalist enterprises, these imperatives are themselves precisely the subjects of class antagonisms which determine the pace and rate of accumulation. That is, because surplus value is contested at the point of production, variations in the degree to which the contestants can control the process of its extraction determine the extent to which the accumulation imperative is fulfilled. The less organised the workforce, generally, the greater the capacity of employers to organise production to maximise surplus value. Thus I am rejecting a linear analysis of capitalist development in which valorisation and its associated sectoral and spatial restructuring occur as manifestations of the logic of capital's internal laws of motion (see, for example, Frobel et al, 1979; Carney et al, 1980). Also, I reject its equally linear inversion such as occurs, for example, in the critique by Tronti of 'capital-logic' analysis where he argues that:

> We too have worked with a concept that puts capitalist development first, and workers second; this is a mistake. Now we have to turn the problem on its head ... and start again from the beginning: and the beginning is the class struggle of the working class. At the level of socially developed capital, capitalist development follows hard behind the struggles ... (Tronti, quoted by Lumley, 1980/81)

or in a recent study of the movement of industry to the

'sunbelt' of the southern USA, where labour force docility is given primacy in the decision to relocate;

> High on the list of factors that comprise (the South's) good business climate is the absence of unions. A South Carolina survey reported that the primary factor attracting firms to that state is the relatively weak position of unions. Another study on business relocation noted that 'when responding to questions "on the record", businessmen tend to put wages and unions at the bottom of any list of reasons for moving south. "Off the record", however, they often admit that unions or "better labour management relations" (a euphemism for "getting out from under union domination") is a prime reason for their decision to move' (Watkins, 1980.

Clearly these statements are a useful antidote to the explanations of decentralisation, relocation and spatial restructuring which stress the magnetic effect upon industrialists of rurality (Fothergill and Gudgin, 1979) or more prosaically, 'deglomeration economies' (Keeble, 1980). However, they display the fault of oversimplifying what is a fundamentally complex labour-capital relation in which on some occasions either protagonist may or may not concede ground depending upon respective calculations of advantage and cost. Capital-labour relations, the social relations of production, develop dialectically and not according to a linear logic. Nevertheless, it remains possible and necessary to analyse tendencies which the law of value comes to exert as a necessary condition for the continued reproduction of capitalist social relations. These tendencies involve the regional redistribution of uneven development and social disorganisation, as well as the valorisation, and hence continued accumulation, of capital. In contradictory fashion, the developing socialisation of production and, more recently, the generation of relative surplus population, supply conditions for the destabilisation of the system. This, in turn, brings forward new pressures and responses towards overcoming these conditions which themselves give rise to contradictory effects. I shall attempt to illustrate the importance of an understanding of class relations to the processes of capitalist development at a regional scale by examples drawn from the Welsh context, and particularly from South Wales. To avoid the accusation of parochialism, I shall refer to such places as. Oxford and Coventry also, where rather fewer Welsh people are found.

INCORPORATION, WORK CONTROL AND UNIONISATION

We have to try to explain, first of all, why some industries appear to give rise to a greater degree of class solidarity than others, (2) and to start this process it is important to examine the organisation of work and the organisation by workers of themselves. In South Wales the

149

two dominant productive industries until relatively recently remained coalmining and the less populous industries of steel and tinplate. As it is put in a seminal paper on classes in regional development:

> The most characteristic element of the class structure of these areas, in terms both of its numerical importance and of its geographical distinctiveness, has been the working class. The very fact of single-industry dominance has had an effect of creating a degree of coherence both in the internal structure of the working class and its organisation. (Massey, 1980)

Now, to the extent that this refers to the coal industry in South Wales (and the North East, and parts of Scotland) it is broadly accurate. However, it is also the case that some coalmining districts, such as the small North Wales field, are less coherent, solidary and defensively well-equipped. But more importantly, other industries in close proximity to and intermingled with the mining communities, are also divisively organised. The difference in South Wales between the coal and steel industries is that while they were characterised by similar work control patterns initially, they evolved differently. This had important effects upon the form taken by unionisation, and hence industrial strength and class solidarity around both workplace and community, the spheres of production and reproduction.

The distinctiveness of the two industries in South Wales, generalisable to other areas in some essentials, can be summarised as follows: variation in the extent of labour process differentiation, differences in class relations within production, and the relative precariousness of the worker in the two industries.

1. Both industries developed their internal task-differentiation on the basis of a <u>contracting</u> relationship. This meant that capitalists made contracts with skilled craft-workers on a tonnage payment basis, and the latter then employed underhands at a percentage of the craft wage. However, whereas in mining this system initially placed a substantial amount of control of the direct labour process in the hands of skilled workers, the basic task of hewing coal did not give rise to a dependence upon skilled expertise for the maintenance of that control. The industry was thus fairly open to a large degree of control at the point of production by unskilled and semi-skilled labour. As deep-mining brought a shift away from small-scale, safety conscious pillar-and-stall working in South Wales, increased production was achieved by increasing the labour intensity of the industry and decreasing the overall differentiation of skills within the labour force, hence keeping wage-costs but also productivity relatively low (Holmes, 1976).

In the steel industry, by contrast, the same contracting system gave rise to a consolidation of craft skills into specialised unions precisely because of the centrality of skilled expertise to the production process of iron in particular. In this way skilled union membership could be controlled much more closely by members than was the case in mining. But the key mechanism which enabled skilled steelworkers to keep a substantial distance between themselves and the underhands they employed was the unique system of collective bargaining developed within the industry. Following a decade of industrial disputes in the 1860s arbitration boards were established in the North and Midlands of England. These had equal representation of employers and union members (who it will be remembered were craftsmen by and large) and in exchange for guarantees on the linkage of wages to market prices for iron, skilled workers agreed to no-strike clauses. Fluctuations in market price were largely borne by the casual labour on which the system ultimately depended but who, as unrepresented and somewhat marginal figures, posed little threat to the agreements struck. In this way, even as general workers gradually became unionised from the 1880s, the craft unions remained an incorporated stratum whose incorporation perpetuated craft-distinctiveness and multiunionism. This, in turn, contributed to the relatively docile reputation of the industry until well into the 1960s.

Nowhere was incorporation stronger than in the newer South Wales mills where, as a case in point, contractors even pressured a Newport company to reverse its decision to abolish contracting. The Ironworkers Union Journal recorded in 1889:

> It is a matter of general congratulation to the whole of the sheet mill workers that the Newport workers have reverted to the general trade custom of the roller having full charge of his own mill and the employment of his own men. (Quoted in Elbaum and Wilkinson, 1979)

But resistance to contracting on the part of underhands persisted, especially on the issue of productivity payments from which they did not benefit, and as general unions secured recognition they gradually negotiated the abolition of contracting. Even so, two-tier bargaining persisted, as did skilled-union control over promotion of unskilled workers into the skilled ranks, through the rigid application of seniority rules and opposition to interplant craft mobility.

2. The differences in the level (in terms of craft skill) at which control of the labour process was maintained in the two industries is crucial in offering guidance as to the varying degrees of industrial conflict between them. As we have seen both industries began with recognisable labour aristocracies, both industries operated on a tonnage payment, sliding scale, wages system, and both came to be dominated numerically by general unions. Yet during the period when the iron and steel industry was undergoing the sort of technologically induced strains, with the passage to open-hearth, then Bessemer and other steelmaking processes, which might be expected to generate sharp conflicts, this did not happen. By contrast when coal was experiencing

151

consolidation after an earlier period of deep-mine investment and changing technological conditions, conflict became
endemic. At the very least this casts some doubt on the
notion that the technical forces of production are prime
determinants of social relations of production; it is
simply not clear that technical change imposes unresolvable
strains in this way. Thus, although wages and conditions
fluctuated in both industries (hence the sliding scale),
the fact that a disorganised, unskilled workforce could be
made to bear the brunt of these effects in iron and steel,
whereas its equivalent was in substantial control of the
labour process in coal, seems to have some bearing on the
form of class relations in the two industries.

Hence, in the South Wales coal industry there was relative
quiescence in industrial relations between the 1870s and
the 1890s when the number of miners increased by about a
quarter, but production doubled, yet severe unrest in the
following two decades when investment had stabilised while
production had doubled yet again. Three major reasons can
be advanced for this change. The first was the severely
competitive nature of the industry in which underselling
exacerbated the erratic price variations endemic to the
industry as a whole. The second reason was the importance
of the export trade in South Wales, which added a further
boost to underselling. And the third was the impact of
competition upon wages through the sliding scale mechanism.
These became major negotiating issues in the years leading
up to the formation of the South Wales Miners' Federation
as workmen's representatives pressed for price controls.
Moreover they were recognised as such by the owners whose
representatives in turn undertook 'to remind each Coal
Owner that so long as the workmen's wages are regulated by
the price per ton of coal the workmen are entitled to expect us to do our best to prevent reckless competition'
(quoted in Holmes, 1976). Nevertheless, the interference
with managerial control - especially where the largest
owners were also often export speculators, selling before
producing - which was thereby signalled, was rejected. The
era of long strikes in 1893, 1898, 1910-11 and 1912, inter-
spersed with Tonypandy in 1910 and 'The Miner's Next Step'
in 1911-1912, followed, to create the reputation of 'a
militant South Wales'.

Experiences in iron and steel could hardly have been more
different, for this was a period of employment growth at a
much lower scale, as large parts of the Midlands' steel
industry migrated to South Wales, to join with the indigenous iron and tinplate industries of the region, and wage-
levels set by the Midlands board were followed by the new
outlying firms. Conflicts such as that led by the underhands to establish standard tonnage rates were settled by
the new Welsh Local Committee of the Midlands board subject
to the underhands joining the Committee and accepting its
judgements. The entry of unskilled workers into a bargaining position led to the further fragmentation of the labour
force on the basis of craft-exclusivity with important

regional variations in membership. Even though membership of unions grew, industry-wide organisation did not, even on an intraregional basis. In most respects, the arbitration boards took the place of the unions _per se_ as the vehicle of worker's representation.

3. These variations in labour process differentiation and class relations in the two industries were, finally, reflected in the degree of _precariousness_ experienced by workers in the two industries. What is being raised here is the extent to which the kind of experience described below has conditioned variations within the working class of South Wales:

> Having had his standard of living fixed in the low-wage days of his youth the highly-paid (miner) therefore regards much of his wages as 'free income' in the sense that nothing has a very firm claim on it. He therefore feels free to spend it on the traditional pleasures of Ashton, in the clubs, in the pubs, and in the bookie's office. And he feels free to refrain from earning it at all - in other words, to absent himself from work... (Dennis et al, 1969)

It is the postwar mineworker in the comparatively less competitive context of a nationalised industry who is being described here, but the allusion to the hardship of earlier days signifies a cultural continuity in his valuation of the cash nexus. That is, it suggests a habituation to the prospect of periodic deprivation which is a strength in that strike action is a less traumatic prospect than for most workers, but a weakness in that the miner has set relatively low thresholds of expectation, themselves narrowed with facility into wage-related issues.

This is precisely the _modus operandi_ of Social Democracy in that it channels concerns having to do with the interaction of the spheres of production and reproduction into narrowly economistic issues resolvable in the workplace by unions and management. As will be seen below, it is only relatively recently and in realisation of the loss of localised working class culture (3) entailed by the pit closures of the 1960s that the wider politics of reproduction have seriously re-entered the agenda of mineworkers' struggles. This has been symbolised most dramatically in the 1981 struggle for reversal of government and NCB policies regarding the closure of coalmines and the direction to be followed in the development of the industry, both of which have taken at least temporary precedence over the hitherto dominant wages issue.

The contrast with the steel industry could, once again, hardly be more stark. For, despite the experiences of the interwar depression, when prices had fallen to 30 per cent of their peak 1920 level, 20 per cent of insured workers were unemployed after 1923, and the real wages of the lowest paid steelworkers fell below their 1914 level (Wilkinson, 1977), the industry nevertheless absorbed the

resultant tensions and increased the wages of the lowest
paid. This was to a considerable extent because of the
slow, though continuous, change in the power relations
between the latter and the skilled grades, as mechanisation
and deskilling produced a gradual erosion of pay differentials. This continued from the 1920s up to practically the
present day. Thus, although employment was precarious in
the interwar period, this consisted of an interruption to
an upward secular trend lasting to the 1970s during which
average wages continued to rise relatively smoothly. The
industry became increasingly capital-intensive, paid high
wages _and_ increased the overall labour force. Nationalisation _and_ renationalisation did little to interrupt these
tendencies; rather, it was the force of growing international competition which demonstrated certain underlying inadequacies in the structure of the industry, most notably a
tendency towards low productivity in basic steel production
and consequent uncompetitive pricing. The travail of the
BSC since 1973 when the 'Ten Year Strategy' was published,
has largely been concerned with the restructuring of this
highly spatially and institutionally fragmented industry.
The effect has been to increase the precariousness of steel
employment enormously and to bring about a serious questioning of the advantages of the kind of incorporation of
the unions into the structure of wage-bargaining which has
been traditional to the industry.

In conclusion, then, what it seems important to say about
the supposed industrial power of workers in industrial
South Wales is that in one of its major industries, iron
and steel, there is scarcely any indication of serious
dispute between management and labour until the late 1960s.
In the coal industry there is evidence of very severe
conflict periodically: notably in the years before 1914; at
the time of the return to the Gold Standard in the 1920s
culminating in the seven-month strike after the General
Strike; unofficially in 1942-3; and most recently in the
early 1970s. On each occasion these were struggles either
to prevent or to reverse real wage reductions, and they
were punctuations in what were often long uninterrupted
periods of industrial peace. Now, while the occasional
headline-gathering series of strikes should not be under-
estimated as a source for refuelling the reputation for
working-class militancy in South Wales, it seems likely
that the danger which the region has held from the viewpoint
of capital is less the strike record of the miners than
something less tangible but culturally of much greater
importance.

For what both steel and coal industries have traditionally
shown - despite their obvious differences - has been their
only partial susceptibility to capitalist control. In both
cases, although probably less so recently for steel, the
labour process has been substantially organised by the
workers themselves. In steel it has traditionally been in
the hands of skilled craftsmen, and their successors the
craft unions and semiskilled general union members; in coal

from an earlier stage the production process has been controlled by members of the general union, despite the attempts of employers to establish industrial unionism in the industry (Francis and Smith, 1980). The effect has been to generalise throughout the culture of the region an expectation that production relations will have a decidedly collectivist rather than individualistic structure on the labour side, and preferably on the side of capital also, through nationalisation (at least until recently). At a theoretical level this seems to relate to the distinction made by Marx (1974), and discussed recently by Hall (1977), Lazonick (1978) and Cressey and MacInnes (1980), between the formal and real subordination of labour to capital. This expresses the transition from the production of absolute surplus value to that of relative surplus value as it affects the labour process. That is, where the working day of the direct producer has already been divided into that part supplying necessary labour and another supplying surplus labour, he or she is exchanging labour-power for a wage, but the control of the labour process remains with the producer and subordination to capital is only formal. However capital's self-expansion requires the reduction of necessary labour and the increase of surplus labour - achieved through the prolongation of the working day, a process with limitations. Not the least of these is state intervention to meet the opposition of labour to this extensive form of exploitation. This forces capital to turn to the appropriation of relative surplus value through the intensification of exploitation by the introduction of machinery. With this development comes the disciplining and control of the labour process itself and the removal of direction and conception of production from the producer. This development replaces the formal subordination of labour with the real subordination of labour to capital.

Unfortunately, this formulation, while supplying an illuminating theoretical insight into the possible explanation for the apparent strength of class consciousness in the steel and coal industries is unsatisfactory. This is despite the appearance that both industries remain relatively unsubordinated in labour process terms. The main problem with the formulation is its proneness to imply a linearity to capitalist development from wage-relation to production-relation. This is to overlook the duality of the capital-labour relation. It also overstates the extent to which the direct producer is actively 'disciplined' under real subordination. This is clearly modified by the existence of unionisation and the informal practices by which workers counter the intolerability of a great deal of their work (Nichols and Beynon, 1977; Willis, 1979), a factor which is sometimes overlooked by neofunctional theorists of class relations (e.g. Carchedi, 1975; Olin Wright, 1980). Moreover, it ignores the extent of reliance of employers upon workers for the appropriation of relative surplus value, since in the last analysis it is the latter who, as individuals, produce commodities through their use of machinery. Lazonick has shown how these problems stem from a rather uncritical reading by Marx of the propaganda of the 'poet' of Modern Industry, Andrew Ure (Lazonick, 1979). The effect is to divert attention, momentarily at least, from the material dualism and indeterminacy accompanying capitalist development, of which, as Hall (1977) has shown, Marx was normally so aware.

The conclusion to this section is that we have to understand regional unevenness in the intensity of class consciousness, organisation and solidarity as the resultant of a range of complex determinations. In the first place, the extent to which the direct labour process remains in the control of the producer seems to be an important basic condition, although as we have seen this need not bear any one-to-one relationship with militancy per se. It is important mainly in decreasing, however slightly, the asymmetry of power in the relations between capital and labour, and increasing the overt dependence of the former upon the latter. Secondly, the extent of relative homogenisation of the labour force seems important in, for example, distinguishing the history and reputation of coalmining from that of steel production. For, whereas both began with substantial internal labour market differentiation, in coal this was quite rapidly eroded, while in steel its erosion was countered by the maintenance of craft exclusivity on a unionised basis. It has been argued that job restructuring of the kind found in steel was precisely a strategy of management to divide an increasingly homogenised workforce (Stone, 1974), although this underestimates the capacity of the unions somewhat. But finally, issues around which· struggles can take place are crucial. As we have seen, the nature of the South Wales coal industry induced wage based struggles, in which growing unionisation was both condition and effect, while in steel, where the wages issue was less salient than production relations, unionisation was nevertheless a central vehicle in the process of consciousness raising and the formation of working class culture. It is because of the relative restrictiveness of the concept of the formal subordination of labour to capital to a concern with the wage relation that it has not been found analytically useful here; and, in a rather different way, it is because of a strong tendency to address the relations of production one-sidedly in favour of capital that the concept of the real subordination of labour to capital has also been rejected. Both seem to miss the complex and dualistic nature of the social relations of production.

CLASS RELATIONS, SURPLUS POPULATION AND THE SPATIAL DIVISION OF LABOUR

It is a striking feature of the development of workplace based social organisation that at the time it was occurring there was a truly massive influx of population to South Wales. As we have seen, to some extent the unskilled nature of much of this population had significant effects upon the relative homogenisation of the mining workforce. However,

the impressive point about the industry to which people
flocked was seemingly infinite capacity to absorb this
surplus population from elsewhere. For, as the following
figures show, unemployment was low in Wales at the point,
around 1912, when immigration was highest.

	1912	1980
South East	7.8	3.8
South West	4.6	5.6
Wales	3.1	8.4
Northern	2.9	9.0
Scotland	1.8	8.4
GB	3.9	5.9

Source: Davies, 1980.

The existence of a substantial labour reserve in the South
East helps us understand the subsequent development of new
industry there during and after the 1914-18 war, but only
to a limited extent. For shortly afterwards the pattern with
which we have since become familiar began to emerge as the
heavy industry regions whose output was markedly export-
oriented began to lose employment. It has become a commonplace to explain the massive generation of surplus population in these regions, and nowhere more so than South
Wales, as failure to adjust, inter alia, to adverse trading
conditions consequent upon Britain's involvement in the war,
sharpened overseas competition, the emergence of new fuels,
and numerous other technical reasons. However, while in no
way wishing to minimise the contributory relevance of these
factors, in keeping with the objective of assessing the
extent to which class antagonisms may also generate variations in capitalist development, I will devote little
attention to them. In any case they will undoubtedly re-
emerge in what follows to some degree since class relations
do not occur in a vacuum but in complex interaction with
various productive forces. What will be aimed for in this
section is an analysis of the processes by which capital
restructuring occurred in spatially distinctive areas not
closely related to those centres of heavy industry such as
South Wales but in often wholly nonindustrialised contexts.
In this the dual nature of class relations in the development of a new spatial division of labour will be given
prominence. I will briefly consider four factors.

1. In the first place, the whole context of political
and economic life in early interwar Britain was predicated
on severe class conflict in which the older working class,
based on the heavy export industries, was centrally important. In discussing this issue Foster (1976) has stressed
the importance of the partial incorporation of labour
organisation within agencies of the state, and its origins
in the persistence of a Victorian labour aristocracy in key
industries divided as between skilled and unskilled workers.
As we have seen, there are certain problems with this
formulation, not least the assumption of permanence implicit

in that kind of simple division in which the working class is conceived as composed of a massified rank and file and a more individuated leadership. But also the theory of the labour aristocracy invites the assumption that skill is the major factor dividing the working class, rather than being one of a number of possible dividing factors along with ethnicity, religion, sex, occupation and industrial specialisation, particularly as these vary by region. What seems more helpful is a conception of the ways in which 'the working class is recomposed around major internal structurations ... within factories, within industries, between occupations, between the sexes and between the employed and the reserve armies' (Johnson, 1979) which retains important elements of Foster's general account of the regionalised nature of the crisis of the interwar economy.

Britain's articulation to the international economy was built on its early domination of world trade, which opened a vast space into which a retreating landed aristo-cracy diverted rent capital to assist in the formation of a dominating financial sector, poorly integrated with industry but closely involved with the state. The state's imperial role was of fundamental importance to capital export, but almost as important to an increasingly uncom-petitive basic industrial sector too, including steel, coal and textiles. It was not, however, the classic finance-capitalism based on the close enmeshing of banks and mono-poly industry. This eventually effloresced under the artificial conditions of the 1914-18 war in which the state monopolised production. One effect of this was high in-flation which halved the domestic value of the currency. It was followed by another burst of inflation after the war as banking credit controls were relaxed to stimulate re-construction, so that sterling had lost parity with the dollar and gold by 1920. By contrast, American, German and Japanese capital was becoming more efficient and competi-tive. However, with, on the one hand, Britain rejecting imperial tariff walls and, on the other, the American dollar maintaining a high value, conditions were ripening for the first steps toward inward investment by US capital. It was principally the lower sterling valuation which delayed any large influx temporarily. The only industries which main-tained wartime tariffs in Britain were those not oriented towards export markets, such as electrical goods and vehicles, in which banks had invested under wartime pro-tection. However, the continuing weakness of the old export industries, increasingly draining short-term banking credit, appears to have convinced Baldwin's government that the future of British capitalism lay in its financial rather than its industrial expertise and a policy of returning to the gold standard was adopted under intense American pressure. Three effects followed fairly quickly: first the basic export industries of coal, steel, textiles and ship-building were decimated, along with the regions in which they were concentrated; second, unrealistically overvaluated sterling now provided the stimulus for American investment

to overcome tariffs on luxury production by direct investment in a Britain which still controlled the largest
market in the world; and third, the severe wage-cuts imposed upon the workers not yet made redundant from the
export industries, nowhere more rigorously applied than in
the export coal industry, ushered in the period of severe
class conflict which culminated in the General Strike of
1926.

2. The second factor which bears importantly upon the
regional unevenness of interwar capitalist development in
Britain involves the interaction of class antagonisms and
technical advance in the USA. American industry was beginning to pull away from its competitors in terms of technological development with, as we have seen, important
implications for the location of new consumer industries in
the South East and Midlands. To situate this factor it is
useful to examine the origins of the 'Progressive Era', as
the 1900-18 period in America is often referred to (Beynon,
1975; Burton and Murphy, 1980). Itself a period of industrial peace and development it followed the emergence of an
embryonic socialist movement, social unrest and strike waves
spearheaded by the railway workers, concluding with the 1894
Pullman strike, and centring upon the movement known as the
'Knights of Labour'. The latter sought to move beyond simple
trade union economism to unite the severely divisive
religious and ethnic mixture that made up the American
working class. Sectarianism, incorporation and varieties of
state action ranging from corruption to suppression, were
capital's responses. These were followed by all-out attacks
on industries, as with the employers' offensive in steel
against skilled unionism begun by the Carnegie Company at
Homestead in 1892. This onslaught had the desired effect of
weakening established labour organisation.

Although violent mass-striking continued as unskilled and
immigrant workers sought recognition in steel, the garment
industry, railways and coal, the years of the Progressive
Era were marked by moves towards a corporatist rapproche-
ment between capital and labour. But the growth of
organised labour had also stimulated the emergence of the
harsher disciplines of Taylorism and Fordism. This meant
that:

> Already by the end of the First World War, the capital-
> ist class in the United States (especially in the
> advanced sectors of the 'Second Technological
> Revolution': vehicles, electrical machinery, chemicals,
> and other consumer durables) was perhaps a generation
> ahead of its European competitors in the degree to
> which skilled labour had been subordinated and frag-
> mented in the labour process (Davis, 1980).

Bearing in mind the weaknesses of the 'subordination thesis'
discussed above, it is nevertheless a crucial moment in the
re-establishment of the cultural conditions of production,
even though, as Gramsci (1971) makes clear in his discussion
of 'Americanism and Fordism', one which is subject to

159

massive contradiction and unevenness in its application
within the USA, let alone its transportation to Europe.

3. To return to the context of interwar Britain, the
third factor in accounting for capital's new division of
labour concerns precisely the nature, requirements and
interests of both indigenous and American capitalists as a
class insofar as these may be judged from their practices in
the new industries. These turn out to be rather straight-
forward, and are illustrated especially clearly in the key
sector of motor vehicles manufacturing.

The first requirement of Morris at Oxford, Austin at
Longbridge, Standard at Coventry and Ford at Dagenham was
nonunionism. The main difference between the British and
American industries centred upon control of the labour process. In the case of Morris, Austin and Standard the
employers were able to enforce a piecework regime and
bonus systems due to their freedom of manoeuvre after the
defeat of the engineering unions in 1922. It also, and
importantly, suited the seasonal nature of the motor vehicle
market. Ford, by contrast, paid a uniform wage to both
skilled and unskilled workers, but of course controlled the
labour process through close supervision. In both industries, technical innovations such as the assembly line were
installed, labour was recruited from outside the engineering
industry, and union membership was not permitted.

The second requirement, a corollary of the first, was
'green' labour. It is no coincidence that greenfield
locations were selected either, as local labour, which comprised an important initial source, was composed either of
wholly unorganised or weakly unionised workers. Thus, for
example, in Oxford workers were normally recruited from the
quasi-feudal college servant or agricultural labour strata,
while in Coventry the main sources were textile workers and
skilled craftsmen from the older metal trades as well as
agricultural workers. The latter were particularly welcome,
for:

> despite periodic upsurges of organisation among
> agricultural workers in Warwickshire and Oxfordshire,
> rural migrants were on the whole cut off from trade
> union traditions, a quality prized by their employers:
> the factory inspector for Oxfordshire noted 'a very
> definite preference ... among contractors and others
> for local workers off farms rather than travellers
> from a long distance' (Zeitlin, 1980).

However, the same could not quite be said for the agents
who fulfilled the third requirement. This was the demand
for large numbers of workers on a scale that could not be
met locally. For the motor vehicle industry was both labour
intensive and rapidly growing so that the total workforce
nearly doubled to 275,000 between 1923 and 1934. This
demand was met by the huge reserves of surplus population
created by the expulsion of labour from the old export

regions of Lancashire, Northumberland and Durham, Clydeside and South Wales, the most industrially experienced work-forces to be found anywhere. These were classic migration streams composed as a first wave of young, single men and childless couples, to be followed after the 1932 unemployment nadir by older men and their families. They suffered most of the characteristic experiences of latter-day immigrants: social disorganisation, low wages, discrimination in the community, and poor working conditions, as the following quotations make clear:

> I was about 18. I didn't know a soul in Oxford but I was lucky enough to get digs with a Mr and Mrs Sawyer up the Cowley Road. It wasn't easy to get digs. In the first place the woman found out I was Welsh and told me to leave. That went on for some time. The Oxford people didn't want the Welsh, because the Welsh were undercutting the English. When the Florence Park housing estate was being built in 1933-4 it was built by Welshmen brought here by the developer, who was also a Welshman called Moss. These men worked for a shilling an hour. When I went to live on the estate the hatred there against the Welsh was terrible (Exell, 1979).

> He found a strong dislike of Welsh people on the part of Oxford men, who thought the Welsh were taking their work and were all 'reds'. Other immigrants were much easier to get on with ...
> Girls were very reserved compared with those at home, and, because Welsh people undercut wages and spoke Welsh, Oxford natives in general were very antipathetic. C. and his friends used to visit public houses in Oxford, but they were stopped from singing there ...
> They complained of the frequent spells of unemployment, the high cost of living, and the loss of small items such as free firewood, wild fruit, etc. Mrs B. had wanted to keep chickens in the garden, but neighbours had stopped her (Daniel, 1940).

What is being observed here is precisely the process by which capital effects the recomposition of the working class both in the direct sphere of production and through the privatised reproduction of labour power. In these ways the necessary conditions for enhanced accumulation are constituted. But, in that process the essential dualism of the capital-labour relation is realised. This occurs as the conditions newly created give rise to opposition in the form of resistance from an individuated workforce. Pressures to modify class relations may operate in both the workplace and the community. This is vividly portrayed by Arthur Exell's experience and practice at Morris Motors and over the Cutteslowe Walls:

> It was easier to organise outside the factory than inside because you weren't so likely to get the sack. That was how I got involved in union work, and how I came to join the CP. Quite soon after I moved house to Florence Park I got involved in a tenants agitation ...

the Florence Park estate were private houses, privately
rented ...One day I saw the concrete floor crack and
a type of wild rhubarb plant come up. Another day when
the chain was pulled the cistern came down off the wall.
Most people had that complaint ...So a few of us held
a meeting in my house ... to discuss the terrible
conditions ... we did find an exceptionally good leader
in Jimmy Kincaid. He lived a few doors from me. And he
said to me, 'I'm going to get some leaflets out. The
Party'll do it for me'.
...So we thought it was about time for a showdown.
Other things in Oxford were also reaching a climax such
as the Cutteslowe Walls Campaign ...The Cutteslowe
Council Estate (adjoined) a private estate known as the
Urban Housing Estate. The UHE decided to put a closely-
boarded fence six and a half feet high, all around their
estate and this fence also went over the two roads that
were part of the roads of the Cutteslowe Estate ...As
in the case of the Florence Park strike the Cutteslowe
Walls helped us in the factory. The union members in
the factory agitated for others to join them at the
walls, and the Trades Council and all the other unions
in the town were involved in this struggle ...Then came
the 1934 strike ...Conditions at Pressed Steel were
probably worse than at any other Oxford factories ...It
was a terrible factory to work in, dark, filthy and
noisy, but men came from all over the country to work
there. In July 1934 we had a heatwave and conditions
were so bad at PS that the men walked out, unable to
stand it any longer. That was the first big strike since
the General Strike ...The strike won union recognition
at PS ...After the PS strike we gradually grew in
strength. In 1935 Jimmy Kincaid, an AEU member tried to
organise in the cars branch of Morris at Cowley but was
sacked. However, we had more success elsewhere ...
(Exell, 1979).

This passage is suggestive of some of the processes by
which, in the absence of formal union representation, semiskilled workers became organised, with little real assistance from skilled unions such as the AEU. They presaged
traditions of strong, plant based, shop steward organisation and job control which have persisted in the vehicles
industry even after the advent of subsequent general unionisation. The response of the eventual Lord Nuffield - in
1931 a heavy subscriber to Oswald Mosley's New Party - to
this development is reported in the following:

The decline in Welsh immigration into Oxford in the
years 1935-7 may not have been due entirely to a
decline in the general prospects of employment in the
area. Labour in the local motor works was unorganised
until 1934, when there were strikes for better conditions of work. Prominent parts in this movement were
played by emigrants from the depressed areas, and
particularly by men from Wales. Thus 16 of the 23 men
on the strike committee are said to have been Welsh, a

162

proportion far in excess of the proportion of Welsh workers to the total employed in the motor industry. It appears that, in following years, vacancies notified by the motor works to Ministry of Labour offices included specific requests for workers who were not from Wales (Daniel, 1940).

4. The fourth and final contributory factor to the uneven development of the interwar and postwar era can be summarised as the TUC's new direction after 1926, which involved two principal political alliances. The first of these was with the advanced section of industrial capital (itself articulated with the finance sector); the second was, through Labourism, with the state. Both movements were predicated on a fourfold reappraisal of strategy. First, the demise of the basic industries was accepted as a 'second industrial revolution', particularly by Citrine (TUC General Secretary) and Bevin (TGWU General Secretary), in part confirmed by the latter's tour of US industry in 1926. Second, the conception of class interests changed from seeing the commonality of working class interests as against those of capital towards seeing a commonality between the interests of labour and capital. Third, the imminence of capitalism's demise was no longer anticipated, and the importance of finding solutions within the existing system was accepted. Finally, the TUC rejected the use of industrial action as a political weapon, isolated the miners and the CP's influence and adopted Labourism as its only mode of political representation (Jacques, 1976).

The alliance with advanced industrial capital began with the Mond-Turner talks of 1928-9 in which the chairman of ICI and thirty or so other employers held joint discussions with TUC representatives on industrial recovery, the status of unions, and the nationalisation of industry through the cooperation of labour. And, although the agreements reached were rejected by the formal employers' organisations (FBI, NCEO) which represented the interests of the older, heavy industries they exerted a formative influence upon the TUC's economic policy, and through it, that of the Labour Party throughout the 1930s. The effects of this redirection were principally reflected in state policies only in the postwar years, but its foundations were laid both before, and during wartime. The new cooperative mode brought the trade union leadership closer to government especially through the newly-formed Ministry of Labour, and, through this, led to the consolidation of the spatial division between growth and declining industries. Even in the staple industry of steelmaking, the application of American strip mill technology would have led to the relocation of new investment away from South Wales into the South East, but for pressure from the Welsh lobby in Parliament. The interests of the right-wing general unions (TGWU and NUGMW) in the new semiskilled industries, and their subsequent involvement in government, most obviously in the shape of Bevin, reflected the regional as well as the sectoral shift that had taken place in the power relations of industrial Britain.

Finally, the role of Bevin in seeking postwar Atlantic unity, especially through his vigorous advocacy of Marshall Aid, helped to set the framework for postwar reconstruction, with its profound regional effects. This appears in the representation of the interests of the Mondist group (especially the motor manufacturers) through the policy lens of steel nationalisation. The American mass consumption economy had inserted the US steel industry into an intensified level of accumulation by confronting its skilled steel workers with the innovation of wide strip mills. If mass consumption were to be fully implemented in a European context, the basic conflict between the steel consumers and the protected, state subsidised, export-oriented steel cartels, especially in Britain, required resolution. The motor manufacturers recognised the value of nationalisation in fulfilling this requirement, as, for reasons of employment maintenance, did the steel unions, the TUC and the Labour Party (Bowen, 1976). The Marshall Plan had two crucial purposes for which the USA was prepared to supply financial aid. On the one hand it turned the European economies away from protectionist, nationalistic, and (insofar as socialists influenced governments) anti-consumerist policies; and on the other hand, it integrated the European steel industries to the consumer sector through the export of strip mill technology. This was only efficient if trade were to expand along consumerist lines. Both purposes served to secure the expanded markets which were so crucial to continued accumulation under the dominance of US capital. In Britain most of the aid to the steel industry went to the Steel Company of Wales, in France to SOLLAC, in the Netherlands to Hoogovens, all suppliers to the motor industry (van der Pijl, 1979; Overbeek, 1980).

It is important to interrelate these points theoretically. To recap, the argument has been that up to 1926 class relations were exacerbated by the intraclass conflict between the finance and industrial sectors which in turn devolved with particular ferocity on the basic industry regions. The failure of the latter heightened class antagonisms between labour and capital over earnings, the solutions to which were migration and a tentative move towards corporatism. This settlement at the economic level followed a pattern established in not dissimilar circumstances in the USA and resulted in a political alliance which defeated the old, imperial industries. The reconstruction of these industries articulated them to an American mass consumption economy in which the working class participated both economically and politically as it recomposed itself in the face of changing social relations of production.

The alliances, forms of political representation, sectionalisms and competing ideologies which have been described above, signify precisely similar processes to those which Hall refers to as:

the forms and relations of the political through which

the various fractions of capital and its political allies can contend, both among themselves and with the subordinate classes, so as to dominate the class struggle and to draw civil society, politics, ideology and the State into conformity with the broad underlying 'needs' of the developing mode of production (Hall, 1977).

This is not to imply a simplistic functionalism, but rather a temporary resolution at the level of classes in and through the state and the economy, of the contradictions entailed in the continuation of the valorisation process. The dualism of which we have spoken earlier is present in the elements of 'double determination' whereby the solution to conflict involved gains and losses for workers, gains and losses for different branches of capital, a displacement of the basically economic struggle between the classes into the state, and the development of its machinery as, increasingly, the direct and indirect guarantor of the reproduction of capitalist relations. It is to an analysis of the further implications of this solution for class relations at the regional level that the last section is directed.

THE DUALITY OF CLASS RELATIONS: WORKPLACE AND COMMUNITY

In what has been said so far, an attempt has been made to underline the essential dualism of class relations. This has direct implications for any theory of class which we would wish to employ to explain the nature and extent of changes in class composition and alignment, and their implications for the developing use made of space by capital. It is also centrally important to the identification of contradictions within capital's spatial division of labour which may raise class consciousness to the possibilities and advantages of noncapitalist relations of production. The double determination of the capital-labour relation whereby capital cannot function without labour exerting some work control, and labour cannot subsist independently of capital, requires a rejection of at least two important theorisations of class identification. On the one hand, the type of analysis which constitutes classes in terms of the 'base', that is, from the perspective of a necessary <u>correspondence</u> between classes and their economic function (Carchedi, 1975) proves inadequate because, as we have seen even the economic is made complex by the intrusion of superstructural factors, such as political alliances, or competing ideologies. But on the other hand, a reverse argument, to the effect that there is a necessary <u>non-correspondence</u> between economically defined classes and their forms of representation in the sphere of class struggle (Hirst, 1977) is also inadequate to our purpose. This is because there is a relationship, but by no means a straightforward one, between the imperatives of valorisation and capital accumulation, and the development of class consciousness and class organisation, most often focussed

165

upon the workplace rather than in the working class as a
whole, but occasionally uniting across the workplace/com-
munity divide.

In this section I want to sketch an outline of the complex
manner in which, in postwar South Wales, a process of reproducing capitalist social relations has been enacted.
Secondly I wish to indicate the centrality of the state in
bringing this process to the point of fruition, and the
contradictory effects of the processes involved upon the
further development of regional class relations. The key to
the reconstruction of the postwar economy of South Wales has
been shown to be state policies towards the coal, steel and
manufacturing industries, the latter via state regional
policy (Morgan, 1979). From the viewpoint of the recomposition of class relations there are three important processes
to be considered; these concern issues of: locality/comm-
unity, mass consumption and feminisation of the workforce.

1. The processes of class recomposition rely centrally
upon the establishment of a pattern of social disruption in
which the cohesiveness impressed upon individuals through
sharing the experiences of locality and community is
gradually, and sometimes violently, fragmented. Put simply,
it is not in the interests of capital's tendency to reproduce its social relations, for non-privatistic modes of
existence to dominate the consciousness of its workforce and
market. We can identify three levels at which the structures
of localism were undercut in the South Wales coalfield.

At the most general level, postwar nationalisation of the
coal industry, and the provision of state welfare services,
undermined the social, welfare and educational roles of the
local union, the SWMF. In addition the union itself was
assimilated to the National Union of Mineworkers, thus
further reducing its regional identity. Nationalisation
placed numerous burdens such as compensation and low-level
pricing, upon the industry which hindered its reconstruction. These burdens also contributed to a slow, but continuous process of pit closure in single industry communities.
Finally, nationalisation did not give rise to noncapitalist
relations of production; rather, the industry became monopolised while remaining under the control of the previous,
private sector management structure. The NUM was however
placed in a markedly more incorporated position vis a vis
management than the SWMF had been in relation to the private
coal combines. Now strikes were often unofficial, involving
conflict between local lodges and the NUM, and doomed to
failure.

Secondly, there occurred a level of undercutting of community cohesiveness which involved, on the one hand reduced morale and insecurity for the mining workforce, and on
the other a motivation to seek alternative employment, to
the extent that it was available. Part of the postwar reconstruction of the Welsh economy, under the aegis of Marshall
Aid, had, it will be recalled, been the establishment of

166

wide-strip steel mills, and to a limited extent the firms that consumed steel, in South Wales. The firms to which the interwar unemployed had migrated had now themselves established branch plants where labour was still in abundant reserve supply. Hence former miners became production workers in the Steel Company of Wales, Fords, Morris Motors, Metal Box, Hoovers and other, non-steel using plants. A result was the further loosening of the ties of localism. Attempts to revive the concept of the politically conscious mining lodge through the reorganisation of the union's education scheme were a belated recognition of the damage reconstruction was doing to a particular kind of working class culture.

The third level is reached with the sudden repercussions upon the local economy and community of rapid closure of coalmines. After 1964 the new Labour Government sharply accelerated the closure programme. Stimulated by its policy of moving towards cheap, clean fuels such as gas and oil, and its aim of modernising British industry, the state-managed rundown of the coalfield in the 1960s began to change the material basis for local alternatives to a privatised consumer culture. For, while the threat of closure only divided communities into 'secure' and 'threatened' categories, the reality of closure immediately removed the economic basis of, for example, the revived miners' welfare schemes with their educational, cultural and sporting activities. Very quickly the associated buildings were transformed from cultural centres of one kind into cultural centres of another kind as the brewing and gambling industries absorbed them into a wider consumer market. The NUM once more adopted the pragmatic stance of leaving what it saw as political issues to be resolved through Labourism, seeking only to pressure for alternative employment in light engineering plants to be brought to pit closure communities. However even its parliamentary influence to achieve this had declined markedly as the number of NUM sponsored MPs was reduced from thirteen in 1945 to two in 1970, and nil in 1974.

The process of 'consumerisation' became widespread even in the 'secure' mining communities, marking a crucial stage in the penetration of new modes of existence into the 'traditional' local community. The relative defencelessness of working class institutions to such a process is symbolic of the power of privatistic and consumerist ideology in the developing relations between capital and labour. The dualism of class relations is not simply confined to labour process, workplace, relations but is equally to be found operating in the sphere of consumption, where, as this experience demonstrated,

it is a process born and conducted in ideological conceptions about 'the market' and the 'consumer' which are the professionalised variants of contemporary ideological and political discourses. Marketing ideologies about the consumer echo political ideologies

about the disappearance of traditional class
differences and the rise of an affluent, middle-class
Britain. In a sense, these marketing ideologies and
practices attempt to 'complete the circle' by producing precisely that affluent middle-class consumer
they claim to have already recognised. Subsequently,
of course, political ideologies register these changes
as the changed conditions of political practice and
debate (Clarke, 1979).

2. Mass consumption ideologies have the effect of filling
the empty spaces left by capitalist development. They
anaesthetise the disruptive effects of social change while
enlarging the market in the process. But postwar South
Wales had been, it will be recalled, partially integrated
into the mass consumption economy from the outset. The
postwar reconstruction of the Welsh steel industry in
conformity with an Americanised blueprint has been explained
and its subsequent development was very different from that
experienced by the coalmining industry. For, whereas the
latter was characterised by secular decline, steel was the
motive force of industrial growth. Employment and output
grew enormously up to the mid-1970s and, importantly, steel
workers continued to enjoy high wages, and steel producers
enjoyed uninterrupted production. Furthermore, between 1948
and 1959 the differential between average earnings in steel
production and those in all other industries increased so
that even during the 1960s when the differential stabilised
there was parity between <u>unskilled</u> process workers in steel
and <u>skilled</u> workers in other industries (Bowen, 1976).

Throughout the postwar period, at least up until the late
1960s, industrial relations, as represented by number of
stoppages, number of workers involved and number of working
days lost, improved in comparison with the record of the
interwar period. This pattern coincided neatly with the
period of least competition on the world market and greatest
demand for the sheet and strip steel for the consumer goods
industries in which South Wales specialised. During this
period of traditionally harmonious steel industry labour
relations, the steel plants had been relocated and concentrated in new coastal locations, geographically close to,
but culturally distant from the coalfield in which the small
iron and steel plants had evolved. The experiences of some
workers (4) involved in this transition focussed upon three
key factors: earnings, deskilling and managerial compliance.

The relative improvement in earnings even for a skilled
employee already within the steel industry is illustrated
in the following: 'When Llanwern opened it was El Dorado.
When I was in Pontymister I earned £13 as a skilled
blastfurnaceman, second from top - the average rate was £8.
When I went to Llanwern on the same grade in 1962, it was
£18 straight away.' With skilled rates setting the pace for
semiskilled and unskilled earnings every new worker was
earning more than in their previous employment. But this
could only last while competition was weak, and once this

began to affect sales, differentials narrowed as productivity increases were sought:

> Around 1966 there began to be problems over the intro-
> duction of new technology. There had been a dip in the
> market as Japan got going and this had led to pro-
> ductivity deals in exchange for de-manning. In Ponty-
> mister we'd had experience of this where skilled grades
> and differentials had gradually been eroded by the
> introduction of machinery. The new processes undermined
> craft skills. At Llanwern most men in these skilled
> categories now only had differentials of about 50p, and
> they were bitter. I wasn't so much because I still
> enjoyed a fair degree of autonomy plus excellent working
> conditions. For others though cash got to be the only
> issue.

In other words the relations of production were changed in
two successive ways in the new plants. First, the traditionally high degree of work control enjoyed by skilled,
craft grades of worker began to disappear at an accelerated
pace, and secondly workers began to replace job satisfaction
with more 'militant particularism' (Williams, 1980). This
is reflected in the changed experience of worker/manager
relations:

> The typical old steel works was part of the community,
> surrounded by houses, like in Pontymister. This is
> where skilled workers like 'melters' were highly paid
> and it was accepted that other grades got less. It was
> amazing, the deference of workers to the manager, and
> especially the owner - I suppose the unions were frag-
> mented and we were each stuck in our own little
> corner. But in Llanwern, because the market was up
> management would give in to almost any claim that was
> put in after the introduction of new machinery.

It is from approximately this point that, as noted in the
Donovan Commission's report: 'the industry's once good
strike record has deteriorated and, in a list of industries
which in recent years have most suffered from unofficial
strikes, iron and steel comes next after the main four,
coal, docks, shipbuilding and vehicles' (quoted in Bowen,
1976). Unofficial militancy grew with the erosion of control
and status of skilled workers, especially in South Wales
where, 'over the twelve month period ending in May 1974 for
example, no fewer than thirty disputes occurred at Llanwern,
BSC's giant and rapidly expanding strip mills at Newport in
Monmouthshire, at an estimated cost of £10m. Two of the
largest strikes were called by craft workers' (Bowen, 1976).

Steelworkers had become well-integrated into the high
wage, mass consumption economy of 1960s Britain. This was
reflected in the new environments created in proximity to
the coastal plants at Llanwern, Port Talbot and near
Swansea. These continue to display abundant evidence of
what Clarke (1979) refers to as 'the more rational reproduction' embodied in mass housing, centralised shopping and
declassed drinking clubs. Yet skilled steelworkers were

beginning to resist their own sectional recomposition, and especially their massification. With hindsight these early struggles can be seen as the preliminaries to more serious campaigns to prevent the steel industry's more recent partial annihilation.

3. The third important element entailing changes in both workplace and community involves the increasing attachment of women to the waged labour force, a process that has developed later in South Wales than many areas but one with important implications for the character of working class culture and organisation in the region.

The first empirical point to be made here is that the participation of women in the Welsh workforce (in which South Wales dominates overwhelmingly) is in some ways different from that found in other UK regions. Although proportionately less women are in employment generally, of those that do work rather more than average are in fulltime manufacturing jobs. Also, and to some extent as a corollary of this, a much higher proportion of part-time female workers are found in services than is the case nationally. The region sharing these characteristics most closely is Scotland where a still smaller proportion of total employment is accounted for by female part-time working than is the case in Wales. Now, while any inference to be drawn should be made with caution, these features are not inconsistent with the observation made by Massey (1980) that 'Not only are women now increasingly absorbed into capitalist wage relations but with the continued decline of the basic industries the men are increasingly excluded from them.' The implication is that, as well as undergoing processes of recomposition, the South Wales working class may be threatened by a process of déclassement as a greater proportion of its population becomes either unemployed, or perhaps subemployed in the black economy and in notoriously unprotected part-time employment, or as fulltime women employees in manufacturing or services where their domestic responsibilities and/or newness to waged work may not lend themselves to committed unionisation (see for example, on services, Heritage, 1980). Certainly the level of industrial disputes in the manufacturing industries with the greatest proportion of women workers, that is textiles, clothing and footwear, is amongst the lowest in industry as a whole (Cooke, 1982).

The increase in female employment in industries which the NUM had sought in exchange for pit closures, and the concomitant marginalisation of many former miners, was probably a contributory factor to the changed attitude towards the NCB which presaged the conflicts of the 1970s. But the closures themselves remained the major emblem of the failure of nationalisation to organise production on a socially useful basis:

> The turning point which made the miners see the NCB as just another employer was pit closures, unquestionably.

> In some parts of the British coalfields they dealt with
> the men ruthlessly. There was no difference between the
> old coalowners and the NCB. They were now turning it
> into state capitalism ... (miner, quoted in Francis
> and Smith, 1980).

Crucially though, given the context of increasing state
intervention in pay, employment and industrial relations
controls, it was the dispersal of fragments of the former
mining workforce, and the recent attachment of members of
miners' families to the new industries, that extended the
networks of class solidarity beyond the confines of coalmining, when the strike action of the 1970s was successfully
undertaken.

Finally, this leads to a consideration of the impact of
the direct and indirect insertion of the state in its many
forms upon class relations in the context of South Wales.
Two features only can be considered here, each having some
relation to the feminisation of the workforce. The first
of these involves reflecting upon the thesis that in
'solving' the problem of regional underdevelopment the state
coopts an increasing proportion of the workforce, either
directly by employing them, or indirectly by making them
dependent through subsidisation of industry. In this way
social stability is maintained, but an increasing proportion of the workforce comes to occupy an ambiguous class
position, with implications for class based action (Pinnato
and Pugliese, 1978). This kind of thesis is sometimes
exemplified by reference to state intervention in the
Mezzogiorno of Italy. However, in that context it seems
likely that direct cooptation occurs mainly with regard to
the male labour force, whereas in South Wales one of the
fastest growing employment sectors is females in state services, often employed in lower order service work in de-
centralised state bureaux. It seems possible to infer that,
rather than being simply employed in a bloated state sector
to offset regional social tensions, these workers constitute
a prized resource, often new to waged work in precisely the
occupations for which labour supplies have all but disappeared in the 'primate region' based upon London. This is
not to say that all such state sector work has this characteristic, for clearly Wales' political identity does give
rise to a state apparatus which meets political demands and
serves a wider requirement for stability as well.

The second side of state involvement in the regional
economy concerns its possible indirect cooptative role
through subsidisation of productive industry. On the one
hand, as we have seen, the class relations of the nationalised industries are complex but seemingly display a
tendency towards less cooptation than in the past. This is
especially true in the coal industry but recent experiences
in steel, where the traditional isolation and divisiveness
of the industry continue to work against solidarity, suggest
that the long process of reorganisation and consciousness-
raising, such as the coal industry experienced in the 1970s,

has hardly begun. (5) On the other hand the state in South
Wales, mainly through the Welsh Development Agency and the
Welsh Office Industry Department has embarked upon a
strategy of 'attracting winners' in the form of inward
investment, especially in the electronics industry, from
foreign countries, notably Japan. In this process one of
the key selling points has been the existence of good labour
relations in the region, a factor which is again being
stressed in the current attempt to attract the Datsun car
plant to South Wales. The important element in the transformation of South Wales labour relations in many of these
new manufacturing industries has unquestionably been the
widespread employment of women in a context, particularly
true of the Japanese plants, of a well-developed 'corporatist' style of industrial management. The formal labour
movement, in the shape of the Wales TUC, has been leaning
over backwards to assure inward investors of cooperation,
notably regarding single-plant unionism. Indirect cooptation could be said to be increasing, albeit slowly and
fragmentarily, as direct state cooptation in older industries has begun to be questioned.

In conclusion, therefore, a twofold creation of relative
surplus population has taken place in South Wales in the
postwar period. The implications of both processes, the
first centring upon the contraction of the core of the
regional working class in the coal industry, the second
upon the other major element in that class culture in steel,
have been to create conditions for further stages of
capitalist development in the region. The involvement of
the state in these processes has been of central importance in, on the one hand, enabling a potentially highly
conscious, unionised, and male dominated working class to
be undercut, and on the other, stimulating its recomposition in ways which have allowed for a markedly increased
level of female labour market attachment. This has further
enabled the state in Wales to present the region as a
fruitful site for future capitalist development. The unanswered questions concern the extent to which the recomposed workforce retains consciousness of 'class in and
for itself', and the degree to which the fragmentation of
workplace and community are transcended in the process.

CONCLUSIONS

This paper has attempted to restore the balance between
analysis of regional and inter-regional uneven development
which stress the immanent logic of valorisation and
accumulation as the central determining mechanism, and
those which, perhaps fewer in number, emphasise the
centrality of class conflict to the processes of capitalist
development. The aim has been to show how capital creates
but also responds to opportunities and obstacles in the
developing social relations of production. The way in which
space is differentially used at different times is one of
many often unanticipated effects of what is nevertheless a

deeply structured process. I have thought it important to stress at various points the importance of conceptualising the basic relation between the two key classes, capital and labour, involved in the development of the process as the product of a double determination, a distinctly relational rather than gradational (Olin Wright, 1980) approach. The dualism which is at the heart of these class relations derives from the condition of interdependence upon which they rely, and it is this which helps account for the indeterminacy of outcomes in many instances.

In examining the nature and extent of class antagonisms it has been of great value to seek the varying bases for social organisation within classes. Though less has been said about the social organisation of the capitalist class than that of parts of the working class, nevertheless the interests which unify and to some extent divide the former appear to have a strongly international flavour and much more so than those of the working class which appear much more meaningful at the subnational than even the national level (Urry, 1980). With regard to the collective bases of organisation within the working class the combination of forms of work control, extent of skill hierarchisation and level of technical development appear to have a considerable bearing not so much upon the extent, but the nature of social organisation, especially as represented by the type of unionisation found in given industries. In the case of South Wales it is likely that the militant reputation of the regional workforce rests upon a relatively few, dramatised and primarily wage related confrontations, whereas the more important and long-established habituation of the workforce as a whole to a culture which includes unionisation as a central feature is what has underpinned the peculiarly restricted form taken by capitalist development in the region, at least until relatively recently.

The latter argument gains some support when consideration is given to the importance for capital restructuring in the interwar years of the absence of workplace based social organisation. However, as is shown particularly clearly in the experience of Arthur Exell, who is probably not wholly unrepresentative of the migrant labour from the older industrial regions, social organisation around the workplace is only one half of the process by means of which working class culture reconstitutes itself. The sphere of reproduction can, perhaps most sharply in the relatively disorganised context of the newly industrialising spatial location (Castells, 1977), take on an importance in the development of class consciousness, in the absence of workplace organisation, beyond that with which it is normally associated.

However, the importance of mass consumption to the post-war reconstruction of European capitalism under American hegemony has had a pronounced effect upon the development of the social relations of production, nowhere more so than in South Wales. The incorporation of the most powerful

173

source of noncapitalist cultural relations, the mineworkers, into a state machinery which was a crucial source of the reproduction of capitalist relations allowed the South Wales economy to be integrated into the consumer economy in a relatively troublefree manner. The state is now the most important and most ubiquitous vehicle of class re-composition in the region, managing consensus, integrating labour reserves with new forms of capitalist development, and 'solving' the problems of regional uneven development by reproducing them in new ways.

NOTES

(1) This paper has been discussed at a Conference of Socialist Economists Urban and Regional Study Group meeting at Bristol University in March 1981 and a conference entitled 'New Perspectives on the Urban Political Economy' held at the American University, Washington DC in May 1981, as well as the BSA annual conference for which it was prepared. I am grateful to those collectives as well as the following individuals for their helpful comments: Ash Amin, Mike Geddes, Mick Dunford, Andrew Sayer, Graham Day, Dai Michael, James Wickham, Ann Markusen, Bennett Harrison, Enzo Mingione and Robb Burlage.
(2) In most of what follows I will focus rather more upon the working class than the capitalist class. This is partly for reasons of space, but also because in South Wales capitalists as a class have been peculiarly under-organised and perhaps under-represented by comparison with labour. This does not of course imply that working class struggles have been any the less real since this lack of class organisation was substituted by a pe-culiarly limpet-like 'possessive individualism' especially on the part of the coalowners. More recently the state has substituted for an organised class of capitalists in South Wales.
(3) By working class culture is meant sets of attitudes of people to each other and of people to things formed out of the relationship of dependency and partial autonomy experienced by the normally dominated class in the capital-labour relation.
(4) The following accounts were given in interviews carried out with Llanwern steelworkers in August 1980 into the effects of the steel crisis, and in particular the 1980 steel strike, upon workers and unions. The inter-views were carried out by Kevin Morgan and Philip Cooke as part of a joint research project with Gareth Rees on the steel industry in South Wales.
(5) This is underlined in the refusal of South Wales miners to adopt the local union recommendation to vote for strike action in sympathy with the striking steelworkers in 1980. Although complicated by questions of coal imports which BSC were increasingly using to cut costs, thereby threatening South Wales coking coalmines, and the inability of the Wales TUC to coordinate union

action on a regional basis, it was the traditional independence and even aloofness of steelworkers from coalminers that contributed substantially to this failure to take concerted action. This was clearly recognised by interviewees at Llanwern who were involved in organising the strike:

> we learned a few things from the strike, mainly that steelworkers' arrogance had got to be toned down. We thought we could be like the miners by following the Scargill model - flyers - but times have changed. We've got to join local trades councils and gain wider support. Next time any action will have to be organised through the Wales TUC.

REFERENCES

Beynon, H, (1975), Working for Ford, EP Publishing Ltd,
Wakefield.
Bowen, P, (1976), Social Control in Industrial Organis-
ations: a Strategic and Occupational Study of British
Steelmaking, Routledge and Kegan Paul, London.
Burton, D. and Murphy, B, (1980), 'Planning, austerity, and
the democratic prospect', Kapitalistate, 8, pp.67-98.
Carchedi, G, (1975), 'On the economic identification of the
new middle class', Economy and Society, 4, 1, pp.1-86.
Carney, J. et al. (eds), (1980), Regions in Crisis, Croom
Helm, London.
Castells, M, (1977), 'Towards a political urban sociology',
in M. Harloe (ed), Captive Cities, John Wiley, London.
Clarke, J, (1979), 'Capital and culture: the postwar
working class revisited', in J. Clarke et al. (eds),
Working Class Culture, Hutchinson, London.
Cooke, P, (1982), 'Dependency, supply factors and uneven
development in Wales and other problem regions', Regional
Studies (forthcoming).
Cressey, P. and MacInnes, J, (1980), 'Voting for Ford:
industrial democracy and the control of labour', Capital
and Class, 11, pp.5-33.
Daniel, G, (1940), 'Some factors affecting the movement of
labour', Oxford Economic Papers, 3, pp.144-79.
Davis, M, (1980), 'Why the US working class is different',
New Left Review, 123, pp.3-46.
Davies, G, (1980), 'Wales: Japan jumps in while Whitehall
hesitates', Business Location File, November, pp.56-9.
Dennis, N. et al. (1969), Coal is Our Life, Tavistock,
London.
Elbaum, B. and Wilkinson, F, (1979), 'Industrial relations
and uneven development: a comparative study of the
American and British steel industries', Cambridge Journal
of Economics, 3, pp.275-303.
Exell, A, (1979), 'Morris Motors in the 1930s, Part II:
politics and trade unionism', History Workshop Journal,
7, pp.45-65.
Fothergill, S. and Gudgin, G, (1978), 'Regional employment
change: a sub-regional explanation', Progress in Planning,
12, pp.155-219.
Foster, J, (1976), 'British imperialism and the labour
aristocracy', in J. Skelley (ed), The General Strike 1926,
Lawrence and Wishart, London.
Francis, H. and Smith, D, (1980), The Fed: a History of the
South Wales Miners in the Twentieth Century, Lawrence
and Wishart, London.
Fröbel, F. et al. (1979), The New International Division of
Labour, Cambridge University Press, London.
Gramsci, A, (1971), Selections from Prison Notebooks,
Lawrence and Wishart, London.
Hall, S, (1977), 'The "political" and the "economic" in
Marx's theory of classes', in A. Hunt (ed), Class and
Class Structure, Lawrence and Wishart, London
Heritage, J, (1980), 'Class situation, white collar union-
isation and the "double proletarianisation" thesis: a

176

comment', Sociology, 14, pp.283-94.

Hirst, P, (1977), 'Economic classes and politics', in A. Hunt (ed), Class and Class Structure, Lawrence and Wishart, London.

Holmes, G, (1976), 'The South Wales coal industry 1850-1914', Transactions of the Honourable Society of Cymmrodorion, pp.162-207.

Jacques, M, (1976), 'Consequences of the General Strike', in J. Skelley (ed), The General Strike 1926, Lawrence and Wishart, London.

Johnson, R, (1979), 'Three Problematics: elements of a theory of working-class culture', in J. Clarke et al. (eds), Working Class Culture, Hutchinson, London.

Keeble, D, (1980), 'Industrial decline, regional policy and the urban-rural manufacturing shift in the United Kingdom', Environment and Planning, A, 12, 945-62.

Lazonick, W, (1978), 'The subjection of labour to capital: the rise of the capitalist system', Review of Radical Political Economics, 10, pp.1-31.

Lazonick, W, (1979), 'Industrial relations and technical change: the case of the self-acting mule', Cambridge Journal of Economics, 3, pp.240-62.

Lumley, B, (1980/81), 'Review article: working class autonomy and the crisis', Capital and Class, 12, pp.123-35.

Marx, K, (1974), Capital, vol.I, Lawrence and Wishart, London.

Massey, D, (1980) 'Industrial restructuring as class re-structuring: some examples of the implications of industrial change for class structure', CES Working Note 604, Mimeo.

Morgan, K, (1979), 'State regional interventions and industrial restructuration in postwar Britain: the case of Wales', Urban and Regional Studies Working Paper 16, University of Sussex, Brighton.

Nichols, T. and Beynon, H, (1977), Living with Capitalism: Class Relations and the Modern Factory, Routledge and Kegan Paul, London.

Olin Wright, E, (1980), 'Varieties of Marxist conceptions of class structure', Politics and Society, 9, pp.323-70.

Overbeek, H, (1980), 'Finance capital and the crisis in Britain', Capital and Class, 11, pp.99-120.

van der Pijl, K, (1979), 'Class formation at the inter-national level', Capital and Class, 9, pp.1-22.

Pinnaro, G. and Pugliese, E, (1978), 'Changes in the social structure of southern Italy', International Journal of Urban and Regional Research, 3, pp.492-515.

Stone, K, (1974), 'The origins of job structures in the steel industry', Review of Radical Political Economics, 6, pp.61-97.

Watkins, A, (1980), 'Good business climates and the second war between the states', Department of Government Working Paper, University of Texas at Austin, Mimeo.

Wilkinson, F, (1977), 'Collective bargaining in the steel industry in the 1920s', in A. Briggs and J. Saville (eds), Essays in Labour History, Croom Helm, London.

Williams, R, (1980), Politics and Letters, New Left Books, London.

Willis, P, (1979), 'Shop-floor culture, masculinity and the wage form', in J. Clarke et al. (eds), <u>Working Class Culture</u>, Hutchinson, London.

Urry, J, (1981), 'Localities, regions and social class', <u>International Journal of Urban and Regional Research</u>, (forthcoming).

Zeitlin, J, (1980), 'The emergence of shop steward organisation and job control in the British car industry', <u>History Workshop Journal</u>, 10, pp.119-137.

9 Technocratic Ideology and the Reproduction of Inequality: the case of the electronics industry in the Republic of Ireland

PETER MURRAY AND JAMES WICKHAM

INTRODUCTION

In the contemporary recession, the states of the western world are apparently convinced that their economic survival depends on the speed with which they adopt the new technology of microelectronics. One particularly dramatic case of such enthusiasm is the Republic of Ireland, where in recent years the electronics industry has been the fastest growing sector of manufacturing industry and where a determined attempt is being made to reorientate the educational system to the needs of the new technology.

When large areas of policy become dominated by discussion of 'the needs of technology', the sociologist reaches for his/her copy of Habermas' 'Science and Technology as Ideology'. (1) Developing Weber's analysis of the spread of instrumental rationality, Habermas argued that in contemporary capitalism science and technology become the most important ideological resource by which the existing society is legitimated: to the extent that political issues become posed in terms of technical issues, soluble only by experts, then the existing structures of power, interests and inequality are removed from critical discussion. In this paper we examine the growth of the electronics industry in Ireland in these terms: the expansion of electronics manufacturing and of state institutions concerned with the industry is analysed as the legitimation of inequality by means of the extension of technocratic ideology.

However, although our argument starts from Habermas' basic framework, it also attempts to develop his analysis. Habermas is concerned with the functioning of science and technology in the society as a whole. For him, science and technology appear as a background ideology, that is, as a set of implicit assumptions which penetrate mass consciousness and induce general acquiescence to the status quo. Habermas is relatively unconcerned with the question of how such an ideology develops and what particular interests are involved in its promotion. By contrast, we assume that science and technology require a material institutional form or forms in order to function as ideology in specific political contexts. Technology therefore has to be analysed as _institutionalised_ ideology.

The first part of the paper shows how the growth of electronics manufacturing in the Republic of Ireland has been presented as transforming the country. For its advocates the industry is based on high technology and therefore involves highly skilled labour. By contrast, we argue that the reality is more mundane: the expansion of electronics in Ireland is due to the way in which the Irish state has managed to integrate itself into the international division of labour; work in the electronics factories is primarily low-skill assembly. Whereas the first part of the paper thus demonstrates a contrast between ideology and reality, the second part analyses the effectivity of the ideology itself. We argue that the electronics industry in Ireland has been used to, firstly, legitimate an industrialisation strategy where national economic development is equated with private enterprise and, secondly, to transform the educational system in ways which ensure that it remains one of the most important (and one of the most legitimate) ways in which social inequality is reproduced.

THE IRISH ELECTRONICS INDUSTRY IN THE INTERNATIONAL DIVISION OF LABOUR

In terms of production and employment the electronics manufacturing industry has expanded dramatically in the Republic of Ireland since the early 1970s. According to the state agency responsible for industrial job-creation, the Industrial Development Authority (IDA), employment in electronic and electrical manufacturing rose from about 5,000 in 1973 to about 10,000 in 1979, and its projections envisage that in 1985 between 25,000 and 30,000 people will be employed in the sector. (2) The IDA's current estimate of about 13,000 employed in electronics (over 5 per cent of the total manufacturing workforce) is broadly confirmed by our own research which located 110 firms engaged in electronics manufacture. All these firms were sent a postal questionnaire in January/February 1981: some 93 firms responded, reporting a total employment of over 11,000 people. Between 1973 and 1978, according to the IDA's own calculations, exports of electronics products rose annually by an average of 52 per cent as against an annual average of 33 per cent for exports of all manufactured goods. (3) In 1980 exports of office machinery and automatic data processing equipment comprised 11.5 per cent of all manufactured exports and 5.3 per cent of total exports. (4)

According to the IDA, this rapid expansion has been due to the importance it has placed on electronics within its general strategy of attracting multinational investment to Ireland. The former Managing Director of the IDA, M.J. Killeen, reported that:

In 1974 the IDA identified the electronics sector as one which at the time was relatively isolated from the impact of the recession and which would expand rapidly in the following years. We prepared a specific development strategy for the sector which has been actively implemented over the past four years. (5)

This strategy was based on a selective approach to the industry which identified 'target sectors' possessing 'high stable growth rates and a strong technological base':

The IDA rejected industries producing consumer goods which would decline in price each year. 'We had no desire to turn Ireland into the Asia of Europe' is how the present head of the IDA electronics division, Dr. Dave Hanna, describes the decision. Pocket calculators and digital watches were to be avoided: word processors, computers and medical equipment were to be encouraged. (6)

The IDA has not only sought to attract the electronics industry: it has also sought to popularise it. No other industrial sector in the Republic has had its rising export figures, its future employment projections or its 'infrastructural' requirements for expansion publicised in a comparable way. It has even been argued that the 'target sectors' of the industry possess characteristics which correspond <u>uniquely</u> with the needs of Irish national development. High technology, high skill, labour intensity, propensity to expand, good working conditions, environmental acceptability, low transport costs and low energy use have been cited as the uniquely suited combination of attributes embodied in the electronics industry. (7) Potential job losses resulting from microelectronic applications are routinely minimised by IDA representatives and it is implied that the growth of the Irish industry will, in the not-too-distant future, become self-sustaining, turning Ireland into the 'Silicon Valley of Europe'. (8) Indeed, some recent pronouncements emanating from the IDA have suggested that Ireland now possesses the 'fundamentals' of an integrated and dynamic electronics industry and that the Authority is now turning its attention to new pastures of high technology such as biotechnology.

At first sight this rapid expansion in electronics manufacturing is simply the continuation of a general feature of recent Irish industrial growth: the domination of manufacturing industry by branch plants of transnational corporations. During the period of tariff protection from the 1930s some Irish-owned manufacturing was created. Since the 'opening up' of the economy in 1958 these 'traditional' industries have declined, while foreign-owned factories have been responsible for the great majority of new industrial projects initiated with IDA assistance (grants and tax reliefs), for the creation of most new industrial jobs and for a continuously rising proportion of industrial output and exports. (9) Today foreign-owned companies employ some 80,000 workers, about one-third of the total manufacturing workforce of around 240,000. (10) In the electronics industry, as Table 1 shows, foreign ownership is even more pronounced: Irish-owned firms make up a small proportion of the total and are nearly all small in size.

Table 1
Electronics manufacturing plants in the Republic

Employees	Irish firms	US firms	Other firms	Row total
Less than 25	17	2	10	29
26 to 50	7	2	2	11
51 to 100	3	12	4	19
101 to 250	2	14	3	19
More than 251	2	9	4	15
Column total	31	39	23	93

Source: Postal survey.

The electronics factories are also similar to other foreign-owned plants in Ireland in that they are merely one stage in an international division of labour organised within the transnational corporation. Foreign-owned enterprises generally process or assemble raw materials imported to Ireland, usually from an affiliate of the parent company, and then export the product, usually again to an affiliate of the same company. This situation is most extreme in the case of the more capital-intensive and 'high technology' sectors of Irish industry. The chemical industry, for example, consists almost entirely of foreign-owned firms. In 1974 some 90 per cent of all the industry's sales were exported, and most of these exports were to affiliates of the same company. (11)

The growth of the Irish electronics industry appears therefore as simply another stage in the development of a branch plant economy: a growth caused by the twin processes of the decomposition of the labour process within the transnational corporation and the increasing competition for production sites between countries. (12) However, such a characterisation needs to be developed by a more detailed examination of, on the one hand, the particular role of the IDA in this overall process, and, on the other hand, the specific nature of the electronics industry.

The IDA's promotion of an Irish electronics industry (in the double sense of the promotion of Ireland as a manufacturing location to multinational firms and the promotion of this industry as a pearl of great price to the Republic's citizens) is comparable to that of the other competing regional or state development agencies of the European periphery. The IDA shares with the principal UK agencies, such as those for Scotland and Wales, the aim of attracting firms in 'high technology' sectors such as pharmaceuticals, electronics and other 'science-based' industries. The electronics industry is seen as a particularly desirable addition by these agencies because of the high growth rate of the western European market for electronic applications over the past few years, a growth rate which at least some industry analysts are predicting will be maintained in spite

of the current recession, (13) and because the fastest-
growing market segments are dominated by US companies which
might be persuaded to locate manufacturing plants in the
peripheral region or state served by the particular agency.
The emergent Japanese presence in the industry presents
similar opportunities.

The similarity of approach to the industry by the various
development agencies can be illustrated by comparing the
IDA's account of its electronics strategy with the strategic
proposals prepared for the Scottish Development Agency (SDA)
by the management consultants, Booz, Allen and Hamilton.
(14) In both cases the selection of 'target sectors' or 'key
areas' is based on similar projections of the likely growth
rates of electronic applications markets: these 'target
sectors' and 'key areas' are virtually identical as are the
specific applications within these 'sectors' or 'areas'
which are singled out for priority in promotional efforts.
(15) The one segment in which the relationship of the Republic to the international electronics industry differs
from that of Scotland is that of telecommunications and
here the difference is equivalent to that between the status
of region and that of nation-state. As a region Scotland is
effectively excluded from this area because the SDA has
little or no leverage on UK post office equipment purchasing
decisions. The Republic, on the other hand, has sought to
use a major investment programme to modernise its telephone
system as a means of promoting joint ventures and the transfer of technology and of 'spinning off' new Irish-owned
firms. (16)

Aside from the special case of telecommunications, what
seems to distinguish the IDA from other comparable state or
regional development agencies is its effectiveness in 'cap-
turing' the largest share of new electronics plants locating
in Europe for the Republic. A study of the attitudes of US
electronics company executives towards European plant
locations carried out for the SDA found that Germany,
Ireland and the UK were consistently preferred as potential
locations:

> Germany would be the first choice of most companies,
> except for the high manufacturing costs and particular
> aspects of labour legislation. Given these constraints,
> Ireland is the predominant first choice, primarily for
> the financial incentives offered. The UK is the pre-
> dominant second choice, but serious concern about
> labour attitudes was the major reservation. (17)

However, taken by themselves, financial incentives do not
seem to provide an adequate explanation of the IDA's
effectiveness. Wage costs and levels of grant assistance
appear to be broadly comparable in the peripheral regions
of the UK and Ireland, while the same study of company
executive attitudes found that the overriding consideration
in US company location decisions was the safety of the proposed investment for the company. This safety factor is

evaluated by these companies in terms of the wider issues of
the political and economic environment of the potential host
country. When the study ranked each preferred potential
location in Europe on the principal company investment
criteria, Ireland did best on those criteria relating to the
policies of the host state (with the exception of the provision of physical infrastructure and the education of
specialist labour), but rather less well on criteria relating to the country's geographical location or the perceived attitudes and attributes of its population. (18)
This positive perception of the Irish state compared to the
UK, we would argue, is the result of the way in which that
state is promoted by the IDA. The IDA is the only significant decision-making state body with which the incoming firm
has to deal - a 'one-stop shop' in the terminology of the
trade. Its autonomy within the Irish state apparatus allows
it to make all the important decisions relating to a project
internally in a manner free from 'political interference'.

This unitary and discretionary mode of operation contrasts
with the overlapping and fragmented promotional initiatives
undertaken not only on behalf of UK peripheral regions but
also by New Towns, local government districts etc. and with
the lack of political autonomy of these bodies. (19) The
SDA study found that US electronics executives considered
UK promotion to be slow and uncoordinated and UK representatives to lack relevant data. In some cases UK promotion
effort seems to have irritated and confused those at whom
it was aimed. (20) Even the major UK agencies do not enjoy
anything like the decision-making autonomy of the IDA: they
are subject to much greater control by the UK Civil Service
and to continuous political 'intrusion' into their activities, a situation which has reportedly led in some cases to
serious demoralisation among the agency staff. (21) The
question of the distinctive space occupied by the IDA within the Irish state is one we will return to in the second
part of this paper: it is now necessary to briefly examine
some general features of the international electronics
industry which are relevant to the Irish situation.

The international electronics industry has become
virtually synonymous with rapid and far-reaching technical
innovation. The potentiality of the ubiquitous silicon
'chip' is widely advertised and some observers have argued
that recent advances in micro-electronic technology are
laying the foundations of a dramatic and thorough-going
social transformation, the 'second (or third, or fourth)
industrial revolution'. (22) The new electronic technology
has been developed in the United States and in particular
on the West Coast in the 'Silicon Valley' area of California. American firms enjoy a substantial technical lead
over their European counterparts, although they now face
increasingly significant competition from Japanese producers. In the United States this rapid technical innovation
has taken place in a highly competitive context. In key
areas of component production and electronic application,
such as semiconductors, wordprocessors and mini-computers

new producers have been able to enter the market with relative ease. Intensive price competition, reflected in dramatic reductions in the cost of electronic components and products, has thus become the norm in an industry where rapidly changing technological conditions dictate high levels of research and development expenditure. (23)

The international mobility of US electronics firms is highly influenced by the interlocking technological and competitive structures of the industry. In order to reduce wage costs, in the 1960s US semiconductor firms developed a 'globalised' system of production. While the more highly skilled sections of the labour process (research and development, final testing) remained in the USA, midway through the manufacturing process components were shipped from the USA to Asia for actual assembly and then re-imported to the USA in built-up form. This decomposition of the labour process therefore not only allowed the firms to take advantage of cheap Asian labour, it also created a polarisation of skill within the now transnational enterprise. (24)

The 'new wave' of US electronics firms have also begun to move production facilities to Europe. This has occurred for rather different reasons than the expansion of offshore assembly in Asia. In order to establish themselves within the large European market, US firms carry out final stage assembly in Europe behind EEC tariff barriers. In addition, the need to service their European customers means that not only is a regional marketing organisation established, but also both final stage testing and some minor R&D (essentially the adaptation of US products to European market conditions and technical regulations) are now relocated outside the USA. However, basic R&D - the genuinely high skill section of the labour process - remains behind in the USA. At the same time, the generous financial incentives in the form of grants and tax reliefs offered by the competing regional development agencies in Europe allow companies to offset the drain on their capital resources from high US R&D costs in a competitive industry by gaining access to European state funds.

While European development agencies tend to claim that they have 'chosen' electronics as a growth area, the reality is the other way round. The electronics industry's ability to relocate its production processes internationally and its desperate need for extra sources of finance have ensured that in fact it has chosen them. The success or otherwise of the different and competing agencies is only a factor within this general situation. However, inside Ireland the electronics industry is being presented not just as creating jobs, but as being an industry that is uniquely suited to national needs. Such statements, as we shall now argue, illustrate the IDA's promotional flair rather than its grasp of reality.

Central to the claims being made for electronics is the

notion that it is a high skill industry. The IDA has laid great stress on its projection that over one third of the manufacturing labour force in electronics in 1985 will be in the professional or highly skilled categories. Table 2 sets out the IDA's current projections for skilled employment in the electronics industry in 1985 and converts these absolute figures into percentages of the projected total employment of 30,000 in the sector. Table 3 gives the current composition of the entire workforce as reported by our survey in early 1981.

Table 2
IDA skill projections for the electronics
manufacturing labour force 1985

Occupational Group	No. Employed	Percent of total labour force
Managerial Staff	2,000	6.6
Electronic Engineers	2,500	8.3
Electronic Technicians	3,500	11.6
Computer Programmers/ Systems Analysis	2,500	8.3
Skilled Craftsmen	1,000	3.3
Total	11,500	38.1

Source: Killeen, 'Electronics Revolution', Table 7, p.15.

Table 3
Current composition of electronics labour force

Occupation Group	Employees	Percent	Females	Percent female in each group
Managers	725	6.4	32	4.4
Supervisors	581	5.1	141	24.3
Administrative	444	3.9	143	32.2
Professional	607	5.3	45	7.4
Technicians	886	7.8	33	3.7
Clerical	848	7.5	609	71.8
Craftsmen	348	3.1	4	1.2
Non-craft Production workers	6527	57.4	4695	71.9
Others	372	3.2	93	25.0
Total	11,338		5795	(51.1)

Source: Postal survey.

The two sets of figures are not entirely comparable owing to the different categories used, but nonetheless our findings do suggest a considerable overestimate by the IDA of skilled employment. Thus the IDA claims that the total 'professional/highly skilled' groups will amount to 38.1 per cent of the workforce by 1985. By contrast, our survey shows that in 1981 only 21.6 per cent of the workforce could be unambiguously so classified: the IDA's proportions can only be reached if the (extremely dubious) assumption is made that our categories of 'supervisors', 'administrative' and 'clerical' workers in fact contain large numbers of the IDA's 'electronic engineers' and 'programmers/systems analysts'. (25)

Our own figures also give, as the IDA's do not, the sex composition of the workforce. Given the unequal access of women to technical and professional jobs, the possibility that the supervisory, administrative and clerical workers are in fact 'professional/highly skilled' becomes even more unlikely when one notices the significant proportions of these workers who are women. Furthermore, as Table 3 shows, more than half of the total workforce of the industry and nearly three-quarters of the non-craft production workers are women: <u>prima facie</u> evidence that much of the workforce is employed in routine semiskilled assembly work.

The term 'skill' has so far been used in this paper in purely conventional terms. However, many studies have argued that official definitions of skill cannot be simply taken for granted. Firstly, there is considerable evidence that in industry as a whole both management and unions tend to overstate skill requirements by regrading jobs upwards while the actual content remains the same; that formal and certified skills may well be required for access to certain jobs but are not necessarily then used in the job itself; and that formal training is required more as a method of inculcating acceptance of managerial authority than for its actual technical content. (26) Since it is largely men who occupy such formally skilled jobs and who possess formally certified skills, our figures which (like those of the IDA) take for granted official definitions of skill, will tend to overestimate the technical skills actually utilised by male workers in the industry. Secondly, for women the situation is the other way round, since here official definitions underestimate 'skill'. In 'light' assembly work in general and in the electronics industry in particular, women are employed for their 'natural manual dexterity'. This dexterity is however not 'natural' at all, but the result of informal training in domestic labour which, because it occurs in the home, does not appear in official definitions. Such processes ensure that in the Irish electronics industry, as elsewhere, 'skill has been increasingly defined <u>against</u> women - skilled work is work that women don't do'. (27)

This sexual division of labour within the Irish electronics industry is hardly unique. As Booz, Allen and Hamilton reported to the Scottish Development Agency:

> Employment in the Scottish electronics industry breaks down into two basic groups: (i) Direct labour and non-professional support staff; predominantly female. (ii) Managerial, professional and technical support staff; predominantly male. (28)

This high proportion of formally 'unskilled' female production workers, together with the low proportion of formally qualified male 'skilled' workers, challenges the

image of a 'high skill' industry as promoted by the IDA.
The image derives its power from the sophistication of the
electronics industry's products, but, given in particular
the international decomposition of the labour process, such
products hardly require a highly skilled workforce at every
stage of their manufacture. There is no necessary and universal connection between 'high technology' products and
'highly skilled' workers. Indeed, the Irish electronics
industry suspiciously resembles what the IDA claims it is
not promoting: the 'offshore assembly' plants of the Far
East with their overwhelmingly female and semiskilled work-
forces, often cited as the classic example of the way in
which the decomposition of the labour process within the
transnational corporation creates an international hierarchy
of skill and gender. (29)

The IDA's claims for the skill structure of the electronics industry are therefore clearly exaggerated. (30) It is
possible, although there is as yet no direct evidence of
this, that its claims that the industry is environmentally
'clean' are equally false. While the IDA has stressed the
attractiveness of working conditions in electronics, recent
US studies have indicated that workers in the industry
face potentially serious health hazards:

> The electronics industry is generally considered to be
> 'clean' and 'light' but many workers face very stress-
> ful working conditions and risk exposure to hundreds
> of toxic chemicals. The tedious hand work that must be
> performed in this space-age industry, coupled with
> exposure to untested combinations of chemicals, create
> potentially hazardous working conditions that few
> scientists have yet investigated. (31)

Research is currently being carried out in California on the
possible increase in the risk of breast cancer faced by
production workers exposed to certain solvents which are in
everyday use in the industry. (32) Equally, the serious eye-
damage that results from assembly work in micro-electronics
in South-East Asia - in plants that would seem to be not so
dissimilar to Irish plants as is usually believed - is well
documented:

> A 1975 study conducted in South Korea by the Urban
> Industrial Mission, an international church group,
> concluded that of the women who work at the micro-
> scopes, bonding super-fine wires to wafer-thin chips,
> nearly half suffered from near-sightedness and 19 per
> cent suffered astigmatism ... In Hong Kong ... from
> extensive interviewing it emerges that at one time or
> another, most workers contract conjunctivitis, a pain-
> ful and highly contagious eye ailment. After three or
> four years of peering through a microscope, a worker's
> vision begins to permanently blur, so that she can no
> longer meet the production quota. (33)

In public the IDA presents trade union representation of
workers in foreign-owned industry as a normal and indeed

required feature of the projects it aids. In practice however this is another area where the IDA's claims for the electronics industry diverge from the reality on the ground. Unlike most foreign industry in the Republic, the electronics industry is concentrated in the major urban areas of Dublin, Limerick/Shannon and (more recently) Cork. Electronics has thus become the major source of new industrial employment in cities whose traditional manufacturing base has been heavily eroded since the implementation of free trade policies. This is most striking in the case of Dublin, where in the last few years the major contribution of the IDA to the restructuring of industry in the region has been the influx of electronics plants. However, despite this concentration of the industry in urban areas, our survey reveals that some 30 per cent of all plants are non-unionised.

As might be expected, non-unionisation is clearly related to plant size, with the bulk of non-union plants employing less than 25 people (Table 4). However, as Table 4 shows, non-unionisation is also related to the national origin of the firm: all Irish firms and all but one 'other foreign' (i.e. non-US) firms employing more than 50 people are unionised, while many large US firms are not unionised.

Further, as Table 5 shows, non-unionised plants are most common in the Limerick/Shannon area. Here in fact the relationship between size and unionisation does not hold. In both Dublin and 'elsewhere' all but one of the plants employing more than 50 people are unionised, but in Limerick/Shannon only 7 of the 13 plants with more than 50 employees are unionised, a level of trade union organisation which is equal to that for plants with less than 50 employees in the region. This regional variation is significant for two reasons, Firstly, Limerick/Shannon is being promoted as a prime location for electronics manufacturing, not least because of the stress on electronics training and research, closely tied to the needs of local firms, at the National Institute for Higher Education in Limerick. Secondly, the Limerick/Shannon area, unlike Cork or Dublin, is a region where industry has been built up almost entirely on the basis of new foreign (largely US) firms and where their factories probably provide a far higher proportion of total manufacturing employment than in other urban areas of the country.

These findings support the view that electronics is internationally an industry characterised by an unusually strong managerial resistance to trade unionism. As the SDA consultants' report cited earlier notes:

The degree of unionisation is also considered to be an important factor by US companies in locating new facilities. Although unions are as prevalent in the US in medium and heavy industry as they are in the UK and elsewhere in Europe, differences appear to exist for the US electronics industry. The belief of US executives

Table 4
Unionisation of plants:
by plant size and national ownership

National Ownership		Plant Size					
		Less than 25	26-50	50-100	101-250	250+	Row total
Irish	Unionised	4	5	3	2	2	16
	Non-unionised	12	2	0	0	0	14
US	Unionised	0	2	11	9	8	30
	Non-unionised	2	0	1	5	1	9
Other Foreign	Unionised	5	2	3	3	4	17
	Non-unionised	5	0	1	0	0	6
Column Total		28	11	19	19	15	92

Source: Postal survey.

Table 5
Unionisation by area

Area		Plant Size		
		Less than 50 employees	50+ employees	Row total
Dublin	Unionised	2	17	19
	Non-unionised	7	1	8
Limerick/Clare	Unionised	7	7	14
	Non-unionised	6	6	12
Elsewhere	Unionised	9	21	30
	Non-unionised	8	1	9
Column Total		39	53	92

Source: Postal survey.

is that companies in the industry have adopted personnel policies and practices that reduce demand for unionisation. As a consequence of this belief, the judgement of US executives is that the majority of successful US electronics companies are not unionised to any great degree. (34)

Interestingly, such executives managed to unite this hostile attitude to trade unionism with a favourable perception of the Republic of Ireland's labour legislation. It is also worth noting that in Scotland, after the Republic the most popular location for US companies within the European periphery, a recent survey shows that up to 30 per cent of all US-owned plants of all sizes in all industries are not unionised. (35)

This characteristic of the industry potentially undermines a central, if largely implicit, element of the national consensus on which acceptance of both the IDA's industrial strategy and its political autonomy has been based: the belief that incoming firms will allow trade union organisation. Hitherto, radical criticism has merely argued against the agreements negotiated between a particular union, the firm, and the IDA. By such 'sweetheart deals', so it is claimed, workers are simply assigned to the union before the factory has even opened. Consequently, critics argue, effective rank and file organisation is prevented, negotiation on non-wage issues effectively precluded and, in particular, working conditions are simply imposed on an unprepared workforce.

Given the lack of systematic research in this area, it is difficult to know how true this widespread perception is. (36) However, not even the IDA's critics have as yet seen non-unionisation as a widespread or significant problem. Their failure to do so is further and startling testimony to the effectiveness of the IDA's promotion of the electronics industry within Ireland.

THE IDEOLOGICAL USES OF ELECTRONICS

The first part of this paper contrasted the ideology of the IDA with the reality of Ireland's electronics industry. The IDA claims to be building an Irish industrial base but its policies lead to increasing dependence on foreign companies. Its promises of attractive and highly skilled jobs prove, when examined, to be questionable, at the very least. In the second part of the paper it is argued that, in spite of the extravagant and untenable claims which have accompanied it, the 'hyping' of the electronics industry has enabled the IDA to legitimate in particularly effective ways its whole broader strategy of private enterprise industrialisation.

Ever since the 'opening up of the economy' in 1958 it has been a basic tenet of Irish government policy that

industrialisation should be based on private enterprise.
(37) The private sector has been constituted as the
dynamic element in national economic growth with a subsidiary servicing role allotted to state enterprises. In
consequence the trade union movement has been denied any
direct influence on industrial strategy. Unlike other
'semi-state' bodies in the Republic, such as the Industrial
Training Authority (AnCO), or the state broadcasting service
(RTE), the trade unions have no representation on the board
of the IDA. Trade union pressure for direct state initiatives in the productive sphere has hitherto produced a
negligible response from successive governments while the
IDA gives no grants or other aid to state-owned industry.
(38)

   The IDA is, literally, a 'businesslike' organisation
committed in its policy and in its mode of operation to the
spirit of entrepreneurial capitalism. It enjoys a remarkable
lack of parliamentary scrutiny, its staffing is distinct
from that of the Civil Service and its personnel frequently
move into the employment of the very companies that they
have attracted to Ireland in the first place. (39) In
similar fashion the characteristic development pattern of
the electronics industry, particularly the proliferation of
relatively new firms, allows US managements to see themselves as reasserting the dynamism of free enterprise. The
rapid technological innovation prevalent in the industry
is frequently attributed by them to the strength of the
spirit of free competition in the USA. As Robert Noyce, a
leading spokesman for the semiconductor industry, put it
recently:

      In the face of a capital shortage (in the USA), and
      lack of new engineering graduates there, the strange
      fact is that there is more venture capital available
      and more new electronics companies being formed than
      ever before. There are many factors contributing to
      this, among them changes in capital gains taxes and
      recognition that electronics leads the second industrial
      revolution which is probably more important than the
      first. Yet I feel the principal cause is the rekindling
      of the pioneer spirit in America (emphasis added). (40)

   Such claims ignore the fact that a major cause of the
dominant international position enjoyed by US electronics
firms has been the technological stimulus derived from
massive state funding of research for military purposes.
(41) Similarly the threat to this dominance posed by the
emergence of intensified Japanese competition has elicited
a distinctly protectionist response from US producers. (42)
Equally the 'pioneer spirit' does not extend to all those
who work in the industry. Production workers in the
'Silicon Valley' are poorly paid but very few are organised
in trade unions. There is evidence of concerted action by
firms in the industry to keep the workforce unorganised.
This workforce is overwhelmingly female and contains a very
high proportion of workers who are immigrants or members of

other disadvantaged ethnic minorities. (43) But the widely disseminated _image_ of 'Silicon Valley' is one of creative, mobile and highly-paid professionals converting their expertise and ingenuity into commercial success. (44) It is this pioneering image (and self-image) of 'Silicon Valley' which converges with the technocratic ideology of the IDA in a conception of 'business' which links private entre-preneurship with technological dynamism and restores the individual entrepreneur to his traditional heroic role. The 'high technology' of the electronics industry is equated with high skill levels in the workforce, and national industrial development, the task of the IDA, becomes identified with a reinvigorated and extended commitment to the privatisation of the economy. The impetus towards such privatisation derived from the ideological fusion of high technology and national development is illustrated by two recent initiatives of the IDA.

In February 1981 the IDA was actively involved in an attempt to create a venture capital company, Eireven, 'for the specific purpose of investing in high technology industries in the USA through a venture capital fund'. (45) Eireven's capital was to be raised in Ireland and its activities would, it was claimed, lead to the eventual establishment of branch plants in Ireland when the time came for the companies in whom the capital would be invested to expand their activities overseas. Exchange control regulations were waived by the Irish Central Bank to allow the company to export capital to the USA. (46) In tandem with Eireven, a second company, McElveen & Mills, was formed to provide investment advice to it. The composition of the Board of McElveen & Mills illustrates the close links between the IDA and both US and Irish private interests:

> (The) company consists of Ivor McElveen, a former IDA man who for five years was its west coast director in the US, Charles Mills, a US lawyer whose particular field is acquisitions, venture capital financing and corporate reorganisation and two other directors, Maurice O'Kelly the managing director of Guinness Mahon (a leading Irish merchant bank) in Dublin and a Mr. George Curran, a director of the California First Bank. (47)

Eireven is at present in abeyance because its shares when offered to Irish financial institutions were undersub-scribed. However, it retains its capital export permission and the project may proceed at a later date. (48)

Also in February 1981 it became known that the IDA had approached a number of American doctors with a view to setting up a luxury medical clinic in Dublin for patients from outside Ireland. The Irish Medical Times reported that two professors at the Harvard Medical School were negotia-ting with the IDA to set up a 300-bed hospital costing in the region of IR£30m. Confirming these reports an IDA spokesman was quoted as follows:

He said that this was part of the Authority's service
industry programme under which it attracted firms to
the country, in areas such as engineering which exported a service instead of a product. The clinic
would be exporting medical care. The consumers would
come here to get it and then go back home again. This
would not be cutting across the existing Irish
hospitals. (49)

The export-orientation of the scheme was further emphasised:

It was likely however that the fees would be closer to
those charged in the United States than private fees
here. (50)

Although private medicine is securely and profitably
entrenched in the Republic the proposal to set up such a
'service industry' clinic represents a new departure in its
complete commodification of health care. The use of state
funds to aid its creation raises political questions about
who benefits from this care since employment could just as
easily be created by the state spending more on health
services urgently required by Irish people. But such
questions are occluded once health care is redefined as a
a 'service industry'; high technology, it turns out, plays
a crucial part in this redefinition:

The idea has come to the IDA as a logical extension of
its present activities according to the spokesman: 'we
are very involved in electronics and in the health care
industry. In the course of our work we realised that a
lot of electronics products are geared towards medical
care. This prompted us to get into contact with people
directly involved in medical care'. (51)

In the event, the project was stymied, for the present at
least, not by considerations of the public welfare, or the
role of state expenditure in promoting that welfare, but by
an affronted private interest - the local medical establishment in the form of the Medical Council, with whom the US
doctors would be required by law to register. (52)

The involvement of the IDA in these projects illustrates
the present institutional constraints on the promotion by
the state of such freewheeling privatisation even when it
is linked to the glamour of high technology. In the one
case Irish private financial interests do not appear to
have found the IDA's venture capital scheme sufficiently
attractive. In the other a powerful Irish professional
interest has succeeded in doing what no trade union or
community group has ever done - frustrating an undesired
IDA initiative. (53) In general however, the IDA has
succeeded in coupling the 'dynamism' of technological
innovation epitomised by the electronics industry to its
private enterprise orientation: since 'everyone' is, of
course, in favour of dynamism it follows that 'everyone'
ends up also being in favour of private enterprise. But,
given the overwhelming dominance of foreign firms in high
technology industry, the problem remains of how this private

enterprise strategy can be presented as a <u>national</u> one.

Like any other development agency in the business, the IDA stresses the contribution that foreign firms make to 'our' economy. Its claims derive considerable plausibility from the reality of industrial jobs in areas where emigration had previously provided the only alternative to the service sector or to agriculture. Given the sophistication of its information management techniques, this plausibility is not necessarily diminished by the frequently exaggerated nature of the claims made nor by the failure to take into account the negative effects, such as large scale redundancies in vulnerable sectors, of the overall industrial strategy. (54) The process of acceptance has also been facilitated by factors specific to Ireland's international situation. Dependent industrialisation has lessened Ireland's historic dependence on the British market, leading to a steady fall in the proportion of Irish exports going to the UK since the late 1950s. Although the UK remains the largest single Irish export market this pattern contrasts with the preceding period during which protectionist policies made little or no impact on Ireland's trade dependence on Britain. At the same time membership of the EEC has given the Republic a political arena broader than the narrow confines of Anglo-Irish relations. Rapid nativisation of local management has also contributed to the acceptability of foreign firms. On the basis of a sample of new overseas firms employing over 100 people at the end of 1974 McAleese estimated that 84 per cent of managers in new overseas industry were Irish and observed that 'in general US firms tend to hire proportionately more Irish managers than European firms'. (55) Thus potential opposition to foreign control of industry along traditional nationalist lines is effectively defused.

In recent years the nativisation of industry through the promotion of small Irish-owned firms has been proclaimed as a central policy objective of the IDA. By the beginning of 1980 small grant-aided firms employed about 23,000 people and, in the same year, small firms accounted for one-third of the IDA's total job approvals. According to the IDA:

> This level of native enterprise - over 90 per cent of small firms are promoted by Irish men and women - illustrates a coming of age of our economy and points the way towards a new era of greater involvement by Irish people as owner/managers in manufacturing industry. (56)

The Enterprise Development Programme, deriving from the Industrial Development Act (1977), offers grant and back-up services to individuals setting up their own businesses. Its formal objective is to encourage Irish persons with technical, managerial and commercial skills to start their own manufacturing industries. Particular stress has been laid on linking the small, new Irish-owned minnows to the foreign-owned whales. As an interview with the IDA's recently-appointed Managing Director puts it:

195

According to White, the IDA has now achieved a growth
period of large and high technology industry which has
in turn opened up completely new opportunities for
smaller companies. The whole of the recent Enterprise
Development Programme which created many small companies was based on technology brought in by the bigger
- and usually foreign - companies. (57)

The electronics industry has been singled out for particular
attention in these small firm development efforts as likely
to produce a wide range of opportunities for such technology transfer through managerial mobility. (58) However
the role of Irish-owned firms in this industry is, as yet
at least, marginal. Irish-owned firms account for only 16
per cent of total employment in the industry; this compares
with roughly 65 per cent of employment in manufacturing
industry as a whole. Irish-owned firms, with the aid of the
IDA's Project Identification Unit, may supply an increasing
volume of materials to the industry. But, just as 'high
technology' products do not necessarily provide highly
skilled work, it can hardly be assumed that all such
locally-purchased supplies embody 'high technology spin-
off'.

The importance of the IDA's commitment to small, supposedly 'high technology' Irish firms lies in the fact that it
promotes the centrality of private enterprise to Irish
industrial strategy in a way that is far more credible than
merely subsidising foreign firms. The likelihood that such
firms will in practice often pay low wages and provide
irregular employment in non-unionised conditions where the
state's weak industrial safety regime is least effective is
obscured in this search for greater involvement of Irish
people in 'our' economy. Given the strong nationalist
current within the Irish trade union movement it is hardly
surprising that there has been little criticism of this
approach. Indeed, at local level, the most common trade
union response to factory closures is that the IDA 'do
something': much publicised visits by IDA representatives
promising replacement jobs then ensure that the impression
is created through the media that something is indeed being
done. Evidence of the failure of the system is thus publicly
transformed into a celebration of its resourcefulness. The
existing strategy is further cemented and a wedge is driven
between local demands for industrial jobs and the alternative development strategies formally advocated through
centralised state bargaining and consultative mechanisms by
the trade union movement. (59) Such activity has helped to
manage growing unemployment politically, even though the
jobs have obstinately refused to materialise in the
quantities promised, while the promotion of private enterprise through the various small industries programmes helps
to ensure that a vital precondition for dependent industrialisation is reproduced - that mysterious 'political
climate' which is so important to foreign firms. It is, in
this context, merely ironic that the continuing level of
state support and 'hand-holding' required by these small
firms effectively gives a new meaning to the concept of

'private enterprise'. (60)

THE ELECTRONICS INDUSTRY AND THE RESTRUCTURING OF EDUCATION

The development of small Irish firms is presented by the IDA as transferring and nativising 'high technology' through the skill and expertise of individual Irish 'entre-preneurs'. But perhaps the most effective initiative of the IDA in the field of 'high technology' is the way in which its projection of electronics as a high skill industry has been mobilised to produce a major reorientation of the Republic's education system. We have already argued that estimates of the skill level in the electronics industry are overestimated even when the existing categories and definitions of skill are accepted, and that the numerically small and quite specific skills and qualifications that are needed within this industry have been treated as defining its whole labour force as skilled. We now suggest that the same process can be seen to operate on an even wider level outside the industry within the state's education system. Here the relatively restricted needs of the industry have been used to promote a whole ideology of education.

Education in capitalist societies serves a dual function: it reproduces the class system and it legitimates the pattern of social inequality produced by that system. The hierarchical class division of labour rests on the differ-ential transmission of technical skills and social re-sources to its different classes. (61) Within this process of transmission different class levels of participation in formal education play a crucial role in the reproduction of class inequality. (62) At the same time schooling, or educational attainment, by appearing to relate differences in wealth and power to formally demonstrable individual achievements, provides, because of its 'objective' basis, perhaps the most powerful tool for the ideological legit-imation of inequality in these societies. (63) As else-where, this is the case in the Republic of Ireland - only more so. As Tussing has argued:

> The Irish educational system is more effective than those of most other countries in perpetuating or re-producing the existing highly stratified social class make-up of Ireland. (64)

In support of this contention he cites the way in which participation rates in Irish education taper off sharply immediately after the compulsory attendance age of 15, the imbalance in the distribution of public money among the three levels of the Irish educational system, the bias in expenditure per pupil at secondary level in favour of the schooling of better-off pupils and the extreme dispropor-tion in the number of students from upper social class backgrounds in the universities. (65) Perhaps most remark-able of all is the evidence from the higher education sector that almost two decades of rapid expansion in the

197

educational system has produced almost no change in the social class backgrounds of university students. Figures from University College Dublin, the Republic's largest university, indicate that the intake of students from working class backgrounds tended to rise between the mid-1960s and the mid-1970s but has since then fallen back to its original level. (66)

The impetus for the expansion of the Irish education system in the 1960s and '70s derived from the wider processes of postwar international economic integration and liberalisation which also provided some of the essential preconditions for the 'opening up' of the Republic's economy – the adoption of free trade policies and membership of the EEC. Thus the key Irish educational policy document of the period, the 'Investment in Education' report, which laid the basis for the introduction of free post-primary schooling, free school transport and means-tested grants for students in higher education, had its origins in initiatives taken by the OECD and, in particular, in a recommendation from an OECD conference held in 1961 that member states should examine their education systems to assess their degree of adaptation to 'the future requirements of scientific progress and economic growth'. (67) Published in 1965, this report explicitly linked a human capital theory of education to an insistence on the need to increase equality of opportunity within the education system. In classic social democratic fashion increased education was seen as ensuring both economic growth and social equality. Although there was some stress on the need to shift educational content in more 'relevant' directions this remained at a fairly general level and occurred within the report's overall emphasis on the importance of a well-educated workforce as a productive resource.

But although the expansion of higher education from the mid-1960s has in fact been characterised by a strong technological and vocational orientation (68) a new and radically different approach to educational policy is evident since 1979. The new emphasis is on a fine tuning of the education system to 'manpower needs' and on the detailed control of educational content in order to greatly increase the supply of specific technical skills. A newly created body, the Manpower Consultative Committee (MCC), has assumed strategic control over new educational investment decisions. Politically, questions about access to education or discussion of its ideological role, whose pertinence has been greatly increased by developments within the system over the past two decades, are occluded by an insistence on the simple technical role of education in servicing the demands which, it is claimed, are being made by rapid economic growth. The agenda for educational change is to be set by the problems allegedly posed by industrial success, not by those of social inequality: under this new regime the Managing Director of the IDA can justifiably claim that Ireland 'has a higher education closely in touch with industry'. (69)

It was largely on the initiative of the IDA that the Manpower Consultative Committee which comprises representatives of employers, trade unions and government agencies was set up in 1978 'to advise on the role of manpower policy in economic development'. Three priority areas for action were identified: shortages of labour in skilled occupations, a bias in social attitudes against industrial employment and the incidence of youth unemployment. (70) In the area of youth unemployment the MCC has to date limited itself to pointing out the inadequacies of existing sources of information about the extent and nature of the problem in Ireland. It has called for more research in the area but it has not carried out or sought funds for any such research. In the case of attitudes to industrial employment, while the MCC's concern may appear eccentric in the context of rapidly increasing youth and general unemployment, it has led to concrete initiatives in the field of education. Diagnosing lack of information as the primary cause of this alleged bias, the MCC has advocated the provision of a careers guidance service to all second-level schools. An already expanding area of professional specialisation has thus found itself, and its further expansion, cast in a key role in a campaign to provide the nation with a technically-trained workforce. The MCC is also seeking to encourage the inculcation of positive attitudes towards industry and towards technological change in general through educational broadcasting and other mass media. (71)

The MCC's major intervention has been at the third (higher) education level where its initiatives have been organised around the estimation of supply and demand trends within the economy for various 'key worker' categories in some cases to the mid-1980s and in others to the end of the decade. (72) The MCC's concrete influence on third level education can be traced in the genesis of the Programme of New Educational Opportunities introduced in the Autumn of 1979 to overcome specific skill shortages identified by the MCC. These shortages fell into two categories. First, apprenticeship-based craft skills, such as fitter, toolmaker, plasterer and bricklayer: here remedial action came under the jurisdiction of AnCO, the Republic's industrial training authority, which coordinates and grant-aids apprenticeship schemes. Second, occupations which usually require formal qualifications obtained through higher educational courses - engineers, technicians, technologists and computer professionals. Projecting supply and demand trends to 1985 the MCC predicted that a current (1979) estimated shortage of 200 mechanical/production/industrial engineers would increase fourfold, a shortage of 250 electrical/electronic engineers would be four and a half times as great and a shortage of 200 electronic technicians would be six times as great. (73) To cope with these projected shortages in the short term, a highly publicised recruitment campaign to induce people with these skills and qualifications to come or to return to Ireland was launched in the UK. (74)

In the medium term, a Programme of New Educational Opportunities was devised. 'Working closely with the Manpower Consultative Committee' the Higher Education Authority, the statutory body responsible for the administration of government funding to higher education, invited the Republic's higher educational institutions to submit proposals for expanding output from existing courses and organising conversion courses for graduates in related subject areas in the specialisms identified as suffering from critical manpower shortages. A package of proposals was then presented, through the MCC, for approval by the Minister for Education. (75) Maintenance grants were paid, at a remarkably generous level by Irish standards, by the Department of Labour to students attending the hastily introduced conversion courses.

The preparation and approval of the 1979 package marked a major shift in control over higher educational policy and finance, and the emergent hegemony of an external 'manpower planning' agency over the established institutions of educational policy-making in the Irish state. The recent White Paper on Educational Development, which sets out the policy framework for the planned expansion of the educational system through the 1980s, confirms this trend by establishing the 'needs of the labour market' as the primary criterion for higher educational investment and formalising the MCC's status as arbiter of these needs. (76) The practical impact of this shift in control can be seen, above all, in the massive expansion in the output of engineering qualifications at both graduate (degree) and technician (diploma or certificate) level which is currently under way in the Republic. The annual output of graduate engineers will virtually double between 1980 and 1990, rising from an estimated 599 (of whom 74 qualified by way of the new conversion courses) to 1,777. The annual output of technicians will grow at an even faster rate, with a projected increase from 950 to 2,540 between 1979 and 1989. (77) Within engineering education, a major shift in the balance of specialisation is also under way. At graduate level, the output in the civil/structural category is projected to fall slightly over the decade: the proportion of engineers specialising in this area will therefore have fallen considerably by 1990. Hence the output in other areas, particularly in the mechanical/production/industrial and electrical/electronic categories, is projected to rise at an even higher rate than the graduate output as a whole.

This expansion of engineering education is, according to the MCC, necessary to meet the manpower needs of the Republic's economy. These needs, it emerges, are IDA projections as transmitted to the education system, apparently without any intervening process of scrutiny or appraisal, by the MCC. This becomes clear when we turn from the supply side to the demand side of this supposed manpower equation. Table 6 sets out the projected sources of demand for graduate engineers over the 1980s.

Table 6
Projected sources of demand
for graduate engineers, 1980-1990

	1981	1982	1983	1984	1985	1986-1990
Total demand arising	977	991	953	969	941	4789
Of which, per cent attributable to:						
IDA manufacturing	37	39	41	40	41	41
IDA services	27	28	28	29	30	29
Incremental Demand non-IDA private sector	8	8	8	8	8	8
Incremental public sector demand	18	14	9	12	10	11
Replacement demand	10	10	10	10	11	10

Source: J. Corcoran, 'Demand and Supply', paper read to the Second Conference on Engineering Manpower for Economic Development, Table 3.

Seventy per cent of the projected demand for graduate engineering 'manpower' is accounted for by the growth of IDA manufacturing and service projects. The obvious conclusion is drawn in the MCC's 1980 Report:

> These projections point to a demand of between 900 and 1,000 for graduate engineers arising each year between now and 1990. A crucial assumption in the projections is the demand arising from IDA activities which account for a large proportion of the demand arising in any year. Any change here would necessitate a revision of the estimates. (78)

More specifically, the selling of electronics as a high technology/high skill industry has played a key role in the subjection of higher education to the 'manpower needs of industry'. IDA representatives have insisted on the relationship between educational change and the full flowering of this most attractive of industries:

> The availability of highly trained personnel is central to the development of electronics in Ireland ... At the moment 100 electrical engineers and 200 electrical technicians graduate annually. Proposals are now being implemented to raise these to 200 and 320 p.a. by 1983. The projections indicate that by the mid-1980s it will be necessary to increase the output of engineers/ technicians fourfold over existing levels. (79)

Indeed the IDA's claims for the existence of a very high skill level in the industry have been built into the MCC's engineering demand projections.

In the case of IDA manufacturing and service industry projects the assumption has been made that 20 per cent of the 15,000 'first time jobs' which will actually be created in each year from 1980 will be in electronics and that 8 per cent of the electronics workforce and 0.5 per cent of the remainder of the manufacturing workforce will be graduate engineers. (80) Again the IDA's firm round projection of the demand for electronic technicians shines like a beacon over the murky 'data base' on which the estimates of overall supply and demand for technicians have had to be made. As the Secretary of the MCC observed in a paper read to the first of two recent conferences on Engineering Manpower for Economic Development:

> While there has been considerable progress made in firming up estimates of present demand and future man-power needs in the various engineering streams the labour market position on engineering technicians is not so clear. The demand position for electronic technicians is probably the exception here since the phenomenal growth of the electronics industry and the success of IDA in attracting new electronics projects here has concentrated sufficient attention on the very key manpower needs of the industry ... (81)

We have already shown that the IDA's projections seriously overestimate the professional manpower requirements of the Republic's electronics industry. Our scepticism concerning the reliability of IDA projections is shared by other investigators. (82) This scepticism is further increased, in the case of the MCC's projections, by the results of a survey of firms carried out by the National Manpower Service which shows that between June 1979 and July 1980 vacancies decreased substantially in all the critical engineering and technical categories in which the MCC had projected rapidly accumulating shortages over the 1979-84 period. (83) Referring to this survey, the Secretary of the MCC has attributed the decrease 'mainly to the recession'. (84) Remarkably, the MCC has not, as yet, revised its projections to take this 'demand' factor into account. Its accumulating shortages continue to hark back, as if in a time warp, to the briefly heady days of 'the Irish economic miracle' of 1978-79. Again, the available evidence on the experience of conversion courses and other graduates in the skill shortage disciplines in finding jobs may be fragmentary but it does suggest that for a substantial number the need of industry for their manpower has proved illusory. It is, for example, reported that almost half of the graduates of University College Cork's Computer Science Diploma conversion course in 1980 had to emigrate to find work. The MCC in its latest report admits that 'preliminary indications are somewhat disappointing insofar as entry to employment is concerned for those completing conversion courses in 1980'. (85) Perhaps as a result of such experiences computer 'professions' have receded into obscurity in the skill shortage literature and maintenance grants were withdrawn from students enrolling for conversion courses in these subjects before the start of the 1980/81 academic year. Recent press comment based on information from the careers advisory services of third level colleges suggests that this problem extends well beyond the occupations of computer programmer and analyst. (86)

The withdrawal of financial support from particular courses at short notice may be a logical consequence of the adoption of a fine tuning approach to educational supply: it appears, however, that labour market demand is not amenable to such precise, if - to the individual student and to the education system - costly, manipulation. If this is the case, then fine tuning may well put Irish education back where it was before the recent period of expansion began in the 1960s, servicing a 'brain drain' of highly qualified professionals to more economically advanced states at the expense of the Republic's relatively impoverished taxpayers. (87) This situation is a common one in other states with a comparable pattern of dependent industrialisation: in these states too a policy of gearing the education system towards the extensive production of scientific and technical manpower seems only to have aggravated the 'brain drain' or led to the chronic underemployment of such graduates. (88)

In relation to the specific question of educational ideology, what matters is not whether the MCC's projections are fulfilled or not, but the fact that the technocratic concerns underlying such exercises effectively set the agenda for all discussions of educational issues in the Republic. This may be briefly illustrated by examining the way in which the question of inequalities of wealth and opportunity is constituted within Irish official discourse. The reduction of such inequality is defined as a priority issue in the recent appraisal by the National Economic and Social Council of the state of Irish social policies. However, having acknowledged the key role played by the education system in the allocation of life chances and the importance of questions of educational attainment to the achievement of social equality, (89) the report makes no attempt to assess the performance of the education system in relation to this objective; instead it focusses narrowly on issues which relate to the administration of welfare benefits and services. Education is thus effectively removed from the terms of reference of the equality debate. Turning to the White Paper on Educational Development, we find that equality of opportunity is referred to only twice throughout the whole document. In the Foreword the introduction of free post-primary schooling and free school transport in the 1960s are said to be rightly regarded as major steps towards equality of opportunity, an assertion which receives little support from the available evidence on class-specific educational participation rates. (90) Later, introducing a discussion of the curriculum at second level, it is stated that educational policy at all levels must try to meet both the needs of the individual and the needs of society. (91) Developing this distinction between the individual and the social, the 'basic purpose' of equality of educational opportunity is defined as being 'to enable each pupil to identify and develop his (sic) talents and thus to help him realise his potential as a human being'. Equality is thus constituted as an individual rather than a social question and it is then contrasted with 'the legitimate expectations

203

of society, which increasingly has come to demand that the
school system be a source of the competences and attitudes
necessary for social, economic and cultural progress'. We
have already seen how these 'competences and attitudes'
become institutionally defined and how 'society's' demands
are transmitted to the educational system. Society, incarn-
ated in the MCC, wants technical manpower and it comes as
no surprise when, reading the White Paper's investment
plans, we find that this demand crowds out the demand for
an equality which merely serves, like hang-gliding or trans-
cendental meditation, to realise the nebulous potential of
the atomised individual.

CONCLUSION

Taking the Irish electronics industry as a case study, we
have argued that technology has to be analysed as an
institutionalised ideology which is developed and promoted
by particular interests. In the Irish Republic foreign
technology has been ideologically nativised by means of an
ostentatious display of strategic planning by state agencies
responsible for industrial development and manpower policy
and by the identification of 'national' characteristics with
the projected nature of the electronics industry. A division
of national labour which identifies national growth with
private enterprise and exploits the mystique of technology
to extend the sphere of privatisation has been institutionalised by the same state agencies.

This identity is affirmed, and the division of national
labour reinforced, by the restructuring of the higher
education system in response to the perceived problem of
skill shortages created by the IDA's 'success': by focussing
attention on the deficiencies of the public educational
'infrastructure' and by then making education responsive to
the 'needs' of the industry to remedy these deficiencies,
the state demonstrates that Ireland is, in the words of an
IDA slogan, a place 'where private enterprise is public
policy'. Such public policy undoubtedly utilises the
mystique of technology to legitimate its operation, but its
attempts to forge a unique link between this cosmopolitan
proprietary technology and the characteristics of the Irish
nation reminds us of the continuing efficacy of other bases
of legitimation. In the specific case of the electronics
industry within the Irish state, the centrality of claims
about the provision of skilled work indicates the consequent
interweaving of technical awe and national pride: through
the ascription of skill - of technological mastery - to the
workforce of this new industry the nation recovers the
sovereignty it has lost over its economy. Engels once alluded to the conception of Ireland as 'the sacra insula, whose
aspirations must on no account be mixed up with the profane
class struggles of the rest of the sinful world': (92) a
similar ideological closure is produced by the construction
of the skilled Irishman of today's electronics industry, a
subject standing apart in splendid isolation from the

interlocking class, sexual and national state hierarchies of the division of labour in today's 'sinful world'.

NOTES

(1) J. Habermas, 'Science and Technology as "Ideology"', J. Habermas, Towards a Rational Society (London: Heinemann, 1972).
(2) M.J. Killeen, The Electronics Revolution: Its Impact on Ireland (Dublin: Industrial Development Authority, 1979), pp.6, 14.
(3) ibid, p.7.
(4) Central Statistics Office, Trade Statistics of Ireland, December 1980 (Dublin: Stationery Office, 1981).
(5) Killeen, Electronics Revolution, p.10.
(6) K. Myers, 'Brave New Island', Technology Ireland, November 1979, p.18.
(7) Killeen, Electronics Revolution, p.11.
(8) 'Japanese Micro Firm Continues to Expand', Technology Ireland, June 1980.
(9) National Economic and Social Council (NESC), Industrial Policy and Development: A Survey of the Literature from the Early 1960s (Dublin: NESC, 1980), esp. p.22; J. Wickham, 'The Politics of Dependent Capitalism: International Capital and the Nation State', A. Morgan and B. Purdie (eds), Ireland: Divided Nation, Divided Class (London: Ink Links, 1980).
(10) Irish Business, August 1981; Central Statistics Office, Labour Force Survey 1979 Results (Dublin: Stationery Office, 1981), p.11.
(11) D. McAleese, A Profile of Grant-Aided Industry in Ireland (Dublin: IDA, 1977), p.28.
(12) V. Froebel, J. Heinrichs and O. Krey, 'The Tendency towards a New International Division of Labour', Review 1.1 (1977): 73-88; idem, The New International Division of Labour: Structural Unemployment in Industrialised Countries and Industrialisation in Developing Countries (London: Cambridge University Press, 1980).
(13) 'European Electronics will Buck the Trend', Financial Times, 5 January 1981.
(14) Booz, Allen and Hamilton, The Electronics Industry in Scotland: A Proposed Strategy (Glasgow: Scottish Development Agency, 1979).
(15) ibid, pp.1-17; Killeen, Electronics Revolution, p.12.
(16) 'The Communications Gap', Irish Times 23 and 24 March 1981; 'Cashing in on the Wrong Numbers Game', Guardian 29 May 1981; Booz, Allen and Hamilton, Electronics Industry, p.8.
(17) Booz, Allen and Hamilton, op.cit, p.33.
(18) ibid, pp.30-5.
(19) For the range of UK bodies engaging in promotional activity, see Electronics Location File 1981 (London: Urban Publishing Co, 1980).
(20) Booz, Allen and Hamilton, Electronics Industry, p.34.
(21) 'Industrial Agencies', Survey on Scotland, Financial

Times, 16 December 1980.
(22) See T. Forester (ed), _The Microelectronics Revolution_ (Oxford: Basil Blackwell, 1980).
(23) 'Delicate Bonds: The Global Semi-conductor Industry', a special issue of _Pacific Research_, XI.1 (1980), pp.2-7, 20-22.
(24) _Ibid_, pp.7-17.
(25) In fact Table 3 _under_-estimates the exaggeration contained in the IDA's projections for skilled labour, since the percentage figures are based on the _upper_ limit projection of 30,000 for total employment in electronics. If the lower limit of 25,000 is taken, the percentages of skilled workers would of course be higher and the discrepancy with our own figures still greater. It should be noted that the IDA claims that the proportion of skilled workers will increase as the industry develops in Ireland, yet this takes no account of the fact that it is usually in the start-up period that skilled employment in new manufacturing plants is highest. Factories commencing operations require, in industry parlance, 'front-end loading': more skilled and professional employees are needed to install and de-bug production machinery than for routine production.
(26) See _inter alia_ C. Offe, _Industry and Inequality_ (London: Edward Arnold, 1976); K. Kumar, _Prophecy and Progress: The Sociology of Industrial and Post-Industrial Society_ (Harmondsworth: Penguin, 1978), esp. ch. 6.
(27) A. Phillips and B. Taylor, 'Sex and Skill: Notes Towards a Feminist Economics', _Feminist Review_ no.6 (1980), p.86.
(28) Booz, Allen and Hamilton, _Electronics Industry_, p.47.
(29) R. Grossman,'Bitter Wages: Women in East Asia's Semi-Conductor Plants', _Multinational Monitor_ 3/80, pp.8-11.
(30) In summer 1981 a draft of an as yet unpublished study of Irish industrialisation strategy by international consultants commissioned by the official National Economic and Social Council (NESC) and leaked to an Irish business magazine was quoted as also criticising the IDA on precisely this point; 'The IDA projections for high skilled job creation fall far short of the reality on the ground'. 'Telesis - an indictment of Irish industrial policy', _Irish Business_, August 1981, p.7.
(31) _Labor Occupational Health Program Monitor_, special issue on Electronics Hazards (Institute of Industrial Relations, University of California, no date), p.2.
(32) _Ibid_, p.7.
(33) R. Grossman, 'Bitter Wages', p.9.
(34) Booz, Allen and Hamilton, _Electronics Industry_, p.31.
(35) P.A. International Management Consultants, _Labour Performance of US-Owned Plants in Scotland_ (Glasgow: Scottish Development Agency, 1979), pp.1, 9.
(36) The only detailed study of trade union organisation in new industry in Ireland is L. Harris, 'Industrialisation, Women and Trade Union Politics in the West of Ireland', L. Harris and A. Morgan (eds), _Republic of_

<u>Ireland: Alternative Politics</u> (forthcoming).

(37) The background to this major policy reversal is set out in 'Economic Development' (Pr. 4893, Dublin: Stationery Office, 1958). On the leading role of private enter- prise see especially p.18.

(38) Under the terms of the 1979 National Understanding (a voluntary incomes policy mechanism in which the govern- ment, employers' federations and trade unions are represented) the trade unions finally won a commitment from the government to set up a National Enterprise Agency to create industrial jobs in the state sector. The priority attached to this undertaking can be judged by the fact that two years had elapsed - and a general election was imminent - before the agency was established. It was initially allocated IR£1m in investment capital by the government: by contrast, a bill circulated a few weeks after its formation pro- posed the doubling of the IDA's borrowing authority to IR£1,500m.

(39) See 'Michael Killeen - Man of the Year', <u>Business and Finance</u>, 4 January, 1979.

(40) Quoted in 'US Plea for Free Trade in Semi-Conductors', <u>Financial Times</u>, 12 May, 1981.

(41) J.E. Tilton, 'International Diffusion of Technology: the Case of Semi-Conductors' (Washington DC: Brookings Institute, 1971).

(42) 'Delicate Bonds', pp.20-22.

(43) See 'Silicon Valley: Paradise or Paradox?' (Mountain View, California: Pacific Studies Center, 1977).

(44) T. Forester 'The Jelly Bean People of Silicon Valley', in T. Forester (ed), <u>The Microelectronics Revolution</u>.

(45) 'Venture Capital Concept Reaches Ireland', <u>Irish Times</u>, 23 March, 1981.

(46) <u>Ibid</u>; see also 'Computer Industry Investors', <u>Irish Times</u>, 29 December, 1980.

(47) <u>Ibid</u>.

(48) 'Eireven Shelves Project', <u>Irish Times</u>, 23 April, 1981.

(49) 'IDA Seeking US Backers for Clinic', <u>Irish Times</u>, 28 February, 1981.

(50) <u>Ibid</u>.

(51) <u>Ibid</u>.

(52) 'How Ireland said Goodbye to 1,200 Jobs', <u>Business and Finance</u>, 17 September, 1981.

(53) The contrast between this, as yet, successful blocking of the IDA's clinic and the failure of campaigns against the virtually unregulated dumping of dangerous industrial waste to secure government intervention is striking.

(54) Manus O'Riordan, 'IDA Plans and Job Losses', Letters to the Editor, <u>Irish Times</u>, 8 July 1981; 'Telesis', <u>Irish Business</u>, August 1981.

(55) D. McAleese, <u>A Profile of Grant-Aided Industry in Ireland</u>, p.57.

(56) <u>Small Firms Annual Report 1979</u> (Dublin: IDA), p.3.

(57) 'New Directions at the IDA' (an interview with Mr. Padraic White, who took over as Managing Director of the IDA in February 1981), <u>Business and Finance</u>, 2

April, 1981.

(58) R. Whitaker, 'How Small Firms can Benefit from the
Electronics Sector', Technology Ireland, October, 1979.
(59) M. O'Riordan, 'IDA Plans and Job Losses'.
(60) See the remarks of Kieran McGowan, Head of the IDA's
Small Industries Division, reported in 'Small Firms.
Can they Survive?', Sunday Independent, 14 June, 1981;
also 'Telesis', Irish Business, August 1981.
(61) L. Althusser, 'Ideology and Ideological State Appar-
atuses: Notes towards an Investigation', in Lenin and
Philosophy and Other Essays (London: New Left Books,
1971).
(62) J. Westergaard and H. Resler, Class in a Capitalist
Society. A Study of Contemporary Britain (London:
Heinemann, 1975), Part 4, ch. 3.
(63) F. Parkin, Class Inequality and Political Order
(London: MacGibbon and Kee, 1971), pp.62-7.
(64) D. Tussing, 'Equity and the Financing of Education',
in S. Kennedy, RSC (ed), One Million Poor? The
Challenge of Irish Inequality (Dublin: Turoe Press,
1981), p.202. See also P. Clancy and C. Benson, Higher
Education in Dublin: A Study of Some Emerging Needs
(Dublin: Higher Education Authority, 1979).
(65) Ibid, pp.201-2.
(66) J.P. McHale, 'The Socio-Economic Background of Students
in Irish Universities', Studies 68 (1979), pp.213-21.
(67) 'Investment in Education' (Pr. 8311, Dublin: Stationery
Office, 1965); A. Wickham, 'National Education Systems
and the International Context: the case of Ireland',
Comparative Education Review 24 (1980).
(68) The White Paper on Educational Development (Prl. 9373,
Dublin: Stationery Office, 1980), paras, 10.4-10.12.
(69) 'New Directions at the IDA'. Admittedly this was not
how US electronics executives perceived the situation
when they were interviewed on behalf of the SDA in
August 1978 (Booz, Allen and Hamilton, Electronics
Industry, p.33). Promotional literature aimed at the
industry currently stresses the availability in the
Republic of a highly-trained workforce - highlighting
the introduction of 38 new electronics courses in
third-level colleges in the state in the late 1970s.
On the general question of skill shortages, it is quite
conceivable that the rapid influx of electronics firms
into the Republic in a short period of time created a
tight labour market for specialised engineers and
technicians and may have led some companies to 'poach'
scarce labour from others. Beyond the electronics
industry the short-lived boom of 1978-9 may also have
created skilled labour 'bottlenecks'. However since
mid-1979 the Republic's economy has slid ever deeper
into recession. The late 1970s boomlet has to be seen
in the context of persistent structural problems in the
Irish economy. As Anthony Coughlan has noted:

> The Republic seems locked into a situation where
> levels of investment similar to those of Japan
> bring about little or no increase in manufacturing

employment (and) where increased service employment depends heavily on public service job-creation
schemes financed by unsustainable levels of debt
creation...'

A. Coughlan, 'Ireland', in D. Seers and C. Vaitsos
(eds), <u>Integration and Unequal Development. The Experience of the EEC</u> (London: Macmillan, 1980), p.132.
(70) <u>Manpower Consultative Committee (MCC) Report 1979</u>
(Dublin: Department of Labour, n.d.).
(71) MCC <u>Reports</u> 1979 and 1980.
(72) MCC <u>Report 1979</u>, Appendix II, MCC <u>Report 1980</u>, Table
IV.
(73) <u>Ibid</u>.
(74) MCC <u>Report</u> 1979, ch. 2; MCC <u>Report</u> 1980, ch. 2.
(75) M. O'Donnell, 'Present and Forecast Capacity', paper
read to the First Conference on Engineering Manpower
for Economic Development, Dublin, April 1980. Mr.
O'Donnell is Secretary of the National Committee for
Engineering Sciences.
(76) White Paper on Educational Development, para. 1.32.
'The Higher Education Authority in consultation with
the Manpower Consultative Committee of the Department
of Labour, the Institute for Industrial Research and
Standards, the National Board for Science and Technology and the Economic and Social Research Institute
will review the needs of the labour market and will
furnish an annual report thereon to the Minister for
Education. The outcome of the forthcoming second
Conference on Engineering Manpower for Economic Development will also be taken into account.' Of the
various agencies referred to only the MCC is actively
engaged in the production of detailed manpower fore-
casts. The MCC was jointly responsible for organising
the two Engineering Manpower for Economic Development
(EMED) Conferences held in 1980 and 1981, and as its
1980 Report observes, 'the information given in previous sections of this chapter on engineering demand
and supply formed a major input to the conference'.
(p.11.)
(77) J. Corcoran, 'Demand and Supply', paper read to the
second conference on EMED, Dublin, January 1981. Mr.
Corcoran is Secretary of the MCC.
(78) MCC <u>Report 1980</u>, para. 2.10.
(79) Killeen, <u>Electronics Revolution</u>, p.15.
(80) See notes to Tables 3 and 4 in J. Corcoran, 'Present
and Forecast Demand', paper read to the First Conference on EMED Dublin April 1980; also pp.8-10.
(81) <u>Ibid</u>, p.16.
(82) 'Telesis', <u>Irish Business</u>, August 1981.
(83) J. Corcoran, 'Demand and Supply', Table 1. Vacancies
in the mechanical/production/industrial engineer
category fell by 44 per cent, for electrical/electronic
engineers by almost 75 per cent and for electronic
technicians by almost 80 per cent.
(84) <u>Ibid</u>.
(85) MCC <u>Report 1980</u>, para. 2.6.

(86) See T. Curtin, 'Programmers: too few or too many?', _Technology Ireland_, June 1980; also 'Has the College System failed for Jobs?', _Irish Independent_, 1 December 1981.

(87) See R. Lynn, _The Irish Brain Drain_ (Dublin: Economic and Social Research Institute, Paper no. 43, 1968).

(88) R. Irizarry, 'Over-education and Unemployment in the Third World: The Paradoxes of Dependent Industrialisation', _Comparative Education Review_ 24 (1980), esp. pp.350-2.

(89) National Economic and Social Council (NESC), 'Irish Social Policies: Priorities for Future Development' (Dublin: NESC, 1981), esp. paras. 2.11-2.13.

(90) Tussing, 'Equity and the Financing of Education'.

(91) White Paper on Educational Development, paras. 6.2-6.3.

(92) Engels to Marx, 9 December 1869, quoted in Karl Marx and Friedrich Engels, _Ireland and the Irish Question_ (Moscow: Progress Publishers, 1971), p.283.

Contributors

Lesley Caldwell: Lecturer in Sociology, Institute of Education.

Philip Cooke: Lecturer in Planning Theory and Urban Politics at the University of Wales Institute of Science and Technology.

Jim Cousins: Senior Research Fellow, Urban Employment Study, University of Durham.

Rosemary Crompton: Lecturer in Sociology, University of East Anglia.

Margaret Curran: Research Fellow in Sociology and Social Policy, University of Durham.

Graham Day: Lecturer in Sociology, University College of Wales, Aberystwyth.

Robert Goffee: Lecturer in Management Studies, University of Surrey.

Gareth Jones: Lecturer in Sociology, University of East Anglia.

Karen Jones: Lecturer, Department of Communication Studies, Sheffield City Polytechnic.

David Hooper: Lecturer in the School of Combined Studies, Bradford College.

Glenn Morgan: Lecturer in the School of Combined Studies, Bradford College.

Peter Murray: Research Assistant, Department of Sociology, Trinity College, Dublin.

Roger Penn: Lecturer, Department of Sociology, University of Lancaster.

Richard Scase: Reader in Sociology, University of Kent.

Diana Smith: Formerly at the Institute of Education, now works with the Family Planning Association.

David Robbins: Lecturer in Sociology, University College of Wales, Aberystwyth.

Hilary Rose: Professor of Applied Social Studies, University of Bradford.

James Wickham: Lecturer in Sociology, Trinity College, Dublin.

H7